Praise for Andrew Lawler
The Secret Token

"*The Secret Token* is a very special kind of popular history. . . . It dives headfirst into the latest developments regarding the fate of the colonists and providing colorful, affectionate portraits. . . . Lawler sheds light on why the story of the Roanoke Colony remains so important today." —*Salon*

"It's not a spoiler to say that Lawler never solves the ultimate mystery, but by the book's end, the enduring legacy of this early colony, from mapmaking to even the far right, is more than enough."
—*Vanity Fair*

"Part detective novel, part historical reckoning, Lawler's engrossing book traces the story of—and the obsessive search for—the Lost Colony of Roanoke. . . . Lawler makes a strong case for why historical myths matter." —*Publishers Weekly*

"[Lawler] creates a vivid picture of the roiling, politically contentious, economically stressed Elizabethan world. . . . In this enjoyable historical adventure, an unsolved mystery reveals violent political and economic rivalries and dire personal struggles." —*Kirkus Reviews*

"This detailed historical inquiry will powerfully intrigue early American history buffs." —*Booklist*

"Lawler compels readers to examine the past in a different light. Accessible and inquisitive." —*Library Journal*

"Andrew Lawler, an award-winning journalist and author, sheds new light on the colony and—equally fascinating—on the myths that have grown up around the mystery and their importance in the national story that Americans tell ourselves."
—*News & Record* (Greensboro, NC)

Andrew Lawler

The Secret Token

Andrew Lawler is the author of the highly acclaimed *Why Did the Chicken Cross the World?* He is a contributing writer for *Science*, is a contributing editor for *Archaeology* magazine, and has written for *The New York Times*, *The Washington Post*, *National Geographic*, *Smithsonian*, and *Slate*.

www.andrewlawler.com

ALSO BY ANDREW LAWLER

Why Did the Chicken Cross the World?:
The Epic Saga of the Bird That Powers Civilization

SECOTAN

Dasamonguepeu

Roanoac

Hatorasck

WEAPEMEOC

The Secret Token

MYTH, OBSESSION, AND
THE SEARCH FOR
THE LOST COLONY OF ROANOKE

Andrew Lawler

ANCHOR BOOKS
A DIVISION OF PENGUIN RANDOM HOUSE LLC
NEW YORK

FIRST ANCHOR BOOKS EDITION, JUNE 2019

Copyright © 2018 by Andrew Lawler

All rights reserved. Published in the United States by Anchor Books,
a division of Penguin Random House LLC, New York, and distributed in
Canada by Penguin Random House Canada Limited, Toronto. Originally published
in hardcover in the United States by Doubleday, a division of Penguin Random
House LLC, New York, in 2018.

Anchor Books and colophon are registered
trademarks of Penguin Random House LLC.

The Library of Congress has cataloged the Doubleday edition as follows:
Names: Lawler, Andrew, author.
Title: The secret token : myth, obsession, and the search for
the lost colony of Roanoke / by Andrew Lawler.
Description: First edition. | New York : Doubleday, [2018] |
Includes bibliographical references.
Identifiers: LCCN 2017045395
Subjects: LCSH: Roanoke Colony. | Roanoke Island (N.C.)—
History—16th century.
Classification: LCC F229 L39 2018 | DDC 975.6/175—dc23
LC record available at https://lccn.loc.gov/2017045395

Anchor Books Trade Paperback ISBN: 978-1-101-97460-5
eBook ISBN: 978-0-385-54202-9

Author photo © R. Plaster
Book design by Maria Carella
Maps in text designed by Jeffrey L. Ward

www.anchorbooks.com

Printed in the United States of America

For Bear

Contents

Cast of Characters

SIR RICHARD GRENVILLE: Feudal lord, admiral, and cousin to Raleigh

GRANGANIMEO: Brother of King Wingina and Secotan elder who lived with his wife on Roanoke Island

KING WINGINA: Secotan leader who controlled coastal mainland of North Carolina

SIR FRANCIS DRAKE: English privateer who brought Africans to the Carolina coast and rescued the first colony

PART TWO: THE SEARCH

JOHN SMITH: Jamestown captain who gathered Lost Colony intelligence

POWHATAN: Virginia Algonquian leader at Jamestown's founding, accused of massacring Lost Colonists

DAVID BEERS QUINN: Twentieth-century Irish historian and dean of Roanoke researchers

IVOR NOËL HUME: London-born archaeologist and colonial America specialist who excavated Fort Raleigh in the 1990s

PHIL EVANS: Founder of First Colony Foundation

NICK LUCCKETTI: First Colony Foundation archaeologist

BRENT LANE: University of North Carolina heritage economist

FRED WILLARD: Former race car driver, wrestling coach, and maverick Lost Colony seeker

DAVID PHELPS: East Carolina University archaeologist who first excavated Hatteras's Cape Creek site

SCOTT DAWSON: Hatteras native who co-founded the Croatoan Archaeological Society with his wife, Maggie

MARK HORTON: Croatoan Archaeological Society archaeologist from the University of Bristol

LOUIS HAMMOND: Purported California retiree and finder of the Dare Stone in the 1930s

HAYWOOD PEARCE: Emory University and Brenau College historian who led the analysis of the Dare Stone

ED SCHRADER: Current Brenau president, geologist, and keeper of the Dare Stone

PART THREE: THE REVELATION

VIRGINIA DARE: Daughter of Eleanor and Ananias Dare and first English child born in the New World

GEORGE BANCROFT: Harvard professor and father of American history who gave Roanoke a romantic twist in the 1830s

ELIZA LANESFORD CUSHING: Boston-born author and later a Canadian who coined the term "Lost Colony" in the 1830s

MARIA LOUISA LANDER: Salem-born sculptor in Rome who created the Virginia Dare "National Statue" in the 1850s

SALLIE SOUTHALL COTTEN: Doeskin-wearing North Carolina author of a popular 1901 Roanoke poem

REVEREND DONALD LOWERY: Present-day Episcopal priest and Lumbee Indian who helped make Virginia Dare and Manteo saints

ROBERTA ESTES: Midwestern computer scientist attempting to trace the Lost Colonists using genealogy and DNA

MARILYN BERRY MORRISON: Current chief of the Roanoke-Hatteras tribe who claims descent from the Lost Colonists and Native and African Americans

Prelude

On August 15, 1590, two English ships, the *Moonlight* and the *Hopewell*, dropped anchor off the Outer Banks of North Carolina. Beyond the slender strip of sand and dense forest, a hazy sun descended over the Pamlico Sound, its calm waters seeming to stretch as far to the west as the Atlantic did to the east. Gripping the rail of the *Hopewell*, as the ship rose and fell on the gentle ocean swells, Governor John White watched with growing elation as a great plume of smoke climbed into the sticky air of the late afternoon sky.

The source of the fire was Roanoke Island, which lay a dozen miles to the northwest in the shallow sound. The signal "put us in good hope that some of the colony were there expecting my return out of England," he recalled later. White had left more than one hundred settlers there, including his only child and her newly born daughter, before embarking on a six-month mission to gather supplies and new colonists. Those six months had become three nightmarish years, comprising a series of mishaps that would have tested Job.

Until spotting the smoke, the middle-aged Londoner had had no way of knowing what had become of his settlers who made up the first English colony in the New World, which Walter Raleigh, an influential knight in Queen Elizabeth I's court, had appointed him to lead. They might have died from disease or starvation or fallen victim to Spanish or Native American enemies. They could have moved to another location or, in desperation, tried to sail back to England in their small boats, only to drown. The rising column seemed a sure sign that the colonists had spotted his ship. He anticipated a happy homecoming.

The governor had already made at least two round-trip journeys to the land that the people who lived there called Ossomocomuck and that the newcomers dubbed Virginia, after their unmarried queen. His return to England in 1587, after landing the colonists at Roanoke, had proved an ordeal. Illness and hunger killed many of his crew on the stormy trip east; only by luck did the ship drift into an Irish harbor. Just weeks before he reached London to organize the resupply effort, Elizabeth I had forbidden any vessel to leave the kingdom without royal permission. Word had just reached the queen that her onetime beau and now bitter foe, the Spanish king, Philip II, intended to launch a vast armada to invade the country and remove the heretic Protestant monarch from her throne.

When White did manage to charter a ship to carry supplies and settlers to Virginia the following spring in a military convoy, unfavorable winds delayed the fleet that was then diverted instead to protect the home coast. Undaunted, he found a privateer—a government-sanctioned pirate—heading for the Caribbean Sea and willing to stop by Virginia on the way back, but he never made it across the Atlantic. French pirates attacked the ship and wounded the governor in a fierce and bloody deck fight off the coast of Morocco. He was lucky to make it back to England alive with a laceration to his head and lead in his buttocks.

Two more excruciating years passed as the armada arrived and was defeated, but the country remained on a war footing with little time to bother about abandoned colonists in a faraway land. The best White could do was obtain a single berth on a vessel that joined a convoy to rob Spanish ships in the Caribbean Sea. After a long hot summer patrolling for plunder, White's ship, the *Hopewell*, accompanied by the *Moonlight*, glided on the Gulf Stream, the warm current that carried them north between Florida and the Bahamas, past the Spanish towns of St. Augustine and Santa Elena that marked the edge of the Spanish Empire, and up the coast to the narrow barrier islands called the Outer Banks. As the land he had departed three years prior came into view, his tribulations finally seemed over. White didn't know they had only begun.

The next morning, the governor and the two ships' captains climbed into two smaller boats to row through the narrow inlet between the barrier islands that would take them from the ocean into the Pamlico and from there "to the place at Roanoke where our countrymen were left."

As they pushed off, the master gunner fired three cannon "with a reasonable space between every shot, to the end that their reports might be heard to the place where we hoped to find some of our people." The ships' guns boomed in the pallid summer sky as the sailors leaned on their oars.

Halfway into their journey another smoke plume blossomed a few miles to the south, along the long thin island called Hatteras that separated the Atlantic and the Pamlico. Because this signal seemed a direct response to the artillery barrage, White and the captains changed course to investigate. The crew pulled the boats up on the marshy western shore of the island, and the men set off on foot to find the bonfire's source.

Distances in the flat landscape of sea and sand proved deceiving. "It was much further from the harbor where we landed, then we supposed it to be, so that we were sore tired before we came to the smoke," White recounts. When they finally found the spot, "we found no man nor sign any had been there lately."

There was also no freshwater. By the time the men returned to the boats after a long midday summer trek without provisions, they were exhausted and desperately thirsty. Digging into the sand beside the shore, a trick White had learned on a previous visit, they were able to procure a drink. The sun had already set into the Pamlico by the time they made their way back through the inlet and climbed back aboard the ships. The governor spent another restless night just shy of his goal.

A boat was sent ashore early the next morning to collect more freshwater, and it was ten in the morning before White could launch a second attempt to reach Roanoke. By now, the ocean had turned rough. The governor set off again with the captain of the *Hopewell*. As they neared the inlet into the Pamlico, "we had a sea break into our boat which filled us half with water," White reports. The soaked crew landed safely on the Hatteras shore, though all their provisions were spoiled and the gunpowder wet. Worse was to follow. As the men made it to land, "the wind blew at northeast and direct into the harbor so great a gale, that the sea broke extremely on the bar, and the tide went very forcibly at the entrance."

The surge caught the second boat carrying a crew from the *Moonlight* just as it entered the inlet. The men on the beach watched helplessly as a wave overturned the vessel on a submerged sandbar, tossing the sailors into the foaming water. The surf pounded those who clung to the gunwales. Some tried to wade to safety, but the water "beat them down, so that they could neither stand nor swim, and the boat twice or thrice was turned the keel upward."

White watched helplessly as the captain and master's mate of the *Moonlight* clutched the boat "until they sunk and were seen no more." Several of the crew members of the first boat stripped and dashed into the treacherous seas but were able to rescue only four of the eleven. "The mischance did so much discomfort the sailors, that they were all of one mind not to go any further to seek the planters," according to the governor. Only an impassioned plea by White and the stern command of the *Hopewell* captain persuaded the men to continue the quest.

The sun was low by the time the two boats could be readied and provisioned anew, but White couldn't bear to wait another night. The expedition set off across the Pamlico Sound toward Roanoke. "Before we could get to the place where our planters were left, it was so exceeding dark, that we overshot the place a quarter of a mile," he reports. As they cruised along the island's north end, the men saw "the light of a great fire through the woods, to which we presently rowed." It seemed another sign the colonists were awaiting White's return.

The men, still shaken from the tragedy earlier in the day, dropped anchor close to the conflagration but decided against landing in the dark. Instead, they sounded a trumpet and sang "many familiar English tunes of songs, and called to them friendly, but we had no answer." It is an unsettling scene: sailors mourning their dead friends commanded to make merry as White peers anxiously into the woods, hoping to spot loved ones after a three-year absence. They spent a restless night in the boats below the slim crescent of a waning moon.

At dawn, White and some of the party climbed up the steep bank. It was the third birthday of his granddaughter Virginia Dare, named for the new land and the first English child born in the Americas. No one appeared, but they were not alone. The men spotted fresh tracks of Native Americans in the sand. Soon after, along the sandy bank on the north shore, White saw the letters *C R O* carved into a tree.

This was a prearranged code, "a secret token agreed upon between them and me at my last departure from them," White explained in his account. If the settlers were to leave the island, he says, they "should not fail to write or carve upon the trees or posts of the doors the name of the place where they should be seated." A cross over the name of their destination would mean that they left in an emergency, but none here was to be found.

Hurrying to the site of the town he'd left, White found the houses dismantled and the settlement enclosed with "a high palisade of great trees." At eye height on one of these posts, the governor saw "in fair capital letters was graven CROATOAN without any cross or sign of distress."

White professed relief. The word, as well as the three letters, referred to the island fifty miles to the south as well as the Algonquian-speaking tribe allied with the English who lived there. One of their number, a young man named Manteo, had visited London twice and had been made an English lord. The lack of a carved cross and the absence of European graves or scattered skeletons seemed to confirm all was well. "I greatly joyed that I had safely found a certain token of their safe being at Croatoan," he wrote. Yet he also added that at his 1587 departure the colonists had planned to move "fifty miles into the main." That meant west, or inland, rather than in the direction of the barrier island of Croatoan to the south.

By then it was afternoon, and a summer storm was brewing. The men abandoned their search and returned to the ships; the tempest blew hard the entire night. The next morning the sea was still rough as the ships prepared to sail the short fifty miles south to Croatoan, "where our planters are." Suddenly the anchor cable snapped in the surging seas, and the ship nearly wrecked on a sandbar before the captain managed to steer into a deeper channel. Only one anchor cable remained. Supplies were low, and the weather grew worse.

White reluctantly agreed to a new plan; the *Moonlight* would return to England while the *Hopewell* would spend the winter in the Caribbean and return in the spring "to visit our countrymen in Virginia." But as they sailed south, a powerful wind from the west pushed the ship deeper into the Atlantic. The ship arrived off the Azores, an island chain three thousand miles to the east, but ill winds prevented a landing to restock the dwindling stocks of food and water. The captain had no choice but to make for England. White landed in Plymouth on October 24, 1590, ending a voyage he called "as luckless to many, as sinister to myself."

There would be no more search-and-rescue efforts by the governor. "Would to God my wealth were answerable to my will," he wrote, keenly aware that he lacked the deep pockets necessary to finance a new transatlantic expedition. The father never found his daughter or laid eyes on his granddaughter again. They, and the entire colony for which he was responsible, vanished from history.

The Secret Token

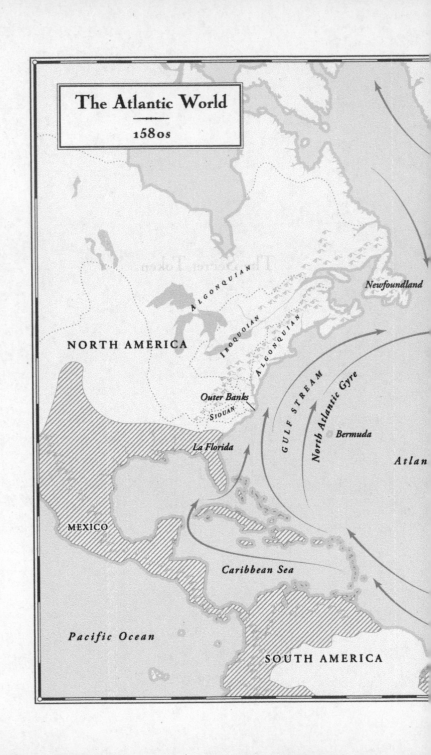

The Atlantic World
1580s

Newfoundland

ALGONQUIAN

IROQUOIAN

ALGONQUIAN

NORTH AMERICA

GULF STREAM

North Atlantic Gyre

Outer Banks

SIOUAN

Bermuda

La Florida

Atlan

MEXICO

Caribbean Sea

Pacific Ocean

SOUTH AMERICA

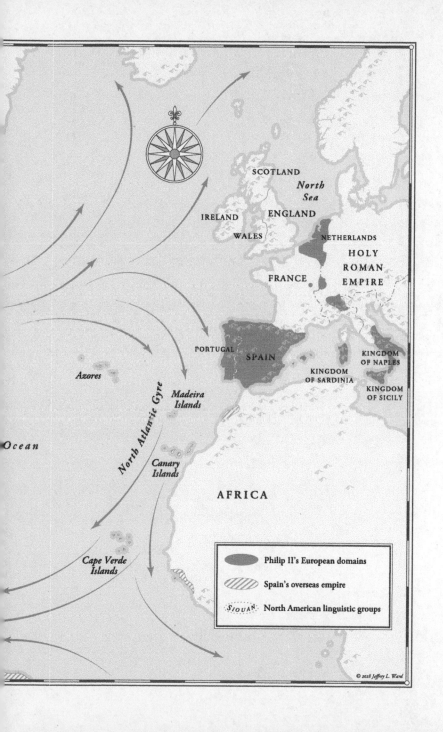

SCOTLAND

North Sea

IRELAND ENGLAND

WALES NETHERLANDS

HOLY
ROMAN
FRANCE EMPIRE

PORTUGAL SPAIN

Azores KINGDOM
OF NAPLES

KINGDOM
OF SARDINIA

*Madeira
Islands* KINGDOM
OF SICILY

North Atlantic Gyre

Ocean

*Canary
Islands*

AFRICA

*Cape Verde
Islands*

	Philip II's European domains
	Spain's overseas empire
SIOUAN	North American linguistic groups

© 2018 Jeffrey L. Ward

Introduction: The Terror Within

Roanoke Island is an unassuming oval of land that today serves as an enormous trestle for the bridges funneling tourists from the marshy North Carolina mainland to the beaches of the Outer Banks. Not quite a third the size of Manhattan, the mostly wooded landscape fringed by swamp is home to a couple of sleepy towns and fewer than seven thousand people.

As ground zero for the mystery of the Lost Colony, it is also inhabited with wraiths and werewolves, enchanted animals and aliens, and all manner of supernatural beings held responsible for what happened to eighty-five men, seventeen women, and thirteen children more than four centuries ago. Roanoke has long been a setting for our national nightmares. Even the U.S. National Park Service trades on this delicious dread. As Halloween approaches, "make plans to brave the haunted trail" filled with "creatures, maniacs, zombies, and disembodied spirits that roam freely on the desolate Fort Raleigh National Park on historic Roanoke Island." It's all part of "PsychoPath: The Terror Within." If the event gets too real, just yell "safety" and you will, unlike the hapless colonists, be promptly rescued.

Our lurid fascination with the disappearance of these Elizabethans stretches back to the early nineteenth century, when a Harvard historian and several women writers transformed an obscure and embarrassing debacle at the nation's dawn into the origin myth of the United

States, adding a twist of gothic horror in the process. Stories of evil Indian warriors and a beautiful but doomed blond huntress—the now mature granddaughter of John White, Virginia Dare—proliferated.

Such tales drew visitors like George Higby Throop, a school-teacher with a delightfully Victorian name, who visited Roanoke (twice) on his 1852 beach vacation in order to savor the island's history of "massacres, murders, and other bloody scenes, on which it is almost sickening to dwell." You can almost feel the self-induced shiver down his spine.

Yet by any measure, the violence in later English colonies surpassed anything recorded during the Roanoke voyages. One hundred miles to the north at Jamestown, the first enduring English town in the New World, settlers resorted to butchering the skull and shinbone of a teenage girl during the starving time of 1609, when eight out of ten perished. A dozen years later in New England, the pious Miles Standish stabbed an Indian to death during a meal, using the man's own knife. He brought the head back to Plymouth to display it with a cloth soaked in the dead man's blood.

Cycles of savage attacks by and on Native Americans in seventeenth-century America, not to mention the list of torments perpetrated on the rising number of enslaved Africans, prompted one historian to dub this period "the barbarous years." Murder, massacre, and mayhem were a way of life as these cultures clashed. Thousands of people, European, African, and indigenous, disappeared or died violent deaths.

But the ones we can't seem to forget, the ones who have since earned the title of *the* Lost Colonists, are the Roanoke settlers. They were mostly middle-class people of no particular distinction: tradesmen, lawyers, and shopkeepers. There was a small-town sheriff. Three of the boys were orphans. A handful of single women and a dozen married ones made the perilous journey. One was nursing a child, and two were pregnant when they stepped aboard the ships bobbing in the Thames. There's not a single portrait of any of them, and most of their identities are blurred by time and the ubiquity of those common English names—Cooper, Powell, Stevens.

The Lost Colonists seem ordinary in a way that makes them more familiar than the incompetent gold-obsessed gentlemen of Jamestown and the sanctimonious Pilgrims who banned Christmas celebrations. These were not people trying to get rich quick or build a fundamentalist refuge but individuals more like the millions who followed in the succeeding centuries seeking a piece of land and a marginally better life. Yet because we know so little about them, and nothing for certain about what they did after Governor White left in 1587, they also make perfect blank slates, encouraging tales of the unfound and the undead to collect on the island. Actress Kathy Bates played White's deranged wife in FX's *American Horror Story* in 2016, terrorizing a nice mixed-race couple on twenty-first-century Roanoke with her bloody knife and Elizabethan brogue. A traumatized historian in the popular series explained that Croatoan "is actually a word of dark power and blood magic." The Zombie Research Society recently warned that "there could be something sinister still in the ground on Roanoke Island, waiting to be released into a modern population that is more advanced, more connected, but just as unprepared as ever."

All this supernatural activity concentrated in one out-of-the-way place is a sure sign that there is something deeper and darker at work than mere historical curiosity or the natural desire to solve a persistent riddle. Our fairy tales are about losing our way in the enchanted forest. In our movies we are looking for Nemo or Dory in the animated depths. Our books are filled with conquistadors swallowed up by the jungles or Arctic explorers disappearing in the ice pack. To die is tragic, but to go missing is to become a legend, a mystery. "Wander off the stage of history and leave only a moving target," writes novelist Charles Frazier. That is why Roanoke exerts such a powerful attraction and why it draws those of us harboring—and who doesn't?— that quiet fear of getting lost ourselves.

Myths cast spells that cannot be broken by facts. They operate in the background, like a computer program hidden deep in a hard drive. Their job is to help us get our bearings in each age, as Aeneas did for Rome and King Arthur still does for Britain. That's why Roanoke does for America what Jamestown and Plymouth cannot. There simply aren't enough facts to get in the way of a good story that can reveal something fresh about who we were, who we are, and who we want to be. This is a haunting as much as history, a spooky tale reinterpreted by each generation to reflect our current national dreams and anxieties.

All these layers of legend can quickly shade into kitsch, delighting horror writers and cable producers but repelling serious academics. Open a book about the nation's past, and it might grant a grudging sidebar to Raleigh's effort before skipping quickly to the firm ground of 1607 Virginia and the inevitable arrival of the *Mayflower*. "This venture had little long-term significance," Philip Jenkins writes dismissively about Roanoke in *A History of the United States,* summing up conventional thinking among scholars. "The fate of the 'Lost Colony' is one of the unsolvable problems with which some modern historians amuse themselves in their moments of leisure," sniffs Oliver Perry Chitwood in *A History of Colonial America*. "But so far, all the efforts in this direction have been no more fruitful than the study of a crossword puzzle." When I told historians what I was pursuing, several rolled their eyes as if to say, *not that again*.

But the public understands intuitively what most scholars do not— that the story of Roanoke is about much more than a dead end or false start. "Raleigh's missing settlers still haunt the American imagination not simply because history, like nature, abhors a vacuum," writes the perceptive historian Robert Arner. "But also because they have not yet imparted all the wisdom that such wayward wanderers may be presumed to possess." The vanished colonists remain lost because, more than four centuries later, they still have wisdom to impart.

The Roanoke venture lasted for six years and involved two dozen vessels and well over a thousand people crossing the treacherous breadth of the Atlantic to establish England's first beachhead in the New World. In size, scope, and cost, it far outstripped the later inaugural voyages to Jamestown and Plymouth. It was the Elizabethan equivalent of the Apollo program. Led by the queen's principal security guard, the Esquire of the Body Extraordinary, Walter Raleigh, the enterprise was born during a cold war that threatened to turn hot, with a technological underdog itching to take on its more seasoned rival in the era's new frontier.

The ambitious effort, which cost the equivalent today of many tens of millions of dollars, began with a reconnaissance mission in 1584, followed two years later by a males-only settlement dominated by a military mind-set that ended disastrously with starvation and severed heads but produced a wealth of scientific and commercial data. It was the next and final try that brought together men, women, and children to create a New World utopia, what we remember as the Lost Colony. Larger forces at work, namely war in Europe, cut the settlers off from their mother country.

While the biographical details of the abandoned colonists are sparse, those who organized and executed the undertaking are not only better known to us but also appear borrowed from an over-the-top production on the rowdy south bank of the Thames. There is a young and preternaturally brilliant Oxford bachelor befriended by a flamboyant courtier and a quarrelsome Portuguese pilot who may be a secret saboteur. The first acknowledged Jew in the Americas is given the impossible job of finding gold in a land lacking even stone, while a rogue with the comic-opera name of Marmaduke Constable stirs up trouble. One Indian youth is charmed by the clamor and chaos of Shakespearean London while another is repelled. A grandfather desperately seeks his family against the menacing backdrop of an enemy invasion. The tale is punctuated by storms, shipwrecks, and surprise attacks gone awry.

Though the colony ultimately fizzled, it generated detailed knowledge of the Americas. The maps produced in those years, as well as descriptions of the plants, animals, and people of eastern North Carolina—including the magnificent watercolors that White himself painted—forged the first link in the chain that came to bind North America and the small island nation. Jamestown followed two decades later as a thinly disguised sequel. Subsequent settlements along Chesapeake Bay and then on New England's rocky coast formed the seedbed for what grew into the American colonies. They, in turn, led to the creation of what became the United States and played an essential part in the rise of the British Empire. By the time of the American Revolution, Britain had surpassed Spain in global power and influence—an outcome that would have astonished even Raleigh, the quintessential Elizabethan conquistador. In his day, English dominance of North

America was an outlandish fantasy maintained only by a few eccentrics. The Spanish and Portuguese had all but sewed up control of the strategic parts of the Americas long before the first ship bound for the Outer Banks sailed down the Thames.

"The profound significance of Raleigh's Virginia voyages to the history and culture of the modern world is often forgotten or undervalued," writes Neil MacGregor, an art historian and former director of the British Museum, which today houses White's drawings of the strange world that he encountered. That has begun to change. Historians believe that these paintings profoundly shaped the European view of Native Americans and the concept of the noble savage. And while scholars long assumed that the venture imitated English outposts in Ireland, archaeologist Audrey Horning of the College of William and Mary argues persuasively that the opposite is true: Roanoke served as a model for the way the English went on to colonize Ireland. It was Raleigh and his cohorts, concludes American literature specialist Lewis Leary, who "gave the most powerful impetus in practice to the idea of English settlement in America." The colonies—and the empire and nation that grew from them—"built on that foundation."

Native Americans, it has also become increasingly clear, were central players in constructing that foundation. Without their food and expertise, England's ambitions to settle the New World would have been quickly thwarted. Roanoke Island is where the complicated and contentious relationship between the peoples of the British Isles and indigenous Americans began. At the start, they traded peacefully while sharing recipes and meals. They learned each other's strange tongues and formed mutually advantageous alliances. Yet this is also where the newcomers impaled their first Native American head on a sharpened post and where vengeful Indians pierced a colonist with sixteen arrows and then crushed his skull with blunt wooden swords. It was from here that the English first spread their microbes that would upend Native life across the continent more ruthlessly than their muskets. D. H. Lawrence might have been speaking of Roanoke when he wrote that American soil "is full of grinning, unappeased aboriginal demons." No wonder we've turned it into our little island of horrors.

There are also intriguing hints of a second, and even more mysterious, lost colony on Roanoke that may have spawned another sort of haunting. Hundreds of enslaved North African Muslims and West Africans, along with South American indigenous women, were brought here to help build the initial English settlement, a third of a century before slaves arrived at Jamestown. Many researchers believe these refugees from Spanish rule were abandoned on the island when the first colony pulled up stakes and returned to England the year before White's settlers arrived. If they are right, then this is where the stage was first set for the drama that was to unfold among the British, Africans, and indigenous peoples that shaped—and still shapes—our national identity.

I can't say that I wasn't warned. "The Lost Colony has a kind of inexorable pull, like a black hole," Brent Lane told me when I set out to pursue this story. He teaches heritage economics at the University of North Carolina at Chapel Hill and has long felt the gravitational attraction of the Roanoke voyages. "You may think you are immune, but if you get too close to it, it sucks you in. You have to run up to the edge and veer off. Or else *you* get lost."

Long childhood exposure made me immune, or so I thought. Once a year, during our summer vacation on the Outer Banks, my parents would drag my sisters and me out of the surf for the thirty-minute drive to Fort Raleigh National Historic Site on Roanoke Island. Dusk fell as we entered the buggy amphitheater lined with hard wooden benches to watch one of the country's longest-running plays, an outdoor drama called *The Lost Colony*. There were Indian dances, sword fights, and fireworks to keep me entertained.

But my strongest memory is what came after the colonists marched off singing to an unknown destiny in the final scene, their voices soaring over the pipe organ's crescendos as they disappeared into the woods. We filed quietly out of the palisaded theater and down a winding path through the dark forest. For a moment, clutching tightly to an adult hand, I would feel the fear and awe of what it meant to be abandoned in a strange land. The sensation struck me more viscerally than anything in the three-hour drama.

When I was a teenager, that sense of magic and mystery turned to adolescent scorn. My sisters and I would mimic the more melodramatic lines in the play. "Roanoke, oh Roanoke, thou hath made a man of me!" exclaims one actor in Ye Olde English. Only much later did I appreciate the influence of this annual pilgrimage. Drifting into journalism, I wrote about space exploration before switching beats to cover the search for ancient lost cities and civilizations in the Middle East. One rainy night in Cambridge in Britain, while attending a meeting on Indian Ocean archaeology for a magazine, I crashed a dinner held for conference speakers. Seated across from me was a rosy-cheeked man who introduced himself as Mark Horton from the University of Bristol.

"Zanzibar," he said cheerily, when I asked where he was excavating. "Oh, and I'm doing a little digging in a place called Hatteras."

"Did you find the Lost Colony?" I responded jokingly. I knew that Hatteras, fifty miles south of Roanoke, was the modern name for Croatoan, the place where White was sure the colonists went.

"Indeed!" he said and then let out a nervous giggle.

When he discovered that I was a reporter, the archaeologist clammed up. "We aren't ready to go public," was all he would say. Horton turned abruptly to his neighbor to chat while I picked irritably at my chicken curry. His evasion stoked my curiosity, but he kept giving me the slip during the meeting. Later, after I returned home, he ignored my badgering e-mails. I couldn't resist the opportunity to pursue the great mystery of my childhood.

Nearly a year passed before I received his abrupt and startling reply: "We have now pretty compelling evidence for the fate of the Lost Colony."

He agreed to chat the next morning on Skype from his home in Britain during his breakfast and long before my dawn. "I'm digging dead Saxons tomorrow," he explained. When his round face popped up on the screen, he told me that his Hatteras excavation team had, among other things, found the hilt of an Elizabethan rapier in a Native American trash heap. I doubted that one lost sword unraveled a four-hundred-year-plus enigma. "Well, why don't you come see for yourself?" he said brightly.

Before signing off to dig his dead Saxons, Horton added, "If you are going to come see me, then ask about Site X." I quickly discovered that another band of researchers in 2012 spotted the image of a fort on a map drawn by John White that the artist had concealed under a patch. A team led by the archaeologist Nick Luccketti and organized by the First Colony Foundation set out to locate the putative fort fifty miles west of Roanoke, enticingly aligned with White's account that said the settlers had intended to travel "fifty miles into the main." Like Horton, Luccketti was reluctant to talk with me. "All those headlines—'Lost Colony Found,'" he grumbled in a gravelly New York accent when I reached him. "How many times can you find the damn thing?" He eventually agreed to let me visit the site, adding confidently, "We think we have the goods on this." He mumbled something about broken pottery.

The two teams, I realized, were locked in a quiet but highly competitive race to find the first hard physical evidence that could determine what happened to the settlers after White's departure. But I learned there was much more to the story than a couple of archaeological digs. Horton and Luccketti were members of a larger cast of modern characters mirroring the colorful Elizabethans they pursued with such passion. There was a gruff amateur sleuth in camouflage wandering in the eastern North Carolina swamps in search of Virginia Dare's tombstone. A Pittsburgh nurse and opera buff had a compelling new theory on the voyages' wicked foreign pilot. I quickly found myself trying to piece together a bevy of smaller puzzles, from tracking down a rumored trove of manuscripts in Portugal to pinpointing the owner of an Elizabethan gold ring found in the Outer Banks sand that lay forgotten in a library vault.

Soon I was immersed in the immense literature that has built up around the Roanoke voyages. I set sail on a reproduction Elizabethan vessel to get a feel for life aboard ship and roamed Raleigh's haunts in Devon as well as archives and libraries in Europe and North America with original maps and drawings. I kayaked the Carolina sounds, took part in Algonquian powwows, and accompanied geologists as they collected cores off Roanoke Island. I sought out those who have devoted much of their professional lives or spare time to solving the mystery. In short, my immunity compromised, I succumbed to the very obsession that afflicted the other modern-day seekers I encountered.

In the first part of what follows, I track the history and characters central to the Roanoke missions. In the second, I explore new archaeological and archival clues to the settlers' fate. When neither amateur nor professional could fully resolve the enigma of the Lost Colony to my satisfaction, I began to wonder just why we remain so haunted by "Virginia Dare and the poor lost white people," as Lane derisively puts it. Their disappearance is, of course, a fascinating riddle that cries out for a solution. But on a planet with a surfeit of missing people and forgotten refugees, this search feels at best quixotic and at worst perverse.

I discovered—in the book's final section—that the settlers exert a disturbing and tenacious grip on our imaginations because they offer a window into two centuries of American angst, specifically about race and gender. Their tale, reshaped by each succeeding generation, tells us far more about us than historians can ever reveal about vanished Elizabethans—why, for example, Virginia Dare, that innocent grandchild of John White, has for well over a century been held up as a heroine to white supremacists.

In the course of investigating this "terror within," I stumbled onto the likeliest living descendants of the Lost Colonists in the unlikeliest place of all. Their remarkable four-century odyssey revealed a story largely hidden in standard histories of the country; another secret token waiting to be read.

There is no way to know for sure what transpired on the North Carolina coast during Governor White's three-year absence or after he watched with a sinking heart as the smudge of land receded from his eyes forever on a hot August afternoon in 1590. But if we want to harvest the wisdom that is the legacy of the long-lost settlers, we must begin with the first European encounters with North America's Atlantic shore and its inhabitants. We must start by asking why an opening act of our national drama played out in the improbable place that it did, on a windswept sliver of swamp and sand.

PART ONE
The Planting

I PRITHEE, LET ME BRING THEE

WHERE CRABS GROW.

—Caliban in Shakespeare's *The Tempest*

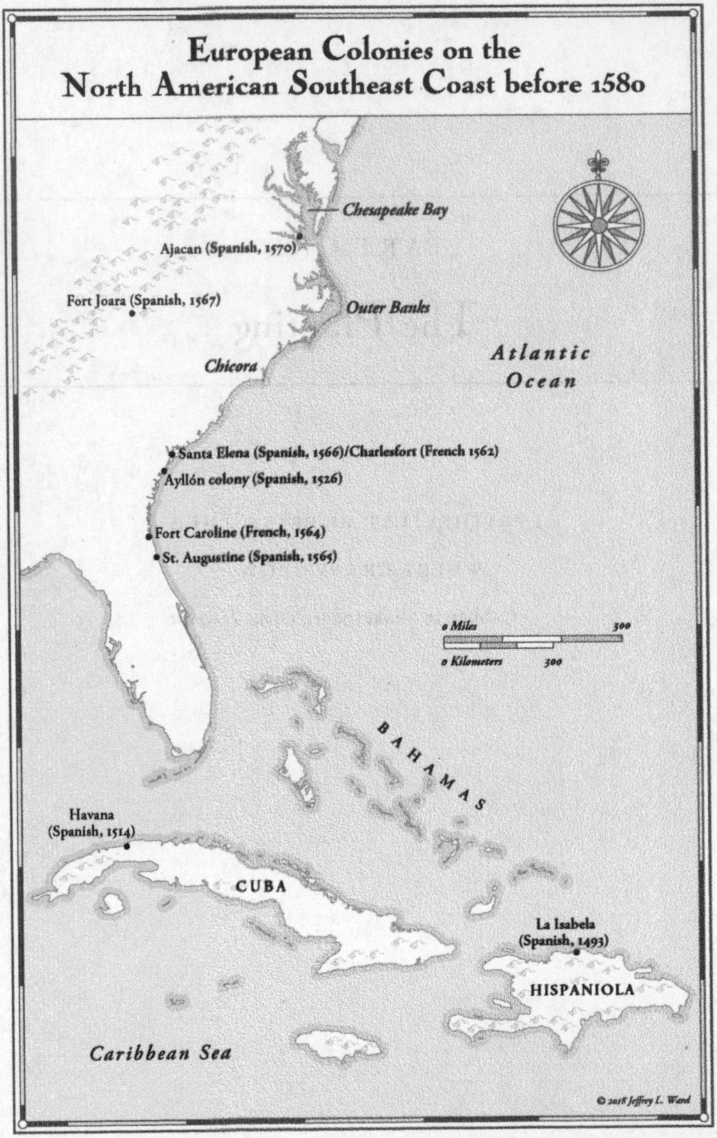

European Colonies on the
North American Southeast Coast before 1580

Chesapeake Bay

Ajacan (Spanish, 1570)

Fort Joara (Spanish, 1567)

Outer Banks

Chicora

*Atlantic
Ocean*

Santa Elena (Spanish, 1566)/Charlesfort (French 1562)

Ayllón colony (Spanish, 1526)

Fort Caroline (French, 1564)

St. Augustine (Spanish, 1565)

0 Miles — 300

0 Kilometers — 300

BAHAMAS

Havana
(Spanish, 1514)

CUBA

La Isabela
(Spanish, 1493)

HISPANIOLA

Caribbean Sea

© 2018 Jeffrey L. Ward

CHAPTER ONE

Some Delicate Garden

First there was the smell, the fragrance of burning cedar on the west wind. Then there was the smoke rising from "great fires because of the numerous inhabitants." As the *Dauphine* bobbed within sight of land on an April day in 1524, Giovanni da Verrazano saw "the sea along the coast was churned up by enormous waves because of the open beach." In a letter to French king Francis I, he described a "seashore completely covered with fine sand fifteen feet deep, which arises in the forms of small hills about fifty paces high." Then came a forest "clothed with palms, laurel, and cypress, and other varieties of tree unknown in our Europe." They gave off a strong scent, he added, "not without some kind of narcotic or aromatic liquor."

After sailing from the port of Dieppe on the English Channel, Verrazano had arrived off the Outer Banks to give us our first description of a gentle Carolina spring day. "The sky is clear and cloudless, with infrequent rain, and if the south winds bring in clouds and murkiness, they are dispelled in an instant, and the sky is once again clear and bright; the sea is calm and unruffled."

Spotting people on the beach "making various friendly signs, and beckoning us ashore," the Italian captain of the French ship sent a small boat, but the pounding breakers made it too dangerous to land. One of the sailors jumped into the water and bodysurfed to shore carrying "some trinkets, such as little bells, mirrors, and other trifles."

But when the locals tried to help him out of the water, he "was seized with terror." They carried him to a sunny spot, took off his soaked clothes, and built a huge fire, "looking at the whiteness of his flesh and examining him head to foot." The ship's crew feared they would roast and eat him; instead, the group warmed him by the fire, hugged him, and retreated politely to the top of a sand dune until the sailor made it back to the boat.

Coasting north after this hopeful and auspicious encounter, the Europeans followed a narrow strip, "an isthmus one mile wide and about two hundred miles long, in which we could see the eastern sea from the ship." Verrazano tried without success to find a safe passage through the isthmus so "we could reach those blessed shores of Cathay." He looked west across the islands of the Outer Banks and saw not the Pamlico Sound, as we now know it, but a vast sea that he proclaimed to be the Pacific Ocean. It was, after all, what he was looking for. "My intention on this voyage was to reach Cathay and the extreme eastern coast of Asia, but I did not expect to find such an obstacle of new land as I have encountered," he explained to the king who had helped fund the voyage, adding, "I estimated there would be some strait to get through." He surely had in mind Vasco Núñez de Balboa, who, a decade earlier, had crossed Panama and found the waters that led to China.

A Florentine and contemporary of Machiavelli's and Raphael's, he named the isthmus Varazanio and sailed on toward the north, earning posthumous fame as the first European to record his entrance into New York Harbor. But his much larger contribution to world history was in making the geographic gaffe of the century. Belief in this Carolinian Panama played a central role in leading the English to the Outer Banks sixty years later. You could argue that the American colonies and the United States are based on a single cartographic blunder.

Verrazano's patron proved too busy fighting a losing war with Spain to authorize a follow-up voyage, so the Italian turned to King Henry VIII across the Channel. To entice the monarch, he either presented or sent a detailed map and globe showing his discoveries. Henry at the time was more interested in divorcing his first wife and marrying Anne Boleyn—soon to be mother of Queen Elizabeth I—than expending scarce crown funds chasing shortcuts to China. He did, however, give the Italian's gifts places of honor in his royal palace on London's western outskirts. Verrazano was killed and eaten by Caribs on the less blessed shores of Guadeloupe before he could correct his error, but his imagined isthmus lived on within Westminster's walls.

As Henry plotted and Francis warred, a wealthy Spanish judge and landowner on the island of Hispaniola—in today's Dominican Republic—quietly launched the first attempt to colonize the east coast of North America since the Vikings. In an eerie harbinger of the plantation culture to come, Lucas Vázquez de Ayllón envisioned turning the Southeast into a feudal empire staffed by Native American workers and African slaves. The North American east coast in that day was seen much the same as the west coast of Africa, a ready source of slaves to work the proliferating sugar plantations of the Spanish Caribbean and Portuguese Brazil. Ayllón sponsored a reconnaissance mission along the Carolina coast that captured more than sixty Siouan-speaking Indians from a land they called Chicora, which lay just south of the Outer Banks in what is now South Carolina. "As for the Indians, they turned out to be useless," Ayllón noted with regret. "For almost all of them died of fretfulness and grief."

One young survivor caught his eye. Dubbed Don Francisco Chicora—we don't know his Siouan name—he was tall and strikingly handsome, and the Hispaniola judge took him to Spain, where he charmed the Castilian court with fantastic tales of the wealth and fertility of his native land. He told of giant kings, men with long tails, and fine cheese made from deer milk.

These compelling stories were enough to win Ayllón a royal grant from King Charles V to settle Chicora. The judge was named governor and given a monopoly on trade in the area for six years, but he had to shoulder the enormous costs of sending and maintaining a colony. He pledged not to enslave the Indians but to "attract them to our service that they will be protected and not molested." Taking along African slaves was, however, permitted. The king also encouraged the new governor to explore the area for a passage through North America to the Pacific.

Two years after Verrazano's voyage, in July 1526, a flotilla of six ships carrying six hundred people, including farmers, priests, women, Africans, two doctors, and a pharmacist, sailed from Hispaniola for Chicora. The exceptionally well-organized expedition carried seven dozen horses, beef cattle, tons of corn, and three thousand loaves of cassava bread. (By contrast, the first Puritans who arrived nearly a century later on the *Mayflower* counted just over one hundred passengers, and no livestock, on their single small vessel.)

Enticing people to leave their familiar homes for an unknown land proved easy. "The entire Spanish nation is in fact so keen about novelties that people go eagerly anywhere they are called by a nod or a whistle," wrote a court acquaintance of Ayllón's, "in the hope of bettering their condition, and are ready to sacrifice what they have for what they hope."

After they sailed twelve hundred miles north from the Caribbean without incident, mishaps plagued the settlers' arrival. The flagship grounded in shoal waters, ruining the bulk of the supplies. The settlement site proved swampy. Upon their arrival in Chicora, Don Francisco promptly defected, his tall tales no doubt designed to ensure his kidnappers would deliver him safely home; he was never seen by Europeans again. The anxious colonists soon moved south to a healthier location near today's Savannah, Georgia. The local Native Americans, initially happy to trade food for valuable European goods, grew tired of feeding the foreigners. Illness and starvation quickly took a terrible toll on the colonists.

"Many persons died of hunger for lack of bread and because in their infirmity they were unable to fish," one account states. Protein from the plentiful seafood, however, was not enough. Without bread or corn, the settlers likely suffered from the lethargy and nausea that can come with eating insufficient carbohydrates. Indians used acorns and roots when maize supplies ran low, but the Spanish seem to have lacked this knowledge. As relations with the local tribe degenerated, the newcomers' situation grew increasingly dire.

Ayllón died in October, and the desperate and leaderless Spanish split into competing factions. Indians infuriated by harsh treatment attacked, and the African slaves rebelled. An unknown number, African as well as European, deserted to the Native Americans. This was only the start of more than two centuries of settlers along eastern North America melting into the indigenous population. The remaining ragged band set sail back home. Stormy seas forced the voyagers to dump Ayllón's body, which they had hoped to bury in Hispaniola, over the side. Less than one-third of the settlers made it home.

The debacle in Chicora presaged events at countless later European settlements along that coast, including Roanoke—grounded ships, inadequate supplies, dependence on and desertion to the locals, and a desperate cycle of hunger and violence. But the legend of a fruitful land akin to Eden woven by Don Francisco spread across Europe faster than the true tale of woe. When French Protestants called Huguenots sought to escape the religious turmoil in France in the 1560s, they looked to Chicora as a welcoming and fertile refuge. A first expedition sent to a South Carolina island collapsed when the governor returned to Europe for supplies in 1562, only to be captured and jailed by the English. The abandoned men made a harrowing journey in an open boat back to France, resorting to cannibalism along the way.

Three years later, a second wave of French settlers led by Jean Ribault built a base a hundred miles or so to the south and fared even worse. Stalked by a Spanish convoy, they launched a preemptive attack, which failed. The Spanish subsequently attacked their fort, sparing only the women and children and a few who claimed to be Catholic. Pieces of the French leader's beard and skin were sent to Spain's new king, Philip II, as proof of the massacre, news of which stunned Europe, given that the two nations were not at war. The message was clear: trespassers on this North American territory, claimed by Spain, faced annihilation. To prevent further intrusions, the Spanish built St. Augustine on the Florida coast. Ribault's head was split into quarters; one part was attached to each corner of the new settlement. On the ruins of the first French colony, they constructed a town called Santa Elena to mark the northern frontier of Spanish control.

There was actually little in eastern North America to interest the Spanish, who focused instead on controlling the wealthy urban civilizations that had already been established in the New World, such as the Aztec and Incan Empires, and expanding sugar plantations across the Caribbean. The region to the north, what was called La Florida, had the wrong climate for growing sugar and held little promise of gold. The indigenous people lacked cities and showed little enthusiasm for Christianity. They also were capable of waging unnervingly effective guerrilla warfare against the slow-moving armored Iberians in the dense woods and swamps. The Spanish, recalling Ayllón's failure, saw no profit in further colonization.

But by the mid-sixteenth century, as a result of geography, the Spanish Empire's jugular vein lay just offshore. In order to arrive in Europe, treasure ships carrying Chinese silks, Indonesian spices, and Bolivian silver first made port on the Pacific coast of Panama or Mexico. Their precious cargoes were then carried overland and stowed on vessels bound for Havana. There, along with ships carrying Mexican gold, South American hides, and the white gold of Caribbean sugar, armed galleons escorted convoys north through the narrow channel between Florida and the Bahamas on the powerful north-moving current called the Gulf Stream. Like an arrow shot from a bow, the convoys surged north on the ever-flowing river within a sea as far as the Outer Banks, where they could catch the prevailing westerly winds to carry them across the Atlantic to the Azores, where they could resupply, and from there to Spain.

The handy Gulf Stream came at a price. Untold numbers of Spanish sailors and passengers drowned in shipwrecks on the treacherous coast, and Native Americans captured hundreds of survivors; St. Augustine was as much a safe haven for castaways as a defense against European intruders. The remote waters were also ideal for pirates eager to seize Spanish treasure, because the course and schedule of the fleets were predictable. Both threats endangered the realm's finances.

The man overseeing this fast-expanding empire, Philip II, came to the Spanish throne shortly before the French made their ill-fated attempts to gain a foothold in the New World. Philip ran not a country but a complicated union of Catholic kingdoms scattered on the Iberian and Italian peninsulas and in what is now the Netherlands, along with the vast colonial domain stretching from the Philippines to Florida. He married a series of queens and princesses—Austrian,

French, English, and Portuguese—to help hold it all together. A formidable intelligence network and well-organized bureaucracy kept this tall and brooding workaholic, who preferred to dress in simple black, apprised of the smallest disturbances in his far-flung domain. His greatest threat lay neither in the New World nor among his European neighbors. Philip most feared the formidable sultan Murad III, who oversaw the sprawling Ottoman Empire from the splendid Topkapi Palace on the Golden Horn in Istanbul. The Ottomans dominated the lands and seas between the Adriatic and the Persian Gulf.

The two mammoth empires clashed in the Mediterranean. Murad used the growing religious rift among Europeans in an attempt to contain Philip's growing power. He colluded with England's Elizabeth, the unmarried apostate queen, adroitly suggesting that her nation's new Protestant faith had more in common with Islam than Catholicism, because both rejected the worship of idols. The English gladly supplied ammunition, along with tin and lead, to the sultan as part of a 1579 commercial deal, scandalizing Catholic Europe. Little wonder that Spain's pious leader saw himself as the only force preventing a Muslim empire from reaching the Continent's Atlantic shores.

The Spanish monarch's luck changed dramatically in 1580. The sultan, embroiled in an expensive war with Persia and facing galloping inflation at home, agreed on a truce that would hold for more than a century. This allowed Philip to turn his attention to rebellious Protestants in the Netherlands. Meanwhile, the Portuguese ruler vanished in a disastrous campaign in Morocco; Philip seized the opportunity and claimed the throne of his smaller neighbor that had its own extensive territories from Brazil to India. With this merger, he found himself at the helm of the largest and wealthiest empire in the history of the world, claiming nearly half of western Europe and all of the Americas as well as ample African and Asian territories. This was the first empire, not that of the British, on which it was said the sun never set. In the New World alone, more than 150,000 Spanish lived in some two hundred bustling cities scattered across the Caribbean basin, Mexico, and Peru. Another 200,000 or so African slaves cultivated their cash crops and did their menial tasks. Millions of Native inhabitants surrounded these growing centers of Spanish power, pay-ing taxes and rents benefiting the new European elite that replaced their indigenous rulers.

Aside from a few fishermen in Newfoundland and farmers in Brazil, there was not a single French or English village in the Western Hemisphere on the day that three hundred Spanish poets competed for a prize in Mexico City. Conquistadors had built forts in the Appalachian Mountains, while Jesuits had settled on the shores of Chesapeake Bay—albeit briefly. Toward the end of the sixteenth century, there was no reason to think that Philip's steamroller wouldn't continue to conquer and cajole its way across Europe while completing his project of dominating the New World. But Verrazano's false promise and the ludicrous myth of Chicora soon fused with surprising, and to Spain disruptive, results.

Elizabeth's cramped and gloomy England was a stark contrast to Philip's gilded Spain. Squeezed between France, with fivefold its population, and a restive independent Scotland to the north, the country could claim only Ireland to the west as a foreign possession, an incessant flash point of conflict where soldiers and settlers clustered behind the protective ditches and fences surrounding the Dublin region. One Englishman at the time described his nation as "a weak, and poor state, destitute of means and friends."

The gulf between Elizabeth's kingdom and other European nations was greater than the English Channel. Her father's decision to declare his land Protestant in 1534 isolated it from a Europe still overwhelmingly Catholic. The Renaissance that began in Italy, with its remarkable advancements in science, technology, and art, arrived here in a belated and sporadic fashion. London was a vibrant capital, the second-largest city in Europe after Paris, but even by the standards of late medieval times the English as a whole were a xenophobic and superstitious lot. "They care little for foreigners, but scoff and laugh at them," a German government official wrote of the capital's citizens during a 1592 visit. He singled out the tradespeople who "seldom go to other countries" and added that street gangs viciously attacked foreigners "without regard to person."

King Philip II of Spain holds a rosary after his 1571 victory over a Turkish fleet; the same year, Virginia Algonquians massacred Spanish Jesuits in their mission on Chesapeake Bay.

On the eve of Virginia's settlement, England's queen, Elizabeth I, carries a sieve in this 1583 portrait that associates her with the Roman vestal virgins.

Navigation by instruments was considered a black art rather than a rational system, and math teachers might be mistaken for devil worshippers. "Books wherein appeared angles or mathematical diagrams were thought sufficient to be destroyed, because accounted popish, or diabolical, or both," an English writer noted a century later. When the Italian friar and renowned scholar Giordano Bruno visited England's intellectual center of Oxford in 1580, where offensive books had been burned in the town marketplace, he was stunned by the "obstinate ignorance, pedantry, and presumption" of the professors, whom he dismissed as "blind asses." (Not that Italy was a freethinker's paradise; Bruno himself was later burned at the stake in Rome's marketplace for heresy.) Two of his English friends begged his sympathy. "Pity the poverty of this country," they pleaded, "which is widowed of good learning in the fields of philosophy and pure mathematics."

England's poverty stemmed from a brewing economic crisis and a fraying social fabric. The country's traditional exports of tin and wool cloth suffered from rising competition and protectionism abroad. By fencing off land to graze more sheep, wealthy landowners forced small farmers into the filthy cities that already bred deadly epidemics. "These enclosures be the causes why rich men eat up a poor man as beasts do eat grass," railed one critic in 1583. Yet the dissolution of the Catholic monasteries by Henry VIII had removed a welfare system of church-funded hospitals and almshouses that the English government had yet to replace.

Elizabeth owned two thousand gloves, but her spectacular wardrobe couldn't mask the nation's destitution, from its bad roads to its woefully inadequate navy. Nor was her throne secure. Would-be assassins stalked her. She was shot at on her royal barge and attacked with a knife in a royal garden. "There are more than two hundred men of all ages who, at the instigation of the Jesuits, conspire to kill me," she complained to the French ambassador in 1583. Mary, Queen of Scots, a staunch Catholic and sometime ally to Philip, was next in line for her job. Though imprisoned by Elizabeth, she was still capable of plotting against her cousin.

England had taken an early lead in New World exploration. Nearly a century prior, when the country had just emerged from a long civil war, Elizabeth's grandfather Henry VII sought to expand his realm's commercial reach. Though he declined the plea made by Columbus's brother to back the Italian's plan to sail west to reach Asia in England's name—one of history's great what-ifs—he did support later American missions by Giovanni Caboto, also known as John Cabot, as well as Portuguese explorers and Bristol merchants. But his son and successor, Henry VIII, squandered that advantage by picking fights with the pope and the French and ignoring the likes of Verrazano.

Henry's daughter learned the hard way that the promise of quick New World riches could be illusory. In 1576, a young Yorkshire seaman named Martin Frobisher set off for China, intending to pass north of the Americas. Ice floes around Canada's Baffin Island forced his return, but not before he picked up black stone that a specialist in England claimed contained gold. Elizabeth unwisely gave Frobisher a thousand pounds—nearly half a million dollars today—and a charter to form his Cathay Company. Other court officials also invested heavily in the venture.

He set off on two major expeditions to establish a mining colony in the frozen north, but the tons of rock carried back to England turned out to be iron pyrite—fool's gold. Instead of filling the queen's treasury, the stone was used to pave a suburban London road in what was possibly the world's most expensive flagstone. The financial fiasco turned Elizabeth and her court into skeptics of American schemes. Merchants got the message; they turned instead to new markets in Russia and the Middle East. But one eccentric figure at court continued to press for a more aggressive New World policy.

Tall and rich, Sir Humphrey Gilbert was well versed in the new science of instrument navigation and deeply obsessed with finding a passage over the top of North America to China. He was also a soldier known for his violent outbursts and brutal tactics in neighboring Ireland. One of his methods was to line the path to his tent with the heads of slain Irish rebels. This brought "great terror to the people when they saw the heads of their dead fathers, brothers, children, kinsfolk, and friends," according to one English observer.

A week after Frobisher left on his second and last Baffin Island expedition, the queen granted Gilbert a charter to explore new lands and settle any place "not actually possessed of any Christian prince"—a warning not to tangle with Spain's colonies, though with no mention of how to handle natives already in possession of the land. Using his large family fortune, he quickly assembled a fleet with eleven ships and five hundred men and set out in the fall of 1578. Gilbert put his half brother in command of a small ship named the *Falcon*.

At twenty-four, Walter Raleigh had a reputation as a libertine; his roommate in London affectionately called him "riotous, lascivious, and incontinent." More than six feet tall, he towered over the average Elizabethan. Slim and handsome, with brown curly hair and pointed beard, he loved fashionable clothes and expensive jewels but came from minor and perpetually cash-strapped gentry in the western county of Devon. In the early 1570s, when not quite sixteen, Raleigh dropped out of Oxford to fight together with French Huguenots against rival Catholics; he might have first heard of the magical land of Chicora on the bloody battlefields of Reformation France.

He had never been on the open sea. Gilbert assigned an experienced forty-year-old Portuguese pilot named Simão Fernandes as his navigator, likely with the task of showing the ropes to his impetuous half brother. Fernandes was a former pirate who barely escaped the executioner's noose and was now intent on improving his social and financial lot in his new homeland.

The fleet's goal was kept secret to avoid detection by the Spanish, though Philip's ambassador in London promptly warned the king that the destination was somewhere in the New World. His specific concern was the presence of the Portuguese pilot, "a thorough-paced scoundrel" who could reveal to the English details of the American coastline, "which he knows very well." From this we know that Fernandes had been in the service of Spain and had extensive experience in the Americas, which made him nearly unique in Tudor England.

Gilbert presumably intended to find the fabled Northwest Passage over North America, but his mission quickly descended into chaos, "frustrated by the usual Elizabethan blend of storms, mischance, quarrels with a second-in-command and desertions," according to one Raleigh biography. All the ships turned back soon after leaving port, save the *Falcon*, which instead of sailing west sped south to the Cape Verde Islands off the African coast. The islands were a common stopping place for Portuguese ships carrying African slaves and gold or Asian pepper. This was, as Fernandes knew, an ideal spot for pirating.

"Desirous to do somewhat worthy of honor, [Raleigh] took his course to the West Indies," a contemporary notes. Short of provisions, however, the young man and his crew returned, limping back to England after "many dangerous adventures, as well as tempests as fights on the sea." Some of the sailors apparently died or were killed in a battle with a Spanish vessel, and the *Falcon* was a shambles when it docked at Plymouth in May 1579.

The country's governing body, the Privy Council, grounded Raleigh, who had learned that the Atlantic Ocean made him seasick. "Man may not expect the ease of many cabins and safety at once in sea-service," he wrote later, adding that ships were "but sluttish dens that breed sickness." But he also learned that pirating could make him rich and famous. "He that commands the sea, commands the trade, and he that is lord of the trade of the world [is] lord of the wealth of the world," he later noted. In addition, six months on the ocean cemented a bond between the courtier and the pilot; Raleigh's ambition and status combined with Fernandes's experience would make a potent pairing in the decade to come.

Though Raleigh subsequently landed in prison twice, once for dueling with a knight and then for exchanging punches with a rival on the Westminster tennis court, his reputation at court grew. Despite (or because of) his brashness, the queen appointed him her chief bodyguard, an unpaid but important position for a monarch threatened regularly with assassination.

An uprising in Ireland backed by Philip and the pope prompted her to send Raleigh to assist in battling the threat. His superiors ordered him to oversee the massacre of more than five hundred prisoners, including women and children, which he accomplished with murderous efficiency. Meanwhile, Fernandes took a small ship named the *Squirrel* on a reconnaissance mission for Gilbert to the North

American coast and returned within three months, an amazing feat of seamanship. He might have passed by the Outer Banks during the course of the voyage.

Meanwhile, undeterred by his previous failure, the single-minded Gilbert planned another New World voyage in 1583. By this time the queen had taken to young Raleigh and forbade him to leave her side. She noted that the enthusiastic Gilbert "was a man noted of not good happ by sea"—that is, plagued by misfortune—and didn't trust him to bring her dashing Devon man back safely. (Despite his knowledge of instruments, Gilbert had found himself lost off the English coast more than once.) Occupied with another mission, Fernandes didn't take part in the voyage either, to his good fortune.

Gilbert's final adventure was part farce and part tragedy. He arrived in Newfoundland's St. John's Harbour to take possession of the land for the queen and to levy taxes, much to the amusement of the rough fishing crews from many nations that regularly gathered there each summer and cared little for royal charters. Storms subsequently sank many of his ships, and Gilbert drowned in a September 1583 storm off the Azores while trying to return to England. In his final hours, he was said to have sat theatrically on the stern of the *Squirrel*—possibly the same tiny ship Fernandes had sailed three years before—while, according to legend, reading from Sir Thomas More's *Utopia*. "Gilbert's scheme was wrecked by his own impatient, unstable, and perverse nature," writes Tudor scholar J. B. Black.

This dramatic death left the field of New World exploration open to a younger generation with fresh ideas. As Gilbert's ship went under in the Atlantic, a thirty-year-old Protestant pastor named Richard Hakluyt was crossing the English Channel to serve as chaplain and secretary to the English ambassador in Paris. This quiet and studious man would play the central role in creating what historian Peter Mancall refers to as "the language and logic that would guide the English colonization of North America."

His father dealt in skins and furs but died when the boy was five. He might have been named for his older cousin who subsequently became his guardian and mentor. This elder Richard Hakluyt collected maps and merchants' stories and likely sent his young namesake to the Westminster School, a short walk from the queen's palace. When the young man was sixteen, he had a road-to-Damascus conversion when looking at his guardian's maps and saw a vast world waiting to be explored, redeemed, and exploited. He went on to graduate from Oxford and became an Anglican minister but held tight to his vision. Still in his twenties, he compiled a book of reports from European voyages to the New World, most of which were unknown in England.

"There is a mighty large old map in parchment, made, as it should seem, by Verrazano," he wrote two years later. The chart "traced all along the coast from Florida to Cape Briton with many Italian names, which layeth out the sea making a little neck of land." He also noted "an old excellent globe in the queen's private gallery at Westminster, which also seems to be of Verrazano's making," marking "the very self same strait neck of land . . . as it doth on Panama."

Hakluyt's 1582 book includes a map of the Americas based on Verrazano's data, in which the Pacific Ocean swoops through the area occupied, we now know, by the Pacific Northwest, Rocky Mountains, and Great Plains. As a result, the hefty girth of North America is portrayed instead as a tiny wasp waist, with Florida below the tightly cinched belt and Canada above it. Hakluyt's excitement grew as he realized that if England could colonize and control this strategic area, this Panama of the North, then it could dominate trade between East and West.

In Paris, he loitered in sailors' pubs and chatted up scholars, buttonholing diplomats from many nations to pump them for information on the wider world, including "five or six of the best captains and pilots, one of whom was born in East India" and a Spaniard just back from Japan. Much of this intelligence was considered classified by Philip, who issued strict orders that maps and descriptions of New World ports and trade routes not fall into the wrong hands. Hakluyt was, in other words, a spy, and he was working for one of the era's great spymasters.

In January 1584, he wrote impatiently to his boss, Secretary of State Francis Walsingham, that the opportunity to settle the Verrazano Isthmus would "wax cold and fall to the ground" without swift action. Building a colony could also, he argued, "stay the Spanish king

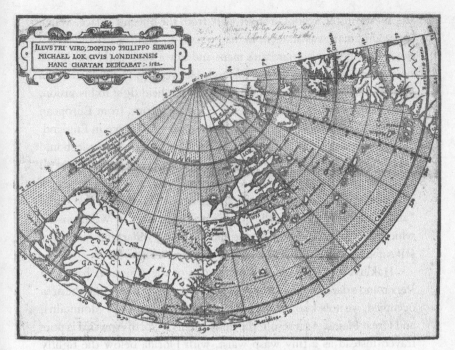

The Sea of Verrazano covers much of North America and laps just to the west of the Atlantic in this map of North America published by Richard Hakluyt in 1582.

from flowing all over the face" of North America. Nor was he content to remain behind. "I am most willing to go now," he added bravely. While appreciating his enthusiasm, Walsingham kept the pastor busy in Paris.

Hakluyt envisioned more than a stopping place to transship goods from the East back to Europe. He saw a land that could also supply raw materials increasingly in short supply in England, such as timber, ores, and pharmaceuticals. And as a pious Anglican minister, he was eager to convert Indians to Protestantism so that the whole of the New World didn't fall into Catholic idolatry. Along with salvation for "the souls of millions of those wretched people," he saw profit in clothing their shamefully naked bodies.

As well as being a political spy in the garb of a pastor, Hakluyt was on the payroll of the Clothworkers' Company of London. He was part of an industrial espionage effort to bribe Turkish and Persian officials to learn about their superior dyeing techniques so they could be copied in England. Cloth was England's prime export—one commentator in 1580 called it the land's "true golden fleece"—and thousands of spinners and weavers depended heavily on foreign markets. By the early 1580s, with the country increasingly a religious pariah across much of Europe, businesses were desperate to find new customers outside the Catholic sphere. Hakluyt saw the ill-clad peoples of eastern North America as a large and untapped market that could turn around the ailing industry.

Three months after Hakluyt pressed Walsingham to move forward on a New World settlement, the queen split the deceased Gilbert's charter between his younger brother, Adrian Gilbert, and his half brother, Raleigh. Adrian won authority to explore and settle the coast from the rich fishing grounds of Newfoundland to the north, where, despite Frobisher and Gilbert's failures, geographers still presumed there was a passage over North America to Asia yet to be found.

In the grant issued March 16, 1584, the queen's favorite seemed to get the short end of the stick. Raleigh received what lay to the south, much of it in land Spain considered its own. He had until 1591 to build and maintain a colony in North America to retain the patent. Elizabeth insisted the colonists "shall be of the allegiance to us our heirs and successors" and enjoy the same rights as other Englishmen so long as they were good Protestants. Raleigh, however, could rule as a feudal lord—much as Ayllón had dreamed for himself six decades earlier—and make all laws as long as they were similar to those in England. The queen was to receive one-fifth of any gold or silver that he found.

There was no mention of the non-Christian inhabitants and what rights they would retain under the new regime. This strange omission, as with Gilbert's charter, reflected English ignorance of the peoples they would encounter. By this time, Spain had undergone a wrenching debate over its early genocidal practices in the New World, and Native Americans had been granted—on paper at least—status as "free vassals of the crown" with rights to land and protection from slavery. (Tragically, this increased the trade in African slaves instead.) The English, quick to criticize Spanish cruelties in the New World, failed from the start to consider the effect of their own policies.

With the queen's patent in hand, Raleigh swiftly organized a reconnaissance mission, one that cost some three-quarters of a million dollars in today's currency. In April, just weeks after receiving his grant, he boarded the larger of two ships docked in the Thames River to deliver instructions to the captains, because he himself was still forbidden to leave the queen's side. His old shipmate Fernandes would serve as navigator, responsible for landing the men successfully in America and bringing them home. They agreed to scout out the promising region visited by Verrazano, which Fernandes likely knew firsthand from his previous voyages. Along with the possibility of a Pacific passage, this area marked the spot where Spanish ships cruising up the Gulf Stream turned away from the North American coast for the Atlantic leg of their journey—and therefore a prime location for English privateering.

The two vessels set sail. By June they reached the Caribbean and caught the warm current north, coasting just out of sight of Spanish eyes at St. Augustine and Santa Elena. This five-thousand-mile journey was to be the course followed by all of the outgoing Roanoke voyages. In words oddly reminiscent of Verrazano's account, one of the captains smelled an odor "so sweet, and so strong . . . as if we had been in the midst of some delicate garden abounding with all kind of odiferous flowers." Two days later, on July 4, 1584, the men caught their first glimpse of the sandy shores that the Florentine spotted six decades before from the *Dauphine*.

CHAPTER TWO

All Signs of Joy

On a midsummer morning, a Native American paddled with two companions across a broad lagoon. They pulled their sleek log canoe onto the sand of the barrier island. Clad only in a leather breechcloth, the man boldly strode to the shore of the nearby inlet where the lagoon met the Atlantic. Just offshore lay two enormous winged ships that dwarfed his tiny craft.

The two English captains, nineteen-year-old Philip Amadas and thirty-four-year-old Arthur Barlowe, hesitated at first. This was their first visit to the New World, and they likely had never seen a Native American. More than twice Amadas's age and well versed in encounters with strange peoples, their pilot Fernandes likely offered words of encouragement because he had a boat prepared to row the three of them to shore. The entire time, Barlowe marveled, the Indian watched calmly, "never making any show of fear, or doubt."

Simple acts of hospitality quickly overcame the language barrier. "After he had spoken of many things not understood by us, we brought him with his own good liking, aboard the ships, and gave him a shirt, a hat, and some other things, and made him taste of our wine, and our meat, which he liked very well."

Then the visitor climbed back into his canoe. Rather than departing, though, he began to fish in the placid waters of the Pamlico

Thomas Harriot says this engraving shows "the arrival of the Englishmen in Virginia" in 1585. "The sea coasts of Virginia are full of islands, whereby the entrance into the main island is hard to find." The Outer Banks are the narrow islands at bottom; Roanoke is center left.

Sound. "In less than half an hour, he had laden his boat as deep as it could swim, with which he came again to the point of the land, and there he divided his fish into two parts, pointing one part to the ship, and the other to the pinnace"—the smaller vessel—as a thank-you for the English hospitality. Then he and his friends paddled away. This amicable encounter between the confident Indian and the nervous Europeans marked the start of a contentious and complicated relationship between the English and the inhabitants of North America that continues to play out today.

The next day, a formal delegation of forty Indians led by an elder named Granganimeo, the brother of the local leader Wingina, arrived on the barrier island. As had the man on the previous day, the elder carefully demonstrated peaceable intentions as if sensing the wariness.

"When he came to the place, his servants spread a long mat upon the ground, on which he sat down, and at the other end of the mat, four others of his company did the like; the rest of his men stood round about him, somewhat afar off," Barlowe recalled. "When we came to the shore to him with our weapons, he never moved from his place, nor any of the other four, nor never mistrusted any harm to be offered from us, but sitting still, he beckoned us to come and sit by him."

Granganimeo's tranquillity as strangers approached carrying swords and guns was a remarkable expression of trust, particularly given the European proclivity to snatch Native Americans for Caribbean slavery. As the two captains warily sat down on the reed mat, the Indian then made "all signs of joy, and welcome, striking on his head, and his breast, and afterwards on ours, to show we were all one, smiling, and making show the best he could, of all love, and familiarity."

The English presented gifts to Granganimeo, and within a couple of days serious trading commenced. Barlowe described the men as "very handsome and goodly people, and in their behavior as mannerly and civil as any of Europe." The chief's brother insisted on dominating the Indian side of the exchange; other Native Americans were not allowed to barter directly with the newcomers. A bright tin dish prompted Granganimeo to "clap it before his breast" with joy. He explained through pantomime that it would serve as a talisman against a rival group with whom they "maintain a deadly and terrible war." Metal was so rare that the Indian leader said they had extracted nails and spikes from a washed-up European vessel, twenty years before, the first reference to a shipwreck along a coast that would claim more than six hundred vessels in the centuries to come and earn the fearsome sobriquet of Graveyard of the Atlantic. Fish teeth commonly sufficed as arrowheads on reed arrows launched with willow bows, while fire-hardened wood made swords and breastplates.

Granganimeo was an elder among a people living in small communities strung along the seafood-rich shores of this watery land of rivers, lagoons, and marshes. Centuries before, as Germanic tribes speaking Anglo-Saxon began to migrate into the British Isles, his ancestors had drifted south from the northeastern coast of North America. They spoke a variation of Algonquian, a language group like the Romance or Germanic tongues of Europe. The women brought particular methods for growing corn, squash, beans, and other cultivated plants, such as the sunflower first domesticated in eastern North America, as well as in-depth knowledge of wild plants and roots for culinary and medicinal uses. The men, trained from boyhood to seek game, roamed the woods for turkeys, squirrels, rabbits, deer, and bear and fished the broad waters in narrow canoes artfully crafted out of single logs.

We get a mouth-watering glimpse of their midsummer diet from Barlowe, who records that Granganimeo provided daily food rations for the visitors that included "fat bucks" and hares as well as plenty of fish. Also on the menu were "melons, walnuts, cucumbers, gourds, peas," and "fruits very excellent good."

As Granganimeo intimated to Amadas and Barlowe, relations among the tribes presented a complex and shifting set of alliances and rivalries. The search for game and fish could spark territorial conflict, and warfare was frequent, but more on the level of skirmishes than European-style slaughters. Hunters doubled as warriors when needed, and the captured women and children of rivals might be incorporated into a community. Like that of Jews and Danes, the Algonquian culture is matrilineal, with kinship passing from the mother to the child. Women hold considerable political power.

Because the Carolina Algonquians of the sixteenth century left no written records of their own, we can only see their world through the cloudy lens of the visiting Elizabethans. For nearly a year, the English mistakenly thought the Indians called their land Wingandacoia; it turned out this was a polite phrase meaning "you wear great clothes." The real name, they discovered later, was Ossomocomuck. The newcomers were not even clear about the nomenclature of the tribe that Granganimeo's brother led; he might have called himself a Secotan or Roanoke.

The Native Americans lived on the swampy mainland fronting the western side of the vast oval of the Pamlico Sound. Most of the barrier islands were not permanently inhabited, except leg-bone-shaped Croatoan Island, where the tribe of the same name lived. "Their towns are but small, near the sea coast but few, some containing but 10 or 12 houses; some 20, the greatest that we have seen have been but of 30 houses," a later settler noted. More populous groups clustered to the west, on fertile lands alongside the freshwater rivers like the Chowan and the Roanoke that flowed into the brackish lagoons.

Once the English and the Indians were at ease with each other, the English set off to investigate the region, in what was more guided tour than bold exploration. Their larger ship couldn't sail through the shallow waters, so the two-masted pinnace carried Barlowe and seven other English for twenty miles across the lagoon "to an island which they call Roanoke." Wedged between the mainland to the west and the barrier islands to the east, it acts like a cork between the broad Albemarle Sound to the north and the Pamlico to the south. The Albemarle, smaller than the Pamlico but still vast, stretched fifty miles into the Carolina interior.

The strategically located island was the home of Granganimeo. "At the north end thereof was a village of nine houses, built of cedar, and fortified round about with sharp trees, to keep out their enemies," writes Barlowe, who had a keen eye for detail. Awaiting them was Granganimeo's wife, the chief's sister-in-law, who had visited the ships with her retainers. Her husband was away, but she ran out "to meet us very cheerfully and friendly."

The warm welcome that the unnamed matriarch gave to a boatful of armed foreigners reflects the powerful role of women among the Carolina Algonquians, as well as the culture's natural hospitality. She ordered villagers to pull the boat close to shore and had the strangely clad men carried to dry ground. She led the Europeans to her spacious five-room house and had their oars stowed inside to prevent theft.

The matriarch ushered them into the central chamber and "caused us to sit down by a great fire." Nearby was a wooden image of their chief deity, "of whom they speak incredible things." The Europeans no doubt gave off a rank odor after months at sea, because she had her attendants immediately remove at least their outer clothes to be washed and dried. Meanwhile, "some of the women plucked off our stockings and washed them, some washed our feet in warm water, and she herself took great pains to see all things ordered in the best manner she could, making great haste to dress some meat for us to eat."

After feasting on wooden platters filled with venison, roasted and boiled fish, melons, various fruits, and what sounds like corn pudding, the men drank wine mulled with ginger, sassafras, and what Barlowe calls black cinnamon as well as "other wholesome, and medicinal herbs." He was impressed by her warmth and solicitude. "We were entertained with all love and kindness, and with much bounty, after their manner, as they could possibly devise."

There was one tense moment during the meal when armed Native men returned from hunting. The alarmed Englishmen reached for their weapons, but the woman ordered the intruders away after having their bows and arrows broken "and with all beat the poor fellows out of the gate." Still fearful of ambush, Barlowe insisted that the English sleep that night in their boat. The distraught hostess sent the English leftovers as well as tightly woven reed mats to protect them from rain. Thirty men and women remained close by throughout the night to keep watch and to entreat them in vain to return to the village.

The courtesy offered to Barlowe by Granganimeo's wife might have been motivated by more than simply hospitality. The island of Roanoke supported only a single village, and a Spanish prisoner later told authorities in Havana that "the land produces little to eat. There is only maize and of that little and poor in quality." It might have been a hunting and fishing preserve for the royal family—Wingina's principal town, Dasemunkepeuc, lay just a couple of miles across the shallow water on the mainland.

The tribal leader himself was said to be at a distant inland town at the time, recovering from a thigh wound incurred during battle, so the English didn't meet him on their first visit. In his absence, though, these strangers handed his tribe a potential political, economic, and military windfall. Wingina was in frequent conflict with tribes to the south, likely made up of Siouan speakers, and his relations with his larger and more powerful Algonquian-speaking neighbors to the north and west were, from what can be gleaned, sometimes fraught. Wingina's people laboriously made shell beads (called *roanoke*; the island may have served as a kind of royal mint), exported inland in exchange for copper and stone, but the many middlemen made such goods expensive. The wealth of material brought by European newcomers promised to alter the regional balance in his favor. To Wingina, Roanoke would seem an ideal place for a new English settlement: a marginal piece of territory under his firm control, one that placed the leader advantageously between the foreigners and his rivals.

Amadas and Barlowe spent six weeks much like modern tourists to the Outer Banks, making excursions and enjoying the sea breezes and shellfish. As summer faded, they set sail for England, with Barlowe praising the locals for a life "after the manner of the golden age." The men had not yet discovered a shortcut to Asia or gold mines, but the mission seemed to confirm the old Chicora legends of a land of plenty.

As a postscript to his report to Raleigh, he says, "We brought home also two of the savages being lusty men, whose names were Wanchese and Manteo."

As a reconnaissance mission, Raleigh's venture was a resounding success, whetting English appetites for a colony in the Americas. But organizing a proper transatlantic settlement demanded teams of experts, not to mention deep pockets. Raleigh's predecessors had had considerable means. Ayllón was a rich planter and well-connected judge, while the Huguenots had the backing of the wealthy French Protestant establishment. Having just turned thirty, the man from Devon didn't even have the funds to buy back his modest family farm. But Raleigh knew how to wield his looks and wits to win royal favor, and in the wake of Amadas and Barlowe's encouraging findings, he went on a charm offensive.

"Fain would I climb, yet I fear to fall," he allegedly scratched on a window in Elizabeth's palace, to which she scratched back, "If thy heart fails thee, climb not at all." It's probably a fable, but the queen gave him a very real boost. In 1583 she granted Raleigh the right to license every one of the thousand wine shops in the country; each had to pay him a pound annually, in an era in which a male servant might earn two pounds in yearly wages. The first English attempt to colonize the New World was paid in large part by a liquor tax. She also let him license exports of wool cloth and lent him a gloomy medieval manor on the Thames called Durham House. Almost instantly Raleigh became one of the realm's wealthiest and most powerful men, suddenly capable of fulfilling his dream of New World glory. But this would-be Tudor conquistador still required additional investors, as well as skilled seamen, navigators, soldiers, and settlers, to pull off his complicated project.

To drum up support, he turned to an ancient institution called Middle Temple—what its present-day archivist, Lesley Whitelaw, described as "a combination of a boy's finishing school and a men's club"—that would serve as a hub for planning English ventures in the Americas for more than a century to come. Middle Temple was named for the Knights Templar, an order of warrior monks founded in Jerusalem during the Crusades. In medieval London, these knights guarded the king's treasury and handled much of his finances. After the pope disbanded the order in the fourteenth century, lawyers rented out the buildings that clustered around the Temple Church, modeled on the Islamic Dome of the Rock. The surrounding buildings, called Inner Temple and Middle Temple, are today in the heart of the British capital, and the Inns of Court that inhabit them still train many of Britain's future top barristers and judges.

In the sixteenth century, the campus lay on the western edge of London, outside the city walls between the Thames and the suburban road leading past Durham House to the sprawling royal palace of Westminster. "The point wasn't always to graduate, like law schools today," according to Whitelaw. "It was just part of general education." In Raleigh's day, "everyone was being sued and suing everyone else. It was also useful for gentry to pick up a background in law since they would be the local justice back on their country estates." Nevertheless, Middle Temple, with about two hundred members at the time, was more a place for elite men to socialize than a formal academic institution. At his later trial for treason, Raleigh claimed never to have read a word of law.

Each inn of court had its own flavor, and the elder Richard Hakluyt, guardian of the young pastor of the same name, helped add the spice of a global perspective to Middle Temple. The bachelor lawyer's rooms there were cluttered with charts and globes that were exceedingly rare in that day, when only one in three English could read and few had ever seen a map. It was here that the younger Hakluyt had his conversion experience, and here that Raleigh and Adrian Gilbert—both of whom kept rooms nearby—talked over their exploration plans.

At mealtimes, the men gathered in the newly constructed Middle Temple Hall, a jaw-dropping piece of Tudor architecture and one of the few extant remnants of Elizabethan London. One hundred feet long and forty feet wide under an arched oak-beamed ceiling and lit by stained-glass windows of heraldic arms, the hall hosted elaborate banquets and long drinking sessions. "You had this convivial social mixing of city money, ambitious lawyers, and people interested in exploration and navigation," Whitelaw said. "It was an important space to be used for all sorts of schemes and ventures."

Today the hall has an antique and hallowed feel, but the scene four centuries ago resembled a raucous frat house. "The members had to be restrained from dining in their hats, and from scrambling for their food," the historical record of one inn notes. "Occasionally they came to fisticuffs, [and] in the hall furniture generally required mending after revels." No laundress or "female victualler" under the age of forty was allowed to enter temple chambers. There was a constant worry that the residents would wreck the place and not pay their bills. "You needed a bond—that is, if you owed money, someone would stand security—for any debts, like rent or damages," Whitelaw explained. Nor was absence from the hemisphere an accepted excuse for late payments. Temple administrators fined the young Amadas for falling behind in his dues while he was on the Outer Banks in the summer of 1584.

Manteo and Wanchese, the Carolina Algonquians who accompanied Amadas and Barlowe to London, likely sat at Middle Temple's long oaken tables, living proof to Raleigh's friends and potential investors of a fruitful land that produced strapping young men. Though Native American visitors were by then a familiar site in Spain and France (writer Michel de Montaigne was impressed with the dignity of the Brazilian Indians he met in 1562 and declared Europeans to be the real savages), they were as foreign as extraterrestrials in England and were probably treated as such.

By then the two men had traded their usual garb of a "mantle of rudely tanned skins of wild animals, no shirts, and a pelt before their privy parts" for fashionable brown taffeta. The elder Hakluyt must be describing them when he writes that Native Americans of the region were "well proportioned in their limbs, well favored, gentle, of a mild and tractable disposition." Not everyone was impressed. "No one was able to understand them and they made a most childish and silly figure," sniffed a German aristocrat who met them shortly after their arrival in October 1584 when they were no doubt still struggling to learn the new language. He added they were "in countenance and stature like white Moors," a reference to North African Arabs.

In November, Raleigh took Manteo and Wanchese to a meeting of Parliament to witness "good government" in operation and testify to their country's wealth. It was the first session in a dozen years, called by an authoritarian monarch who did so only when she was in dire need of additional revenues from taxes. Legislative minutes from the House of Commons mention "some of the people are brought into this realm, and thereby singular great commodities of that land are revealed." Those commodities included pearls and furs obtained by Amadas and Barlowe and possibly pharmaceuticals like sassafras and tobacco thought to cure any number of illnesses.

Of course, the two men might have exaggerated the riches of the New World, like Don Francisco Chicora before them, to ensure themselves a ride home. Raleigh might have encouraged that exaggeration. He had his own agenda, because he wanted Parliament to give its stamp of approval to the charter granted him by the queen. The House did so on December 14, but the House of Lords refused on the grounds that it was not in the members' jurisdiction. No matter. Raleigh's real goal was to drum up publicity and investors to launch a full colony. The legislation highlighted his desire to convert the Indians to Christianity and find "merchantable commodities."

Two weeks later, Elizabeth called Raleigh to her Greenwich palace, downstream from London, to attend her at dinner. She had recently been briefed by the young pastor Hakluyt on the advantages of English colonization of the Americas. Another gossipy German noble noted the courtier's presence along with a dozen other leading courtiers. The fifty-one-year-old queen at one point called the dashing Raleigh over as she sat on a beanbag-sized cushion on the floor watching others dance.

"Pointing with a finger at his face," she noted a smudge and moved to wipe it with her own handkerchief, the nobleman remarked, but Raleigh rubbed it away first. "She was said to love this gentleman above all the others; and this may be true, because two years ago he could scarcely keep a servant, and now with her bounty he can keep five hundred." Many of them wore liveries adorned with chains of gold, and he lavishly appointed the dark rooms of Durham House, the home he'd been lent, with silver-laced tablecloths and a massive four-poster bed covered in green velvet with white feather plumes and spangles set into each corner.

Ten days after the dinner, on the last day of the twelve days of Christmas, Elizabeth knighted Raleigh in a ceremony that Manteo and Wanchese likely attended; almost certainly they were presented at least once to the monarch, whose gender might have given them less pause than it did many of her own subjects. We don't know if it was the brainstorm of Raleigh or the queen, but she announced that the new land would be called Virginia, after the Virgin Queen. Raleigh's new grand seal stated proudly, "Arms of Walter Raleigh, Knight Lord and Governor of Virginia." If Raleigh's idea, it was a canny way to entice the queen to support the venture.

The queen's infatuation with the man she delighted to call "Water," in reference to his thick Devon accent, didn't interfere with her practical judgment. Frobisher's fiasco no doubt still on her mind, she refused to help finance another New World gamble that might also inflame tensions with Spain; for Philip, the Outer Banks was part of La Florida and not Virginia. Elizabeth did, however, provide Raleigh with gunpowder and use of a ship and gave him the right to seize idle men for a crew. She also appointed a Middle Temple member and former parliamentarian, who also was cousin to the lord chancellor, as the colony's governor (its first, though not the last). Ralph Lane was a professional soldier then fighting in Ireland, and he would cast the venture in a military mold that would prove its undoing.

Raleigh lobbied to persuade influential figures at Middle Temple and the court to contribute money to the venture. The recent rise of cloth and mining magnates created an eager pool of investors. Secretary of State Walsingham signed on; he had backed efforts by English merchants to expand their reach in Spain, Russia, Venice, and Turkey and liked the idea of developing a global network of English trading centers that would allow him, in turn, to expand his formidable spy network. William Sanderson, a wealthy financier who had just married Raleigh's niece, helped cover the mission's remaining up-front costs. A fellow Middle Temple member, Sanderson proved a critical partner for the courtier. By the spring of 1585, Raleigh had raised the equivalent of nearly four million dollars in today's money to launch the Virginia colony across the Atlantic.

When he wasn't cornering courtiers in Westminster's halls, he was assembling one of the most formidable and influential scientific exploration teams of the era. He seemed to follow Hakluyt's advice to hire a geographer, a painter, and an alchemist. After Frobisher's folly, Raleigh knew that he needed a competent metallurgist on-site. Walsingham, who governed the royal mines, likely recommended Joachim Gans.

A Jew from Prague famed for a novel method for using the waste from copper processing for dyeing textiles, Gans had won the equivalent of an H-1B visa to work in England, which had banned Jews since 1290. He appears to have been the close relative of a famous Jewish historian, a man who befriended the German astronomer Johannes Kepler and the Danish astronomer Tycho Brahe. Gans would be the first acknowledged Jew to set foot in America, because the Spanish excluded all practicing Jews from their New World domain.

Raleigh also needed an expert in the art of instrument navigation to train his captains, as well as a competent mapmaker and a person capable of analyzing potential New World products. In addition, he wanted to know as much as possible about the Native Americans of his future fiefdom, including their language, traditions, and beliefs. He found a twenty-four-year-old scholar fresh out of Oxford named Thomas Harriot who could do all of that and more.

From a working-class family—his father might have been a blacksmith—Harriot became Raleigh's intellectual muse and one of

(Left) Dressed as an English conquistador, Sir Walter Raleigh was at the height of his influence when this portrait was painted in 1590, as John White sought the Lost Colonists. (Right) Oxford graduate Thomas Harriot was barely twenty-five and already fluent in Carolina Algonquian when he left for the Outer Banks in 1585.

England's first and most accomplished scientists. Unlike his handsome and fashionable patron, the young man was a perpetual bachelor in black, with a pointed red goatee accentuating a bony face and thin lips. His list of accomplishments by the time he reached middle age is mind-boggling. He made major advances in algebra. Harriot pioneered binary notation instrumental in the later development of computers. He solved the problem of how to match compass readings as a ship changes direction and location, and his resulting rhumb line charts were in use by the Royal Navy well into the twentieth century. He wrote an entire textbook on navigation, now lost; one chapter title was "Effect of Longitude on Declination." Some scholars believe he invented the < and > symbols (for "less than" and "greater than"), now standard on all keyboards.

The man from Oxford also revived the atomic theory posed by the ancient Greeks. He was the first Englishman to own and use a telescope. He mapped the moon and saw sunspots before Galileo (Gans might have facilitated his later correspondence with Kepler). He was the first to figure out the sun's rotation rate. The careful observations he made of Halley's comet allowed later astronomers to calculate its path. His surprising obscurity is due to his failure to publish; because he always had a patron, he didn't make a public show of his achievements. He also feared potentially lethal accusations of witchcraft and atheism in a nation that was, he complained to Kepler, "stuck in the mud."

The voyage to Roanoke would open Harriot's eyes to the wider world in the same way that the trip on the *Beagle* changed the life of the young Charles Darwin. Like the nineteenth-century biologist, Harriot encountered a bewildering array of exotic plants and animals, as well as stunningly different people and challenging beliefs. But while Darwin weathered charges of heresy, Harriot lived in a day when the death penalty awaited those guilty of "invocations or conjurations of evil spirits."

The third senior member of Raleigh's scientific team was a middle-class Londoner and minor gentleman artist with the forgettable name of John White. In an era before photography, an artist was essential for any serious exploration venture. White, who might have been aboard the 1584 expedition, was tasked with recording the people, plants, animals, and landscape of Virginia. The son of the famous Dutch painter Cornelius Kettel appears to have served as his apprentice. The mission included a surprising number of other foreign nationals besides Gans and the Dutchman; there were also several French, Irish, Welsh, and Flemish participants, as well as the Portuguese-born Fernandes. A Danish officer also came along to train in naval warfare at the personal request of King Frederick II. Though an English-funded mission, the colony was by necessity a multinational venture; the country lacked the homegrown talent required to transport the settlers to the New World and conduct credible scientific experiments.

With his experts and financing now in place, Raleigh chose a distant cousin as the expedition's admiral. Sir Richard Grenville, a forty-two-year-old merchant, was the feudal lord of the western Devon port town of Bideford and a man of "intolerable pride and insatiable ambition," according to Governor Lane, who would become his nemesis. Grenville (who later threatened to imprison Lane) was known for a prickly temperament and strong stomach; he was said to take "glasses between his teeth and crash them in pieces and swallow them" for the amusement of his fellow drinkers.

Raleigh's precise purpose for the colony remains opaque; he might have avoided a paper trail to keep from alerting the Spanish. But the knight seemed to favor a multipurpose settlement that could prey on passing Spanish ships while extracting resources from the land. Given that he was in touch with Hakluyt and chose the Outer Banks as his destination, a desire to control a northern Panama was also likely a factor (years later, he told the queen that by controlling the Panama Isthmus, "you will wrest the keys of the world from Spain"). A Spanish pilot captured by Grenville and held prisoner off Roanoke in 1586 later told authorities in Havana that the English chose this location "because on the mainland there is much gold and so they can pass from the North to the South Sea"—that is, from the Atlantic to the Pacific "which they say and understand is nearby; thus making themselves strong."

Beneath the personal animosity pitting Lane against Grenville, some scholars perceive two rival camps that collaborated in the Roanoke voyages. The Devon cousins Raleigh and Grenville sought quick wealth by extracting gold and raiding Spanish ships, while a second group made up of Walsingham, Lane, and the pilot Fernandes seem to have favored a trading center that could provide long-term profits. The two factions formed an uneasy alliance.

Unlike the colonies planted by Ayllón and the Huguenots, however, there would be no women or children, and there doesn't seem to have been a focus on cultivating subsistence crops, both of which were critical for establishing a permanent settlement. These would prove the same mistakes that nearly destroyed the later attempt at Jamestown. This was nevertheless the largest colonization attempt on the Atlantic coast of North America since Ayllón's voyage to Chicora six decades earlier. The ships carried provisions for a year, including six thousand loaves of bread, three thousand dried fish from Newfoundland, and two tons of strong wines. A virtual apothecary shop of drugs and dyes were stowed away, as well as pikes, longbows, guns, and personal armor to fight off a Spanish attack. Stevedores loaded Gans's mining and metallurgical equipment and Harriot's navigational instruments on board the flagship, the *Tiger*. "This was really a science team with a big security detail," said Brent Lane of the University of North Carolina at Chapel Hill.

At last, on April 9, 1585, five vessels crowded with at least four hundred and possibly as many as eight hundred men set sail from Plymouth on England's southern coast. The destination was kept a strict secret except among those with a need to know; the Spanish ambassador in London promptly reported the departure to Philip, though he believed the fleet was heading for lands in New England or Newfoundland.

The flagship was rated at between 160 and 180 tons, which meant it could carry that many casks, each of which had a capacity of 252 gallons of wine. About the same size as the *Mayflower* that would later carry the Puritans to Plymouth, it was a typical Elizabethan merchant ship. The length of a good-sized modern yacht, the vessel was much taller and wider, with its rear or stern rising thirty feet or so out of the water.

With two full decks below for storage and accommodations, the ship could carry two hundred passengers or so, though in tight and squalid conditions. "Betwixt the decks there can hardly a man fetch his breath by reason there arises such a funk in the night that it causes putrefaction of blood and breeds disease much like the plague," wrote Jamestown colonist William Capps four decades later, when conditions were much the same. The sole latrine projected from the bow, where a wood lattice let human waste fall into the sea. The only place to wash was in the ocean itself, but this wasn't a popular practice. One man doing so on the voyage lost his leg to a shark.

Though designed to haul cargo, the *Tiger* was outfitted to fight; five guns lined each side and a cannon faced fore and aft, with nearly ten thousand pounds of the queen's gunpowder stored below. The three-masted ship was square-rigged, which meant it sailed most effectively with the wind from behind, though its ability to maneuver was limited. Fernandes, as chief pilot, was in charge of getting the vessels safely to and from the Outer Banks, while Admiral Grenville oversaw the mission at sea, and Lane would be in charge once the colony was situated on land. A Spanish gentleman later held captive aboard the fleet reported that the admiral dined on plates of gold while serenaded by musicians. The instruments, he added, were also designed to please the Native Americans they would encounter, because "they said the Indians were lovers of music." The Spaniard also noted the presence of Manteo and Wanchese, returning home after eight months in London, and remarked that they were well treated and "already spoke English." The two had taught Harriot Carolina Algonquian, and the lessons likely continued on board, with White and Gans possibly taking part as well. Ten days out, the Native Americans as well as the crew likely watched with curiosity as Harriot observed a solar eclipse from the rolling deck as the ship sped south to catch the current and winds off Africa that would then carry them west.

A fierce storm off the Portugal coast scattered the ships and sank one of the two pinnaces. The *Tiger* later halted at a remote beach on Puerto Rico to construct a new one; the punctilious Lane insisted on building and fortifying earthworks around their temporary settlement. Grenville also stopped at the first European town built in the New World, La Isabela (in present-day Dominican Republic), and hosted a sumptuous feast for the local Spanish authorities, who in turn held a bull hunt in honor of their unwelcome but heavily armed guests.

White, meanwhile, busied himself on the deck of the *Tiger*, capturing the brilliant colors of a dolphin and a Portuguese man-of-war in the bright subtropical sun so shockingly different from that of England. As they cruised the Caribbean, the armed marauders bought and stole island livestock as well as sugar, salt, and spices, dodging Spanish patrols. Once their holds were filled, the *Tiger* and two other vessels caught the Gulf Stream north.

At the end of June, nearly three months after leaving Plymouth, the ships anchored off Ocracoke, an uninhabited barrier island sixty miles south of Roanoke and adjacent to Croatoan Island. Even before setting foot in Virginia, however, the newcomers faced a crisis that ominously echoed Ayllón's doomed expedition.

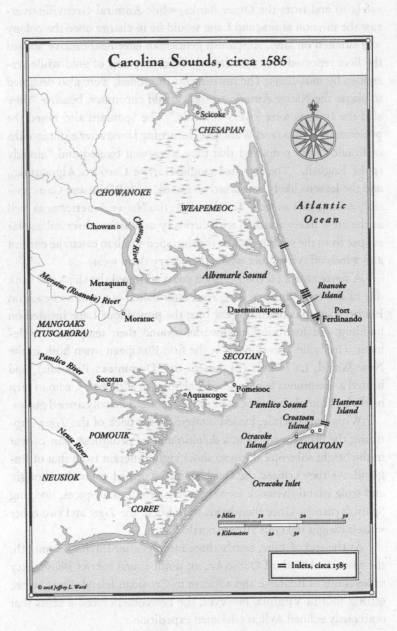

Carolina Sounds, circa 1585

CHESAPIAN

Scicoke

CHOWANOKE

WEAPEMEOC

Chowan

Chowan River

Atlantic Ocean

Albemarle Sound

Metaquam

Moratuc (Roanoke) River

Moratuc

MANGOAKS (TUSCARORA)

Dasemunkepeuc

Roanoke Island

Port Ferdinando

Pamlico River

SECOTAN

Secotan

Aquascogoc

Pomeiooc

Pamlico Sound

Croatoan Island

Hatteras Island

POMOUIK

Neuse River

Ocracoke Island

CROATOAN

NEUSIOK

Ocracoke Inlet

COREE

| 0 Miles | 10 | 20 | 30 |
| 0 Kilometers | 20 | 30 | |

▬ Inlets, circa 1585

© 2018 Jeffrey L. Ward

CHAPTER THREE

Firing Invisible Bullets

The barrier islands called the Outer Banks are like a child's beach dam that holds back a shallow pond of water from the ocean. The ponds are brackish lagoons or sounds, fed from the swift and clear streams that run out of the distant Appalachian Mountains. The waters converge in broad and sluggish rivers that flow through the marsh-fringed coastal plain and into these vast inland seas. You could drop Delaware and Rhode Island into Pamlico Sound, the largest lagoon along the North American east coast, and still have room to spare. Verrazano was not completely deluded in mistaking the Pamlico for the Pacific. Yet it is also shallow enough in parts that you could stand on the sandy bottom in the middle of this vast body of water, out of sight of any land, and still feel the breeze in your hair.

Though they are called inlets, the narrow breaks in the barrier islands siphon more water into the Atlantic than comes in. Storms play them like organ stops, opening and closing them abruptly. A single hurricane in 1846 opened today's Oregon and Hatteras inlets. Even in calm weather, the sand is constantly in motion, altering depths and turning today's safe channel into tomorrow's hazardous shoal. Despite electronic depth finders, GPS, and the Coast Guard standing by, navigating the inlets of the Outer Banks makes for white-knuckle skippering. Verrazano, though tempted by his belief that China lay just on the other side, had not dared to pass through one of these treacherous openings.

On the morning of June 26, 1585, the *Tiger* tried to slip through Ocracoke Inlet to gain a safe anchorage. With Fernandes at the helm, the ship containing most of the expedition's supplies hit a submerged sandbar. "We were all in extreme hazard of being cast away," Lane wrote later. He anxiously counted as eighty-nine ocean swells slammed against the hull, "which all the mariners aboard thought could not possibly but have been broken in sunder."

Disaster was averted only in a daring two-hour effort by the other ships to tow the *Tiger* to safety. No one was injured, but "the ship was so bruised that the salt water came so abundantly into her that the most part of his corn, salt, meal, rice, biscuit, and other provisions" were spoiled, one contemporary chronicler noted. Opinions differed on whether the pilot was to blame. An anonymous account accused Fernandes of "unskillfulness," though Lane later insisted that he "has truly carried himself with great skill and great government all that voyage."

Early July was spent on a nearby beach assessing and repairing the damage. With less than three weeks' worth of food remaining, Lane had to scale back dramatically the number of settlers. Even then, those who remained would have to rely heavily on Native Americans to survive.

The English did not immediately recognize a second crisis. Wanchese vanished from camp and subsequently refused all contact with the Europeans, much as Don Francisco had upon reaching Chicora. There is no record of any European seeing him again, though his presence would be keenly felt. He emerged as a determined and knowledgeable opponent of the invaders. His disappearance coupled with the loss of provisions put the colonists in a precarious position even before they had established a firm beachhead.

Manteo, meanwhile, traveled north to meet with the Indian leader Wingina or his representatives to discuss a permanent home for the newcomers and returned to the flagship soon after.

Strangely, the party did not then head north to meet with the paramount chief and negotiate a place to build their town. Instead, on the morning of July 11, sixty men—including White and Harriot—pushed off from the west shore of Ocracoke in three open boats to cross the Pamlico and explore the mainland to the west, on the southern fringe of the leader's territory. Grenville sailed in comfort aboard a broad-beamed wherry designed for use as a Thames taxi, complete with a canvas canopy for shade. The vessel navigated the shallow waters well, but the heavier pinnace built in Puerto Rico that carried Lane kept scraping the sandy bottom.

Manteo served as their guide. His people on nearby Croatoan seem to have been nominally under Wingina's jurisdiction, but their home on a barrier island gave them some measure of independence. Days earlier, the Croatoan had conducted a quick reconnaissance trip across the Pamlico with an Englishman, presumably to prepare the locals for guests. Grenville and Lane might have wanted to seek alternative settlement sites and allies before meeting with Wingina, an idea that Manteo could have suggested or at least encouraged. He must have had close ties, or even relatives, at their destination. The young man was now a vital player in the English effort, which he might have calculated could benefit his small and vulnerable tribe immeasurably. Like Wanchese, he had seen the enormous numbers of the newcomers on their own turf, but he had come to a radically different conclusion on how best to deal with the English.

After a full day's sail, the men arrived the following morning on the low-lying shore near the village of Pomeiooc. Thanks to White, we know in startling and intimate detail how the Native Americans they encountered in the summer of 1585 dressed, fixed their hair, and went about their lives. In fact, we have more likenesses of individual Carolina Algonquians than we have of the English who met them; only Harriot and Grenville left behind their own portraits. White's images provide us with a rare glimpse into a Native American society at first contact, the very moment when its tragic unraveling began.

The newcomers entered a circular palisade of regularly spaced poles protecting eighteen rectangular houses with arched roofs, built with a framework of small poles and enclosed with mats and furnished

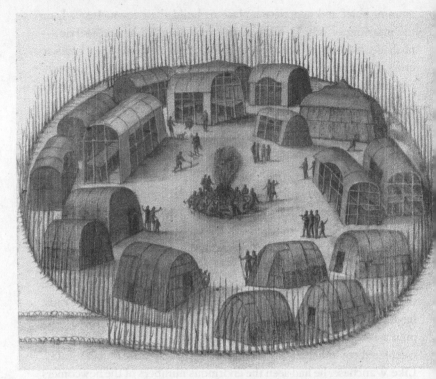

John White drew the town of Pomeiooc on the western shore of the Pamlico Sound during a summer 1585 visit; in the upper left is the first known image of the native Carolina dog that was the Indians' sole domesticated animal. *British Museum*

with wide benches. The mats shed rain and could be rolled down to block the sun yet still admit a breeze during the hot Carolina summers, just like the roll-up reed blinds still popular in the coastal South. At the center of the village was a fire pit for communal cooking and rituals, and a mortuary temple to one side held the skeletal remains of the town's elite dead. White drew a dog—the first American canine depicted in English art—as well as what may be a stone ax. The artist also sketched the chief's wife, who wore black beads or pearls and a fringed deerskin skirt and carried a gourd. Her full lips seem about to form a smile, and elaborate tattoos decorate her biceps. Behind her stands her nearly naked daughter—"of the age of 8 to 10 years"—

proudly showing her mother a black-clothed Elizabethan doll that was perhaps a gift from White to encourage her to stay still as he rapidly drew. The doll and the gold coin on a red necklace around her neck are the only hints of a European presence in all of his images of Carolina Algonquians.

The English spent the night and then visited the village of Aquascococke, which lay to the southwest, before arriving that afternoon in the town of Secotan, which lay to the west up the Pamlico River. Unlike Pomeiooc, this settlement was built along a central street without an encompassing fence, and surrounded by corn and tobacco fields and game-filled forest. That evening, the hosts put on a feast, and one Englishman records the men "were well entertained there of the savages." Their arrival coincided with a festival, because White paints nine male Indians waving gourd rattles and dancing around a circular row of wooden posts carved with faces—what Harriot called "a ceremony in their prayers with strange gestures and songs."

The cordial relations between guests and hosts came to an abrupt halt the next morning, when one of Lane's party found a drinking vessel missing. While the party continued to explore the coast, Grenville sent Amadas the same captain who had visited the previous summer—to Aquascococke "to demand a silver cup which one of the savages had stolen from us." Sending the young man who was barely twenty and known for his flashes of temper—he was once charged with battery after a fight on a Thames ferry—proved a terrible mistake.

The villagers might have thought the cup was a gift or just payment for hosting the guests and likely did not grasp the strict European concept of private ownership. They promised to return the item. But when Amadas's deadline was not met, "we burnt, and spoiled their corn, and town, all the people being fled." The reckless act, which marked the first record of violence between the two peoples, would have disastrous repercussions.

Soon after, the expedition recrossed the Pamlico to board the *Tiger* and sail north. Passing along the forested dunes of Croatoan, where Manteo was raised, the vessel came to anchor at the north end of the next barrier island, the narrower and uninhabited Hatteras,

(Left) This woman was the wife of the Pomeiooc chief; her daughter, aged eight to ten, carries a heavily clothed Elizabethan doll and wears a gold coin on a red necklace, contrasting sharply with her spare summer wear. *British Museum*
(Right) This White painting of a Carolina Algonquian chief may be a portrait of Wingina; copper, such as the large plate he wears, was reserved for royalty. *British Museum*

where the two ships that had been lost in a storm off Portugal months earlier were now waiting. The inlet here seemed the one best suited for shuttling in and out of the Pamlico Sound, so the English established a small base here, called Port Ferdinando after their pilot, to serve as the primary gateway to the interior.

Wingina's brother Granganimeo and Manteo boarded the *Tiger* to meet Grenville and Lane and offer the English land on Roanoke. In addition to its benefit for Wingina and his tribe, this easily defensible location, with quick access to the ocean but invisible to Spanish patrols, made strategic sense for the English. Lane agreed. The newcomers unloaded equipment on the beach as teams of soldiers built wells and slipways and possibly a small redoubt. Material was then shipped in small boats to their new home that lay a dozen miles to the northwest.

Meanwhile, Amadas led a party to explore the Albemarle Sound to the north, which supported denser populations, its wide rivers lined with villages and maize fields. At one settlement the visitors claimed to witness seven hundred revelers at a green-corn festival marking the start of the harvest, an Algonquian tradition still celebrated in August in New England and Canada.

An expedition member named Richard Butler later wrote that the English at one point encountered "enemies of those of Port Fernando"—an apparent reference to rivals of Wingina's people—and killed twenty men in a battle. The soldiers captured some women, whom they presented to their allies. The official reports are silent on the incident, but the claim suggests that the English quickly became embroiled in local conflicts.

Lane orchestrated construction of the English settlement on the island's north end, presumably close to Granganimeo's village. "You can do nothing til you have a strong town, as a magazine of victuals, a retreat in time of danger, and a safe place for the merchants," wrote London trader Sir Thomas Smith the Elder in 1572. The governor likely heeded this advice. He was an accomplished military engineer familiar with the latest in Italian defensive techniques. One of his first actions was undoubtedly to build a fort, which he had done twice during brief halts in the Caribbean. This was territory claimed by Spain, and the entire expedition would have been aware of the massacre of the French colony two decades earlier. They had to be ready for an enemy attack at any time.

In mid-August, Lane was writing letters to investors in London from "Porte FerdyNando in Virginia." By early September, work on Roanoke was sufficiently complete for him to address his missives from "the new fort in Virginia." The structure likely became the center of the English settlement. White, meanwhile, painted "one of the wives of Wingina" in her deerskin fringed skirt and wearing an elaborate blue necklace, tattoos on her wrists, biceps, and calves, and her face stippled with dye. His watercolor of a werowance, or a Carolina Algonquian leader, may be of Wingina; the lean older man has a Mohawk and wears a copper plate the size of a salad plate on his chest and large blue earrings. His expression is placid and his arms folded; he looks serene but a little weary.

The lack of provisions meant that only one hundred or so men would remain in Virginia. Having discharged their duties, Grenville and Fernandes set sail for England on the *Tiger;* the admiral intended to return with supplies in the spring. A few miles off the coast they captured a Spanish ship filled with tens of millions of today's dollars in gold, silver, sugar, ginger, and hides as it lumbered offshore. This bonanza allowed Raleigh to pay off all his investors while demonstrating the usefulness of a New World colony as a handy base to harass the Spanish. One of the queen's spies, William Herle, advised her in December 1585 that a Virginia port would make it possible "to possess Philip's purse."

The loss alarmed the Madrid court and confirmed Spanish fears that the English were building a pirate hideout that threatened the empire's economic lifeline, though they didn't yet know its location. Historian Kenneth Andrews describes English operations in the Atlantic as a "predatory drive of armed traders and marauders" intent on getting their share of New World wealth. War loomed as Philip imposed an embargo on English shipping and Elizabeth turned her pirates into legal privateers. In an effort to chase the Spanish away from the fishing grounds of Newfoundland, the queen diverted a ship with supplies and additional settlers bound for Roanoke. That move would deny Lane and his men critically needed provisions for the winter.

Unaware of the political crisis rapidly unfolding across the ocean, Governor Lane remained optimistic. When the last ship of the fleet eased out of Port Ferdinando on September 8, 1585, he sent along with it a rough sketch of the area, the first known map made by the English in North America. The unpolished drawing, clearly dashed off in a hurry, marks Roanoke as "the King's Isle"—clearly a reference to Wingina—but fails to note the location of the Roanoke settlement or Port Ferdinando. This omission was likely done to keep sensitive information from Spanish spies, but it has since frustrated generations of historians and archaeologists.

The drawing identifies the location of silk grass, grapevines, and good fishing spots, evidence that the English were already searching for possible exports with the help of Manteo and other locals. The artist cites the presence of oak galls, tree deformations that secrete a substance that formed a major constituent of Elizabethan ink. In letters, Lane assured London investors that the colony was based in "the goodliest and most pleasing territory of the world, for the soil is of a huge unknown greatness and very well peopled and towned, though savagely." The governor predicted that Virginia products would replace the Mediterranean goods that conflict with Spain was already making increasingly difficult to obtain.

It was a common misconception of the time. The English thought that because Virginia's latitude matched that of Gibraltar, its climate would be similar. Lemons and limes would flourish, as would olive trees and even sugar. Lane envisioned a bright future. "If Virginia had but horses and kine"—cows—"in some reasonable proportion, I dare assure myself being inhabited with English, no realm in Christendom were comparable to it."

Another misconception was that the Native Americans were not true landowners. Lane noted that "being savages that possess the land, they know no use of the same." For the English, used to neat wheat and barley fields bordered by stone walls, the sophisticated Native American approach to growing corn, beans, and squash together seemed chaotic, and their habit of collecting roots, nuts, and berries from the woods, though carefully timed with the seasons, appeared haphazard. The absence of domesticated animals, other than the dog, seemed uncivilized, as did the indigenous practice of moving around. "The savage people rule over many lands without title or property; for they enclose no ground, neither have they cattle to maintain it, but remove their dwellings as they have occasion," wrote John Winthrop four decades later in Massachusetts. In fact, the indigenous people prepared for lean seasons by storing food, and their knowledge of game and prowess at hunting typically provided them with ample animal protein and clothing material.

The newcomers, however, saw this way of life as not just wasteful but depraved. In Thomas More's 1516 *Utopia,* which Gilbert was said to be reading when he drowned, the author argued that dispossessing indigenous people of their territory was a moral imperative. The recent discovery of the New World inspired More's book, in which the Utopians drove out any who didn't till the soil properly to claim the land for themselves, "for they count this the most just cause of war." Raleigh enthusiastically backed More's ruthless philosophy. "If the title of occupiers be good in land unpeopled, why should it be bad accounted in a country peopled over thinly?" he argued.

A sixteenth-century Portuguese scholar wasn't fooled. He dismissed More's ideal society as "a modern fable" designed "to teach the English how to rule." Well into the seventeenth century, many English landowners lacked documentation; settling the land was often enough to make it yours. ("Possession is nine-tenths of the law" is a particularly English concept.) Territory considered vacant was, in effect, theirs for the taking. This was the genesis of the argument used to deny Indian land rights and justify westward expansion for the next four centuries.

Wingina might have let Lane and his men use Roanoke as their base, but he almost certainly did not intend to transfer the island permanently to the newcomers. Native Americans would often accept payment for land, but they typically did so with the assumption that it was a temporary lease rather than a final purchase. "For a copper kettle and a few toys as beads and hatchets, they will sell you a whole country," marveled John Smith at Jamestown, misreading the Algonquian approach to land use.

Yet Lane did not advocate removing the indigenous people; he recognized that trade with them was essential. "The people naturally are most courteous and very desirous to have clothes, but especially of coarse cloth rather than silk." This news no doubt was music to Hakluyt's ears. To Elizabethans, proper clothes, like tilled land and grazing sheep, were the very essence of civilized life. Ever since Amadas and Barlowe bestowed a shirt and a hat on the lone Indian, the Algonquians held wool and cotton in high regard, as Europeans of the day viewed rare Chinese silk. Here was a vast and untapped market for English textiles.

At first, relations with Wingina and his people seemed cordial.

We don't know if Lane applied a strict code—suggested in an undated and anonymous set of notes, apparently made prior to sailing, with regard to the 1585 colony—that called for three months' imprisonment for any Englishman forcing an Indian to labor unwillingly and twenty blows with a cudgel for striking one, "in the presence of the Indian stricken." Even entering a Native American's house without leave entailed six months' imprisonment or enslavement. The author, who might have been the elder Hakluyt from Middle Temple, had read enough history of European colonization to know that alienating those most familiar with the country would prove calamitous. Elsewhere he warned with prescience that "seeking revenge on every injury of the savages" would result in the English being "rooted out with sword and hunger." Lane ultimately failed to heed this advice, with dire consequences for his colony and the one that followed.

White seems to have returned with the fleet to England, where he worked on his portfolio of watercolors. But Gans and Harriot stayed behind to embark on an ambitious effort to explore and meticulously catalog Virginia's resources. They tested metals and botanical samples and set out to search for ores and medicinal plants, all the while visiting Native Americans to draw on their knowledge. Harriot marveled at plants most Europeans had never seen and that would become important staples of the Old World, from the sunflower to the potato. He encountered his first caffeinated drink in a cup infused with yaupon leaves (coffee and tea had yet to reach England). Evening primrose and nasturtium promised important health benefits, while sassafras—native only to eastern North America—was well on its way to becoming the wonder drug of the sixteenth century. The New World offered not just gold and silver but "a botanical philosopher's stone with which to transmute disease to health," historian Ralph Bauer writes.

Along the way, traveling in a small open boat crammed with cartographic equipment, Harriot and his assistants made maps. On torturously humid and hot days, batting away the swarms of mosquitoes and huddling under canvas in fierce squalls, the young scientist and his team performed complex calculations, using the new method of triangulation to produce charts better than almost anything that existed in England in that day. The maps that resulted, which John

White later drew based on Harriot's data, remained the most accurate of the region for almost two centuries.

What makes Harriot so unusual, aside from his insatiable curiosity and scientific gifts, was his easy rapport with the indigenous peoples. No Englishman at Jamestown or Plymouth would garner so much trust or gain such privileged access, and few Westerners in the century that followed reported indigenous life with so little judgment. He was still a product of his time, proselytizing for "the true and only God" and hoping the people he met "may be in a short time brought to civility, and the embracing of true religion." He was not above showing off the technological marvels of the day, such as sea compasses and "spring-clocks that seem to go of themselves" in order to impress his audience, who wondered if they were more "the works of God than of men."

Manteo, no doubt, provided crucial introductions that gave him insight into crops and pharmaceuticals that could benefit Raleigh and his investors. But Harriot was fluent enough in the Secotan dialect of Algonquian to speak directly with the women who farmed and gathered wild plants as well as the men who fished and hunted. He established "special familiarity with some of their priests" as well as with "conjurers" who could predict the future. While collecting practical information on potential exports, he studied the preservation of the corpses of leaders in special mortuary temples and recorded local belief in the immortal soul and heaven and hell. Mindful of Amadas's harsh treatment of the Indians, Harriot insisted that his team avoid conflict, "because we sought by all means possible to win them by gentleness."

Yet, in a tragic irony, he and his party unwittingly wreaked far more damage on their hosts than the ill-advised July raid over a missing cup. They spread deadly disease that decimated the very culture Harriot sought to understand. Native Americans lacked the immunities to pathogens that Old World people developed over long time spans. Even today, this lethal aspect of the Columbian exchange remains a crisis. A simple cold or flu inadvertently spread by oil workers or television crews seeking isolated tribes can quickly devastate peoples in the Amazon jungles.

Ever the scientist, Harriot noted the disturbing trend, though he lacked a germ theory to grasp its origin. "Within a few days after our departure from every such town, the people began to die very fast, and many in a short space; in some towns about twenty, in some forty, in some sixty, and in one six score, which in truth was very many in respect to their numbers. This happened in no place that we could learn but where we had been."

The epidemic began less than a month after the last of the English fleet departed; we know this because Harriot mentions that the illness spread within days of a comet's appearance in the sky that can be dated to mid-September to early October 1585. Such a celestial event foretold disaster among both Europeans and Native Americans. The sickness was likely influenza, then raging in the Caribbean, and it was unlike any illness the Carolina Algonquian healers had encountered. None of their herbal remedies could halt its spread or cure its symptoms. They presumed—correctly—that the English could kill "by shooting invisible bullets into them."

Wingina himself twice fell sick. When his practitioners failed to find a cure, he called on English prayers. The leader's recovery reinforced Indian perceptions that the newcomers' powerful tools extended into the spiritual realm. He asked the English to unleash this powerful weapon against his enemies. With every visit to a neighboring tribe, they did. The raging epidemic that spread from village to village likely hindered the fall harvest, reducing the surplus available for trade with the English as winter approached.

Before the New Year, Harriot joined an expedition to the southern shore of Chesapeake Bay, about one hundred miles north of Roanoke Island. A glance at any modern chart shows that the Chesapeake and the Carolina sounds are isolated from each other. That was not obvious in the 1580s, even among the Spanish who had settled a Jesuit mission briefly on Chesapeake shores in the previous decade. The sketch map sent by Lane noted that the colonists' landfall on Ocracoke was at "St. Mary's Bay," or Bahía de Santa María in Spanish. Historians long assumed that Bahía de Santa María was synonymous with Chesapeake Bay, but other maps of the era suggest that Europeans saw the bay and the sounds as one large system. Harriot's data established that the

Chesapeake region was in fact a separate body of water, with more fertile soil and deeper waters, as well as large concentrations of Indians amenable to trade. This discovery, immortalized in John White's map of eastern North Carolina and southern Virginia, later turned English attention north, leading two decades later to the settlement at Jamestown that gave the English their first firm foothold in the New World.

Lane, meanwhile, remained cooped up on Roanoke, in part because of food shortages and unrest among what he called with exasperation the "wild men of mine own nation." One ringleader might have been the nineteen-year-old Oxford graduate Marmaduke Constable; on his return to England he was accused of leading an armed gang of Elizabethan punks who tore down hedges and attacked livestock.

The worried governor issued strict rations, but it proved increasingly difficult to secure corn to tide the men over until spring. The English were now almost wholly dependent on the Secotan for their survival. The Indians stored surplus crops, but they were not prepared or able to feed a hungry English multitude for six months or more, particularly given the impact of the devastating illnesses ravaging their villages. The apparent listlessness of Lane's men during the winter suggests that they, like Ayllón's settlers sixty years earlier, might have suffered from carbohydrate deficiency.

Relations between Wingina and Lane worsened as the food shortage grew more acute. The English governor set out in early March to explore the interior that lay beyond the chief's control, in order to gather provisions and possibly forge fresh alliances. He dreamed of finding the Pacific and valuable ore deposits. Thirty men sailed west from Roanoke to the head of the Albemarle Sound and up the Chowan River. Their goal was the capital of the Chowanoke people, the region's most numerous and populous tribe.

Manteo accompanied the expedition, but Wingina supplied his own guides—a sign of his growing distrust of the Croatoan—while warning Lane that the Chowanoke chief, Menatonon, planned to ambush the English. Wingina was no doubt reluctant to let the English create an alliance with a more powerful neighbor, and the guides doubled as spies. Upon their arrival, Lane, battle hardened from the

Irish wars and not given to diplomacy, stormed the beach at Menatonon's main village and seized the chief; no difficult feat given that he
was an apparent paralytic. The commander then declared him, "for a
savage, a very grave and wise man." Menatonon claimed no intent to
harm the English and blamed Wingina for attempting to create ill will
between the newcomers and the Chowanoke. He filled Lane's eager
ears with tales of pearl fisheries to the north, in an apparent reference
to the Chesapeake, as well as copper mines to the west controlled by a
fierce Iroquoian-speaking people. Beyond the setting sun, he assured
the eager English commander, was a rock on the shore of a great sea.
Excited by the prospect of metals and a passage to the Pacific, Lane
released Menatonon but as a precaution sent his son, Skiko, to Roanoke Island as a hostage.

A few days later, the English conquistadors donned armor and
began their journey up a nearby river called the Moratuc—today's
Roanoke River—that snaked west to the alleged copper sources and
the great sea. Finally they had a chance to find glory or wealth or both
in this land that seemed rich only in mosquitoes and marsh. The men
made a gallant pact that "whilst there was left one half pint of corn for
a man that we should not leave the search."

The expedition proved an unnerving trip into an American heart
of darkness. The villages they encountered as they rowed upstream
were strangely deserted. Food ran low. The current grew stronger,
forcing the anxious soldiers to pull harder at their oars, and the banks
lined with tall trees narrowed with each twisting mile. The men soon
realized with unease that they were being watched. Finally, a human
sound broke the silence. "We heard certain savages call," reported
Lane. Heartened, he urged Manteo to propose a meeting. At that
moment, male voices began to sing. Manteo warned it was a war chant
and grabbed his English gun. Before he could fire, a volley of arrows
whooshed out of the trees but "did no hurt." The English landed and
pursued their attackers, who utterly vanished in the thick brush. The
eerie silence returned.

Shaken and hungry, the expedition members agreed it was time
to turn back. They killed and roasted two mastiffs they had brought
along to terrify the locals. It was the last of their food. By the time they

emerged back into the broad Albemarle Sound, they were reduced to picking sassafras leaves to stave off the gnawing in their stomachs. It was the Saturday before Easter Sunday, "which was fasted very truly," says Lane, in one of his only wry remarks.

The next day, the famished men raided an Indian fish trap and by Monday were back on Roanoke. "We be dead men returned into the world again," Lane wrote, referring to Wingina's shock that the English had survived their ordeal.

But the situation had deteriorated in their absence. There was still no sign of a resupply ship. Two of the key elders sympathetic to the English, Granganimeo and a respected council member named Ensinore, were dead, "the only friend to our nation that we had amongst them," lamented Lane. Harriot notes that some of the Indians "seem to prophesy that there were more of our generations yet to come, to kill theirs and take their places"—a chillingly accurate prediction.

A faction among the Carolina Algonquians advocating removal of the English was gaining ground; Wanchese, hostile to the English after his experience in London, was now a senior adviser to Wingina. The chief changed his own name to Pemisapan, or "one who watches," though Lane doesn't seem to have picked up on this ominous detail. The newcomers were wearing out their welcome. Their trade goods had lost their appeal, and the Europeans were building alliances with his rivals that threatened to cut Wingina and his tribe out of the equation.

At Lane's surprise return, the Secotan leader evacuated Roanoke and halted all food distribution to the English; Indians also broke the fish weirs they had made for the settlers, who were unable to repair them. The newcomers' lack of skill is remarkable, given that the Thames, from London Bridge to Windsor, was at the time said to be nearly unnavigable due to the salmon and shad nets. Harriot later blamed ill-prepared urban dwellers for their desperate plight. While some of the colonists were common soldiers, many were small London businessmen—basket makers, carpenters, and merchants. "Because there were not to be found any English cities, nor such fair houses, nor at their own wish any of their old accustomed dainty food, nor any soft beds of down or feathers, the country was to them miserable," he wrote scornfully. Of course, the young Oxford don and his scientific team spent much of their time traveling from Native American village to village, no doubt enjoying elaborate meals like the one Barlowe experienced on Roanoke Island in 1584. His men likely felt far fewer hunger pangs than those forced to do time on Roanoke.

Desperate for food, Lane broke up his company so that his men could forage, trade, or beg in smaller groups. A dozen crossed the Pamlico to Port Ferdinando "to live upon shellfish," while twenty men led by Captain Edward Stafford sailed south to Manteo's home island of Croatoan. With only a skeleton crew manning the Roanoke settlement, the English were vulnerable to attack. Lane learned from his prisoner Skiko, Menatonon's son, that Wingina was organizing an alliance that included the tribes to the south, intending to wipe out the weakened settlers. Not surprisingly, warriors from the village that Amadas had burned a year prior signed up. The captive also told the commander that Wingina intended to meet with Lane under the guise of friendship, while his men lit bonfires to alert allies on the mainland. That was the signal for the warriors to canoe over to Roanoke and set fire to the thatched huts belonging to Lane, Harriot, and other senior members of the colony, who apparently lived in cottages outside the fort—a sign that the English had until then felt little threat from their neighbors and hosts. As they fled their homes, the Indians would pick them off. Once the leaders were neutralized, the warriors would attack the protected enclosure.

Lane again planned a preemptive attack. As darkness fell on May 31, 1586, a squad of Englishmen seized Algonquian canoes to use in a surprise amphibious operation against the Indians. A struggle broke out with the boat's outraged owners. The English beheaded some of the Native Americans in view of others, who raised the alarm.

Though he had lost his element of surprise, Lane landed quietly on the mainland with his men early the next morning, sending word that he wanted to complain to Wingina about the previous night's incident, which he claimed was the fault of the chief's warriors. He also said, falsely, that English reinforcements had arrived at Croatoan.

Once ushered into the village center, Lane cried out, "Christ our

Victory," the signal for his soldiers to attack. They drew their pistols and took aim at the Native Americans. Amadas fired at the chief, who fell on the spot. Lane claimed that during the skirmish he was busy protecting Croatoan Indians, who happened to be visiting the mainland village, as well as those tribe members friendly to the English. His men, meanwhile, ensured that "none of the rest should escape."

Wingina, only wounded and waiting for the right moment, suddenly sprang up and ran for the woods, but not before he was shot "thwart his buttocks" by an Irish mercenary. The leader vanished in the trees. Another Irishman named Edward Nugent, who had served with Lane in the Irish wars, ran after him. Lane and a party of soldiers anxiously followed. On the path they spotted Nugent marching back with Wingina's bloody head in his hand.

As was the English practice in dealing with the Irish, Lane had the head thrust on a pole outside the fort. The same people who two years earlier welcomed the new arrivals "with all love and kindness," sharing their land and food, were now implacable foes.

Exactly one week after Wingina's assassination, Stafford strained his eyes on top of a Croatoan Island dune facing the Atlantic. What he saw spelled either rescue or death. Nearly two dozen sails crowded the southern horizon. In the early summer haze—the telescope's invention was still two decades away—he couldn't be sure if the enormous fleet was a Spanish expedition sent to snuff out the nascent colony or the English resupply mission. It turned out to be neither.

He sent word to Lane of the fast-approaching ships. Finally, after spying English pennants, Stafford torched the dry grass and tinder piled on the beach. The smoke caught the attention of the fleet's flagship, which sent a small boat to investigate. The next day, Stafford raced up the coast to Port Ferdinando and then across the sound to Roanoke with a letter from the renowned English sea captain Sir Francis Drake, promising "not only victuals, munitions, and clothing, but also barks, pinnaces, and boats."

On June 10, Lane rowed out to meet the famous admiral of the fleet assembled off Port Ferdinando. Not until the American Civil War, nearly three centuries later, would such a large number of warships cluster on this perilous coast. Drake was returning to England after devastating raids in the Spanish Caribbean that marked the start of official armed conflict with the Spanish Empire. A friend of Raleigh's, he decided to check in on the courtier's settlers at Roanoke.

The forty-five-year-old Drake, short and bearded, came from a Devon clan that fell on hard times; he grew up on an abandoned hulk near the mouth of the Thames. As a young pirate, Drake cruised the Caribbean for loot. Later he attacked Spain's rich and largely unde-fended ports on the Pacific coast of South America while making the second circumnavigation of the world. He came home to fame and fortune, and the man who grew up in an abandoned boat bought Sir Richard Grenville's grand Devon mansion.

Pirates traded in all commodities, including slaves. Along with his cousin John Hawkins, Drake raided West African ports and the ships of Portuguese merchants who dominated the business to sell the human cargo to Spanish plantations in the Caribbean. Yet he allied himself with escaped slaves in Panama in the 1570s to steal several tons of Spanish gold and silver. That one raid put more money into the queen's treasury than all the taxes collected in England that year, and one of the African men subsequently served with the privateer for many years.

As Lane's colony slowly starved during the long winter at Roa-noke, Drake was attacking Cartagena. This was one of Spain's most important Caribbean ports, on what is now the coast of Colombia, protected by armed galleys rowed by enslaved Ottoman Turks and North African Muslims, or Moors. A stone fort bristling with cannon overlooked the harbor. Along with gun-toting Spanish soldiers were Native American troops carrying poisoned arrows. Stakes dipped in poison lined the land approaches.

The overwhelming English force quickly routed the untested defenders. The invaders looted the wealthy homes and churches and methodically burned portions of the city until the Spanish citi-zens agreed to a ransom to make them stop. According to an English report, Drake ordered his men to treat French, Turks, and Africans in the city—most of whom were slaves or captives—with respect.

A Spaniard later blamed the disaster on God's wrath for the "unrighteous intercourse" between the Moors and the West Africans as well as Christian Indians in Cartagena—"and even other women of every sort, moved to desire which overmasters every other consideration." The comment gives us a fleeting glimpse into the dizzyingly diverse nature of a port where people from the Americas, Europe, and Africa mixed, if not freely, then frequently.

Drake's fleet stayed two months. As Lane and his men searched in vain for copper deep in the Carolina interior, the admiral departed Cartagena, carrying with him the cathedral's massive bronze church bells. An Englishman who took part in the raid wrote that "we had many Turks, Frenchmen, Negroes, Moors, Greeks, and Spanish with us from this town" when the fleet departed. How many remains unclear. "Most of the slaves and many of the convicts from the galleys went off with the English as did some of the Negroes belonging to private owners," one Spanish report states. Another Spanish document confirms that Moors deserted to Drake, "as did the black slaves of the city, whom they find very useful."

Estimates of the number of refugees on board range from 80 to a staggering 1,200. The most reliable reports suggest that Drake transported 200 Moors as well as 150 male and female West Africans. Whatever the precise numbers, the English fleet was filled with people from three continents.

The ships sailed east but failed to find Havana, missing a chance to lay waste to Spain's most important Caribbean city. But they did land on Cuba. The crew suffered from scurvy and dysentery, and legend has it that South American indigenous women on board went ashore to obtain rum and limes, along with mint, to make a soothing medicinal concoction dubbed *El Draque*—the dragon—the Spanish nickname for the feared admiral and privateer. (Today it is Britain's favorite cocktail, recast as the mojito.)

By late May, with the crew on the mend, the fleet cruised north to St. Augustine on Florida's Atlantic coast. A landing party arrived at the town and fort, only to find both abandoned; the residents had been warned of an impending attack and fled into the swamps to the west. The men torched each of the town's 250 houses (no English town in North America would grow that large for well over a century). St. Augustine's destruction rid the English of the primary threat to Roanoke. But first Drake's crew stripped the buildings of their locks and other valuable hardware. "The Spanish Caribbean was his Ikea," said historian Adrian Masters at the University of Texas at Austin. "You go there to pick up your raw materials."

The hardware, Drake reasoned, would be useful at the new Virginia colony that his friend Raleigh had founded. So would the slaves. Three Africans left behind at St. Augustine told Spanish authorities that Drake "meant to leave all the negroes he had in a settlement [established] by the English who went there a year ago. He hinted to leave the 250 blacks and all his small craft there, and cross to England with only the larger vessels." Another report circulated in Havana corroborates the numbers and notes that the refugees on board "who do menial service" were not apparently destined for England, because "they are not useful to [Drake's] country." There were black servants in England, but few slaves.

The fleet glided five hundred miles north on the Gulf Stream before sentries spotted Stafford's smoke signal. When Lane and Drake met in the luxurious stern cabin of the forty-seven-gun flagship the *Elizabeth Bonaventure,* one of England's most impressive ships, the privateer could afford to be generous. Drake also knew that Raleigh, an ally at court and a fellow privateer, would repay his efforts. The admiral invited Lane's treasurer and quartermaster on board to make an inventory of their needs, including desperately needed gunpowder and clothes. The settlers by then were reduced to rags. Drake was willing to part with enough supplies to feed the hundred-plus colonists for four additional months, by which time resupply vessels would surely have arrived. He also agreed to leave behind a medium-sized ship along with six smaller boats. These would help Harriot expand his range of exploration and Lane to continue his search for the Pacific and copper.

But as they spoke, clouds thickened in the south. Soon "a great storm . . . extraordinary and very strange" blew up, according to one sailor's journal. Several of the larger ships hastily weighed anchor to escape being driven onto the shore at Port Ferdinando amid "thunder and rain, with hailstones as big as hens' eggs." Cables tethering other vessels to the sandy bottom snapped in the fierce wind and strong currents. Waterspouts—tornadoes whipped up on the sea—traveled across the ocean's surface until it seemed "heaven and earth would have met."

For three days and nights the storm raged, and several of the smaller boats were smashed into splinters on the beaches. Lane lamented that the weather did more damage to the little colony than all the efforts of Spain. It was the first record of a hurricane hitting the Outer Banks. When the tempest passed, the ship that was to remain behind with supplies and a crew had vanished; its captain sailed for England rather than do more time in the awful place that offered precious little shelter for men and ships alike.

The colony's governor and his men held a hurried meeting. With no sign of Grenville's resupply ships and surrounded by hostile Native Americans, Lane suggested that the only option was to abandon the colony. "Considering the case we stood in, the weakness of our company, the small number of the same, the carrying away of our first appointed bark"—the designated ship to be left behind—"with those two special masters, with our principal provisions in the same," wrote Lane, "by the very hand of God, as it seemed, stretched out to take us from thence."

The young Hakluyt later obtained an account that instead saw divine retribution for Lane's violent behavior. The unknown author said the English "left all things so confusedly, as if they had been chased from thence by a mighty army, and no doubt so they were, for the hand of God came up on them for the cruelty, and outrages committed by some of them against the native inhabitants of the country." Harriot came to a similar, though more muted, conclusion, apparently unwilling to criticize Lane directly. He wrote delicately that several colonists "showed themselves too fierce in slaying some of the people, in some towns, upon causes that on our part, might easily have been borne with all." The enemy, he said, were not the Native Americans but "carelessness of our selves."

Drake agreed to take the bedraggled settlers home; he and his crew were eager to be away from "their long and dangerous abode in that miserable road." Boats were sent from Port Ferdinando to evacuate the fort and settlement. In the chaotic scramble, sailors heaved into the still-choppy waters heavy chests that threatened to swamp the small vessels. "The weather was so boisterous, and the pinnaces so often on ground," Lane lamented, "that the most of all we had, with our charts, books, and writings, were by the sailors cast overboard." Even today, scholars rue the sailors' actions. The lost items likely included invaluable data gathered by Harriot during nearly a year of travels, interviews, and experiments. The young polymath had compiled an English-Carolina Algonquian dictionary and transliteration that recorded English words using a modified thirty-six-letter English alphabet that one linguist calls "an astonishing feat for his time." This method, now commonly used, became an essential tool as the British Empire expanded. All that remains of this innovative and herculean effort is a single yellowed sheet of paper rediscovered four centuries later at a London prep school.

Manteo spontaneously decided to join the fleet, and another Indian named Towaye, possibly his servant, accompanied him. The fleet left in such haste that three of Lane's men either were abandoned or refused to go; they might have decided to join the locals. They were never heard from again.

Were it not for the hurricane, American history might have unfolded along a different course. When a hundred-ton ship sent by Raleigh and filled with provisions anchored off Port Ferdinando a few days later, the crew searched in vain for the colonists. The vessel soon departed for England. Two weeks later, Grenville arrived with half a dozen ships and four hundred men and supplies for a year. These reinforcements, combined with Drake's contributions and Raleigh's relief ship, would have given the English a secure base. The baffled admiral likewise sought some sign of the settlers, who seemed to have vanished into thin air. A Spanish prisoner on board one of the vessels later told authorities in Havana that Grenville's men found the putrefying bodies of a Native American and an Englishman hanged in the Roanoke settlement. Neither Lane nor the admiral mentioned the grisly executions.

Grenville's men eventually kidnapped three Indians, hoping to extract intelligence. Two escaped, but the third, later baptized "Rawley," was brought back to England to live in the admiral's new mansion in Bideford. We don't know what he told the English, and the Algonquian died in April 1589, the only known Native American from the Roanoke voyages buried in England. His grave in the local churchyard, as with so much else associated with the venture, is lost.

Unwilling to abandon the island completely, Grenville left fifteen unlucky men and sailed back to England. The next expedition would learn something of what happened to them.

But the most fascinating and unresolved question about the Lane colony is the fate of the hundreds of refugees on Drake's fleet when it arrived at Roanoke. Most of those from the Ottoman Empire, Spain's mortal enemy, returned to England and were repatriated. Less than a week after the ships arrived in England, the queen's Privy Council noted "100 Turks brought by Sir Francis Drake out of the West Indies (where they served as slaves in the Spanish galleys)." But only one black African is recorded as arriving with the fleet, and he apparently did not see the English as saviors; he immediately fled for France and sought sanctuary with the Spanish ambassador. An English diplomat in Paris wrote Walsingham that the man had a cut on his face and claimed to have returned from the New World. He added that "he would be glad to hear whether any such hath escaped away from Sir Francis Drake or not." Nothing more has been found in British archives to answer his query.

As to what happened to the remaining Africans and South Americans, "the saddest part of the story and perhaps the most revealing is that no one bothered to say," notes historian Edmund Morgan. It is unlikely Drake brought hundreds of slaves to London in the 1580s, given the limited market there for humans in bondage. There are also no records of a large sale after his return. Some might have drowned in the hurricane off the Outer Banks, though there is no mention of casualties. And while a crew might dump slaves into the ocean if supplies dwindled, there is no evidence that Drake committed or countenanced such acts. Though quick to kill mutineers, Spanish soldiers, and Irish rebels, the admiral did not have a reputation for indiscriminate slaughter for no obvious gain. "The only reasonable explanation is that a considerable number of Indians and Negroes were put ashore on the Carolina Outer Banks and equipped with the pots and pans, locks and bolts, boats and launches of Saint Augustine," concludes David Beers Quinn, the late University of Liverpool historian and dean of Roanoke researchers.

Grenville doesn't mention seeing anyone during his brief stopover save for the three Indians he kidnapped. If the refugees were left on Roanoke, however, they would surely have scattered with the appearance of European sails, to avoid detection and a potential return to slavery. Native Americans may have absorbed them. Whether they would have made their presence known to the Lost Colonists who arrived a year later—or even made common cause with them—is unknown. But these scores, perhaps hundreds, of West Africans, Native South Americans, and North African Moors form a mysterious *other* lost colony, one that left an even thinner paper trail than their English counterparts. Their presence on Roanoke would mean that the bulk of the first permanent settlers of England's initial New World colony were neither Christian nor European but North African Muslims as well as followers of West African and South American traditions.

To this day, rumors persist from eastern North Carolina to the Appalachians of an influx of southern Mediterranean people predating the English settlements. They might have been remnants of Ayllón's colony or other Spanish and French expeditions, or castaways from shipwrecks. Yet Quinn notes the strong possibility that the refugees from Drake's fleet were "left to form an isolated colony in what is now North Carolina." If they did, then they were soon joined by a fresh batch of Europeans intent on making Virginia their home.

CHAPTER FOUR

Small Things Flourish by Concord

The raucous celebration must have felt like a public humiliation. The elaborate dinner on August 4, 1586, came just one week after Drake's fleet arrived back in England to national rejoicing. Having burned and looted his way across Philip's Caribbean, the admiral was London's most highly sought-after guest. Ralph Lane sat at a long oaken table in the candlelit twilight of Middle Temple Hall, in the heart of his own club, as toast after toast congratulated El Draque on his triumph.

The governor and his men had returned from the New World looking like refugees themselves, ragged and thin, bearing no crates of Spanish silver or bronze church bells. Already, word of the Virginia debacle was spreading in the pubs along the docks near the Tower of London on the other side of town. Rather than finding Eden, the men had been plunged into hell.

Thomas Harvey, a merchant who had made the trip in hope of profiting in trade with the Indians, publicly complained about "one whole year and more in very miserable case" that drove him to bankruptcy. Others told hair-raising tales of starvation and Indian attacks. Harriot later railed in print against "slanderous and shameful speeches bruited about abroad by many that returned from thence."

Lane quietly returned to Ireland, where he attempted, again without success, to create a colony while continuing his penchant for displaying the heads of enemies on pikes (eventually winning a knighthood and the castle of Belfast). He never again ventured across the ocean. Before departing London, he submitted a report to Raleigh at odds with his glowing accounts sent the previous summer from the new fort in Virginia. "The discovery of a good mine, by the goodness of God, or a passage to the South Sea, or some way to it, and nothing else can bring this country in request to be inhabited by our nation," he bluntly concluded. Productive fields would require hard work clearing and manuring land, while the governor only grudgingly admitted that some of Harriot's potions, such as sassafras, might "make good merchandise." He knew that Raleigh wanted gold, or at least copper; all he could offer were roots. The only hope that he saw was in the area north of the Outer Banks, along the shores of the Chesapeake, "for pleasantness of seat, for temperature of climate, for fertility of soil, and for the commodity of the sea, besides multitudes of bears, being an excellent good victual, with great woods of sassafras and walnut trees, is not to be excelled by any other whatsoever." Pinned down at Roanoke, he had not seen the region for himself; this was based solely on reports from Harriot's expedition. But laying out the prospect of another Eden just a hundred miles to the north must have been easier than admitting simple failure.

We don't know how Raleigh reacted to Lane's surprise return, but the governor's abrupt abandonment of Roanoke after only nine months must have been a bitter blow. Profits from the Spanish ship captured by Grenville the previous fall cushioned the impact. Yet after pouring a fortune of his money and that of his investors into the venture, the courtier had nothing to show.

In any case, the time for colonizing the New World was passing. Drake's raids all but ensured open war with Spain. With pirating not only legal but patriotic, speculators saw fat returns for a small investment. Fitting out a privateer cost only a fraction of what was needed to organize and support a colony. As summer turned to fall, Raleigh waffled on whether to pursue a new Virginia venture.

"This brilliant, ruthless, and sardonic creature," as one biographer describes him, was at the height of his influence. Like his passion for flashy jewels, the knight's attention drifted to the next shiny object. Even as Lane and his men were climbing aboard Drake's ships in retreat, the queen granted Raleigh thousands of acres in southern Ireland. With enemy ships prowling the ocean, the short trip to Ireland was both safer and cheaper. By the time Lane arrived in London, the courtier was already deeply immersed in organizing thousands of English farmers and artisans to settle his new lands. As with Virginia, the queen granted Raleigh the territory without reference to the indigenous people. Audrey Horning concludes that the first Roanoke settlement served as an important model for the way Raleigh, Lane, and others sought to colonize Ireland—and with similar disastrous results that echo down to this day. Within a few years, a rebellion by the displaced Irish upended Raleigh's new venture, and he would set out instead for South America to find El Dorado.

But Sir Walter's Virginia brain trust that included Hakluyt, Harriot, and White pestered him to not give up the New World effort so quickly. Hakluyt dedicated a volume of exploration reports to Raleigh, reminding him that "you freely swore that no terrors, no personal losses, or misfortunes could or would ever tear you from the sweet embraces of your own Virginia," and predicted that "if you persevere only a little longer in your constancy, your bride will shortly bring forth new and most abundant offspring." Along with applying public pressure, he urged a second colony in private correspondence. "If you proceed, which I long much to know, in your enterprise of Virginia, your best planting will be about the bay of the Chesapians," Hakluyt wrote to Raleigh from Paris on December 30, 1586.

His extraordinary reasoning was that Chesapeake Bay offered an easy route to the rich silver mines in the American Southwest that the Spanish were rumored—falsely—to have recently discovered. He still clung to the notion of a narrow-waisted North America. "I am fully persuaded that the land on the back part of Virginia extends nothing so far westward as is put down in the maps of those parts," he insisted, although by then he had surely been briefed by Harriot and White on the geographic realities. He could not or would not give up an illusion that would persist for another full century.

A week later, January 7, 1587, Raleigh approved an ingenious plan to continue the Virginia colony under his name and royal charter while limiting his financial exposure. He immodestly called it "the Cittie of

Raleigh." This first American corporation mixed a medieval mind-set with modern capitalistic innovation. It also freed Raleigh from investing huge sums of money, or that of his friends, while retaining his position as absentee landlord. The incorporation papers have not survived, but from scraps of information it appears that the new settlers could purchase a share in exchange for five hundred acres of land—a staggering amount in an era when a thirty-acre farm was considered large in land-hungry England. As far as we know, there was no stipulation that the corporation was required to buy or trade the land from the Algonquians, who had lived there since the days Anglo-Saxon speakers arrived in Britain.

The financial burden as well as the physical risk fell primarily on those willing to invest in building a new home across the ocean. Those who could not afford a share, such as small farmers and the urban poor, might have had the option to sign up as indentured servants. They would labor in Virginia to pay back their expenses. This novel approach ultimately proved the model for later English colonies. A second inspiration, which proved just as vital in later successes, was to include women and children to ensure long-term stability and survival.

This time the queen didn't meddle in the choice of a governor, and Raleigh made a surprising selection of a chief operating officer. The man who would lead the second colony would be John White, an artist with no known managerial or military experience—the polar opposite of Lane.

White lived down the street from St. Paul's Cathedral and went to church at St. Martin Within Ludgate, dedicated, appropriately, to the patron saint of travelers. He might have come from Cornwall in western England—his common surname makes it hard to be sure—but he was clearly of modest origins. What seems certain is that he trained as a painter of miniatures, a fashionable style in that day, and was a member of the painters' guild. We don't, however, have an image of the man who painted so many sensitive portraits.

Long before sailing to Roanoke Island as the expedition artist in 1585, White was fascinated with the New World. A copy of his earliest known watercolors is a striking action scene of Elizabethan soldiers firing muskets on Eskimos floating in kayaks amid ice floes as they deftly aim their arrows at the intruders. The image is so realistic that White might have witnessed the battle that took place during Frobisher's voyage to the Canadian Arctic in 1577.

By then, he had been married to Thomasine Cooper for more than a decade. Their son, Tom, died in infancy, and a daughter named Eleanor was the only surviving child. Eleanor had just turned fifteen when she wed Ananias Dare, a member of the bricklayer and tilers' guild, in June 1583, in a church a few blocks from Middle Temple. White quickly became a grandfather when the couple had a son named John and a daughter named Thomasine.

The family lived the comfortable life of middle-class guild members in an upscale neighborhood in the bustling Tudor capital, yet White seemed fatally drawn to North America. An expat French painter who escaped the slaughter at Fort Caroline lived nearby and might have served as his mentor. We know little about White's travels; in addition to the possible Frobisher trip and the 1585 voyage, he might have been on the reconnaissance mission with Amadas and Barlowe a year earlier. He worked closely with Harriot, on the scientist's return in 1586, to convert the surveyor's cartographic data into maps that are both accurate and beautiful.

White had a deep and abiding interest in the strange forms of life he encountered in the New World, from swallowtail butterflies to "a fly, which in the night seemeth a flame of fire," one of the earliest descriptions of the firefly. His portraits of Carolina Algonquians betray an unusual willingness to present the Indians as they were rather than as devilish brutes or idealized Renaissance figures. The watercolors reveal a man who, like the younger Harriot, saw Native Americans as comfortable and competent in their world rather than the barbarous savages imagined by many Europeans of their day.

White oversaw planning for the venture, recruiting colonists and organizing logistics in a frenzy of activity in the winter and spring of 1587. Unusually for that time, the new colony's leadership team included no gentry, so Raleigh placed a rush order with the College of Arms, which quickly granted each a coat of arms. Despite the widespread rumors of Virginia's horrors and the impending threat of war with Spain, White seemed to have had little trouble in quickly assembling 150 people willing to make the voyage. A few dozen got cold feet, but about 115 prepared to sail that spring.

Who would leave the safety of Elizabethan England for the uncertainty of the Atlantic and the strange lands beyond? Until recently, we had few clues because most of the settlers were simply names on a list. Given Raleigh's and White's ties to the western English counties of Devon and Cornwall, coupled with the plight of dispossessed farmers, most historians guessed that the colonists were country villagers eager for land, with a few London orphans in the mix. That reflects the assumption that you would have had to be desperate to climb aboard a ship bound for the New World in the spring of 1587. After all, a full third of the first Jamestown settlers were gentry, mostly younger sons with no hope of inheritance, and another third were common soldiers who needed employment when the Spanish war finally subsided. The bulk of the passengers on the *Mayflower*, bound together by a strict set of fundamentalist beliefs, sought refuge as the French Huguenots had done two decades earlier.

But painstaking research of wills and parish records, pioneered by the late historian William Powell, proved otherwise. The 1587 venture was an Elizabethan back-to-the-land movement powered by middle-class Londoners much like White. Many were small-business men, including tailors, lawyers, goldsmiths, and college professors. Some were neighbors near the docks close to the Tower of London, while others worshipped in the same parish on the western end of town near Middle Temple.

The colonists as a whole were remarkable in their sheer ordinariness. They were overwhelmingly middle-class people who owned a house, rental property, or bit of land they could sell to gain a berth on the Virginia voyage. Their goal seems to have been neither to find easy gold nor to worship in peace. They appear driven by an aspiration to climb the social ladder, which in that day meant to become landed gentry. In this practical desire for a better material life, they resembled the Europeans who would follow in their wake in later centuries more than their immediate successors, the Jamestown and Plymouth colonists.

There were four sets of fathers and sons and seven single women. Nine were children, three of whom appear to have been orphans. Six married couples are recorded. The seventeen women included Jane Pierce, who might have been the same person as a Jane Pierce listed as a Londoner who was daughter of a Portuguese merchant named Balthasar Pierce and sister of "Fornando Simon," suggesting an intriguing link to the pilot Fernandes. At least one nursing mother and two who were pregnant were among these women, including White's only surviving child, Eleanor Dare. She was in her first trimester and would make the journey with her husband, Ananias, who was also one of White's assistants. They would leave their young son and daughter behind in London.

They would also be leaving behind one of Europe's biggest cities, with more than 200,000 people packed into a strip of land three miles long bordering the Thames River. It was famous for its entertainments. Baiting chained bears with ferocious dogs was a "sweet and comfortable recreation" that thrilled Londoners, including Queen Elizabeth. Cockfights provided constant gambling opportunities, while foreign visitors were shocked not just by the plethora of pubs but also by the presence of respectable women eating and drinking within. William Shakespeare was poised to make his entrance into the thriving theater scene; the year the colonists departed, the Rose theater opened on the south bank of the river as one of the country's first dedicated playhouses. "This city of London is not only brimful of curiosities," a contemporary Swiss visitor noted, "but so populous also that one simply cannot walk along the streets for the crowd."

Those crowds, however, made the capital both expensive and deadly. Upper-crust Elizabethans obsessed over the rising numbers that increased rents and spawned regular epidemics of malaria and typhus. Tuberculosis was rampant. In 1593, plague swept the city and killed more than ten thousand people. Less than half the babies born reached their fifth birthday. The queen, scarred from smallpox while still young, complained in 1580 of the "great multitude of people . . . heaped up together." These circumstances no doubt made it easier for White to recruit candidates for the Virginia adventure.

The absence of an organized military force and the addition of women and children, along with a civilian leader and the promise of land, gave the White colony a wholly different flavor from the Lane effort. Though he could not have known it, the governor had hit upon a formula that would prove the winning model for the later successes at Jamestown and Plymouth. "Military outposts always failed," writes Karen Ordahl Kupperman, a New York University historian. "Settlers must come expecting to devote themselves to providing food, shelter, and supplies for the colony." And that, she adds, was possible only by offering acreage and encouraging families to ensure long-term commitment.

We have only the haziest notion what White hoped to accomplish, but he seems to have envisioned creating an English village on the shores of the Chesapeake, where Harriot had been welcomed the previous winter. They would presumably set to work growing their own food while trading cloth and copper to the Indians in exchange for deerskins, sassafras, and other exports. They clearly intended to stay. White even brought along framed pictures to hang on the walls of his new Virginia home.

Like any back-to-the-land movement dominated by city people, this effort was no doubt powered by a shared vision of a better society. More's *Utopia*, long a best seller and itself inspired by New World settlement, might have been a model. The regular practice of slavery and the harsh bias against the indigenous people that More touted might have given the new settlers pause. But his imagined society of prosperous farmers and small-business people who are religiously tolerant and hold no private property likely held strong appeal for White and his colonists.

The new governor was both knowledgeable about and sympathetic to the indigenous people; he also must have known that without their help no English settlement could possibly survive. White might have seen the new colony as a chance to side with Elizabethan England's better angels after the disastrous death of Wingina. "The whole 1587 project," asserts Quinn, "paid tribute to his belief that not only were Native Americans and white Europeans compatible, but also that in the future they could look forward to living side by side." If he is correct, then the venture was envisioned as an attempt to exist in harmony with rather than in opposition to the indigenous peoples of North America. Instead of focusing on striking it rich or creating a feudal plantation economy, the second Roanoke colony seems the first English experiment in realizing the Eden promised by Chicora. The corporation's humble motto emblazoned on its coat of arms was "small things flourish by concord." Of course, "utopia" translated as "no place."

A month and a day after Raleigh's corporation was created, Mary, Queen of Scots, lost her head. While under house arrest by her cousin Elizabeth, Mary had sought to overthrow the Protestant ruler so that she, a pro-Spanish Catholic, could take the throne. Walsingham orchestrated a plot in which secret missives from her confederates were hidden in beer barrels and delivered to the castle where Mary was confined. Then they were carried out, her treasonous responses hidden within. The revelation forced the queen's hand. Elizabeth's decision to execute a person of royal blood under her protection—and Philip's ally—ensured a massive Spanish reprisal. It also doomed White's settlers before they even left home.

Rumors quickly spread that a multinational fleet would invade England. Two months after Mary's death, Drake set sail to plunder the Spanish coast, making a preemptive strike on its armada. He called it "singeing the King of Spain's beard." In April, he created havoc in the strategic Spanish port of Cádiz, setting back Spain's planned invasion by a full year.

Meanwhile, London stevedores were loading three ships just below the Tower of London with the provisions and gear that White's colonists would need to make it through the following winter. The flagship, the *Lion*, was a sturdy vessel of 160 tons accompanied by a fly boat, a cargo carrier that could accommodate bulk supplies. A smaller pinnace completed the little fleet. Though dwarfed by the Lane expedition, this single mission still exceeded in tons and personnel the Jamestown expedition that would sail two decades later as well as the *Mayflower* voyage a dozen years after that.

Departing, the ships worked their way down the river and around the underside of England to the southern harbors of Portsmouth and Plymouth. On May 8, after the final passengers were aboard and the water casks topped off, the vessels began their two-month journey across the Atlantic. Along with the settlers and crew were Manteo and Towaye, returning home after more than half a year in England.

Most of White's settlers had never been to sea, and the conditions could be stomach churning even when the ocean was calm. Only officers had bunks; the rest made do with a bit of floor space and a wool blanket. The useful Carib innovation of the hammock had yet to catch on. Blankets hung from a line provided the only privacy. Hot food was possible only when the water was not rough, because of the danger of fire. Passengers subsisted mainly on dried biscuits called hardtack along with cheese and beer. Urine and feces collected in the bilge, and storms stirred up the rats that inevitably stowed away.

The ships, navigated by Fernandes, made their way south past the French coast to pick up the trade winds off Portugal to carry them to the Caribbean. Off Portugal, a dreadful storm lashed White's ships, separating the fly boat from the flagship and pinnace. The rough seas likely produced nightmarish bouts of nausea for passengers (no less for the heavily pregnant Eleanor Dare and Margery Harvye) in their dark and filthy hold as their vessel careened over the surging waves.

They likely passed Drake's fleet as it returned to England after the admiral's assault on Cádiz. The war had now come to Spain, but Philip remained concerned about reports of an English pirate haven on the North American east coast. His formidable intelligence network had informed him of Lane's expedition two years prior, though not the exact location of the settlement or that it had been abandoned the previous year. Spanish intelligence suggested the second colony was to be placed in a different spot. "It is to be feared that, if [Grenville] has established a settlement on the coast, the fact that he has changed its site is no indication of a decision to abandon it, but rather of his intention to improve his position," Philip wrote in a memo. And so, the day before White and his colonists set sail, Florida's governor departed St. Augustine with orders from the king to find these English trespassers. If the Spanish had their way, they could eliminate this menace to their treasure ships before the invasion of England was under way. He and

White's settlers made their way toward the Outer Banks at the same time, unaware of each other.

As the settlers endured the rolling deck and bad food, White and Fernandes bickered their way across the Atlantic. In his account of the voyage—the only one we have—the governor hints darkly that the Portuguese pilot sabotaged the mission at every turn.

Tension came to a head on July 22, 1587, two months after their departure, when the flagship and the pinnace at last anchored in the Outer Banks off Port Ferdinando (White pointedly insisted on calling it Hatteras rather than pay tribute to his pilot). According to the governor, he intended only a brief halt at the former Lane colony in order to check on the fifteen men Grenville left behind and to gather intelligence on "the state of the country and savages." After that, the ships would continue north "to the Bay of the Chesapeake, where we intended to make our seat and our fort, according to the charge given among other directions in writing, under the hand of Sir Walter Raleigh."

What took place next is one of the most mystifying moments in early American history. As a party of settlers led by White boarded the pinnace for the short trip across the Pamlico Sound to Roanoke, "a gentleman by the means of Fernandes"—sent, it would seem, as a messenger to do the pilot's dirty work—"called to the sailors in the pinnace." This unnamed person "who was appointed to return to England" leaned over the flagship's rail and ordered the pinnace crew "not to bring any of the settlers back again, but leave them in the island, except the governor and two or three such as he approved, saying that the summer was far spent, wherefore he would land all the planters in no other place."

White does not identify the mystery man, but adds that Fernandes then "persuaded" the sailors to follow these orders. The shocking news that the settlers were to be dumped on an island surrounded by vengeful Indians, in direct opposition to Raleigh's orders and White's well-laid plans, is as astonishing as the governor's response to the sudden crisis. "Wherefore it booted not the governor to contend with them," White writes haughtily in the third person, "but passed to Roanoke."

By meekly accepting the decision, he helped undermine the entire venture. Wingina's assassination the previous year by Lane and his men made Roanoke Island a dangerous place for the English, as the new governor would have heard firsthand from Harriot. The Europeans had been welcomed warmly during the first two voyages but could now expect quite different treatment. Ever since, historians have chastised White for weak leadership and lambasted Fernandes for his betrayal of Raleigh and the innocent colonists—a view that lay unchallenged for centuries.

After conceding the fight to Fernandes, White and his ill-fated party arrived on Roanoke at sunset and made camp. The next morning, they walked warily to the island's north end, "where Master Ralph Lane had his fort." The settlement was strangely quiet. None of the fifteen men Grenville had left behind were to be found, alive at least. There was a set of bleached bones of a person "which the savages had slain long before." The fort was "raised down," or dismantled, while the houses stood intact but vacant. Deer grazed on melons that had grown up in the ruins. Making the best of a bad situation, White ordered the settlers to repair the existing homes and build new cottages.

Two days later, the third ship arrived at Port Ferdinando, and all the colonists disembarked after the long sea voyage. Three days after that, White's assistant George Howe, who might have been the colony's designated artist, foolishly took a solo walk. After strolling along the shore for a couple of miles, he removed his clothes and waded into the warm water to spear crabs. A party of Indians riddled him with sixteen arrows and crushed his skull with their wooden swords. His son, also named George, became the first English child orphaned in America.

The murder was clearly revenge for Wingina's death and a message that the English were no longer welcome by his people or their allies. A shaken White sent a delegation of twenty-one men led by Stafford, the man who had spotted Drake's fleet, to Manteo's people on Croatoan to find out what happened to the rest of Grenville's men "and the disposition of the people toward us." When the English beached their vessel, the inhabitants aimed their bows and arrows at the party "as though they would fight with us," but fled when the English raised their guns.

Manteo, dressed as a European, intervened, calling out in his native tongue. They rushed forward to embrace the visitors and begged the English not to "gather or spill any of their corn, for that they had but little." This was either a sign of famine, brought on by a drought that researchers suspect began that year, or a response to Lane's demands that they feed his settlers the previous year.

The Croatoan took the English to a nearby village, where, despite their worries about the corn supply, they "feasted us after their manner." They also pointedly showed their guests a paralyzed man whom the English shot during the attack on Wingina. The Indians used tattoos to mark their clan and tribe, markings that White had carefully drawn the previous year. Knowing that the English couldn't read these markings, they asked for a "token or badge" they could wear to avoid mistaken identities in the future and prevent bloodshed. Unfortunately, no one acted on the practical idea.

The next morning, the Croatoan elders explained that after Grenville departed, a coalition of mainland tribes sent thirty men to ambush the remaining English. As the others hid, two Indians stepped forward to greet the Europeans. While embracing, one of the Native Americans pulled out a wooden sword hidden under his cloak and killed the colonist on the spot. His English colleague managed to escape and warn his companions.

The surprise attack turned into an extended Wild West shoot-out. The English rushed into their building containing food supplies and ammunition. For an hour they held off the enemy, shooting through its windows and doors. Then the Indians set the structure on fire, forcing them to flee. For another hour the two groups battled it out within the thick forest. One of Grenville's men was shot in the mouth and died, while a "fire arrow"—evidently from an English bow—killed an Indian. Though we associate bows and arrows with Native Americans, every Englishman of the day between ages seven and sixty-two was required to know how to use the weapons.

Eventually, the nine remaining English were able to scramble into a nearby boat and make for Port Ferdinando. On the way they picked up the four others, who had been oystering in a nearby creek. Rowing hard, they reached a sandbar close to the port and stopped to rest. Then they left, "whither, as yet we know not," reported the Croatoan. This group of thirteen men was never heard from again.

The attackers were Wingina supporters led by Wanchese, the same Indian who had spent much of a year in London and who vanished as soon as he returned to America in 1585. His allies included members of other villages on the mainland. The English naively wanted bygones to be bygones and proposed a peace conference. Croatoan leaders agreed to let them know within a week if their enemies would be willing to negotiate.

White waited impatiently at Roanoke for a response to his proposal, worried that not responding to Howe's murder invited more retaliation. When the week passed without word, White, borrowing from Lane's playbook, prepared a preemptive attack on Wingina's people at Dasemunkepeuc. At midnight on August 9, he and a party of two dozen men, including Manteo, crossed the same water separating Roanoke from the mainland that Lane had a year before. Before dawn, they crept toward a low fire burning in the village center where a few figures squatted around the flames.

When the English charged, the surprised Indians quickly scattered into the thick reeds nearby. Following close behind, the settlers managed to shoot one man before an Indian recognized Stafford and called out. These were not their rivals after all, but Croatoan, subjected yet again to friendly fire. White offered the weak excuse that the mistake was inevitable, "it being so dark . . . and the men and woman appareled all so like others."

In fact, Wanchese and his people had fled their village after Howe's death, fearing just such an English reprisal. The Croatoan were busy looting what was left behind. Manteo had inadvertently guided an attack against his own people, including a Croatoan leader and his wife, who was carrying an infant on her back. While Manteo was "somewhat grieved," he "imputed their harm to their own folly." If the tribal leaders had kept their promise and reported to White within a week, he scolded, they would have avoided harm.

A series of joyous celebrations the next week took the colonists' minds off their tenuous situation. At Raleigh's request, White had Manteo baptized and named Lord of Roanoke and Dasemunkepeuc "in reward of his faithful service." This move gave him ostensible control over what had been the core of Wingina's territory.

Five days later, on August 18, Eleanor Dare gave birth. "Because this child was the first Christian born in Virginia, she was named Virginia," her grandfather wrote. It is the only mention we have of the girl. The baptism, presumably by White because no pastor is known to have come with the company, took place less than a week later. Soon after, Harvye gave birth to a child as well, although the gender and name went unrecorded.

With the settlers now situated, Fernandes prepared the ships to depart for England, his work complete. But "some controversies rose between the governor and the assistants," wrote White, again using the third person. The colonists felt they needed additional provisions and colonists to improve their long-term prospects. White at first persuaded Christopher Cooper, possibly a relation, to depart with Fernandes and act on the colony's behalf, but his friends persuaded him that evening not to leave. Instead, the next day, the entire community went to White and "with one voice requested him to return himself into England."

White refused, saying his enemies would "slander falsely both him and the action." The governor feared he would be accused of leading "so many into a country in which he never meant to stay himself, and there to leave them behind him." This is to say nothing of what surely, on a personal level, must have been an agonizing thought: the prospect of abandoning his daughter and infant granddaughter on a remote island amid Indians intent on driving them out.

White had trunks containing his armor, framed drawings, and maps, and he argued that his "stuff and goods might be spoiled and most of it pilfered away" were he to leave. The governor noted that the settlers "intended to remove 50 miles further up into the main presently." This is the first mention of a plan to abandon Roanoke Island and move into the interior, a Plan B evidently hammered out when it became clear they would not be going to the Chesapeake after all. Whether this was to be a temporary move to inland winter quarters with Native American allies or a permanent resettlement is unclear.

The colonists promised to safeguard White's trunks and signed a formal document addressed to the queen's subjects explaining the governor's departure as "most requisite and necessary for the good and happy planting of us." He reluctantly yielded. White never mentions who was to take charge in his absence. Nor does he record his farewell to Eleanor and baby Virginia two days later. He would never see any of them again.

The governor refused to travel back to England on the flagship with the detested Fernandes, choosing instead the smaller fly boat. A voyage normally lasting six weeks or so proved a three-month nightmare of sickness and starvation, and when the ship miraculously drifted into an Irish harbor, many of the crew were dead or dying. The delay proved devastating. By the time he reached London in November, word that the Spanish Armada was nearing completion had arrived before him. The queen had just issued an order prohibiting all vessels from leaving England until the threat of Spanish invasion passed.

White doubtless pleaded with Raleigh to obtain an exemption for an immediate resupply mission. The courtier was in a position to do so; as the new captain of the Queen's Guard, he filled a prestigious post that kept him by her side. He was, however, busy with court politics and his ambitious new Irish colonization scheme. White and his settlers would have to wait.

That winter, Sir Richard Grenville secured a waiver to attack the Spanish in the Caribbean, and the governor won a green light to tag along with the convoy. He rapidly pulled together a ship, supplies, and additional colonists to travel in the safety of the fleet and then peel off north to Virginia. In March 1588, the ships bobbed in the harbor just below Bideford in Devon, but contrary winds kept the ships in port.

Orders arrived from London on March 31 commanding Grenville's fleet to join a defensive force being assembled by the navy in Plymouth. Yet again, White was delayed. When the Royal Navy deemed two of the smaller ships unworthy of military action, the desperate governor cut a deal with the captains to take him to Virginia, along with seven male colonists and four women and provisions. Carrying letters of encouragement from Raleigh, he set off in late April aboard the little *Brave*, accompanied by a second ship. Traveling without a convoy during a war, on vessels run by privateers, was an enormous risk. As soon as the ships were offshore, the crews began to hunt for merchant prey. On May 6, off the Moroccan coast, they crossed a larger and better-armed French ship that chased and caught the *Brave*. A bloody deck fight ensued.

"I myself was wounded twice in the head, once with a sword and another time with a pike, and hurt also in the side of the buttock with a shot," White reports. One of the would-be settlers fared worse, receiving a dozen wounds. In all, nearly two dozen of the crew were killed or grievously injured. The victors stripped the ship of all its weapons and the colonists' supplies, and the crew and passengers limped back to Bideford. All England was preparing for a Spanish invasion, and a further mission was out of the question until the danger passed. A disconsolate White remained in England, imagining the Virginia planters "were not a little distressed" at his absence.

A day after the governor's pirate battle off Morocco, the Spanish launched a second attempt, from Florida, to locate the English trespassers on the eastern coast. The effort the previous year by St. Augustine's governor had failed to reach Chesapeake Bay. Now, with rumors in the Madrid court that the English had found a mountain made of diamonds, as well as a passage to the Pacific, their search took on an added urgency. A Spanish sailor taken prisoner by Grenville in 1586 and later released reported "the reason why the English have settled there is . . . because on the mainland there is much gold and so that they may pass from the North to the South Sea, which they say and understand is nearby; thus making themselves strong through the discovery of great wealth." Philip ordered an experienced forty-five-year-old commander named Vicente González to conduct another reconnaissance mission. González and his crew of thirty left St. Augustine and reached the Chesapeake, possibly traveling as far as today's Washington, D.C., but they found no sign of the English.

A powerful west wind caught the ship as it sailed back into the Atlantic for the long journey home. Fearful that they would be pushed far out to sea, González ordered his crew to furl the sails and take down the two masts to reduce wind resistance. Then they began the arduous task of rowing for land, in the middle of the night and into the teeth of the sharp gusts whipping over the dark waves. All the while they had to keep a lookout for the treacherous shoals lining the coast south of the Chesapeake. As dawn broke on July 1, 1588, the exhausted men sighted land. They made for a cove that promised refuge from the wind and waves.

On a nearby barrier island, the crew spotted a wooden slipway used for repairing small vessels and several wells sunk into the sand with English-style barrels. Along with these telltale signs of a colony were "other debris indicating that a considerable number of people had been there," according to a later Spanish account of the voyage. Through sheer luck, González had rowed blind through a stormy night and stumbled on Port Ferdinando.

The once-bustling staging point for the Roanoke settlement now lay deserted; nearly a year had passed since White and Fernandes had weighed anchor there. Yet González did not pursue his serendipitous discovery by seeking out the main settlement, though he describes seeing a wooded arm of land that almost certainly was Roanoke. He reports no cooking fires that would signal the island was then occupied. Had the settlers abandoned their town? Were they dead? In hiding? Or were they waiting in ambush for the Spanish to investigate? Rather than find out, González and his men spent the midsummer's day on the beach before eventually departing.

The same day, across the ocean, Philip ordered the Spanish Armada to proceed against England. "Pressed as I am by financial and other difficulties," he wrote, "I am resolute to overcome them all with God's aid." The immense convoy of 130 ships crowded with thirty thousand Spanish, Portuguese, French, and Dutch as well as English soldiers soon headed out of Spanish waters and toward the

English Channel, the flapping banners of Christ and the Virgin Mary heralding a crusade against the northern heretics. Their plan was to rendezvous with Philip's forces in the Netherlands and land troops on the island's southern coast.

But by the end of that month, bad weather and England's more maneuverable vessels had inflicted a calamitous defeat on the multinational invasion force. Two out of three armada sailors and soldiers perished, and only half of the fleet's ships made it back to Spain. Raleigh and Grenville remained on land during the battle, but Fernandes, returned from the Americas, served aboard the largest English warship.

With González's lucky find, Philip now knew the location of the English settlement. But the virtual destruction of his armada delayed his intention to snuff out the pirate base. The following year, in response to reports by Spanish spies that the English planned to mass ships at their American base—likely English propaganda designed to divert enemy resources—he decided again to take action. The king ordered a third expedition to seek out the colonists. This time he wanted the English settlement destroyed once and for all.

In the flush of victory after the armada's defeat, the English showed less interest in the Roanoke colony than their enemy did. The country remained on a war footing. The ban on shipping remained, and the luckless governor White could not persuade Raleigh or his Cittie of Raleigh associates to win a waiver and fund a relief mission to Roanoke. And so another year slipped by. All attention was on a 1589 English armada, led by Drake, designed to attack Spain and deliver a decisive blow. The effort foundered amid storms and illness, ensuring a long and drawn-out conflict.

It wasn't until the following spring that White at last succeeded, after nearly three years, in joining a Caribbean-bound convoy. Raleigh twisted the arm of a major investor in a privateering syndicate, and two ships—the *Moonlight* and the *Hopewell*—were assigned to carry the governor to Virginia, but only after a summer spent cruising for Spanish loot in the Caribbean. At the last minute, the crew barred him from bringing supplies or additional settlers, or even, to White's indignation, a single servant. He would return to Roanoke from his resupply mission empty-handed and alone. By then, despite his intervention, Raleigh was putting more distance between himself and the Virginia settlers; he had turned the Cittie of Raleigh over to another set of investors.

Meanwhile, in preparation for his assault on the English colony, Florida governor Pedro Menéndez Márquez went to Cuba to assemble a fleet of war galleys powered by convicts and enslaved Muslims from North and West Africa. These flat-bottomed boats, designed for the Mediterranean, were well suited to the shallow waters of the North Carolina sounds. The galleys would call at St. Augustine to take on a large complement of experienced soldiers and then move up the coast to destroy the Roanoke settlement pinpointed by González. Afterward, Philip would have Menéndez sail to the Chesapeake and build a new fort to accommodate three hundred men. The Spanish would send out teams to search and seize the mines of precious metals and diamonds that the English were rumored to have found. The bold strategy would secure Spanish control of the all-important shipping lanes as well as the potential resources inland. If successful, the effort would ward off all future trespassers, securing the North American east coast for Spain.

Yet the king's plan was nothing more than an elaborate ruse, designed to fool the English spy network. The Florida governor's secret mission was not to attack colonists but to guide the year's treasure ships in the Caribbean up the North American coast and safely to Spain. Philip still wanted to extinguish the English colony, but more important was to transport safely the revenue to pay off his mounting debts. On July 20, 1590, the scheme succeeded as Menéndez triumphantly sailed into a Portuguese harbor with a fleet of vessels loaded with silver, gold, and other valuable goods for the depleted Spanish treasury.

That same day, White was sailing past St. Augustine on his way to what he hoped would be a happy reunion with his family and colonists. He had spent the long Caribbean summer with privateers itching to capture the very ships that Menéndez had already shepherded to Spain. As hurricane season approached, the English dispersed and White's two ships sailed north for the Outer Banks. The race to find the Roanoke settlers, initiated by a sixteenth-century Spanish king and pursued well into the twenty-first century, was under way.

August began stormily as the *Moonlight* and the *Hopewell* cruised north on the Gulf Stream through "much rain, thundering and great spouts, which fell round about us nigh unto our ships," White reports. Two days later the vessels were in sight of the barrier island of Ocracoke, where Grenville's flagship *Tiger* grounded five years before. But "the weather was so exceeding foul, that we could not come to an anchor near the coast" for nearly a week.

When the storm passed, the ships halted a mile or so off a barrier island south of Ocracoke, and the men went ashore to fish in the Pamlico and gather freshwater. They spent two full days there before resuming their journey, anchoring off the northeast end of Croatoan on August 12. The next morning, the ship's boats were sent to measure the depth of a breach between the Atlantic and the Pamlico. This seems to be Chacandepeco Inlet, separating Croatoan from Hatteras and close to the site of a Croatoan town.

Just why the men spent so much time mapping depths when they were less than a day's sail shy of their goal of Port Ferdinando is perplexing. Was White hoping to leave a clear trail for future rescue missions? Even more bizarrely, White doesn't mention going ashore to look for someone. He records no sign of any human, European or Native American. Yet even before he found the "secret token," this was the obvious place to seek out the colonists or information about their fate as he had done in 1587.

Two days pass before White resumes his account, noting that the ships anchored off the north end of Hatteras the evening of August 15. This would seem an unreasonably long time to travel less than fifty miles, but what happened in the intervening time we're left to guess. Before the sun set, the crews spotted smoke rising from Roanoke Island, which White read as a sign the colonists had seen their arrival and awaited their visit. The next morning, the governor and the two captains diverted their two small boats on the way to the island when they spotted another "great smoke" to the south along Hatteras—

the very area they had sailed past the day before. When they reached the spot, "we found no man nor sign any had been there lately." Was it a natural brush fire? Again, White gives no indication, though he uses the same term—"great smoke"—that he does for the Roanoke column.

The second attempt to reach the colonists' settlement was interrupted the next morning by the tragic mishap in which seven men in one of the boats, including the captain of the *Moonlight*, drowned in the inlet. White pleaded with the shocked survivors to press on, and they reached the island in the dark. Though they overshot the landing place by a quarter of a mile, they spotted "the light of a great fire through the woods, to which we presently rowed."

Rather than risk going ashore in the dark, the men spent the night in the boats, sounding a trumpet and singing "many familiar English tunes of songs." Only silence greeted their efforts. At dawn, they found "grass and sundry trees burning about the place," but, again, White doesn't specify if the blaze was natural or made by people. If it was made by lightning strikes, he doesn't say as much.

The search party led by White hiked through the woods to the island's west side, facing Wingina's village of Dasemunkepeuc. Was he looking for more smoke or signs of life on the mainland shore? Or was there an English fort or settlement here he wanted to investigate? In either event, the English then walked up the beach that curved around to the north shore. By then it was clear they were being watched. "In all this way we saw in the sand the print of the savages' feet of two or three sorts trodden [during] the night," White recorded. Perhaps, then, the fires were designed to alert the English or warn others of their approach.

While trudging along the beach of the north shore, the men once again climbed the sandy bank and saw a tree with the carved letters *C R O*. At the nearby settlement, where the houses were "taken down" and the site "very strongly enclosed with a high palisade of great trees," was another carving. At eye height at the right entrance of this fortified complex, the governor saw "in fair capital letters was graven CROATOAN without any cross or sign of distress."

White explains that this was an agreed-upon signal, "a secret token" that the settlers agreed to leave if they abandoned the settle-ment. A Greek cross would mean they were in distress, but neither carving showed such a sign. Grenville's frustration in not finding Lane's men on his return to Roanoke in 1586 might have prompted this plan. The place had clearly been deserted for a time; only a few heavy objects, such as small artillery guns and "two lead ingots," were to be found. Everything easily portable was gone.

The party's next route took them again along the shore, this time eastward, to look for the colony's small boats at a landing site—presumably the one they overshot the night before. White found no signs of the vessels or the small cannon and ammunition that were there when he left. As the group doubled back to the settlement, a squadron of sailors—evidently the men had broken up into two groups, one likely to guard the boats—intercepted them with news that they found five looted trunks.

They had been dug out of a trench. Three were White's, left behind when he returned to England, "and about the place many of my things spoiled and broken, and my books torn from the covers, the frames of some of my pictures and maps rotted and sailed with rain, and my armor almost eaten through with rust." As with the thick brush growing in the settlement, the rusted armor suggested the colo-nists had been gone for some time.

The governor blamed "the savages our enemies" for the looting and speculated that hostile Indians had waited until the colonists left Roanoke to pillage what was left behind. "But although it grieved me to see such spoil of my goods, yet on the other side I greatly joyed that I had safely found a certain took of their safe being at Croatoan." The statement, seeming to balance loss of his stuff with the fate of more than one hundred people, feels jarring. "The whole existence of the colony—its population, its habitation, its past, and its potential future—was concentrated into this 'secret token,' and yet John White believed that it was a history he could read," note authors Margaret and Dwayne Pickett.

If he was certain the settlers were safe at Croatoan, why does the governor mention that they had planned to move "fifty miles into the main," which likely meant to the head of the Albemarle Sound to the west? If he thought they might be there, he made no move in that direction. Instead, "when we had seen in this place so much as we could, we returned to our boats." The sky, he reports, was overcast, and the crew feared a stormy night ahead. The entire party climbed into the two boats, and White left Roanoke forever.

The governor was no Sherlock Holmes. He seems to have felt the carvings on the tree told him all he needed to know. But why leave so abruptly without attempting to make contact with those he knew were shadowing him? As noted before, Grenville spent a full fourteen days looking for clues to the missing Lane colony, not knowing they were safe in the holds of Drake's fleet. It is possible that the governor and his men feared ambush or that the sailors demanded to return to the ships to mourn their dead mates.

"The same evening, with much danger and labor, we got ourselves aboard, by which time the wind and seas were so greatly risen that we doubted our cables and anchors would scarcely hold until morning." The next morning the ocean was still rough, but the captain of the *Hopewell* agreed to sail back to Croatoan—where both ships had been only days before. This was, White is explicit, "where our planters were." Then disaster struck again when the men were hauling up the anchor and the cable snapped, sending the ship careening toward a sandbar. "If it had not chanced that we had fallen into a channel of deeper water, closer by the shore," White recalls, then the ship would have been beaten apart by the waves.

With only one cable and anchor out of the original supply of four, they had to abandon the planned Croatoan visit. Without a spare anchor, the risk of shipwreck was too great. In addition, the weather seemed to be worsening, and this was hurricane season. Food supplies were running low and the sea was too rough to retrieve a cask of water still onshore. The crew of the *Moonlight,* complaining of a leak in their hull but also no doubt eager to be far from these treacherous waters that had killed seven of their men, headed home that same day.

Apparently moved by what the governor called "my earnest petitions," the captain and crew of the *Hopewell* compromised with the distraught governor. They agreed to winter in the Caribbean and then come back in the spring fully stocked with provisions "with hope to

make two rich voyages of one"—that is, to snag Spanish prizes—
"and at our return to visit our countrymen in Virginia."

The *Hopewell* made its way out to sea and then turned south,
leaving Roanoke and Croatoan in its wake. It would be White's last
glimpse of the New World. Two days later, the wind swiveled to the
west-northwest and blew hard, pushing the small ship deeper into the
Atlantic. Unable to get back on course for the Caribbean, they set sail
instead for the Azores Islands three thousand miles due east.

In that Portuguese archipelago controlled now by Spain, the ship
found protection under the guns of an English fleet led by Admiral
Sir John Hawkins, the pirate and slave trader. Unable to make landfall to replenish their food and water because of a contrary wind, the
captain instead set sail for England. The governor landed at Plymouth
on October 24, 1590, never, so far as we know, to venture across the
Atlantic again. Tragedy struck again a few months later when Thomasine, his wife of a quarter century, died.

After writing up his account of the voyage, he summed up his
misadventures in a letter to the pastor Hakluyt three years later, blam-
ing bad weather and ill luck as well as "cross and unkind dealings"
with ship commanders for his failure. The tone is touched with bitter irony. "Thus you may plainly perceive the success of my fifth and
last voyage to Virginia, which was no less unfortunately ended than
frowardly"—perversely—"begun, and as luckless to many, as sinister to myself."

For White, the search was over. In the centuries to come, a slew
of historians, archaeologists, genealogists, and amateur gumshoes
would take up the hunt for traces of the missing settlers. But while the
colonists might still have been alive, several rescue missions produced
intriguing clues to the fate of the vanished Elizabethans. Their trail
was not yet cold.

PART TWO

The Search

NO MATTER TO WHAT HAZARDOUS LENGTHS
WE LET OUR LINE, THEY STILL WITHDRAW, AGAIN AND
FURTHER INTO THE DEPTHS.

—Thomas Mann, *Joseph and His Brothers*

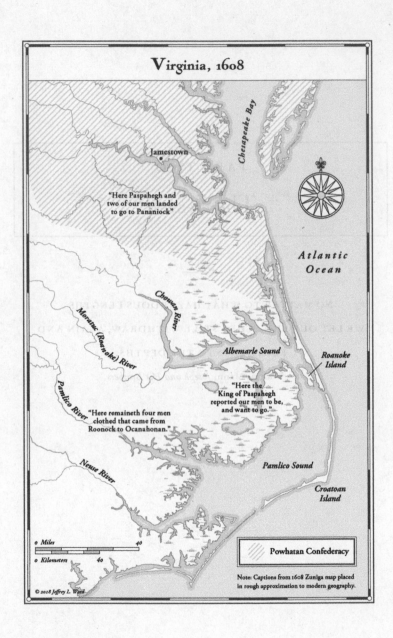

CHAPTER FIVE

A Whole Country of English

Governor John White's account of his 1590 voyage remains our single best source for determining what happened on Roanoke. Yet the more I scrutinized the brief report, the more its inconsistencies and elisions made it feel as mysterious as the fate of the Lost Colony itself. The record White left behind has a hallucinatory quality unlike almost anything in early American literature. Bonfires ignite as if by ghosts. There are footprints in the sands of a silent forest. Hidden trunks are plundered, scattering rusty armor and torn maps. The only clue is a word carved on a tree. Men drown in the morning in a freak wave, the survivors made to sing songs that evening to their phantom countrymen.

There is an otherworldly detachment to his tale, as if the governor were a disembodied witness rather than the main character in an emotionally wrenching journey. After three years fighting bureaucracy and pirates, he spends several precious days fishing south of Roanoke. After finally reaching his long-sought destination, White fusses over his looted possessions yet never mentions his daughter or granddaughter or any colonist by name. Then he abandons the search after a few hours because of a summer storm.

Strangest of all, the governor was actually in sight of the very place he came to believe the colonists to be, and a boatload of sailors from his two ships—perhaps accompanied by the governor—came within hailing distance of a Croatoan village. Yet he doesn't mention stepping ashore on the island that was home to the only known allies of the English, the same island he sent a delegation to in 1587 in order to learn "the disposition of the people toward us."

Nothing adds up in the governor's cursory and contradictory telling, yet we have—so far—no other record of what took place those August days on the Outer Banks except for a short letter he wrote to Hakluyt in 1593. Until a long-lost ship's log or Spanish deposition of some English sailor surfaces from a European archive, all that remains of this strange voyage are White's words.

I began to wonder if the confusion was deliberate. It's possible the governor was trying to throw off the Spanish, not wanting to give the enemy intelligence that could result in a massacre of the settlers, including his loved ones. He might have recast actual events to make himself appear a tragic figure rather than one culpable for the disastrous loss of the settlers for whom he was, after all, responsible. His patron Raleigh, fearful of losing the charter for his New World fiefdom if the colonists were declared dead, might have forbidden White to reveal the full truth in writing. Grief, age, and time might also have played tricks with the governor's memory. After his missive to Hakluyt, written from a Raleigh estate in Ireland, he vanishes from history as completely as his colonists.

What do we make of this man who left us with too many riddles, this innovative artist, curious explorer, and bold idealist who persuaded more than one hundred people to leave their conventional lives for an unknown shore? The governor showed tremendous tenacity and bravery, yet he was also a poor manager and incompetent military commander with a marked tendency to blame others, and even given to flashes of paranoia.

His greatest legacy was not in taking the Lost Colonists to North America but in bringing the New World to the Old. While White was still at sea in 1590, Flemish publisher Theodor de Bry released *A Briefe and True Report of the New Found Land of Virginia*, which combined copper engravings based on White's 1585 drawings with extended captions by Harriot. An immediate best seller in English, French, German, and Latin, the volume was the first and most popu-

lar in a series introducing the New World to a broad European public. Though the Spanish and Portuguese sent accomplished artists on
many of their New World missions, both before and after the Roanoke voyages, most of the results remained the equivalent of classified
material, stored at secure sites like Philip II's sumptuous royal library
at El Escorial outside Madrid.

Because of this relative dearth of publicly available images from
the Americas, and because de Bry published the White engravings
as the first in his series (thanks to the urgings of his friend the pastor
Hakluyt), the Carolina Algonquians and their way of life came to represent Native American life for centuries to come, long after disease
and violence all but wiped out the people of Ossomocomuck. "If you
saw those books in 1590, it was like seeing television for the first time
would be for us," explained Larry Tise, a historian at East Carolina
University at Greenville, as we leafed through a first edition at the
John Carter Brown Library at Brown University. "These are action
scenes." The leather-tooled volume indeed was as large as a desktop
computer screen. Though the engravings gave White's portraits a
Renaissance makeover, the images still illustrate an entire way of life
foreign to Europeans and yet familiar in their everyday activities of
hunting, eating, and celebrating that struck a universal chord.

"They were the best portrayals of American Indians available for
centuries, and they were reproduced many times to illustrate studies
for Indians far removed from Roanoke," writes Kupperman, the New
York University historian. One later Dutch engraving of an Indonesian village looks suspiciously like Pomeiooc, while an Italian portrayed a dancing West African in 1690 in a pose identical to White's
Algonquian shaman. Some scholars believe the engravings played
a role in European concepts about the "noble savage," a phrase that
first appeared not quite a century after Roanoke in a poem by John
Dryden, who was almost certainly familiar with the men and women
the governor depicted who smiled, danced, and prayed in a kind of
Edenic innocence. Not until the great nineteenth-century painters like
Frederic Remington and George Catlin did the Plains Indians assume
the role of the iconic North American indigenous people.

White, however, had to live with the knowledge that he was the sole European to lose an entire colony in the New World; even some of Ayllón's settlers survived their ordeal, as did a few of the French in their misbegotten efforts in the 1570s. Still, the governor ultimately did more than any other single person to shape the way Europeans and European Americans viewed the continent's Native inhabitants. And as researchers would come to find four hundred years later, his maps still had secrets to reveal.

No sooner did White return than theories about the fate of the Lost Colonists began to accumulate like blowing sand, settling around White's single statement: "I greatly joyed that I had safely found a certain token of their safe being at Croatoan." His acquaintance the botanist John Gerard argued in 1597 that the settlers survived, but only if "untimely death by murdering, or pestilence, corrupt air, bloody fluxes, or some other mortal sickness hath not destroyed them." In subsequent centuries, the spectrum of alternatives grew to include peaceful assimilation with the Indians and a fatal attempt to flee to Newfoundland or England aboard small boats. More recently, intricate conspiracy theories to rival those of the Kennedy assassination have emerged, including a plot at Elizabeth's court to destroy the colony and thereby damage Raleigh's standing. One investigator is convinced that Raleigh himself conspired to hide the colonists so that they could harvest sassafras for his personal gain without attracting potential competitors. Then there are the perennial pop culture suggestions that typically involve blood and gore and a heady dose of the supernatural, including, of course, vampires. With no accepted academic wisdom, any theory seems as credible as another. This is one of those chapters in American history that invites democratic speculation. "It's the Area 51 of colonial history," said Adrian Masters, the University of Texas historian.

In White's day, there was one person who expressed surprisingly little interest in the fate of the Lost Colonists: their feudal lord Sir Walter Raleigh. When the governor was searching Roanoke, the knight's power was at its zenith. But shortly after, he impregnated and secretly married one of the queen's attendants. The furious Elizabeth, who clearly still had personal feelings for the handsome if haughty knight, threw them both for a time into separate cells in the Tower of London. Raleigh's star went into a long eclipse.

Unwelcome at court, he crossed the Atlantic for the first time in 1595. His goal was not to locate his abandoned settlers but to gain gold and glory by finding the realm of El Dorado in the Amazon. During a visit to the Caribbean island of Trinidad before plunging into the Venezuelan jungle, Raleigh plied Spanish traders with bottles of good wine to pump them for intelligence. Not wanting them to know his real destination, he told the men he was "bound only for the relief of those English which I had planted in Virginia."

This was, he admitted, merely a convenient way to cover his tracks. After his futile search for treasure, he sailed up the Gulf Stream and right past the Outer Banks. He claimed that "extremity of weather" kept him from landing. Critics of Raleigh, who were legion, sniped at his indifference. Two years after he returned from the Americas, his nemesis Sir Francis Bacon acidly noted, "It is the sinfulest thing in the world to forsake or destitute a plantation once in forwardness, for besides dishonor, it is the guiltiness of blood." Everyone knew whom he was alluding to.

Raleigh, by then restored to the queen's favor, ignored the flack. None of his correspondence after White's 1590 return mentions the vanished settlers. There was more than callousness in the knight's lack of interest in searching for the abandoned colonists. His charter from Elizabeth required that he settle Virginia by 1591 to keep his monopoly. If the English there could not be proved dead, then they could be presumed to be alive, and Raleigh's charter would remain intact. If Raleigh's attitude is seen in that light, even White's upbeat statement about the settlers' certain home on Croatoan might conceivably have been dictated by a powerful patron intent on keeping a hand in the North American game.

Shortly before Raleigh left for South America, a London court declared White's son-in-law, Ananias Dare, legally dead so that the settler's son, John (who was apparently estranged from his presumed grandfather and namesake), could inherit his father's property. As far as England's courts were concerned, the settlers were no more. In this era, however, the patronage of a monarch trumped a lowly magistrate's ruling.

Raleigh's charter suddenly seemed potentially lucrative again when the price of sassafras rose to dizzying heights on the European market in the late 1590s. The smooth and slender tree noted by Harriot grows naturally from northern Florida to Maine and prefers the sandy coastal soil. Native Americans made an orange-colored tea with its root to cure everything from acne to urinary-tract infections. The Choctaw of Louisiana later showed French settlers how to use it to thicken their gumbo (filé powder is still made from dried and crushed sassafras leaves). Today we know that in excess sassafras can cause cancer, but in sixteenth-century Europe it was considered a miracle drug. A Seville physician publicized its wonders in the 1570s. Harriot touted its "rare virtues in medicine for the cure of many diseases." It was rumored the root could even remedy the dreaded French pox, the syphilis then ravaging Europe. Soon desperate patients would pay whatever the price to obtain this magical substance. The primary alternative was a heavy dose of mercury, feared for its horrific side effects, which included loss of speech and hearing and, frequently, a slow and painful death.

At the time of the Roanoke voyages, a pound of sassafras sold for eighteen English pounds a ton. A decade later, the same amount was worth more than three hundred English pounds, or nearly a hundred thousand dollars in today's currency. With his charter covering much of the North American east coast, Raleigh held a monopoly over other English competitors. He even impounded the stock of one merchant who obtained more than a ton of sassafras in New England. He sued the interloper, citing his legal claim to the shipment. "All ships and goods are confiscate that shall trade there without my leave," he wrote to a member of Elizabeth's Privy Council, adding that his competitor's attempt to dump a huge cargo on the market would depress prices and ruin his own profits.

Raleigh's interest in Virginia, dormant for well over a decade, swiftly revived. "I shall yet live to see it an English nation," he valiantly wrote in 1602. This patriotic sentiment coincided with the collapse of his ambitious Irish colony, which he sold the same year.

Raleigh was desperate for cash. Under the guise of seeking the vanished settlers, he sent a ship that same year to the Outer Banks. What was stuffed into its hold reveals the mission's real purpose: thirty-two pounds of copper to trade with Native Americans, along with knives, hatchets, shovels, and saws useful for harvesting sassafras roots.

The vessel's itinerary offers further proof of Raleigh's priorities; the crew arrived at a cape far to the south of Croatoan and spent a leisurely month trading for and collecting the pharmaceutical. Only when the hold was filled did the captain turn north. In a replay of White's misadventure, bad weather snapped at least one of the anchor cables, which "forced and feared them from searching the port of Hatarask, to which they were sent," according to a contemporary account. The cargo, some of which was shipped to Germany, would have earned Raleigh a handsome return. But before he could collect the proceeds, Elizabeth died. Her successor, King James I—son of the beheaded Mary, Queen of Scots—revoked his Virginia charter and locked him in the Tower. The new ruler despised Raleigh's arrogance and aggressive stance toward Spain. Before the year was out, the courtier had been charged, tried, and found guilty of treason. He kept his head—for now—but spent the next dozen years inside the Bloody Tower, albeit in relative luxury, composing his *History of the World* in a high-backed chair in front of a comfortable fire and with frequent visits from his family and friends, including the loyal Harriot. He never directly mentioned the Roanoke settlers again in writing.

Londoners, however, did not wholly forget their deserted countrymen. Memory enough remained for the famous playwright Ben Jonson to co-author a 1605 smash comedy referencing the Lost Colonists. *Eastward Hoe* relates a botched effort by two naive shysters with the telling names of Spendall and Scapethrift to sail for the New World and make their fortune. (Curiously, one of White's vanished settlers was a man called Spendlove.)

Captain Seagull assures them that in Virginia "gold is more plentiful there than copper is with us." Even the chamber pots, he maintains, are pure gold. This skewered not just Virginia's notorious lack of gold but Thomas More's *Utopia*, in which prisoners are bound with golden chains and citizens do their nightly business in golden chamber pots. What for Elizabethans had begun as the promise of a New World Eden was now an illusion to be mocked.

"Why, is she inhabited already with any English?" asks Spendall, playing the straight man.

"A whole country of English is there, man, bred of those that were left there in '79," replies Seagull, misstating the correct date but revealing that the colony's loss was still common knowledge in London's pubs. "They have married with the Indians, and make 'em bring forth as beautiful faces as any we have in England; and therefore the Indians are so in love with 'em that all the treasure they have they lay at their feet." The racist assumption that the English added welcome beauty to the Native American gene pool posited that the settlers not only survived but prospered by joining the indigenous people. This was the first recorded suggestion that the colonists didn't die, but assimilated with the indigenous people. During the play's extended run, Virginia Dare, if she still lived, would have turned eighteen.

Precisely twenty years passed from the time the Lost Colonists arrived on Roanoke until the English launched a new venture in the Americas. The next generation of leaders ended the long and costly Anglo-Spanish war. Pirating was again illegal and no longer as profitable. Investors once more cast an eye toward the North American shore. By then, the elder Hakluyt at Middle Temple was dead, while Grenville had perished in a Spanish attack and Fernandes vanished off the Azores. White faded into Irish obscurity; no one knows where or when he died and was buried. Lane died a few months after his queen, though his tomb in Dublin's St. Patrick's Cathedral has since been lost.

Despite the long interval, the revived effort was in many ways a continuation of Raleigh's vision. Pastor Hakluyt, now a middle-aged cleric, was deeply involved. "You must have great care not to offend the naturals," he warned the newly formed London Company, which also called in Harriot for consultation. Many of the organizers were again Middle Temple members, and the place they chose to settle was the one originally intended for the 1587 mission: Chesapeake Bay.

Ironically, instead of the Cittie of Raleigh, the name for the first permanent English settlement in the New World would be the City of James, named for the old knight's jailer. Odder still, it was a family friend of Raleigh's who found the first fresh evidence of the lost settlers since White noted the carving on the tree at Roanoke.

Tall and sickly, the twenty-seven-year-old George Percy had a long pale face on which he wore a short dark mustache. Percy's older brother, the Earl of Northumberland, shared the Tower with Raleigh for his suspected ties to Catholic terrorists. Known as the "wizard earl" for his interest in chemistry and math, Northumberland became his close friend and Harriot's new patron. The loyal scientist paid frequent visits to his jailed benefactors while living on Northumberland's grand estate on London's outskirts. A "blackamore" lived there with the earl for a time, before his incarceration; this may be a reference to a stay by Manteo during his second trip to England in 1586 and 1587.

If so, then George Percy might have met the Indian as a young child. He certainly knew all about the Roanoke voyages from Raleigh and his father, as well as from listening to his elders tell stories in Middle Temple Hall, when he too became a member of this inn of court. Like many younger sons with little hope for an inheritance, and perhaps fired by the talk of the New World that dominated his childhood, Percy joined an expedition bound for Virginia to seek his fortune.

In 1606, James granted the London Company the right to settle the area between the southern tip of the Outer Banks and present-day Long Island. Wary of irritating Spain, which still claimed most of North America, the king declined to support the venture, which was funded solely by private investors. But he did issue a charter granting territory that was not his to give. "They shall have all the lands, woods, soil, grounds, havens, ports, rivers, mines, minerals, marshes, water, fishing, commodities . . . whatsoever . . . and shall and may inhabit and remain there." As with Raleigh's charter, this blanket gift ensured conflict with the Algonquians they would encounter. The following April, three ships loaded with 143 men and boys anchored off a swampy peninsula upriver from Chesapeake Bay, one hundred miles northwest of Roanoke Island.

The territory controlled by a small tribe called the Paspahegh was part of a larger confederation that dominated much of the coastal plain of today's Virginia and led by the king the English called Powhatan. A week after landing along the Powhatan River, which the English renamed the James, the newcomers organized a party to explore upriver with the hope that the Pacific lay within easy reach. (Hakluyt was still beating that dead horse.)

As the expedition made its way inland, Percy spotted "a savage boy about the age of ten years, which had a head of hair of a perfect yellow and a reasonable white skin, which is a miracle amongst all savages." Many historians have long taken his sighting as confirmation that some of the Roanoke colonists migrated to the Chesapeake, spreading their genes in the process.

As with so many Lost Colony myths, this one came to be accepted through centuries of repetition. What was not understood until recently is that albinism is far more prevalent among Native Americans than other groups. Among today's Hopi in the Southwest of the United States, for example, the rate is one in two hundred compared with one in thirty-six thousand for European Americans. Yellow hair and white skin are the hallmarks of the genetic trait. Percy is much more likely to have seen an albino child than the progeny of Raleigh's settlers.

A more solid lead appeared a few months later, in December 1607. This time it was Percy's hated rival, Captain John Smith, who stumbled on exciting intelligence that pointed to surviving colonists.

Smith was Percy's age, but that is where the similarities ended. The stocky redhead with a full red beard was a hardy mercenary who'd left his family's small farm in eastern England to battle Ottomans in central Europe. He served as a cavalry captain and won a knighthood from the grateful Christian king of Transylvania. Later captured by Turkish soldiers and enslaved, he escaped and walked to Russia before returning to England. Bored with life in London, he joined the Jamestown expedition and became the practical and experienced leader the colony needed.

While mapping the area, Smith and two English companions, with their Indian guide, were attacked by an Indian hunting party. The others were killed in a brief but fierce fight, and Opechancanough, the brother of the confederation leader, Powhatan, captured Smith. Later described as "a man of large stature, noble presence, and extraordinary parts . . . perfectly skilled in the art of governing," the elderly warrior was impressed by Smith's courage. He not only spared the Englishman's life but told him of "certain men clothed at a place called Ocanahonan, clothed like me." By clothed, the Indian meant they wore European-style dress.

When Smith was brought to Powhatan's capital, ten miles north of Jamestown, the king confirmed his brother's report and added that they wore "short coats, and sleeves to the elbows, [and] passed that way in ships like ours." They lived "to the south part of the back sea," six days from Roanoke.

Powhatan also told Smith of an intriguing country to the south called Anone, "where they have abundance of brass, and houses walled as ours." Whether this referred to Lost Colonists or Spanish towns in South Carolina and Florida wasn't clear. But the news fired Smith's resolve to look for the vanished settlers.

After he was inducted as an honorary tribal leader—a scene that Smith later rewrote as an execution halted in a dramatic intercession by Powhatan's daughter Pocahontas—the captain returned to Jamestown the day after New Year's 1608. Nearly two out of three men were dead from sickness and starvation, and a fire soon broke out that damaged their dwindling supplies. Despite the dire situation, Smith pursued his Roanoke leads. This enthusiasm might have been more tactical than humanitarian; linking up with Raleigh's settlers might have strengthened the rapidly weakening position of the English.

What happened next depends on which John Smith you are reading. He wrote several versions of his time in Virginia, culminating in his 1624 tract with the Pocahontas scene that reads like a romance novel, in which Smith is the indomitable hero. His earlier accounts of Jamestown are terse but seem more reliable. "We had agreed with the king of Paspahegh to conduct two of our men to a place called Panawicke beyond Roonok," he wrote in a 1608 report, "where he reported many men to be apparelled"—dressed in the European style.

Panawicke was apparently a place southwest of Roanoke Island on the mainland, west of Croatoan Island, and more than a hundred miles due south of Jamestown. They barely made it across the James River. After crossing, their guide, "playing the villain, and deluding us for rewards," went off on his own. He returned three or four days later with no news. Taking strangers into the territory to the south, outside Powhatan's confederation, might have proved too dangerous.

A slightly later account by Smith mentions that "southward we went to some parts of Chawonock and the Mangoags to search for them left by Sir Walter Raleigh." The Chawonock, or Chowanoke, were the same tribe Lane encountered in 1585 along the Chowan River. The Mangoags, or Mangoaks, were Iroquoian speakers who lived to the west and went by the name Tuscarora ("Mangoak" was a Carolina Algonquian epithet meaning "rattlesnake"). Smith apparently didn't feel whatever information he gleaned was solid enough to warrant a further search. When he set off in June 1608 to explore the region, he headed north instead, up Chesapeake Bay, rather than south to Albemarle Sound and Roanoke Island, to locate the presumed Lost Colonists.

But before Smith left on this mapping expedition, he mailed a letter to England that included a large rough-drawn sketch of eastern Virginia and North Carolina. The original has long since vanished, but in a major intelligence coup Spain's ambassador in London, Don Pedro Zúñiga, copied the classified document and sent it to King Philip III. It includes the only known image of the triangular Jamestown fort.

The table-sized chart, rediscovered in a Spanish archive in 1890, offers a marriage of Smith's clues with his cartography. The Chesapeake Bay region of Virginia is drawn with surprising accuracy. On the south bank of the James River is the notation "Here Pasaphege and 2 of our own men landed to go to Pananiock." This is a reference to the expedition mentioned by Smith that stalled on the south shore of the James River. But the rivers and sounds in North Carolina are pictured with imprecision. A tiny circle off the coast marked as "Roonock" marks Roanoke Island. But the long stretch of the Outer Banks, including Hatteras and Croatoan, is entirely missing. The broad Albemarle Sound—more than ten miles in width—is drawn as narrow as the James River. No European who actually crossed this body of water could make that mistake. This is mapmaking by hearsay, based on secondhand Native American information rather than on-site exploration.

A river flowing into the Albemarle has the word "Ocanahonan" scribbled alongside it, the name mentioned by Powhatan and his brother as a place where men in European-style dress were said to be. To the south is another stream called the Morattic. This is no doubt the Moratuc River that Lane and his men explored in their search for copper and a path to the Pacific. Between these two rivers is another notation. "Here the King of Pasapahegh reported our men to be, and want to go." Finally, in an area on the mainland south of Roanoke, along a river called the Pakrahwick, is this last and strangely specific note: "Here remaineth four men clothed that came from Roonock to Ocanahonan."

By the fall of 1608, after he was elected colony president, Smith wrote to London that he was skeptical the Jamestown settlers would find "the south sea, a mine of gold, or any of them sent by Sir Walter Raleigh." Instead, he focused on securing food and building a fragile peace with Powhatan. He taught his men the Virginia Algonquian phrase for "I am very hungry. What shall I eat?" Injured the following year in a gunpowder explosion, Smith left Virginia in August 1609 and reluctantly turned over leadership to the incompetent Percy. The young gentleman ordered the Paspahegh queen killed and her children executed "by throwing them overboard and shooting out their brains in the water," he noted without regret. The settlers, meanwhile, descended into "the starving time" and "a world of miseries." Despite his personal ties to Raleigh and Harriot, there was no time for the new commander to continue the search for survivors. He and his men would be lucky enough to survive the winter.

Jamestown was poised to go the way of Roanoke, another expensive private venture that failed. Spain's military and intelligence leaders urged Philip III to strike while the settlement was weakened, but the cautious monarch bet that the latest English effort would collapse of its own accord, like its predecessor. He didn't want to risk war over this remote edge of empire. Instead, he sent a reconnaissance mission to gather intelligence on the English.

Shortly before Smith left Virginia, in July 1609, the Spanish ship encountered an English vessel guarding Chesapeake Bay and turned back to St. Augustine as a deadly hurricane moved up the coast. The same storm pummeled a fleet of large London Company ships on their way to reinforce Jamestown with new settlers and supplies. The three-hundred-ton flagship *Sea Venture* wrecked on Bermuda, seven hundred miles east of the Chesapeake.

The castaways included Sir Thomas Gates, the new acting governor for the colony, as well as Machumps, who was returning from England as a representative of his brother-in-law Powhatan. Smith later reported that while on Bermuda, Machumps murdered another Native American, a young favorite of the chief's, and "made a hole to bury him, because it was too short he cut off his legs and laid them by him." He had little good to say about this "villainous" youth, whom he must have known during his Jamestown days. Some scholars believe that Machumps is Shakespeare's model for the wild man of *The Tempest*, Caliban, enslaved by the magician Prospero.

The bard's inspiration for the story itself, which takes place on a distant island after a shipwreck, can be traced to a letter written by another castaway, William Strachey. A literary man down on his luck, the thirty-seven-year-old Londoner had matched wits with Jonson, poet John Donne, and possibly Shakespeare himself at the famed Mermaid Tavern. He surely knew the story of Roanoke and would have seen Jonson's play *Eastward Hoe*. But debts led him to board the ship to Virginia to start fresh; one can imagine Jonson and his friends teasing Strachey before his departure for chasing after golden chamber pots.

The stranded men built two boats on the Bermuda beach and limped into Jamestown in May 1610, horrified to find only sixty of the colony's three hundred inhabitants alive. An extended drought likely exacerbated the suffering, along with Percy's poor leadership. Gates ordered Jamestown immediately abandoned, as Lane had done on Roanoke in 1586. But while Lane missed the long-awaited supply vessel by days, Gates spotted an English fleet arriving in the Chesapeake just as he and his men were departing. With three hundred new colonists and plenty of provisions, he ordered his ship to return to Jamestown. Of such near hits and misses is history often made.

Gates's instructions from London contained startling news. The document provided detail on the whereabouts of the Lost Colonists and called for him to move Virginia's capital to their territory in the south. He was to engage Indian guides and travel south to "a town called Ohonahorn" or "Oconahoen," located upstream from the Albemarle Sound. This seems to be the same English settlement mentioned to Smith by Powhatan and his brother. One oddity is that the latitude mentioned is that of Croatoan Island and the western mainland rather than that of the Albemarle Sound. "You shall find a brave and fruitful seat every way inaccessible by a stronger enemy" and abundant in silk grass and other commodities, the company men wrote. "Here we suppose, if you make your principal and chief seat, you shall do most safely and richly."

A capital here had two advantages. First, it lay near "the rich copper mines of Ritanoc," and, second, it lay near "Peccareamicke, where you shall find four of the English alive, left by Sir Walter Raleigh who escaped the slaughter of Powhatan of Roanoke, upon the first arrival of our colony, and live under the protection of a werowance," or tribal leader. This chief, said to be an enemy of Powhatan's, would never give up his English captives. "If you find them not, yet search into the country," apparently meaning more to the south. Not only were some of White's settlers alive, the London document suggested, but Powhatan murdered many just before the English arrived in 1607. The instructions blithely move on to discuss the proper manner of manuring the settlers' fields.

A second and just as curious piece of intelligence emerged in England while the castaways were still on Bermuda. Worried about the negative publicity around Jamestown, the London Company drafted a "true and sincere declaration" including the dramatic news that "some of our nation planted by Sir Walter Raleigh, yet alive, within fifty miles of our [Jamestown] fort, who can open the womb and bowels of this country."

That would have placed the surviving Lost Colonists near the upper Chowan River in the vicinity of today's state line separating Virginia from North Carolina. The bombshell allegedly came from two Jamestown men sent to find the Roanoke settlers. Though "denied by the savages speech with them," the expedition found "crosses and letters the characters and assured testimonies of Christians newly cut into the barks of trees." This astonishing announcement, with its mention of carvings on trees like the ones White observed, implied that Raleigh's survivors could help the struggling Jamestown colony locate copper, iron, and silk grass that would prove profitable exports.

Despite these dramatic revelations, interest in searching for the Lost Colonists cooled after Smith left Virginia in the summer of 1609 and the dreadful starving time commenced. Captain Samuel Argall apparently led an expedition to the Chowan River the following year, but the outcome is unknown. Jamestown remained the capital, and the area to the south remained largely unexplored by the English. Despite rumors of their survival, the Roanoke colonists remained elusive.

By the time Strachey left Virginia in 1611, the search for the Raleigh settlers was effectively over. In 1612, Strachey wrote his *Historie of Travaile into Virginia Britannia* (dedicated to Percy's older brother, who was still incarcerated in the Tower with Raleigh), echoing the claims in Gates's instructions and the London Company declaration and including a few more choice details.

Strachey blames Powhatan's priests for persuading Powhatan to murder "men, women, and children of the first plantation at Roanoke." This was done, he adds, "without any offense" to Raleigh's settlers, who for "twenty and odd years had peaceably lived intermixed with those savages, and were out of his territory." (The secretary also takes John White to task for abandoning his search for "these unfortunate and betrayed people" in order to go pirating.) He reports that James I was apprised of the gruesome massacre. The king agreed to spare Powhatan but demanded the death of his priests who led him to "that bloody cruelty." Strachey goes on to say that four men, two boys, "and one young maid" escaped the Virginia Algonquian leader's wrath and lived under a chief's protection at Ritanoe—apparently the same as Ritanoc—where they "beat his copper."

London Company officials, however, refused to publish Strachey's account; the work did not go public for nearly two centuries. There is no evidence that his shocking charges led to any immediate reprisals against Powhatan's people. In fact, the leader's beloved daughter Pocahontas, kidnapped by the English in 1613, married Jamestown settler John Rolfe —an odd match if the father of the bride was suspected of having the blood of English innocents on his hands. She was treated with respect on her later visit to London, where she had a tearful reunion with Smith and died of a European sickness.

Smith, who knew Powhatan better than any European, never publicly accused the Native American leader of any such massacre, even after the leader's death in 1618. Nor did Smith give much credence to surviving Raleigh colonists.

Who, then, was the source of the intelligence? All signs point to Machumps as the one who fed both London Company officials and Strachey with the details of the massacre and the enslaved survivors. He was in London prior to the sailing of the *Sea Venture* on a diplomatic mission. Whether the intelligence is reliable, however, is another matter.

We know almost nothing of the young man, aside from his alleged role in murdering a compatriot. Smith clearly felt that Machumps was, at best, a person with his own hidden agenda. The language barrier might have led to misunderstandings. This ambitious member of the royal family might also have been playing a strategic game to knock Powhatan off his throne and benefit from English support. Encouraging the English to shift south would take the pressure off the confederation that was struggling to cope with the unpredictable invaders. Likely less monster than Machiavelli, Machumps remained close to the English even after his return from England—and, tellingly, kept his distance from Powhatan.

In the four years following Powhatan's death, the English population surged from a few hundred to nearly fifteen hundred people. With tobacco as a kind of "vegetable gold" driving an economic boom, commerce with Native Americans grew less important than clearing forest and appropriating Indian fields. Virginia Algonquians were increasingly unwelcome strangers in their own land, debilitated by Old World disease while drawn to the exotic material goods, including alcohol, offered by the Europeans in exchange for pelts and much-needed corn. As late as 1621, a directive from London warned the settlers to cease their dependence on the locals, a dependence that made the English vulnerable. The next year, Opechancanough—the same man who first captured Smith—executed a bold and carefully coordinated attack on the English settlements up and down the James River. Nearly one in four of the settlers died. The massacre ended all English pretensions to living peacefully with the indigenous people.

Meanwhile, an Anglican cleric named Samuel Purchas took up Hakluyt's colonization cause when the latter died, but he ignored his predecessor's admonition that the settlers should "have great care not to offend the naturals." In a popular 1625 book, he blamed the Indians for "devilish treachery" in decimating not one but three colonies— the fifteen men left by Grenville, the Lost Colony, and the nearly vanquished later Virginia settlers. All this spilled blood proved, wrote Purchas, "this our earth is truly English, and therefore this land is justly yours O English." These massacres, in other words, justified English extermination of the Indians. Purchas asserted, "Powhatan confessed to Cap. Smith, that he had been at their [the Raleigh colonists'] slaughter, and had divers utensils of theirs to show," referring to the barrel of a musket, a bronze mortar, and a piece of iron said to belong to them.

Yet Smith himself remained silent. Never a man to resist embellishing a dramatic tale, his 1624 book on Virginia included the fanciful story of Pocahontas saving his life when he was still a young man. When he does mention the Lost Colonists, it is only a passing reference to his effort to secure a guide to take one of his men "to search of the lost company of Sir Walter Raleigh, and silk grass." The soldier returned from the Chowan region with "little hope and less certainty of them who were left by Sir Walter Raleigh . . . [T]he river was not great, and the people but few, the country mostly overgrown with pines." European sickness and strife among tribes had decimated the bustling and populous towns described by Lane. Smith also notes a trip south made by three Jamestown colonists who questioned a tribe of Iroquoian speakers. "But nothing could they learn save that they were all dead."

While Smith seems sincere in his conclusion that the Jamestown settlers found no hard evidence of Roanoke survivors, rumors of a bloody massacre masterminded by Powhatan persisted. Not for the last time, the desire to solve the mystery of the Lost Colony masked other, darker motives.

Raleigh died six months after Powhatan. James let him out of the Tower for a second trip to Venezuela on a last-ditch attempt to find El Dorado. Instead, the still-impetuous knight tangled with the Spanish and his son died in battle. Once again he passed by the Outer Banks on his return to England but made no recorded landfall. Once he was in London, James ordered him beheaded. Standing on the scaffold on a chilly late October morning, he called himself "a man full of all vanity, and having lived a sinful life, in all sinful callings, having been a soldier, a captain, a sea captain, and a courtier." Few at the time would have disagreed. One of his myriad enemies at court damned him as "the greatest Lucifer that have lived in our age," a man who would "lose a friend to coin a jest." But Raleigh and the steadfast Harriot remained close until the very end; the scientist appears to have written out the notes for his first patron's final speech.

The bachelor scientist tried to keep a low profile, no easy task in a world where one's fate was inextricably linked with that of one's sponsor. "Our situation is such that I still may not philosophize freely; we are still stuck in the mud," Harriot explained to Kepler while Smith was exploring Chesapeake Bay. "I was never ambitious for preferments," he wrote during a brief stint in jail while himself under suspicion for treason. "But contented with a private life for the love of learning that I might study freely."

What finally rooted England to North America was neither the Pacific passage that so obsessed Hakluyt nor the gold sought so maniacally by Raleigh. It was the common New World herb Harriot helped publicize, praising it because it "preserves the body." One of his contemporaries called it "the sovereign remedy to all diseases" but also "the ruin and overthrow of body and soul." It proved Harriot's triumph and his undoing. An inveterate smoker, he found a small ulcer on his lip that morphed into a painful tumor. The red hair of his youth long gone, the sixty-one-year-old died in 1621, the first recorded victim of tobacco-related cancer. He passed away in the London house of one of his colleagues from the Lane expedition that so shaped his life. The man who unwittingly brought so much death to the people he studied eventually succumbed to the New World plant that his victims had taught him to use.

By then, the Puritans had celebrated their first Thanksgiving in Plymouth, five hundred miles northeast of Jamestown. Three decades later, there were more than fifty thousand northern Europeans settled up and down the North American coast, with English in Virginia and Massachusetts and Dutch, Swedes, and Germans scattered in between. Enslaved Africans trickled in; there were three hundred in Virginia. Meanwhile, the Native American population in the region plummeted dramatically amid disease and societal disruption, though exact numbers are hard to ascertain.

Geography colluded with the final passing of the Roanoke generation to consign the fate of the vanished settlers to oblivion—at least among Europeans. Sailors steered clear of the treacherous shoals of the Outer Banks, considered the most dangerous waters south of Nova Scotia. Several of the inlets that provided access between inland waters and the ocean began to close up; in any case, the marshy interior offered few deepwater ports along long stretches of fertile land. Virginia settlers and their tobacco culture spread north up the lung-shaped Chesapeake in the first half of the seventeenth century rather than into the boggy lands and shallow sounds to the south.

It was Native Americans rather than Europeans who kept alive the memory of the first English settlement. When a beaver trader arrived on the island in 1653, the "emperor of Roanoke" showed him "the ruins of Sir Walter Raleigh's fort." Shortly after, the leader sent his son to Virginia for an English education, and his people retreated south and west to the more inaccessible mainland. Roanoke Island became a backwater of cattle ranchers and fishermen for the next two centuries.

Not until an English explorer named John Lawson traveled through the area in 1701 is there another reference to the Lost Colonists. He reported on members of an Indian tribe called the Hatteras who lived on the Outer Banks. "These tell us, that several of their ancestors were white people, and could talk in a book, as we do; the truth of which is confirmed by gray eyes being found frequently amongst these Indians, and no others."

He relates "a pleasant story that passes for an uncontested truth amongst the inhabitants of this place." A ghost ship under sail often appeared off their shore "which they call Sir Walter Raleigh's ship." Lawson speculated that the Roanoke settlement "miscarried for want of timely supplies from England" and "we may reasonably suppose that the English were forced to cohabit with them, for relief and conversation." Roanoke's first supernatural spirits date from this distant time.

A deadly epidemic had swept the Native American communities in eastern North Carolina in 1695, and alcohol took a terrible toll on the dwindling community. "The smallpox and rum have made such a destruction amongst them that . . . there is not the sixth savage living within two hundred miles," Lawson reported. "These poor creatures have so many enemies to destroy them, that it's a wonder one of them is left alive near us." White settlers from Virginia and colonists from Switzerland moved into the region to snap up available land. War followed, ending with Indians forced to leave the region or confine themselves to reservations.

As Europeans crept west and the American colonies broke with what was now Britain, the new nation eagerly heralded its founders but left its early colonial past in the shadows. Typical is William Robertson's 1796 *History of America*. He passes quickly over the Roanoke venture, briskly noting they "perished miserably by famine, or by the unrelenting cruelty of those barbarians by whom they were surrounded," and concludes that "there was not a single Englishman settled there at the demise of Queen Elizabeth in 1603." As late as 1830,

John Howard Hinton repeats this conclusion almost verbatim in *The History and Topography of the United States*, noting that because "no trace was ever found of this unfortunate colony, there is every reason to apprehend that the whole must have miserably perished." Raleigh's failed effort was a fiasco best forgotten, rather than a mystery to be solved. Roanoke was relegated to a historical footnote.

That changed dramatically in 1834, when a young Harvard-trained historian named George Bancroft published his magisterial work *A History of the United States*. It is difficult to overstate his impact on the way that we see Raleigh's colony today. A New Englander steeped in German Romanticism, Bancroft was the first person to study American history in a comprehensive way. As a young man traveling in Europe, he met thinkers like Goethe, Hegel, and von Humboldt, absorbing new ideas about progress and the evolution of societies.

Bancroft was the first writer to dwell at length on the early settlement attempts on the North American east coast. They contained "the germ of our institutions," he writes in his preface. "The maturity of the nation is but a continuation of its youth," he adds. From this novel perspective, the gestation of the country was just as important as its revolutionary coming of age. And Roanoke was the germinating seed.

He studied Hakluyt's documents and rewrote the Roanoke story as a compelling gothic drama, led by a splendid Tudor knight and betrayed by a greedy Portuguese pilot and cruel Indians. In this influential telling, "disasters thickened" and "a tribe of savages displayed implacable jealousy." After the armada's defeat, the honorable Raleigh desperately tries but fails in his repeated efforts to resupply and rescue the brave settlers.

Unlike those before him, Bancroft cast a lurid glamour over the venture's finale. The colonists, as they "awaited death in the land of their adoption," might have "become amalgamated with the sons of the forest" or encountered some other unknown fate. "The further history of this neglected plantation is involved in gloomy uncertainty," he writes in a style worthy of Edgar Allan Poe, who was just starting his literary career. There simply were not enough facts to come to a definitive conclusion. Speculation was inevitable and, indeed, enticing. "Imagination received no help in its attempts to trace the fate of the colony of Roanoke."

Bancroft was a friend of the son and nephew of the Brothers Grimm, who were then collecting Teutonic folktales with their disturbing themes of lost and hungry children in dark woods. Germans in this era drew on a mythical past to define their emerging identity. By reframing the Roanoke story as one of mystery and allure—a lost white child in a wilderness of dark savages—Bancroft did the same for the United States by turning an obscure failure into the start of the American experiment as well as our original national folktale.

He made what appears to be the earliest recorded reference to Virginia Dare since John White's brief mention. She was, Bancroft writes, "the first offspring of English parents on the soil of the United States." This was a brand-new way of seeing the governor's baby granddaughter, as a symbol of the fledgling country destined to grow up to conquer a continent. Roanoke was, in essence, the nation's humble Bethlehem, and Virginia Dare was its infant savior destined for sacrifice.

Bancroft's radical new assessment of the forgotten colony quickly captured the attention of both scholars and the public. The country was hungry for an origin story more enchanting than the spoiled fops of Jamestown or the straitlaced Puritans of Plymouth, neither of which measured up to a romantic legend like England's king Arthur and France's military hero Roland, leaders felled by overwhelming odds but whose sacrifice helped forge a common identity. Roanoke, with its knights and villains and its brave but outnumbered few facing an alien culture, provided all the elements for a national myth.

Shortly after Bancroft's work was published, the *Raleigh Register* bemoaned the fact that Roanoke Island's contemporary inhabitants were ignorant of the fact that this was "that paradise of the new world, in which Providence has decreed the nativity of a great and mighty people." A few months later, just before the Battle of the Alamo, the president of the American Historical Society gave a talk at the U.S. Capitol in Washington echoing Bancroft's reassessment of Roanoke.

"The fate of this last colony was never ascertained," said Lewis Cass, referring to John White's settlement. "It disappeared, but why, or how, was unknown then, and is unknown yet." Such questions, he noted, lend "to the narratives of these early efforts that romantic interest, which is equally delightful to youth and age."

For the remainder of the nineteenth century, imagination indeed dominated the strange tale of the lost settlers. The Roanoke story spawned a whole genre of dark romances about a blond-haired Virginia Dare, a beautiful huntress roving the Carolina woods while fending off Indian suitors and evil shamans. Bancroft resurrected interest in Raleigh's venture that spawned the very term "Lost Colony." But it wasn't until the end of the century that this mythic kindling reignited the search for the vanished settlers.

There is no approaching the mystery of Roanoke without passing the Cerberus of David Beers Quinn. By all accounts a compact and polite man with a quick Irish temper, this historian from the University of Liverpool did more than any person since Hakluyt to collect every shred of documentary evidence he could find relating to the Raleigh voyages to the coast of North Carolina. An Irishman teaching in a working-class English city in the aftermath of World War II, Quinn was an outsider in the clubby world of British historians at a time when American colonial history was, at best, a peripheral topic. "He was not interested in scholarly esteem, or in being one of the boys," one of his many protégés told me.

For six decades, with his wife, Alison, who won awards for her proficiency in the art of indexing, Quinn systematically scoured European archives. He recovered the long-lost stories of sailors deposed by Havana inquisitors and obscure English contracts that shed light on the voyages' financing and organization. He tracked wills and letters providing insights into overlooked figures like Fernandes and assiduously cataloged thousands of details, from the number of cannon on the *Tiger* to North Carolina stone sources.

"I have thought of myself very much as a historical work horse," he once said, "clearing the way through documentary tangles for others to follow." In so doing, Quinn transformed Raleigh's venture into a credible research topic, though academics remained leery of what is still seen by many as a cheesy romantic legend. "He was the first scholar to put Roanoke on the map," said NYU's Kupperman. Quinn sailed the sounds and tramped through the sands of the Outer Banks to get a feel for what the settlers encountered, carrying a suitcase of Virginia Gentleman bourbon to ensure a warm welcome at remote Coast Guard stations.

In several thick volumes nearly biblical in their authority, Quinn wrote concise explanations to guide those who came after through the thicket of primary accounts, letters, and reports, often written years after the event, that can be hard to decipher. What for an Elizabethan was a creek, for example, we would call a harbor. Even something as straightforward as a list of passengers on a Virginia-bound ship proves to be deceiving; some said to be in the New World never went, while others not on the list might have been there. "The attempts to knit together the scraps of hard information, vague tales, and carefully judged speculation has not been an easy task," he once acknowledged.

No history, least of all one that touches on Roanoke, comes fully formed. He learned that he could "restrict himself to what is exactly, or more or less exactly, known" or "let his fancy ride free from the documents and fill the gaps with whatever theories may cross his mind in order to make a good story." Instead, he chose a sensible middle ground—"to stick as closely to the documents as they will permit, but to point out carefully their limitations, ambiguities, and omissions, and then attempt, cautiously, to fill them."

Yet even Quinn could not resist the temptation to solve the mystery of the colonists' disappearance. In 1984, on the four hundredth anniversary of the voyage by Amadas and Barlowe, he made headlines by announcing that he had clarified the fate of White's settlers "with reasonable certainty" based on "what now appears to be a measure of solid history."

He began by dismissing White's insistence that the settlers were at Croatoan as "clouded by sentiment," given that the island was "unsuitable for an agricultural colony." He asserted that "the main body of the colonists had indeed joined the Chesapeake Indians as early as 1587." These were the people Harriot met during his sojourn on the southern edge of Chesapeake Bay in the winter of 1585 and 1586. The historian insisted "with some confidence" that the Cittie of Raleigh was built not on Roanoke Island but near the site of today's port city of Norfolk just south of the great bay.

Quinn envisioned the settlers using their small pinnace to haul building materials scavenged from Roanoke to the new site, where they built a proper English village protected by a palisade, complete with "enclosures for breeding rabbits." White's settlers, he seemed to suggest, succeeded in their utopian vision until disaster struck when the Jamestown settlers appeared at the mouth of the Chesapeake in the spring of 1607. The arrival of a second batch of English prompted Powhatan to destroy the little settlement before their fellow countrymen could join forces with them. It was a dramatic end to a stubborn band of valiant Englishmen.

This pronouncement was the academic equivalent of tablets from Mount Sinai. But the more I examined Quinn's reasoning, the more I realized that he had failed to point out the "limitations, ambiguities, and omissions" of his sources.

The historian relied heavily on the words of Strachey, a man who spent barely a year in Virginia, and Purchas, a vitriolic Indian hater who by his own account never traveled more than two hundred miles from his village in Essex. They, in turn, got their information from Machumps, a man with a motive to misinform the English in order to accrue power. The London Company also had reason to insist the colonists were still alive, to reassure nervous investors and prevent financial collapse. Quinn ignored Smith's accounts and rejected White's conclusion that the settlers moved to Croatoan or, possibly, fifty miles inland. Nor was there archaeological evidence to back up his notion of a Cittie of Raleigh near Norfolk (full disclosure: my childhood hometown).

Even Quinn's closest acolytes, I learned, were skeptical of his conclusion, which failed to win wide acceptance among other scholars. "I don't find much evidence for that theory," said historian James Horn, president of the Jamestown Rediscovery Foundation. Of course, Quinn was modest—and savvy—enough to know that his word on the Roanoke voyages was not likely to be final. "The story of the colonies is a continuing process of discovery and interpretation, to which an end is not in sight," Quinn wrote before his death in 2002 at age ninety-two. He predicted, however, that the new insights would have to come not from rummaging through archives, which he had picked over so thoroughly, but from digging in the ground.

Since definitive evidence still eluded the historians, I set out for eastern North Carolina, where archaeologists claimed to have new and compelling clues to the settlers' fate.

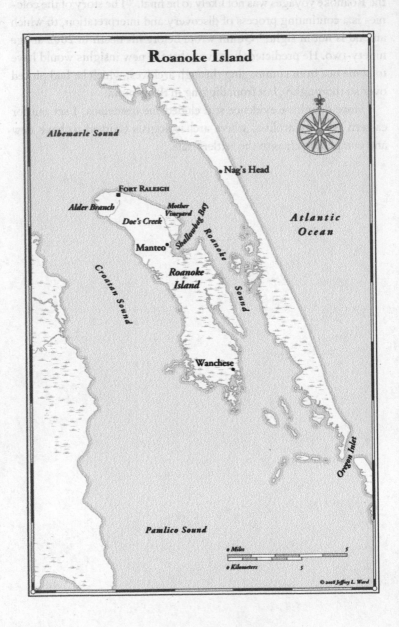

Roanoke Island

Albemarle Sound

Nag's Head

FORT RALEIGH
Alder Branch   *Mother Vineyard*
          Doe's Creek
                              Shallowbag Bay

Manteo

          Roanoke Island

Croatan Sound   *Roanoke Sound*

Atlantic Ocean

Wanchese

Oregon Inlet

Pamlico Sound

Miles   5
Kilometers   5

© 2008 Jeffrey L. Ward

CHAPTER SIX

Child of Science and Slow Time

If you look at the maps long enough, Roanoke Island can begin to take on the shape of a question mark, as if geography set the stage for a riddle. At the south end of the island is the fishing village of Wanchese, a cluster of piers, warehouses, and mobile homes with easy access to the Pamlico Sound. People have lived and fished here for at least two thousand years. Midway is the arc of Shallowbag Bay that faces east, bordered by the neat grid of the Dare County seat of Manteo, with its Uppowoc Avenue and Sir Walter Raleigh Street lined with tourist shops. Adjacent is a state park with mock-ups of a Carolina Algonquian village and Tudor settlement dominated by the masts of the *Elizabeth II*, a reproduction of one of the sixteenth-century ships that carried the 1585 settlers to Roanoke. At the northern tip of the island, where it begins to bend to the west, sits Fort Raleigh National Historic Site.

One spring morning, I pulled out of the parking lot of the faux half-timbered Elizabethan Inn and followed the two-lane highway running north out of Manteo to the park's entrance road that snakes through the shadows of dark green longleaf pines, ending in a parking lot butting up against Albemarle Sound.

There is not much to see. If you didn't know better, you might swear this was America's most boring national park, or at least the one that requires the most imagination. Unlike every other unit in the

National Park Service, this one has no old home or venerated battle-field, no breathtaking vista or famous fossils, no unique ecosystem or dramatic volcano. There isn't even a vending machine in the visitor center. The star attraction is a small grassy mound shaped like an irregular star that takes up no more area than the footprint of a modest suburban home. It was built in 1950 to re-create what was thought to be the 1585 fort built by Ralph Lane, but what's underneath may not even be Elizabethan. On Roanoke Island, where the Lost Colony mystery began, excavators haven't found enough artifacts in a century of digging to pack the trunk of a compact car, even using extra bubble wrap. The big question here is not where the settlers went but where they started.

"It's frustrating," said Eric Deetz, an archaeologist at the University of North Carolina at Chapel Hill who has worked on Roanoke on and off for years. We stood amid blooming dogwoods in an open meadow next to the mound. "For every artifact on Roanoke, you find ten thousand at Jamestown. We have so little, and the historical texts are so ambiguous. Where were a hundred people living?" Even an English colony in Maine, established at the same time as Jamestown but which lasted barely one winter, produced more than two hundred pieces of plate armor as well as thousands of other objects.

Deetz worked with a team that recently uncovered a couple of pottery fragments from an apothecary jar at Fort Raleigh. It made news all over the country, and one London newspaper spun the minor find as a major discovery. "Did Disease Drive Off Colonists on Roanoke Island?" blared the large-type headline. "Medicine jar pottery may provide clues to fate of lost 16th century settlers." That was nonsense, but the breathless coverage hints at the hysteria that even the slightest find can unleash.

No one knows exactly where, but Lane and his men landed on Roanoke in the summer of 1585 and set to work building a proper English town and a modest wooden stronghold. This was no temporary camp. "As soon as they had disembarked, they began to make brick and tiles for a fort and houses," according to a deposition by an Irish soldier who later defected to the Spanish. There was a warehouse to store food and trade goods, as well as an armory to secure weapons.

Soldiers lived in barracks, and a jail and gallows loomed over the town center. Senior officers lived in thatched houses outside the compound.

The colonists also brought tons of equipment to plant and harvest crops and mine for ore, including shovels, spades, sledgehammers, wheelbarrows, and iron hoops for barrels. Each male settler was expected to carry along two sets of light armor, along with a musket, sword, belt, bandolier, and sixty pounds of lead shot, and that doesn't include what was in the armory. There were primitive guns called arquebuses, pistols, and small cannon to protect the fortified area. The colonists packed most of their goods in chests with padlocks and hinges; even books from this era often had copper fittings apt to survive for centuries even in damp soil.

And then there was garbage. Elizabethans produced a small fraction of the 4.3 pounds thrown away each day by the average American, but Lane's men would have gone through twenty bushels of oysters in a single dinner and discarded the thick shells, which decay slowly. White's settlers would have eaten no less. At least two thousand meals were prepared here, leaving tons of oyster, scallop, and clam remains along with deer, bird, turtle, and fish bones. Plates cracked and bottles broke. Cooking pots toppled over and smashed on the ground. This stuff, much of it impervious to water or insects and of little interest to human scavengers, piled up somewhere.

Even if Native Americans thoroughly scavenged the site for metal and glass, at least the garbage pits would remain. Deetz, an affable man with a wide face and thick hair, grew up the son of a colonial archaeologist in Plymouth, Massachusetts. He trained early in the art of reading dead people's rubbish, a key skill in the discipline. "I would hunt around old bottle dumps as a teenager," he recalled. Most of his finds were mid-twentieth-century mayonnaise jars. "But here," he asked, looking at the ground around his muddy boots as if he had lost his car keys, "where did they put the trash?"

White made the first archaeological finds on Roanoke in 1590 when he recorded the presence of lead ingots, cannon, and looted trunks. No known sixteenth-century map marks the exact settlement site, and there are no known drawings of the town. All we can say for sure is that it was on the north end of the island, possibly near Granganimeo's village, where Amadas and Barlowe were fed their sumptuous meal in 1584. But no one knows where the Algonquian settlement was either.

More than a century later, when Lawson passed through the area, he noted "some old English coins which have been lately found; and a brass gun, a powder horn, and one small quarterdeck gun made of iron staves." Long after the colonists' departure, their stuff was still strewn around and had apparently held little interest to Native Americans.

Lawson also refers to the ruins of a fort, apparently the same one shown to the beaver trader half a century earlier. The historic site was already a tourist attraction when President James Monroe visited on the morning of April 7, 1819, while inspecting coastal defenses and ports. According to the *Edenton Gazette*, he and his staff went ashore "to view the remains of the fort, the traces of which are distinctly visible, which is said to have been erected by the first colony of Sir Walter Raleigh."

An 1850s visitor, reflecting the new romantic notions about the vanished colony, noted that the remains of the settlement "are but scanty; and therefore the remains of the fort, glass globes containing quicksilver, and hermetically sealed and other relics occasionally discovered there, give rise to a thousand conjectures destined never to be solved."

On the eve of the Civil War, Edward Bruce, a writer for *Harper's New Monthly Magazine*, arrived by steamer and made his way through "dense copses of live-oak" and past the occasional homestead to the site to sketch what remained. All he could make out was a shallow trench about forty yards square, "in many places scarcely perceptible," with the outline of a small bastion. "A fragment or two of stone or brick may be discovered in the grass, and then all is told of the existing relics of the city of Raleigh."

In 1862, the Union army scored its first major victory against the Confederacy when ten thousand men invaded Roanoke Island, which stood between the ocean and the rebel interior. The sleepy home of ranchers and fishermen quickly turned into a busy community housing thousands of Northern troops and enslaved African Americans fleeing mainland plantations. A soldier named Charles F. Johnson drew an image of "Earth-work Built by Sir Walter Raleigh's Colony on Roanoke Island," though it is hard to make out its form in his drawing. He acknowledged that "anyone who was not shown the place would probably pass over it a hundred times without discovering anything so unusual as to warrant the thought of a fortification." After all, Johnson added, "this has been here some hundreds of years, and in that time the elements have reduced it." A Northern newspaper described the remains of a star-shaped moat "well worthy of the visit of the antiquarian."

Such visits, however, proved destructive. Another soldier stationed on Roanoke published an article mentioning that treasure hunters had dug holes around the fort's ruins, "but with little success, a vial of quicksilver being the only relic said to have been found." (He also made the prescient observation that "this article was doubtless to be used in discovering deposits of the precious metals by the old adventurers," later confirmed by archaeologists.)

The island again slipped into obscurity after the war. Then, exactly three centuries after the Lost Colonists arrived, a vacationing thirty-eight-year-old writer from Philadelphia stepped out of a boat and began to explore. His arrival launched the first scientific effort to find physical remains of the vanished settlers and resolve a mystery that increasingly fired the public's imagination.

Reporters remember Talcott Williams as the first dean of Columbia University's journalism school. Art historians recall him as one of the naked bathers in Thomas Eakins's famous 1885 painting *The Swimming Hole*. Largely forgotten is his pioneering work on Roanoke, which launched the archaeological search for the Lost Colony.

Williams grew up in the midst of the world's first major excavations. Son of New England missionary parents, he spent his childhood in Mosul. The walled city in northern Iraq, then part of the Ottoman Empire, lay across the Tigris River from the great Assyrian capital of Nineveh, where British excavators were hauling massive stone statues of forgotten kings and mythical beasts out of the ground. "My early memories are of the trenches in Nineveh," he recalled, "and its monuments fill my earliest vision."

An iconoclast who befriended Walt Whitman and supported the largely unpopular cause of Negro rights, Williams visited the island in 1887. Whitman's brother had been stationed there in the Civil War, and the poet might have suggested the trip. Williams was interested not just in the English colony but in the Native Americans who lived on the island before, during, and after them. He discovered, on that first visit to Roanoke, an Indian burial thick with skeletons and first noted with alarm the erosion eating away at the island's north and east shores. He returned half a dozen years later with permission to excavate the fort, which had recently been put under the protection of a memorial association that he helped inspire.

"By little short of a miracle of accident," wrote the delighted researcher, "this crumbling mound, 'child of science and slow time,' has escaped destruction." Unlike the Plymouth and Virginia settlements, where later development obscured the colonial past, rural Roanoke seemed the perfect time capsule. His optimism proved short-lived.

Fully expecting to find loads of artifacts, he proceeded to dig thirteen long and deep trenches, moving tons of dirt and sand with the help of a team of local workers. Like so much else connected with the Roanoke voyages, Williams's notes and excavation report are missing. But in a brief paper to the American Historical Association, he described the site as "singularly barren." Other than a single nail, some bits of iron, and a few sherds of Indian pottery, he found nothing. He left the island, baffled by his failure.

The child of science and slow time suffered badly in the years that followed. In the early 1920s, a crew filming a silent movie about the Roanoke voyages constructed a temporary log fort atop the fragile remains of the original. Soon after, a state highway crew used bulldozers for a road intended to give visitors easy access but which further damaged the site. "Today half of the old entrenchment is gone," mourned Raleigh's *News and Observer*. As autumn rains fell on the unprotected soil, "the joy-riding public is cutting deep furrows in a spot that should be hallowed by a nation." The outcry prompted the state to move the road, and it used dynamite to do so.

In the following decade, the State of North Carolina built charming if fanciful juniper-log houses chinked with Spanish moss to resemble the colonists' homes around what remained of the fort and added a chapel thatched with native reeds that became a "matrimonial Mecca." Inside the earthwork's much-abused foundation, Civilian Conservation Corps workers constructed a tall wooden blockhouse. A log palisade enclosed the entire area, which was graded and crisscrossed with trenches for underground power, water, and sewer lines. A paved road was created to carry President Franklin Roosevelt to the site for celebration of Virginia Dare's 350th birthday in 1937 and to see a performance of *The Lost Colony,* the new outdoor drama held in the adjacent amphitheater, carved from the wooded dune sloping to the Albemarle. The result was more a set for a Western B movie than an authentic Elizabethan village.

Tourists and locals loved it. Archaeologists, none of whom were present during all the major construction to see what might have been disturbed or destroyed, were appalled. "By the time this 'restoration' was completed," one later commented, "all visible traces of the ditched fort seen by President Monroe and by other nineteenth-century visitors had been obscured."

Not until after World War II did Jean Harrington, known as Pinky for his red hair and pale skin, begin modern archaeological work on the site. Harrington was hired at Jamestown in the 1930s to prevent the occasional brawls between excavators eager to dig and architects tasked with restoring historic sites for tourists to enjoy. There he met his wife, Virginia Sutton, the first female historian park ranger, and the two pioneered a new field called historical archaeology, which combined knowledge of history and architecture with the latest methods in excavation.

By then, the log cabins had been dismantled, to the outrage of locals who argued that tourists needed *something* to draw them to this out-of-the-way forest. Harrington assured them he intended to pinpoint the Lane and White settlements and reconstruct the structures where they once stood. He assumed that the settlement was adjacent to the fort and so focused on that area. As Williams had before, Harrington began work confident of success.

The team shoveled more than half a mile of trenches yet recovered only an iron bar, a bronze weight, a scattering of lead musket balls, an auger, some nails, and an iron sickle. Along with two dozen pieces of Spanish and northern European pottery, he found a bit of brick and roofing tile and a small lump of worked copper. It was a shockingly small haul for such a major excavation.

His prize discovery was three small copper disks made in Nuremberg. "These little objects have a unique historical significance, for they are among the very few objects from the site of Fort Raleigh that unquestionably go back to the period of its founding and brief existence," Harrington wrote, with what seemed relief. The little round artifacts showed, "beyond reasonable doubt, that the site is that of the Raleigh settlements on Roanoke Island."

He was referring to what are called casting counters. These look like coins but were used, abacus-like, to do math using Roman numerals. In this era, most people in England had yet to learn the newfangled Arabic numerals (they actually originated in India) already favored by other Europeans. Because each manufacturer used unique mottoes, names, and symbols, they are valuable dating tools for archaeologists. "True good fortune comes from God," reads the German motto on one. Harrington dated the counters to a decade before the first Roanoke reconnaissance trip, so, he concluded, Raleigh's settlers must have brought them.

Even these proved illusory. Later archaeologists and art historians pegged the counters' minting to 1586 or later, and therefore unlikely to have made it into the pockets of White's colonists early the following year when they departed England. Their origin now seems much more likely to be from later traders, those based in Jamestown.

Harrington never doubted the little mound was a remnant of an Elizabethan fort. But where was the town? He could not pinpoint its location, much less what it looked like. "No physical remains of the settlers' homes were found, nor was there encountered sufficient building or household refuse to indicate the proximity of a habitation area," he wrote. Using White's drawings of Lane's 1585 Caribbean fortification as well as the results of his own dig, Harrington rebuilt the fort in a best-guess effort. A park service sign confidently proclaimed it the work of Ralph Lane. Visitors finally had something to see.

In the 1960s, Harrington returned to investigate a spot where workers, installing a new water pipe a few yards west of the fort, found brick fragments. His team quickly uncovered a nine-foot-square structure once supported by hefty log posts at each corner. Circular

Using the latest Italian Renaissance style, Ralph Lane designed this temporary Caribbean fort, which was built by the 1585 voyagers as protection as they collected salt. *British Museum*

fire pits were buried inside, with locally made bricks mixed up with broken European and Native American pots and roofing tiles. The archaeologist was perplexed: Was it an Indian sweat lodge? A small defensive structure? He concluded the building was part of an extension to the fort, perhaps part of the palisade that White noticed the colonists built when he returned to the abandoned settlement in 1590.

By the following decade, a new generation of excavators developed a radically new approach to detect the early European presence in the region. One of the field's rising stars was Ivor Noël Hume, known by his last two names. A self-taught British archaeologist, he began his career as a teenager sifting through the bombed-out landscape of World War II London. Immigrating to the United States, he eventually led and strengthened Colonial Williamsburg's archaeology program in Virginia. Noël Hume demanded that every shovelful of dirt pass through mesh to capture the tiniest glass bead or sliver of metal. Seeds and animal bones, long ignored as so much trash, could reveal secrets of diet, ethnicity, and climate, while pottery could pinpoint a specific date. Each artifact required careful cataloging and analysis.

He taught how to read the subtle changes in soil to spot building remnants. Foundation posts stuck deep into the earth attract tree roots eager to suck up the organic matter in the sandy soil. A root might be a ghostly remnant of a colonial structure, or it could be just a root. Telling them apart required patience and skill. Gone were the massive trenches and unskilled workers of the days of Williams. Digging was now only the start of archaeology; it was careful analysis of the finds that mattered, and Noël Hume's definitive volumes on colonial artifacts are still the most dog-eared books on every colonial archaeologist's shelf.

In 1982, Noël Hume joined Harrington and Quinn at Fort Raleigh to hear a presentation by a young historian and park ranger named Phillip Evans. Before his distinguished elders, Evans postulated that Harrington's pit found in the 1960s was almost certainly a watchtower on the palisaded edge of the Cittie of Raleigh. He cited a remarkably similar shape found by Noël Hume at a 1622 settlement on the James River.

Excited, the historian and the archaeologists urged an intensive investigation. Using state-of-the-art metal detectors and magnetometers that detect the magnetic properties of underground material, park service researchers spotted a wealth of exciting outlines—even what looked like a large triangular fort—that promised to reveal the missing settlement at long last. As so many had before, the excavators began their digs optimistic that at last they had found the town. They were quickly humbled. One of the most promising features they observed yielded only a 1969 Pepsi bottle.

Archaeologists subsequently kept their distance from what seemed to be America's colonial sand trap. But Noël Hume's wife, Audrey, an accomplished archaeologist in her own right, remained intrigued by the challenge. She shared a birthday with Virginia Dare, which spawned her lifelong fascination with the Lost Colony story. As a child, she even begged her parents to change her name to Virginia. At her urging, the couple paid a visit to Fort Raleigh in 1990, precisely four centuries after White recorded the first Roanoke artifacts.

"Every archaeologist dreams just once in his life he'll find treasure," Noël Hume wrote years after his work was done. "Mine substituted copper for gold and antimony for silver, and it came not from a sunken galleon or an Egyptian tomb but from Roanoke Island." What he ultimately found proved to be "the most exciting in a lifetime of discoveries."

Excavating a space no bigger than a beach towel near Harrington's pit during a cold and stormy January, Noël Hume's team uncovered more than one hundred artifacts, an unprecedented bonanza for the archaeological void that was Roanoke Island. For the first time in more than four hundred years, an intimate glimpse of life in Raleigh's colony emerged. A spilled drop of copper still clung to the side of a broken crucible, a vessel designed to withstand heat from molten metal. Later analysis revealed traces of zinc, copper, and silver in the shattered remnants of at least six of these triangular-shaped vessels. Each stood only three inches high. One had a peculiar rim that Noël Hume traced to the Austrian Tirol. The excavators also carefully extracted a small chunk of antimony used to purify metals like copper, silver, and gold, an unmistakable marker of an Elizabethan metallurgical tool kit. There were bits of English coal suggesting a forge, as well as tiles that

An archaeology team led by Ivor Noël Hume (in jacket) in 1992 excavates the workshop used by Joachim Gans and Thomas Harriot on Roanoke Island. The earthwork reconstructed by Jean Harrington in 1950 rises in the background.

could withstand high heat. The bricks unearthed previously at the site had been shaped, they could now see, for use in a forge.

Noël Hume realized this wasn't a corner of a fortification or a watchtower. This was the very workshop where metallurgist Joachim Gans conducted his work during the 1585–86 mission. In his thick report, which remains unpublished, he envisioned the structure as "a carport-like shed with a slightly sunken floor and perhaps breast-high log walls to control draft and allow smoke to escape from one or more brick built furnaces within the structure." Four posts at each corner likely supported a thatched roof to protect the workers from the elements. A 1556 German manual on metallurgy includes an engraving of just such a building, with the chemist on a stool within preparing his experiments. Another engraving depicts a furnace foreman sampling butter from a pot, "that the poison which the crucible exhales may not harm him, for this is a special remedy against that poison." Remnants of a butter pot from western England were found strewn on the workshop floor. "There is, of course, no proving that Gans and his workers sat around in their laboratory eating butter," Noël Hume wrote, "yet it is hard to dismiss the West of England jar's presence as purely coincidental."

The trench team, led by William Kelso, who would go on to redis- cover the 1607 Jamestown fort, also identified seeds and nuts, as well as blue-and-white pharmaceutical jars, the medicine bottles of the six- teenth century. Gans likely shared the space with Harriot, who spent much of his time on Roanoke analyzing potential pharmaceuticals that could prove popular in England. It was these—in particular sassafras and tobacco—that ultimately secured England's control of eastern North America.

Kelso and the excavators also recovered fragments of a clay pipe, including a mouthpiece, "where it had almost certainly been between English—or maybe German—lips," Noël Hume noted. Harriot learned that the Indians dried the leaves and turned them into pow- der, which they used by "sucking it through clay pipes into the stom- ach and head." He believed "the fumes purge superfluous phlegm and gross humors from the body by opening all the pores and passages."

Harriot passed the pipe-smoking practice that he learned here, and that would eventually kill him, to Raleigh, who in turn popular- ized this method of smoking in Elizabeth's court. Despite attempts by her successor, James I, to stamp out the practice, even today the use of pipes remains closely identified with Englishness. (The Span- ish, by contrast, picked up the Caribbean habit of rolling tobacco into cigars.) More important, the English craze for tobacco eventu- ally made the later Jamestown settlement—and English settlement of North America—financially viable.

Noël Hume's dig provided a visceral picture: an English Christian and a German Jew working side by side in a state-of-the-art labora- tory, drawing on Native American expertise and an eclectic mix of French, German, Spanish, and Indian equipment to investigate New

World resources. This was where Gans sweated while stoking a forge in the Carolina heat as Harriot quizzed a Native American elder on the healing properties of local plants.

But the excavation raised a perplexing question: Why would Lane's men build a smoky workshop *next to* their fort, rather than inside it, or in an open area to diffuse the fumes, as was done at Jamestown? Curious, Noël Hume dug into the earthwork's original ditch, deep inside the reconstructed redoubt. There he found bits of crucible and other pottery resembling those discovered in the workshop.

"The ditch cuts through the debris from the research center, which then turns up inside the fort," he told me shortly before his 2017 death. By then nearing ninety, he retained a sharp mind and tongue. "I can't prove the date of the fort, but it is after 1585. Harrington was a dear man, but he didn't get it right." Harrington had also found a piece of smelted European copper below the fort parapet in the 1940s, which reinforced Noël Hume's suspicion that the earthwork was built *after* the workshop—and probably long after Raleigh's colonists had abandoned the site.

The archaeologist's contention that the centerpiece of what many consider the nation's spiritual birthplace was an illusion vexed the National Park Service. "If a bunch of fellows were building a fort in the 1700s, then someone would have left behind alcohol bottles," scoffed Guy Prentice, an archaeologist from the park service's Southeast Archeological Center in Tallahassee. Their absence can only mean it was built in the Elizabethan era. Even Kelso is skeptical of Noël Hume's assertion that Fort Raleigh has nothing to do with the Cittie of Raleigh. He told me that Lane's soldiers might have used crucibles to make lead shot, thus explaining the pieces found in the trench. In 2016, Prentice led a dig to resolve the controversy but found "everything was jumbled and mixed."

The morning I met Deetz, his small team was re-excavating a parking-space-sized area at the workshop site, just across the path from the fort. "Harrington didn't dig deep, and he wasn't here every day," he explained, adding that Noël Hume's team might have missed something. "So here we are, digging for the *third* time." There is a piece of virgin ground nearby, but park service policy is to leave something for future generations.

He and two students took turns shoveling the sand-flecked soil into a screen propped on two sawhorses as another sifted through it by hand to spot any stray artifacts. Deetz held up a piece of asphalt from the 1920s road and sighed, throwing it over his shoulder. There was also an electrical casing of indeterminate age and a 1952 penny. He recognized the remnants of a Fireball wrapper as the favorite brand of one of Noël Hume's team members nearly three decades earlier.

In the afternoon, players in the still-running outdoor drama arrived at the nearby amphitheater for rehearsals. The choir voices drifted over the trench: "O God that madest earth and sky, and hedged the restless seas." At that moment, one of Deetz's students plucked a mottled gray bit of ceramic no bigger than a quarter from a sifting screen. Deetz eyed it with interest, then with something like excitement.

I followed as he rushed down the wooded trail to the visitor center with its small display of the few Roanoke artifacts. Within a Lucite case was a small shallow dish dug up by Noël Hume that was missing a piece. The broken bit of pottery recovered minutes before seemed to fit as perfectly as the slipper on Cinderella. "Brought from Europe, this shallow dish, known as a palette, may have been used during alchemical trials," read the description. It was clearly part of Gans's metallurgical equipment.

By the end of the day, the team had four slivers of Elizabethan-era pottery, including part of a crucible and a bit of French stoneware. "That's a good haul for Roanoke," Deetz said, allowing himself an easy smile. "That's more than you sometimes find in an entire season!" As the team packed up, I walked over to a new sign beside the fort that reads, "At this spot, Lane busied his men with constructing such an earthwork." It was a retreat from the old claim that it was Lane's Fort, but still inaccurate from the perspective of Noël Hume. There was no marker commemorating the workshop that the archaeologist considered his single greatest find.

Later, I visited Fort Raleigh's cultural heritage officer, Jami Lanier, to pick up an archaeology booklet. She extended it to me, only to abruptly pull it back as I reached out. "I'll give it to you, but only if you write that the fort is Elizabethan." I smiled at the joke. Then I noticed she wasn't smiling back. The park service never published Noël Hume's workshop findings—a rare copy sits covered in dust on a high shelf in a ranger's office—and the standoff continues even after his death. Take away the earthwork, I realized, and Fort Raleigh National Historic Site is nearly as lost as the Lost Colony itself.

Even as archaeologists were busy digging just west of the fort in search of the settlement, the Cittie of Raleigh might have been in the act of vanishing just a few hundred yards away. Not long after his 1982 meeting with Noël Hume and Harrington, Evans played hooky and made a serendipitous discovery that fired up a new generation of seekers. It was a sunny spring morning, and the young ranger took a walk on the beach below the parking lot a hundred yards or so northeast of the earthwork. "I saw a ring in the water and wondered, what the heck is that, so I waded out and realized it was a barrel."

He knew that colonists in coastal areas commonly sank barrels into the ground to create a well. These features were a reliable marker for early European settlements. The fragments of wood he discovered went into a water-filled bucket in the maintenance shed. Two days later, the park superintendent's son found another round shape off the beach, about fifty yards from Evans's discovery. It turned out to be a hollowed log. It joined the barrel ring in a trash can of water. ("Otherwise they would have turned to powder," Evans explained.)

Later, when they were analyzed using radiocarbon methods, the dates fell well within the Elizabethan period. The finds suggested that archaeologists had been looking in all the wrong places. Rather than west of the fort, perhaps the settlement was to the northeast. But erosion was quickly eating away the fragile bluffs, a problem that Williams observed and that was noted officially in 1972. The park service response was to dump massive granite blocks along the shore by the amphitheater, which only sped up erosion along the adjacent beaches. Evans left the park service for law school and then opened a practice in Durham but continued to return to the island regularly. He couldn't shake his fascination. He walked the woods repeatedly in an attempt to trace White's 1590 steps. When a 2003 hurricane tore away huge chunks of land, he grew worried that the first English settlement in the New World was disappearing before it could be found. He organized the First Colony Foundation to conduct emergency archaeological digs. The results along the bluffs were a few pottery pieces, and underwater archaeology just offshore was inconclusive. But Evans, his hair now white, doggedly continued the work, using his own funds and those raised from friends and other enthusiasts. His quiet and courtly demeanor, longtime acquaintances told me, was deceiving. "Phil is like a moray eel," said Nick Luccketti, one of the archaeologists he tapped to do the job. "You have to cut off his head to make him give up."

Luccketti grew up in New York and went to college at Virginia's College of William and Mary in Williamsburg to take advantage of the longer baseball season. He soon fell under the spell of Noël Hume and cut his archaeological teeth on some of his breakthrough colonial Virginia excavations; he also took part in the early 1990s dig at Fort Raleigh. Inspired by the workshop find, Luccketti joined forces with Evans to continue the search for the Cittie of Raleigh. Yet he grew so frustrated with the dearth of artifacts that he once resorted to a psychic.

A Canadian tourist named George McMullen and a companion stopped one afternoon in 1995 to watch him dig yet another barren trench northwest of the fort. McMullen had no formal scientific training but told the excavator that he was an intuitive archaeologist who practiced psychometry. This, he explained, is the use of extrasensory perception to intuit the history of an object. "That is to say, I hold an object in my hand and information comes to me as to who made it, where it was made, and the time it was made—often far in the past," he writes in his book *One White Crow*.

"These guys showed up and we weren't finding anything," Luccketti recalled. "And so we said what the hell! Tell us where things are."

According to park service documents, McMullen used his psychometric abilities to sense a longhouse surrounded by a palisade. The inhabitants were twenty-five of the Lost Colony gentry who lived separately from the common settlers. Nearby he envisioned barracks for soldiers along with a shed for storing gunpowder and a dock with a small warehouse. McMullen also intuited a nearby well and three bodies. A hand-drawn map made by his assistant Sam Sumner notes that it is "unknown whether fallen bodies or graves. George stated one body died of snake bite."

When the Canadian pointed out the specific location of the fort's corner and the well, "we said, okay, we will dig a hole there," Luccketti, who has the build of a bulldog, told me later. His team excavated four small test pits based on McMullen's intuition. "We didn't find anything," he said. "McMullen said we didn't dig deep enough." Park service records note dryly, "Since no mention is made regarding any notable discoveries . . . it appears safe to conclude that Luccketti's ground truthings were not corroborative with McMullen's predictions."

Undaunted, McMullen and Sumner requested an excavation permit of their own, submitting the hand-drawn map as data. The request was denied, but the park service did approve use of ground-penetrating radar. The pair felt the results were promising, but the park service disagreed and denied a dig permit. Two years later, however, park service archaeologists quietly conducted their own radar survey in the same area. Briefly they thought they had found "structures or some features associated with the original colony." When they dug, however, all they found was a ceramic insulator.

Luccketti fared better in 2008, when his First Colony Foundation team returned to this area northwest of the fort and uncovered Indian pipes, bits of sixteenth-century French flasks and Spanish jars, seventeenth-century glass beads, and eighteenth-century Pennsylvania crockery. The most sensational find was a set of thirteen copper plates, each pierced by tiny holes and nestled among oyster shells. The plates looked nearly identical to necklaces worn by the tribal leader painted by White.

When analyzed, the copper proved to be European. Luccketti pictured Joachim Gans hammering out the copper as a gift for Wingina or in exchange for corn or deer pelts. But because it was hard to date the finds precisely, it was also possible the material was traded south after Jamestown was founded.

The earthwork remains the magnet that has drawn archaeologists to this part of Roanoke Island since Williams's day. But what if it is like the streetlight under which a drunk looks for his keys? Asked why he's looking there of all places, he replies, "Because that's where the light is." I decided to widen my search beyond Fort Raleigh.

One autumn afternoon I visited Hubby Bliven, the curator of the Roanoke Heritage Art Gallery and Military Museum, a rambling wooden shed in the backyard of his century-old family home on a backstreet of Manteo. His collection includes a Pleistocene horse tooth and captured Nazi regalia and most epochs in between.

Treasure hunting and the Roanoke voyages run in his family's veins. An ancestor on his father's side was Blackbeard's quartermaster, he said. "On my mother's side we've been told by numerous sources that we are kin to Eleanor Dare and John White from Devon," the gray-bearded sixty-eight-year-old added. "And one of the men that came over was a Mann, which is my mother's maiden name."

He showed me case after case of Indian artifacts laid carefully on red baize. "That's a platform pipe from the Archaic period about four thousand years ago," Bliven said. "My wife found that in her chicken yard. And these arrowheads, well, the oldest is dated about nine thousand years." He had never, however, found a recognizably Elizabethan object in all his decades of collecting.

I asked where he thought the settlement was built. "If I were on a ship and I saw a natural harbor like Shallowbag Bay, that's where I would put my boat. It is easier than going to some other part of the island." He predicted it is under today's Manteo, specifically on the outskirts in a neighborhood called Mother Vineyard that is home to an ancient scuppernong vine also nicknamed Sir Walter Raleigh's vine (though horticulturalists say it actually dates to the eighteenth century). The vine has long been linked to a romantic tale about Virginia Dare.

When I asked Prentice and Luccketti about this option, they agreed it was promising. Unfortunately, the upscale neighborhood on the eastern shore of Roanoke is covered in ranch homes and split-levels set off by carefully tended lawns and azalea beds. Owners are reluctant to let archaeologists dig up their turf.

A second possible location is on the western side of the island. In 2007, a local named Scott Dawson stumbled on an unusual feature while tramping through the woods with an eye out for Civil War material and Indian pottery. Dawson, who grew up on Hatteras—the island Elizabethans referred to as Croatoan—is a thirtysomething with a surfer's build. At the time he worked as a blacksmith at Manteo's Roanoke Island Festival Park. Like Bliven, he grew up hunting for artifacts and claims relation to a Blackbeard crew member.

Beachcombing along the Outer Banks is more than a leisurely pastime for tourists. Locals call it progging, an old British term for foraging. The Carolina Algonquians told Barlowe that they scavenged nails from a European shipwreck. Later islanders built their houses from beached vessels and survived by selling washed-up merchandise. They were often accused of stealing goods claimed by insurance companies or even of allowing shipwreck victims to drown so they could plunder their belongings with impunity. When a northeaster in 2006 pushed a cargo container of Doritos into the ocean and thousands of small bags littered the beach, school was let out early so the children could collect the snacks. (A local teacher told me, "I had a kid bring me a knee bone, and I said, 'Please don't bring me human remains!' ")

One brisk winter day, Dawson took me to a wooded area less than a mile from Fort Raleigh that is quickly succumbing to a suburban development. Part of the land is owned by the park service, but much of the area has been bulldozed to make way for homes and culs-de-sac without any oversight by archaeologists. I tried to keep up as he strode through brambles that grabbed at my coat and pants. "I started to think that I was crazy wandering through the woods," he said. "Then I found this."

We had emerged into a small clearing. Through bushes and tall pines, I could make out the marsh where a creek met the water separating Roanoke from the mainland. Wingina's village would have been directly opposite. At my feet I spotted a barely discernible depression about a foot wide and nearly filled with a cushion of pine straw. The ditch ran in a straight course into the thick brush where the clearing ended. We used an iPhone app to draw a crude map as we followed the ditch as it curved through the trees.

Dodging low branches and brambles, we walked in single file and discovered that one side alone stretched nearly eighty feet. In a few minutes we found ourselves back where we started. "It is an enclosure!" Dawson said with excitement. "But it's a weird shape," he added. "Maybe it was built to follow the landscape." He called it Fort Blob.

"This is a cove, a nice place to put a longboat," Dawson remarked as a cold wind blew off the water to the west. "Imagine that Lane is trying to defend against Spaniards. The Spanish were on their mind. They robbed two Spanish ships on the way here, sacked Puerto Rico, and stole salt. He wants to be tucked in." From this vantage point, Lane could also keep an eye on Wingina.

Williams would have agreed. "This harbor is the natural site for a settlement on the island," he wrote in 1895. The creek also supplied freshwater, a vital commodity in short supply on the sandy island. There is also an undated document found by Quinn that makes recommendations on how Lane should construct his 1585 settlement. If based on an island, he should build a second fort in another location in case of attack. Also, a Spanish captive on Grenville's fleet in 1586 reported a fort "of little strength" on Roanoke Island located "inside by the water." Quinn suggests that he may be describing a fort situated on the western shore facing the mainland. There is the added detail that White mentions coming to this side of the island in 1590.

When park service archaeologists briefly examined the trench that Dawson showed them, they found in it "no discernible pattern" and dismissed it as a possible animal path or a drainage ditch. Animals don't walk in circles, and drainage ditches don't form rough enclosures. As I walked the spongy depression with Dawson, the site struck me as an obvious place to build a fort or settlement. And the narrow and shallow trench was remarkably similar to the one that archaeologists in the mid-1990s finally recognized at Jamestown after a century of looking for the fort, leading to the greatest find in American colonial archaeology.

For a brief moment, I felt a thrill that the first English town in the Americas might lie undisturbed under my feet. Then I noticed a bright pink ribbon tied to a stake that was poking out of the ground. Later I learned that the Lost Colony Research Group, an organization of enthusiasts that includes a professional pianist, a retired engineer, and a self-confessed "obsessive genealogist," secured a permit in 2015 to examine the ditch using nondestructive methods. Tom Beaman, an archaeologist at Wake Technical Community College in Raleigh hired by the group, conducted ground-penetrating radar and metal-detecting tests on the site. When I called him he said, "The early results didn't meet any of our hoped-for expectations." The only way to know for sure is to dig, but three years later he had yet to submit his data, a necessary step before the park service would consider granting an excavation permit.

There was a third possible location for the settlement, but it was one that I had been avoiding.

I think John White would still feel at home here," said J. P. Walsh when I visited the gleaming new Coastal Studies Institute between the towns of Manteo and Wanchese. We were standing on a balcony at one end of a building that looked like a white skyscraper that fell on its side. We had a panoramic view of the marsh and sounds beyond.

With his stocky build, shorts, and sunglasses pushed back on his baseball cap, Walsh looked more like a local fisherman than a sedimentary scientist. "The basic form and character is there, like when you go back to your hometown and the road and the curves in it are the same, but what's alongside it may be different." This immutable feeling of the land is an illusion, as Walsh well knows. That's why he's here. Few places in North America undergo such rapid and fundamental change as the Outer Banks and Carolina sounds. White drew several inlets that no longer exist, while in 2017 a crescent-shaped hundred-acre island suddenly appeared off Cape Hatteras.

Later that breezy summer afternoon, he and a colleague took me along on their boat to draw cores out of the Albemarle Sound. Their goal was to understand how the landscape has altered over time. We anchored a few miles off the north end of Roanoke. The distant white granite monument marking the Wright brothers' first flight shone like a beacon in the hot sun on a distant grassy knoll. The scientists stuck a simple plastic tube with a homemade plastic handle over the side. After screwing it into the mud, they hauled it back up and used a putty knife to cut sections the size of a thick silver-dollar pancake.

"Sometimes it gets stuck and you have to jump in to wrestle it out," Walsh said. "That's no fun in January." Sealed in plastic bags, the environmental time capsules would be analyzed later in the lab.

Research suggests that the English arrived in a stormy era that punched a host of holes through the narrow barrier islands. In a 1585 map, White depicts nearly a dozen inlets in the vicinity. Today there are just three. Ocean water poured in to mix with the freshwater flowing down from the interior of North Carolina and Virginia, altering the habitats of fish and shellfish in the process. Battered by waves and tides, the forests at the island's southern end began to give way to swamp.

A century or so later, as the second wave of English settlers appeared, most of those openings began to clog with sand, and the waters of the sound became less brackish, yet again changing the forms of life below and above the water's surface. "The closure of inlets, mostly over the last two hundred years, reflects a more stable climate, fewer storms, and a decrease in wind and wave intensity in the North Atlantic," he said.

President Monroe's 1819 visit was, in part, to see if the rapidly closing inlet between the Atlantic and the Albemarle might be artificially widened. The plan was abandoned as too expensive.

When that inlet filled in, the Albemarle rushed down the west side of Roanoke and into the Pamlico, dramatically altering the flow of water. The new currents abraded the sandy bluffs along the north end of the island. Just how much land has been lost is a topic of fierce debate between geologists and archaeologists. Walsh pulled up the anchor as his colleague started the boat. We sped back toward Roanoke's northern shore. Gray bands marked the rocks dumped by the National Park

Service to protect the historic site and a nearby old cemetery. I could plainly see how the hard barriers diverted the water to the neighboring shores, gouging large hunks out of the crumbling bluffs.

We veered away from a set of rickety posts stuck in the shallow water used to attach fishnets, remarkably similar to those used by the Native Americans that White drew. "This was all land back then," shouted Walsh over the engine's roar. He pointed at the depth finder, which had read ten feet and suddenly dropped to seven and then six. We were still more than half a mile offshore.

"Twenty-five hundred feet," he replied, when I asked how much land had been shaved off Roanoke's northern end in the past four centuries. If he is right, then nearly half a mile of the shore where the colonists likely settled was submerged long ago. Swift currents and storms would have buffeted, broken up, and buried the tons of artifacts and trash the settlers generated. If so, then we will never know what the first English village in the Americas looked like. The lanes and homes, the fields and public buildings, the cottage where Virginia Dare was born—all will have vanished.

Locals have little trouble believing the north end of Roanoke Island is sinking under the waves. Williams himself noted the water rise when he visited more than a century ago. One Manteo shopkeeper told me that the streets are underwater so frequently now that the town places "No Wake" signs along the roads so that cars don't splash water into the buildings on either side.

Later I pored over the latest geological maps of Roanoke. According to the data, the top part of the island, the north end, had been progressively shaved away in the past several centuries. The change seemed hard to deny, but archaeologists are reluctant to accept the judgment of geologists. "If you look at the maps from the 1700s, the island's geography has not changed much," Prentice from the National Park Service told me. "And it hasn't changed much since the Civil War. I just don't buy that a couple of thousand yards are gone." Jamestown, after all, was said by geologists to have been washed away by the James River, a conclusion that Kelso proved wrong when he uncovered the original fort. And Noël Hume's workshop proved that major activities took place on what is still land. Evans from the First

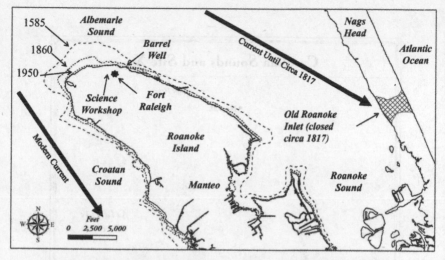

The closing of old Roanoke Inlet altered the currents in the Albemarle Sound, and geologists estimate that two thousand feet or more of Roanoke Island's north shore has been lost to erosion—possibly sweeping away all remnants of the colony settlement. *J. P. Walsh and Ian Conery of East Carolina University/UNC Coastal Studies Institute*

Colony Foundation remained confident the mystery of where the Lost Colonists first settled could still be solved.

But the discovery of a dramatic clue overlooked by centuries of historians—even Quinn—turned the spotlight away from Roanoke Island and swung it instead to one of the two destinations mentioned by White, a place that lay "fifty miles into the main."

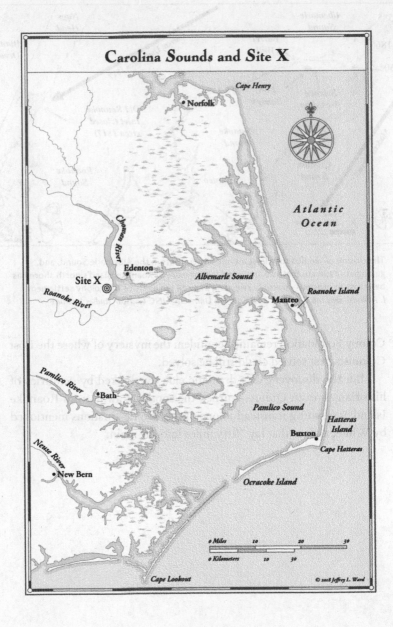

Carolina Sounds and Site X

Cape Henry

Norfolk

Atlantic
Ocean

Chowan River

Edenton

Site X

Albemarle Sound

Roanoke Island

Manteo

Roanoke River

Pamlico River

Bath

Pamlico Sound

Hatteras
Island

Buxton

Cape Hatteras

Neuse River

New Bern

Ocracoke Island

0 Miles · 10 · 20 · 30

0 Kilometers · 10 · 30

Cape Lookout

© 2018 Jeffrey L. Ward

CHAPTER SEVEN

A Four-Hundred-Year-Old Cover-Up

The atmosphere was gloomy when the First Colony Foundation board met the day before Thanksgiving 2011 in Chapel Hill, North Carolina. After more than half a dozen years of intensive excavations to find remnants of the Raleigh colonists on Roanoke, Evans's group had little to show. No one could agree on what to do next.

One of their newer board members, Brent Lane of the University of North Carolina, enjoyed volunteering at the excavations, but he was weary of digging dry holes. "It's an astoundingly sterile place," he told me later. "Dig under the theater! Dig under the parking lot! It's been eating away at these guys. I realized that the broader story wasn't going to be told by working exclusively on Roanoke."

Lane is a bearish man with a trimmed white beard and a voice like a Tar Heel Garrison Keillor. His presence tends to fill a room. Though he grew up in a suburb of the state capital of Raleigh, his father was from the Albemarle Sound region. As a youth he fished eastern North Carolina waters and as a college student mapped the area's extensive peat bogs. "We worked in small boats and four-wheel drive trucks," Lane recalled. "On foot, you had to hack your way through with a machete. I knew this area the way the Roanoke colonists did."

While he doesn't claim a blood relation with the leader of the first colony—his ancestors arrived here in the 1630s as indentured servants—Lane admitted "the affinity of a shared name inevitably draws you to a person." The business aspects of the 1585 expedition particularly appealed to his professional interest in the growth of the global economy. He didn't truck with romance. "The Roanoke voyages have nothing to do with Virginia Dare and the poor lost white people—the lost cause of the sixteenth century and all that southern gothic shit. The real story is geopolitics, colonization, the advancement of science, and the development of investment."

So in 2006, after reading a newspaper story about the foundation, he called Evans, and the two hit it off. They shared a deep fascination with the Roanoke voyages and were equally excited by the challenge of finding physical clues left by the colonists. Evans invited him to join the board.

In an attempt to nudge the foundation away from its Roanoke fixation, Lane put Evans in touch with Tom Thompson, the economic development chief of rural Beaufort County, one hundred miles southeast of the state capital. The county spans both sides of the Pamlico River, which flows into the sound of the same name. This was the area that Grenville and Lane's expedition explored during the summer of 1585 before settling on Roanoke and also where White made some of his most compelling drawings of Native Americans and their villages. An engraving of his watercolor of Secotan, reprinted innumerable times, heavily influenced the way Europeans imagined an Indian community. Anthropologists still consider the image a masterpiece of their field, because it captures in one scene the way the locals hunted, prayed, farmed, ate, celebrated, and honored their dead. Eager to draw tourists to a county suffering from high unemployment, Thompson asked the foundation's archaeologists to identify the location of Secotan, in order to reconstruct the settlement.

They agreed and turned to White's map of eastern North Carolina, called *La Virginea Pars,* or "the parts of Virginia," for hints to its precise location. They zeroed in on a point of land across the creek from Bath, a colonial North Carolina capital famed as the home of Blackbeard the pirate. The Canadian potash company that owned the site, however, refused to allow excavations. Soon after, Thompson left his job. "It all fell apart," said Lane. "But it demonstrated the value of the map."

White's watercolor is a work of art. Elizabethan ships glide across the sounds below long fluttering banners as Native American log canoes float in the light blue rivers. The painting is part of a collection of White's New World drawings owned by the British Museum. But the image that covers the landscape between the southern Chesapeake Bay and the southern terminus of the Outer Banks is as much science as art. White based the drawing on the meticulous cartographic work done by Harriot, and its faithfulness to the complicated shorelines wasn't equaled for at least two centuries.

"It was incredibly accurate and precise," said Lane. "I found that it hadn't been used much as a tool for investigation." Lane brought a reproduction of the map, along with his father's fishing charts, when the board met that November day in 2011. As the group debated where to excavate next, he idly scanned White's drawing for the hundredth time.

"Why are there patches on the map?" he asked abruptly, looking up at the other board members.

There were two. The first was a long oval one in the bottom third that covered part of Beaufort and surrounding counties, about fifty miles west of Hatteras Island. A smaller round patch covered the spot where the Roanoke and Chowan Rivers merge to form the Albemarle Sound, about fifty miles west of Roanoke Island. No one in the room had noticed the coverings before. Lane said he would contact British Museum curators to get their opinion. If they were lucky, he figured, what lay under the patch might provide new information that could revive the effort to locate the Secotan village that locals had hoped to reconstruct.

Lane got in touch with a Harriot scholar he had met in London, Stephen Clucas, who taught at the University of London, just a short walk from the museum. The museum curators, however, ignored him. "They thought this was a request from a crank, so they gave me the cold shoulder," Clucas told me later. Lane wasn't surprised. He was well aware that the Lost Colony mystery was a magnet for amateur sleuths who often harbored theories ranging from unconventional to unhinged.

Undeterred, Clucas discovered that Kim Sloan, the head of the

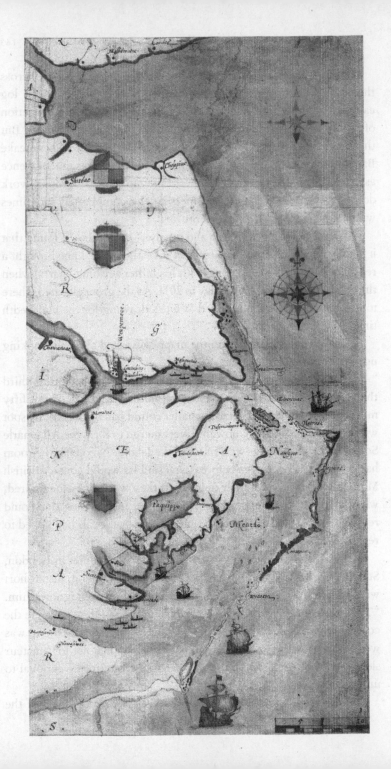

print department that oversees the White drawings, had a daughter studying at Chapel Hill. Through this connection and dogged persistence, he got Sloan's attention and convinced her that he was a legitimate researcher. She promised to look into the matter. When I contacted the curator, she was at first reluctant to meet and discuss what happened next, but eventually relented. I flew to London to see her and White's drawings.

The print room at the British Museum is well hidden from the thousands who mill through the endless maze of exhibit rooms. I wandered through the labyrinth, thoroughly lost, until a guard directed me to a nearly invisible entrance in a small gallery on the top floor. Stepping through the doorway was like entering the wardrobe in the C. S. Lewis novel.

Inside was a room as big as a train station, lit by Victorian skylights and supported by Ionic columns. Mahogany shelves filled with tall red-bound books and boxes lined the walls nearly to the ceiling. At one end stood a platform with a desk surrounded by a wooden rail. From here, the librarian in charge surveyed the room in a glance like a judge in a courtroom.

After I signed in, a curator appeared, introducing herself as Alice Rugheimer. She had been on the team that analyzed the map and said Sloan was in a meeting but would be along soon. "Would you like to see the drawings in the meantime?" A few minutes later she rolled a metal cart to a long polished table and unloaded four red boxes. The curator then handed me a pair of white cotton gloves and left me alone with the entire collection of seventy-five John White watercolors.

Their survival is itself a dramatic tale of loss and recovery, a rare example of something related to the Lost Colony that was never fully lost. The delicate watercolors vanished into a private library in Ireland

(Facing page) This magnificent White watercolor called *La Virginea Pars* is based on Harriot's precision cartography and provides a remarkably accurate view of eastern North Carolina; Virginia's Chesapeake Bay is at the top. Note the outline of two patches applied near the bottom and left of center. *British Museum*

some time after White's death. In 1865 they were brought to London to be auctioned at Sotheby's. Just before the sale, a catastrophic fire swept through the warehouse where they were stored. All seventeen thousand volumes of German naturalist Alexander von Humboldt's library and nearly every first edition of the English classic *The Pilgrim's Progress* went up in smoke before firefighters could pump thousands of gallons of water to extinguish the blaze.

A few days later, a Vermonter named Henry Stevens poked through the wet and smoking ruins. Stevens specialized in buying books about early America for wealthy patrons. He had been eager to purchase the White drawings that were the basis of so many famous engravings about the New World. According to Lane, Stevens stumbled on the singed and waterlogged White volume and took it to his bookbinder, who cleaned and rebound the material and returned it to Sotheby's, where he subsequently purchased the set. When he failed to drum up interest among American buyers for the drawings—there were few buyers in the immediate aftermath of the Civil War—he sold the lot to the British Museum. "How miraculous this stuff ever survived!" Lane had remarked.

I opened the first box and pulled out the top image. Each painting is only ten inches by five inches. They are among the few objects that we know were handled—and, in fact, created—by a member of the Roanoke voyages. I looked into the kindly face of a grizzled old man huddled in his winter garment of soft deerskin and worn moccasins. The artist clearly persuaded his subject to haul out his cold-weather clothes, because he met him in the muggy Carolina heat of the 1585 summer.

"One of their religious men" looked as dour as a Puritan preacher except for the earrings and topknot. I imagined him debating theology with Harriot over a cup of sassafras tea. There was "the flyer," a muscled and clean-shaven holy man with feathers in his hair and his arms aloft as if in an ecstatic trance. I came to the painting of Secotan, with its neat rectangular houses and their arched roofs made of reed mats, lacking any defensive wall. The villagers were busy in a host of daily activities, from scaring birds away from the maturing corn to "dancing about poles carved on the tops like faces of men."

Sloan arrived then in gray tweed and a black turtleneck, a slim woman with her silver hair pulled back. Like Brent Lane, her last name is tied to the Roanoke voyages; Sir Hans Sloane founded the British Museum and also purchased a separate set of drawings associated with John White that are dominated by New World flora and fauna. "I'm not directly related, but all Sloans are related eventually from a Scottish clan, and my father is from Northern Ireland," she said.

The curator explained that White drew on fine French paper, later mounted on thin boards, which made it impossible to examine the reverse side. After many decades of handling, splotches left by greasy fingers dappled the edges; small tears had become evident. So in preparation for an upcoming 2007 exhibition, Sloan decided to replace them.

Her staff laboriously removed the mounts that had stuck to the edges of the fragile drawings. Using a light box of the sort once common for sorting slides, they pinpointed weak areas and fixed tears using a gluten-free wheat-starch paste that can easily be removed. Lightweight Japanese paper replaced the board backings, and the drawings were then fitted into cream-colored acid-free mounts. For the first time in more than a century, the backsides of the drawings were easily accessible.

At the time, the curators didn't take any special note of the patches on the White map. Patches, after all, are not unheard of in paintings of the day. "I have some examples from Pre-Raphaelites where they have done a detailed drawing and want to fix one bit," Sloan said. "They will draw it on another piece of paper, cut it out, and stick it on." It was the delete key of that era. Unlike oils, watercolors are difficult to paint over. "My automatic assumption was that White got something wrong and he corrected it."

I asked how she went about examining the White map after Lane made his request. "It was a Friday," she said. "It's always on a Friday. We were both so busy, but Alice said, 'Let's do this!' We thought with a strong light behind it we might be able to see if the inlets and villages were in a different place underneath." She took the map to a museum conservation lab and laid it in the light box they had used to repair the drawings in order to examine the patch laid over the area of Secotan.

As she spoke, Sloan removed the White map from its box and placed it on the table in front of us. Its colors were pale but beautiful, the shorelines outlined in a slightly deeper blue than the offshore waters. Rugheimer had brought a portable light box and plugged it in at the long table where we sat under the gray London afternoon filtering through the skylights above. The outlines of the patches were clearly visible.

Sloan slid the box under the bottom part of the map, around Secotan. "You see the little lines there? That looked like pencil. White changed it, as if there was a river going in the wrong place and he made a correction. It all seemed to make sense." The patch over the area around Secotan alters the shoreline and placement of one village. Perhaps Thomas Harriot, White's colleague and the mathematical mind behind the map, insisted that the artist make the correction after revising his own calculations.

Later analysis found that both patches adhered so strongly to the drawing that they could not be removed without risking a tear. By using a camera with filters for infrared and ultraviolet imaging, the team was able to enhance the watercolor. The infrared light picked up White's initial pencil sketches underlying the entire image. Most of the changes he made from drawing to painting were minor. There was the ghost outline of a ship riding off the coast that was never actually painted, and the rigging altered in one that was.

White had easily painted over his pencil drawings, but it was more difficult to cover the blue outlines of the shore and the village placement along the squiggly coast of the Secotan area. He apparently covered the entire region with a patch. Then he could make small changes to the shore and move the location of the settlement called Secotaoc, located downstream from Secotan on the Pamlico River. The blue pigment used for both the original and the correction appears to be the same, suggesting that it was White or an assistant who made the alteration.

"We thought that was what Brent wanted to know," Sloan added. "But we said while we are at it, we would look at the other patch. It's not that easy to see unless you have it under the right kind of light." The team had a camera to photograph their finds, and Sloan was looking through the viewfinder that day when an assistant moved the map up to the patch on the northern end.

"I said to Alice, 'I think we just discovered the intended site of the Cittie of Raleigh.' Then I swore." Her tone was of dread rather than delight.

"I've looked at enough old maps, and I knew the symbol. I had that 'Oh. My. God.' moment. As in 'Oh my God' there are going to be so many people asking about this damn thing. I knew the first question would be about the Lost Colony. I didn't want to be the person who discovered the patch and therefore would be the go-to person for the answers to everything. And we don't know the answer. Because without more documentation, there is no answer to why he covered it up."

She slid the upper part of the map over the light, just where the Albemarle Sound split into the Roanoke and Chowan Rivers. What seemed a blank space suddenly revealed a bright star-shaped lozenge in deep red and outlined in a royal blue.

By placing the White map on a light table, Sloan and Rugheimer revealed this image of a fort hidden underneath the upper patch covering the head of the Albemarle Sound. Circles indicate Native American settlements. *British Museum*

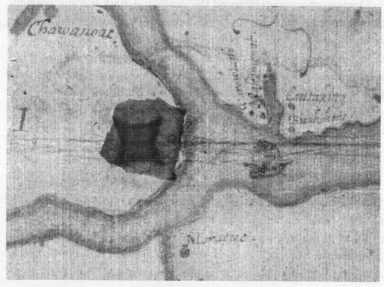

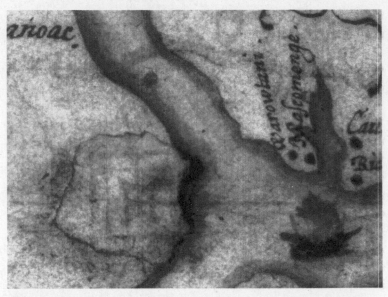

Ultraviolet analysis of the White map reveals not just a fort symbol hidden beneath but a separate outline of a fortification, likely outlined in urine-based invisible ink, on top of the patch. *British Museum*

Image processing enhanced the symbol. A dark feature, possibly the outlines of a square, sits in the center of the lozenge. There was no mistaking the form. White had drawn, and then hidden, a common representation of a Renaissance-era fort, located about fifty miles inland from Roanoke Island. It recalls his mention that the settlers intended to move "fifty miles into the main." The blue pigment proved similar to the paint White used for the coastlines, again suggesting the change was made by the artist himself. After more than four centuries, a secret that John White so carefully concealed was revealed.

But what did it mean?

"Most people think that history provides definitive answers," Sloan said as we gazed at the long-hidden image of the fort. "But finding real proof is something else. What this did say to me was that this was an intended site of the Cittie of Raleigh. This is Raleigh's crest and the queen's," she added, pointing to the elaborate coats of arms that White had placed prominently on the map. "It is about finding financial backers and settlers. And it was also White's purpose to convince people to come and settle, to say that I have permission from Raleigh. Here's his seal and I'm the governor—let's go!" Others, however, saw it as far more than a promotional gimmick.

Lane was coming out of the dentist's office in February 2012 when he got the news. "My mouth was still numb, and I had two images from Sloan—including a big red-and-blue symbol—on my phone." He sat on the news for half an hour or so, wondering what it meant.

He approached the revelation from the perspective of a venture capitalist. Like Sloan, he assumed at first the symbol simply showed where Raleigh planned a settlement. "I said to myself, don't get too excited; this is just a place they wanted to build a fort."

But there was one more secret hidden in plain sight. Archaeologist Clay Swindell from the Museum of the Albemarle, who worked with Evans's foundation, dug through his hard drive for high-resolution images that he had taken of the map during an earlier British Museum visit. In one, he noticed a faint outline of a similar symbol that seemed to be *on top* of the northern patch. "I e-mailed Kim that she sent us more than she knew," said Lane.

The clue required no modern imaging to spot. "If you stand here and look on top of the patch, can you see something very faint?" said Sloan, motioning me to hover just above and to the side of the map. A distinct outline swam into view when I turned my head so that the gray London light hit the map at the right angle.

"You can see it with the naked eye!" I exclaimed. I felt the eyes of the librarian at her elevated desk on me.

"It's a fort," Sloan replied in a more subdued voice. "That is on top of the paper and not underneath. And it is smaller than the image below. It is also in a slightly different place and a slightly different thing."

Within a week of the initial discovery, Sloan's team used ultraviolet light to investigate the faint postage-stamp-sized outline on top of the patch. "It appears to have a central cross shaped feature and to be surrounded by two concentric squares, incomplete on the coastal side," stated the technical report. Analysis of the thin and shadowy outline, however, proved challenging. The results, the report noted blandly, "are difficult to interpret."

Under a microscope, "the lines give the impression of being stains or areas of localized damage rather than being due to the deliberate application of a particulate pigment." But the faint outline was not made by the underlying symbol bleeding through the patch. It was, as Sloan said, "a slightly different thing." Further analysis with ultraviolet light showed that the lines were not faded pencil markings like White's ghost ship. The outline seemed made by organic material, just nothing like the watercolors that White used.

"Urine," said Sloan, when I asked. Conservator Janet Ambers, who worked with her, had walked to the nearby British Library to research a theory that would soon figure prominently in headlines. "One other possible, if rather romantic, explanation is that these lines could reflect the use of an 'invisible ink' (an ink which would only be revealed when treated in some way, usually by applying heat)," the study noted. "Such materials are well recorded from the period, with inks based on alum, milk, citrus juice, or urine being the most frequently mentioned."

There was nothing romantic about the cloak-and-dagger world in which White moved. This was an era when revealed secrets could easily lead to indefinite imprisonment, horrific torture, and death by methods such as public disemboweling and drawing and quartering in which the victim's four limbs were tied to horses, then sent off in different directions. Walsingham's agents arrested Sir Francis Throckmorton—a cousin of Raleigh's future wife—as he encoded a letter to the imprisoned Mary, Queen of Scots. While Amadas and Barlowe enjoyed their summer visit to the Outer Banks, Throckmorton was drawn and quartered in London. Abroad, the English confronted innumerable enemies, from the pope's influential court in Rome to Inquisition judges in the Caribbean with their own methods of persuasion. "In these doubtful times wherein so much malice is born against England, men are loathe to have their names or exposition known," an English diplomat told Walsingham.

The secretary of state employed specialists adept in the art of hiding secrets from unwanted eyes. They drew on the medieval tradition of alchemy and the emerging discipline of chemistry. One, Arthur Gregorye, advocated using alum to write letters that would then appear with a sprinkling of coal dust. He even proved his point by sending the secretary of state a sample. "If your honor rub this powder within the black line, the letters will appear white." The dark smear on the letter, which still exists in the British Library, shows that Walsingham did as he was told.

In 1586, his expert team lured Mary and her fellow plotters against Elizabeth to correspond using the beer barrels arriving and departing from the jailed monarch's castle. They sprang the trap that led to her execution. Mary prided herself on her knowledge of invisible inks, and she shared her favorite recipe with the French ambassador in London. "The paper must be dipped in a basin of water, and then held to the fire; the secret writing then appears white, and may easily be read until the paper dries," she advised.

The use of invisible inks extended beyond diplomatic dispatches. English Catholics faced arrest if incriminating letters were intercepted, while businessmen sought to hide questionable transactions in an era of piracy and fenced goods. Secrecy was a way of life among the Elizabethan elite. Given that the Spanish stood ready to destroy any rival settlement in the New World, there was nothing out of the ordinary about White or one of his associates resorting to invisible ink. He was, after all, part of a circle that included Walsingham and Harriot, a young chemist who no doubt was familiar with the covert technology of his day. White himself told the colonists to leave behind a secret token designating their destination, in the hope that if Spanish forces discovered the settlement, they wouldn't notice a word carved on a tree.

But Sloan was wary of the public response to the revelations from the White map. "It's dangerous when you put out there all the options and people leap to conclusions," she said as she carefully set the map back in its box and replaced the lid.

The situation, Brent Lane told me, reminded him of the 2004 film *National Treasure,* in which Nicolas Cage plays a historian who deciphers a coded map on the back of the Declaration of Independence.

"We had to have credible research behind this," he said. "It was all rather sensational. We wanted it covered methodically and soberly."

White or his assistant drew a fort and then hid the image under a patch. Someone then drew another fort symbol in what certainly seems invisible ink on top of the concealing patch. The fort might have been planned but never built, or a mistake that required fixing, as White had done with the patch over Secotan. Yet if it was simply to cover something that was never built, why use invisible ink to draw a similar image on top of the patch?

There was only one way to find out. Archaeologists had to go to the X marked on the map and dig.

The search for the colonists didn't start this decade; it didn't start this century," Brent Lane told reporters at a crowded 2012 press conference in Chapel Hill three months after Sloan first slid the map onto the light table. "It started as soon as they were found to be absent from Roanoke Island . . . I would say every generation in the last four hundred years has taken this search on." But, he added, "none of them had this clue on this map."

Sloan declined to attend the event in person, appearing instead on a screen set up at the university's Wilson Library. On the stage, it was clear that the scholars associated with the First Colony Foundation interpreted the discovery differently. Principal archaeologist Eric Klingelhofer suggested that "parts of Raleigh's exploration in North America were a state secret, and the map 'cover-up' was an effort to keep information from the public and from foreign agents."

Historian James Horn felt vindicated by "a pretty amazing piece of evidence from a source that has been staring us in the face all along." He had long advocated the view that the colonists went fifty miles inland as White suggested. "We believe that this evidence provides conclusive proof that they moved westward up the Albemarle Sound to the confluence of the Chowan and Roanoke Rivers."

"This is really a good solid lead," countered Lane, "but it's not conclusive, and it won't be until we find something." The fort symbol was just a mark on a piece of paper until archaeologists could find

Members of the First Colony Foundation following the patch discovery; clockwise from bottom left, James Horn, Brent Lane, Phil Evans, Eric Klingelhofer, and Nicholas Luccketti. *Briana Brough for The New York Times/Redux*

physical remains in the ground. And it was not drawn to scale; the red-and-blue lozenge covered territory on the ground amounting to thousands of acres in rural Bertie County. This was no simple treasure map.

Though they said nothing about it at the press conference, the foundation already had its eye on a specific parcel of land fronting the Albemarle, between the mouths of the Roanoke and Chowan Rivers. Luccketti had dug there in 2006 when a massive housing development was planned that required an archaeological survey before construction could commence. His team uncovered a mix of Native American and European artifacts, including gray and green English pottery common in the seventeenth century and wine bottles manufactured after 1650. None of this was surprising, because a Virginian named Nathaniel Batts established the first European trading post in what is now North Carolina near there in the 1650s.

With the onset of the Great Recession, the development plan collapsed. Luccketti still had the artifacts from the site boxed up in his

Williamsburg office. When he and colonial pottery expert Bly Straube took a closer look at the finds, they concluded that they were of a sort that *could* date to the late sixteenth century. "Here was a suggestion that there may be something at this site relating to the Roanoke colony," Luccketti told me.

Another piece of evidence pointing to the region was a red dot hidden under the patch that marked the site of an Indian village almost precisely where they dug. Some historians believe the red dots and markings on White's map show where the English visited. As at Roanoke, the settlers would be likely to build close to a Native American village that could offer food and protection.

Another map provided an additional clue. As part of his 1590 volume on Virginia, the Flemish engraver Theodor de Bry published a black-and-white map of the region that is more detailed than White's. He likely based this copper engraving on a more precise map since lost. The engraving features more inlets into the Carolina sounds, as well as sixteen additional place-names. The place where Luccketti dug matched the location of an Indian village marked as Mettaquem on de Bry's reproduction, located at the same spot as the red dot on White's watercolor.

Ralph Lane mentions leading an expedition past Mettaquem, which may mean "big trees" or "great woods" in Carolina Algonquian, in 1586. It was under the control of King Okisco, ruler of the Weapemeoc who dominated the northern side of the Albemarle Sound. They were subject to the larger and more powerful Chowan tribe, to the north and west. Lane reported that Okisco later sent two dozen of his "principalest men" to Roanoke Island and that he pledged obedience to Queen Elizabeth, at the order of his Chowan chief. By placing the fort symbol in the vicinity of Mettaquem, White might have been suggesting that the English had their eye on the area. In his 1586 report to Raleigh, Lane suggested building a series of small forts, called sconces, to protect a passage between the Chowan River and Chesapeake Bay to the north. There is no evidence that he did so, but Mettaquem was at a strategic juncture that an experienced military engineer like Lane would surely have appreciated.

In part to keep its location secret and in a nod to the treasure-map nature of their hunt, Luccketti and his colleagues called the place of their prospective dig Site X.

Like Sloan, Luccketti was reluctant at first to talk with me. Given the publicity frenzy surrounding the map, he was wary of reporters and wary of making claims before the results were fully analyzed. Publicity, however, is a key method for nonprofit groups like Evans's foundation to attract funding for future excavations, given the paucity of government grants for archaeological work. He finally relented, but he refused to give exact directions to the site because of worries that artifact looters might learn of the location.

One still and humid summer morning, in a fittingly clandestine manner, I rendezvoused at a local country store with Swindell and followed his truck down a back road dotted with farms between pine woods. He turned onto an unpaved road and waved me through a gate that he locked back up once I had passed. My car bumped between rows of soybeans before we parked on a grassy slope. Beyond, to the east, the orange glare of the midsummer sun lifted above the still expanse of the Albemarle Sound, which stretched to a hazy horizon. Roanoke Island lay just over the earth's curve.

When I got out, the air already felt viscous. Immediately in front of me was a narrow meadow framed by thick woods and punctured with half a dozen rectangular holes.

"No social media!" Luccketti barked by way of greeting. "No Facebook, no tweeting, no texting!" Short and stocky and given to a downcast expression and low-key manner, he earned the nickname Eeyore, after the pessimistic donkey in *Winnie-the-Pooh*. Today, however, he was uncharacteristically on edge.

Just then, a tall middle-aged man in a polo shirt walked up. "He's our leak," the man said quietly to Luccketti, nodding discreetly over his left shoulder. "He's been taking pictures."

I turned to see a worker in jeans and a T-shirt shoveling dirt from a neatly cut trench. Another was standing over a mesh screen boxed in plywood laid on top of two sawhorses, sorting through the dark earth for artifacts like pottery or bone. "He told the guy with metal detectors where this place was," the man added. Luccketti frowned. "I'll take care of it," he said, and stalked off toward the trench.

He returned without comment and walked me down to the beach that bordered the Albemarle. On either side of the field was a cypress swamp. To my left, across a mile or so of flat water, were the gables of Edenton, a sleepy North Carolina colonial capital that marked where the Chowan River entered the sound. To the right was a small cove formed by the mouth of Salmon Creek. A golden eagle soared by. It was easy to imagine lookouts peering down the sound as an English pinnace rode nearby at anchor, invisible to any Spanish ships that might venture into the interior in their hunt for the trespassers.

Walking back up the gentle slope, Luccketti led me to a folding table set up in the full sun of the open field. On either side, close to the trees, volunteers were busy shoveling and sifting. He rifled through a stack of binders and pulled out a map of the site. Swindell, a specialist in Native American archaeology, joined us. "It makes sense as a location," he said in the melodic drawl of eastern North Carolina. "You've got a Native American settlement right next door. We've found 275 pounds of Indian pottery from very early until the seventeenth century. This land has been intensively used for a thousand years."

The team dug six trenches during their first season in 2012, uncovering more English and Indian pottery and several Native American pits possibly used for storage. There was a scattering of iron slag and bits of brick. A dog burial came to light. This was clearly a place where the two cultures met. Some of the excavators thought they could make out postholes and ditches in the damp soil. The excited archaeologists speculated that they were finding remnants of Lost Colonists who had built a new settlement adjacent to the indigenous village. But to be sure, they needed to find artifacts and remains of buildings that could be precisely dated.

When the team returned the following summer, they brought along what looked like a jogging stroller that held a ground-penetrating radar device. Guiding it around the site, the expedition members mapped metal and disturbed soil under the field. The results were dramatic. Long shadowy lines under the earth, and the outlines of rectangular and circular structures or enclosures, suggested there had once been architecture here. Though there was no definitive proof yet, and they all knew of the failures of radar at Roanoke, the team was encouraged. "Evidence of an early colonial presence is definitely there and with it the real possibility that it occurred in the late sixteenth century," their 2013 report noted, adding that "an Elizabethan presence at Mettaquem opens up for us an opportunity to change the traditional, simple image of Settler vs. Indian." Indians and early Europeans here seemed to mingle together freely.

While researchers examined the earth, an underwater archaeologist used a similar radar tool to map the bottom of Salmon Creek, identifying the outline of what appeared to be a wooden ship. "The possibility exists that it is Elizabethan, and none of the boats left with the Lost Colonists has ever been found," the report noted. The scientist planned a future dive to examine the wreck and determine its age and origin.

As on Roanoke Island, however, the promising outlines in the soil turned out to be of later origin. What looked like postholes were roots of long-fallen trees. The iron-working areas dated much later. And some of the Indian pottery was made centuries before Columbus left Spain.

Undeterred, Luccketti and his team dug further. During the 2014 season, his excavators uncovered a few small L-shaped bits of metal that resembled similar artifacts found at early colonial Virginia sites. They could have been used to stretch the canvas of a tent or animal skins. These small pieces offered further hope. Two priming pans from firearms also appeared in the sorting screens. The archaeologists found one pan too worn to identify, but the second appeared to be from a popular late sixteenth- and seventeenth-century firearm. There was also an iron buckle that could date from either the sixteenth or the seventeenth century, as well as a lead seal similar to one found by Noël Hume at Fort Raleigh. These seals were fastened to bolts of finished cloth to certify their length and quality: a likely sign of trade goods.

The archaeologists also picked out aglets, the tiny tubes of metal used to secure a lace. Today they are the bits of plastic at the end of a shoelace, but in Elizabethan times they were common on clothing. Similar objects had been found on Roanoke during Luccketti's dig in the woods just northwest of the earthwork in 1995. A few have turned up at Virginia sites dating to the 1640s, but they appear less frequently after the time, suggesting the Site X artifacts could be Elizabethan.

Luccketti reached into a plastic bag and pulled out what he felt was their ace in the hole and handed it to me. The triangular-shaped piece of ceramic had a green and smooth outer surface, while the interior was reddish and rough. This was, he told me, one of several dozen bits of ceramic, made on the boundary between Surrey and Hampshire in southern England and therefore called Border ware.

It wasn't much to look at. Luccketti read my mind. "The mundane nature of this is what makes it important," he said. "If it was a pretty object, then the Indians might collect it." Native Americans viewed most European goods as exotic and therefore desirable. White found this out when his trunks, carefully hidden in a deep trench by the settlers, were dug up and looted by the time he returned in 1590. The Indians took everything they found useful. Even broken glass could be turned into arrowheads, which is why early English traders at Jamestown could sell rum, but not the bottles, to Indians.

Simple pottery, by contrast, was of little value because the Indians had their own. Luccketti felt confident that I was holding part of a bowl used by a Lost Colonist. "We think this was where they came after Governor White left," he said confidently. I handed the bit of ceramic back. "But couldn't this pottery be from one of Lane's 1585 and 1586 explorations?" I asked. "After all, we know he was in this area."

He slowly shook his head as he slid it back into the bag. The air was growing hot, and we were both sweating. "Lane's visit was too brief to produce lots of broken pots. The only likely owners were English who spent a good deal of time here, and that could only be the 1587 settlers."

But wasn't Border ware made long into the seventeenth century?

Yes, he acknowledged, the English imported Border ware well into the seventeenth century, so its presence alone doesn't necessarily point to Elizabethans. In fact, archaeologists dug out four pieces at a 1660s plantation house just a mile down the road. But, he said, its presence diminishes over time. Border ware accounts for more than a quarter of the ceramics found in a Jamestown well used from 1607 to 1610. A well used between 1616 and 1619 contained less than one in ten pieces. At a nearby settlement dating between 1630 and 1650, the figure drops to only one sherd in fifty. After 1650, it is a rarity—literally one piece in a thousand.

"Here, we've opened up forty square feet and found thirty sherds of Border ware making up three or four vessels," he said. "We think this represents the Roanoke colonists."

Later I asked Jacqui Pearce at the Museum of London Archaeology for her opinion. Pearce literally wrote the book on Border ware in 1992. At the time of the Roanoke voyages, she told me, potters began to make vessels in this style for cooking, eating, and drinking, as well as for bedpans, candlesticks, ink pots, and even chicken-feeding containers.

The pottery found at Site X, she added, appeared to be from a common form of dishes. This particular style, she explained, changed little from the sixteenth to the seventeenth century. That makes it difficult to assign even an approximate date to manufacture. Luccketti's claim hinges on the argument that if the pottery were from the post-1650 Carolina frontier, it wouldn't be found in such large quantities.

It was a good scientific theory, but a slim thread to carry the full weight of a Lost Colony solution. Pottery unearthed here that comes from a tall jar made in Devon may be a better candidate for an undeniably Elizabethan artifact. But the other material found so far at Site X—the hooks, the lead seal, the guns, the belt buckle—could conceivably be goods traded south from Jamestown decades later. Like the material Luccketti found on Roanoke Island, such as the European copper plates of an Indian necklace, the objects are intriguing but can't definitively be linked to the Lost Colonists.

Nevertheless, a few days after my visit, the First Colony Foundation announced at another crowded press conference that it had sixteenth-century artifacts pointing to the Lost Colonists. Luccketti's 2015 report maintained, "It cannot be a coincidence that the Indian village site labeled by the Elizabethans as Mettaquem, and identified as such by First Colony Foundation archaeologists, also contains English artifacts attributable to the period."

He stopped short, however, of claiming to have solved the mystery. "Our working hypothesis is that the Elizabethan artifacts at Site X represent perhaps a small group of survivors." This was not necessarily the Cittie of Raleigh, he suggested, but a smaller settlement built after White left and the colonists decamped upriver. Many of the resulting headlines and stories, however, didn't capture the nuances of "working hypothesis" or "perhaps." One Australian paper announced, "England's Lost Colonists 'Went Native' in America."

The notion that at least some of the settlers went where White suggests they planned to go, fifty miles inland, was a reasonable one. But I was skeptical that a few pieces of Border ware were enough to clinch the case. Subsequent excavations found more pottery but no sign of the fort suggested by the patch. Nor was there a silver bullet; there wasn't, say, the skeleton of a woman buried on her back, in an east-west orientation, reliably dated to before 1650. Such a find would be strong evidence for a Lost Colonist, because Indians placed their corpses on their side in the fetal position, and the Lane expedition was all male.

In the summer of 2017, Luccketti and his team donned hip waders to look for artifacts in the marsh just west of the main excavation site and recovered a few more pieces of the same pottery. "I think we've done enough work here at Site X," he told me, a note of natural pessimism in his voice. "We don't know exactly what we've got here. It remains a bit of an enigma." Luccketti said the foundation planned a new excavation—back on Roanoke Island. But, he added, "we would have to raise the money first." Meanwhile, the owner of Site X sold the land to a trust that intends to turn it over to the state, which will convert it to a park.

Unhappy with the direction that the work was taking, Brent Lane had by then resigned from the board. "It was getting too claustrophobic," he told me. "And I'm tired of the competition with the Hatteras folks." While the foundation focused on Site X, another team was working fifty miles south of Roanoke, on Hatteras Island. Lane made an annual pilgrimage to that rival camp to volunteer for a day or so, and the next time I saw him he was happily sifting through the sand and mud there.

"I greatly joyed that I had safely found a certain token of their safe being at Croatoan," Governor White had written after he found the carving on the post in 1590. Amazingly, it was only recently that anyone bothered to look for the Lost Colonists in the very place they said they went. Even then, it took a ferocious hurricane and a persistent wrestling coach to get the attention of archaeologists.

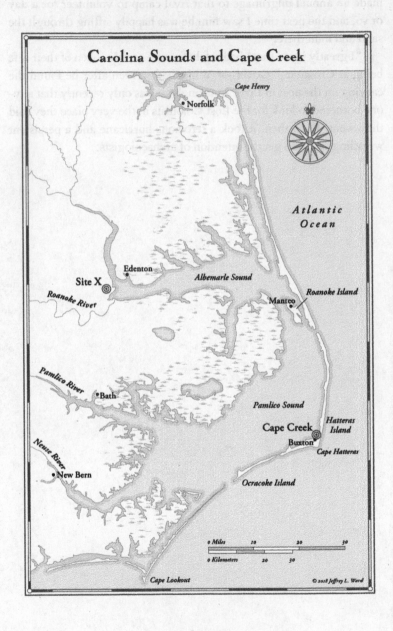

CHAPTER EIGHT

Pot of Brass

The name Croatoan, and its later equivalent, Croatan, has an exotic ring to it, akin to Atlantis or Shangri-La, but with a menacing undertone. In the long-running TV series *Supernatural*, in which two brothers hunt evil beings, it is a blood-borne virus created by "a demon of plague and pestilence." Lucifer himself releases the illness in order to kill off humans in a kind of demonic germ warfare. Stephen King evokes a haunting scene of bewitched islanders in the miniseries *Storm of the Century*, in which the awful word is carved not on a tree but on their foreheads as they jump, one by one, into a raging ocean.

It was, in fact, a dark and stormy night that launched the first concerted effort to find evidence of the settlers on Croatoan, what is today known as Hatteras Island. Just after midnight on September 1, 1993, a ten-foot surge of water driven by hundred-mile-per-hour winds rushed out of the Pamlico Sound and over the middle of the exposed barrier island. Boats lodged in trees, and a house floated half a mile away. The flood even wiped away rain gauge data on a chart at the National Weather Service station. No one on the island drowned, but Hurricane Emily left a quarter of the population homeless.

"It was terrifying," said Fred Willard, a hulking onetime Maryland marina owner and race car driver nicknamed the "Wildman" who had relocated to the island a few years earlier to fish and coach the high school wrestling team (including a young Scott Dawson). "I never want to live on that island again."

After the storm passed, Willard and his then-girlfriend, Barbara Midgette, walked down a gravel road that runs between the Pamlico Sound and a little waterway called Cape Creek, at the bend in the L-shaped Hatteras. Amid the half-buried car tires and broken kayak paddles, they spotted fragments of pottery, clay tobacco pipes, and other Native American objects. "We picked up all the artifacts that we could," he said later. "Everyone told me that I needed Dr. Phelps."

Dr. David Phelps was an archaeologist at East Carolina University in Greenville, a three-hour drive west of Hatteras, and nearing retirement as a preeminent authority on prehistoric Indians in eastern North Carolina. Willard called the academic and urged him to visit. Months passed. "He kept postponing," said Willard. In August 1994, Willard loaded some of the objects in his truck and drove to Greenville to confront Phelps in person. "We almost had to put him in a body bag to get him to come."

When Willard showed up at his office door, Phelps already knew that Native Americans had lived for centuries on this stretch of rolling dunes covered in dense stands of gnarled water oaks bordering the Pamlico. Archaeologists first recorded the site in 1956, and Phelps did a brief excavation there three decades later, uncovering intriguing evidence of fish- or meat-smoking racks, windbreaks, and possibly a longhouse along with Native American pottery mixed in with shellfish remains and animal bones. He already suspected the site could shed light on the Roanoke voyages. Quinn had noted long before the oddity that except for one stray casting counter unearthed by a local on Hatteras in the early twentieth century, no artifacts associated with the Elizabethans had been found there.

"The Cape Creek site offers one of the best opportunities to thoroughly investigate an English-Algonquian contact town . . . which figured prominently in friendly relations with the 1587 colony," Phelps wrote at the time. "Every effort should be made to conduct excavations there." He was more interested, however, in learning about the Native Americans than in pursuing Lost Colonists, and no other researcher dared infringe on his turf.

At the time of the Roanoke voyages, a shallow inlet severed Hatteras to the north from Croatoan to the south. The village was perched just southwest of this waterway. The location provided easy access via the creek to both the Pamlico and the inlet, and plentiful freshwater ponds drew migrating birds, while thick forests were home to possum, squirrel, and herds of deer. Patches of loamy soil made it possible to cultivate corn, beans, and squash. Whelk hoes recovered by excavators make it clear the land was suitable for growing crops. Unlike most of the Outer Banks, this area could support full-time human occupation in prehistoric times; according to a de Bry engraving based on a long-lost White map, there were three villages strung along the fifteen-mile island. Quinn was wrong when he maintained that Croatoan was "unsuitable for an agricultural colony."

The English were nearly as familiar with the island as they were with Roanoke. Amadas and Barlowe almost certainly visited in 1584, and twenty men landed here with Grenville's fleet the following year. This is where Lane sent a group of his starving men in the spring of 1586 to keep watch for a resupply vessel and live off Croatoan hospitality. The next summer, White dispatched a delegation here to gather intelligence on the political situation after Howe's slaying. It also was the home of Manteo, who the governor said "had his mother and many of his kindred dwelling in that island." This unusual notice given to a woman may signal that she was an important figure in this matriarchal culture. Which village was Manteo's birthplace is not known, though Cape Creek is an obvious candidate.

Despite this well-known history, it took Willard's tenacity to prompt the archaeologist to launch a large-scale excavation of the site in 1995. While Phelps's focus was on Native American life, the possibility of finding artifacts relating to the Roanoke voyages made it easy to round up volunteers to help with the dirty work of digging, sifting, and sorting. "Everybody who lives here has a theory about what happened to the Lost Colony," one said to a reporter at the time. "And, secretly, in everybody's heart, there's a hope that we'll find something to link them here."

On a fall afternoon in 1998, the team finished digging a trench in a small clearing surrounded by water oak. One worker hoisted a bucket of soil into a screened box, while another sprayed the mix of mud and sand to expose any artifacts. A lump of earth dissolved into a metal form: a chunky ring. It was incised with the image of a prancing lion on its round setting. There was a sheen that looked to some like gold. Nothing like it had ever been found anywhere in the region.

The discovery transformed the sober, elder academic, a specialist in Native American prehistory and a man who quietly disdained those chasing after the Lost Colony, into an excited schoolchild. "Dr. Phelps just went totally ballistic," Midgette told a local reporter shortly after the find. "He danced around. There was just sheer elation." Charles Heath, a graduate student working at the site that day, remembers it a little differently. "We all realized it was special and mysterious," he told me, "but I really don't remember Phelps dancing around the site." The archaeologist himself, with what the journalist called "a broad smile," acknowledged that "everybody was screaming and excited, let's put it that way."

The find bore all the hallmarks of a signet ring used by an Elizabethan man of rank to place his mark on documents using hot wax. In his unpublished field notes, Phelps described tersely what happened next. "Took signet ring from Sq M0H, Zone IIIA, Level 2 to Frank Riddick Jewelry in Nags Head for assay." Phelps returned with the exciting news that the jeweler determined it was made from 18-karat gold. No gold signet ring of this sort had ever been found in North America. Only one has been found since; owned by a Jamestown colonist who arrived in 1619, it features a skull and crossbones with the owner's initials.

The Cape Creek ring came from an Indian trash pit that had other European goods dating to the late seventeenth and early eighteenth centuries, or a century after the Roanoke voyages. Phelps, however, assigned it a late sixteenth-century date because it resembled pre-1600 rings in British collections. The artifact "is the first direct tie-in we'd had with the Roanoke colonies," he said to a *Virginian-Pilot* journalist, who described his voice "wavering with excitement." Phelps added, "That doesn't mean the Lost Colony was here, but this begins to authenticate that." The ring, the story added, "offers breathtaking new clues to the 400-year-old mystery of the Lost Colony."

The archaeologist had the first physical clue pointing to the settlers on Croatoan since Lawson mentioned the gray eyes of the Hatteras Indians. Newspapers soon reported Phelps had found a link between the ring and the Kendall family, two of whom were associated with the voyages. Yet he published no research paper on the artifact, which exerted a Gollum-like response in its finder. He kept the ring for years at his Florida retirement home. Locals groused that the archaeologist had absconded with an Outer Banks treasure. Only when East Carolina University officials threatened to take legal action did he grudgingly return it—in unregistered mail.

Much more was found in five seasons of excavations, including thousands of bits of bone and pottery and the small figure of a human cut out of European copper but clearly made into a Native American design. Phelps never published a single word on any of it. Squirreled away in plastic bags and boxes, the trove remains locked away and largely unstudied in an ECU storage room. "Signet Ring Crowned N.C. Archaeologist's Career" was the headline of his March 2009 obituary. Meanwhile, its prancing lion languished in a campus library vault.

The fall after Phelps's death, a new team arrived on the scene at Cape Creek. "Pity that the colonists have been lost twice—first by the English and then by the archaeologists," Mark Horton said. "Ironic that now there's a Brit on the case. We lost it, so I guess it is up to us to find it again." He was sitting at a folding table under a canopy of live-oak trees, peering at a tiny circular piece of metal that had just come out of a small trench close to where Phelps found the ring. "From Virginia Dare's bodice?" he asked, holding it up and looking at me mischievously.

It had been more than a year since I'd first met Horton, the University of Bristol archaeologist whose offhand comment at a dinner in Cambridge had inadvertently sent me down the Lost Colony rabbit hole. Horton is inexorably drawn to hard-to-solve mysteries. In a Panamanian swamp, he uncovered Scotland's version of the Lost Colony, which had brought financial ruin to that country a century after

Raleigh's voyages. "It's an interesting parallel to Roanoke," he said. "Another grand scheme that went awry." Now he was drawn to the place that Hakluyt and Raleigh had bet would prove to be England's Panama.

Though he's over sixty, Horton's round figure and red cheeks are those of an overgrown English schoolboy, as is his irrepressible enthusiasm. He is the antithesis of the Harrison Ford image of an archaeologist. He hates hats and, to the dismay of his dig team, refuses to wear a belt around his perpetually sagging trousers. His lackluster hygiene is a source of constant distress to his fellow excavators. Disliking cold, he prefers excavating comfortably close to the equator. Given to spontaneous exclamations like "Right!" and "Cheers!" Horton is a human Google on most matters historical and archaeological.

The voluble archaeologist is also a minor media star in Britain; it is difficult to walk down a village street without an elderly woman accosting him with the phrase "Haven't I seen you on the telly?" His credits include appearances on a show about the British coastline as well as *Julius Caesar and the Druids*. He consulted on a mercifully short-lived drama called *Bonekickers*, with Hugh Bonneville of *Downton Abbey* fame playing a character based on the Bristol archaeologist (the *Guardian* called it "a clattering bag of madness" that "was utterly bonkers but curiously satisfying").

Horton was drawn into Roanoke's vortex as a result of a comic mix-up. Years earlier, a representative from the town of Manteo showed up in the little west English port town of Bideford with an elaborate brass clock. It was meant as a goodwill gift to Manteo's sister city, home to Sir Richard Grenville, who led the fleet carrying the Lane expedition. The gift puzzled the Bideford town clerk, because no one in city hall could recall the American twin. Nor had he heard of the North Carolina city. "I googled Manteo and saw it was colonized by the English during the exploration of the New World, but couldn't find a link with us," he told a reporter. Newspapers in both countries picked up the amusing story. "Twin Town Twits U.S. Man," read London's *Daily Mail*.

Stung by the publicity, the mayor, Andy Powell, invited Horton to lecture on Bideford's link with the New World. Fascinated, Powell began to read up on the voyages. Eager to know more, he was put in touch with Scott Dawson, the man who discovered Fort Blob on Roanoke Island. Dawson grew up near Cape Creek on Hatteras, and he watched with alarm as wealthy outsiders bought up land in the area to build massive summer homes with views of the sound. Despite being designated by the State of North Carolina as an important archaeological site, no state or federal laws protect the site from destruction.

Dawson told Powell that construction workers claimed to find old swords and human bones as they dug foundations. "One crew said they filled a bunch of black Hefty trash bags with bones and reburied them, so they wouldn't have to stop working," Dawson recalled later. "They were probably Indian, but the guys said they were buried in a row"—a European rather than Native American tradition. When Powell and Horton visited Hatteras at Dawson's invitation in late 2009, he urged them to organize a professional excavation before it was too late.

The wooded lot where Phelps dug had not yet been developed, but the owner refused to allow the archaeologists access. Many locals were still bitter that Phelps hauled away their island's heritage. Dawson's status as a local helped secure permission, however, from the owner of a nearby lot. With funding from a philanthropist and volunteer help, Horton and his team of British students began digging.

Almost nothing was known about the early history of Croatoan, which was renamed Hatteras in the late seventeenth century after a storm filled in the inlet separating the two barrier islands. Lawson noted the presence of Indians on his visit in 1701; they fought on the English side in the subsequent Tuscarora War and were rewarded with sixteen bushels of corn. By then, European settlers had begun to encroach on their land, and in 1731 only half a dozen or so remained in "Indian Town." Within another few decades they had all but vanished. Horton's finds revealed that the two groups traded with each other while retaining their own separate communities.

But the British archaeologist itched to dig closer to where Phelps found the ring and other artifacts that dated a century or so earlier. When bulldozer operators building a driveway on an adjacent lot sliced through a three-foot-high thick deposit of Native American material, Dawson wrangled approval from the owner to excavate a trench nearby, starting in the spring of 2013.

By then Dawson, now a schoolteacher, and his wife, Maggie, a nurse, had formed the Croatoan Archaeological Society to oversee the work. Organizing cookouts and concerts, they raised money to fly the British team to the United States and pledged to keep the artifacts on the Outer Banks. They recruited friends and family to assist Horton's students. By giving talks at the local library and conducting excavations behind the local secondary school, the team overcame the community's initial wariness.

Vacationing BBC reporter Nick Knowles volunteered to work the sieves that March. "The Lost Colony is a story I had been slightly obsessed with for years," he recalled. "So I jumped at the chance to take a few days off from work to fly out and join the dig." That day, "just as the next bucket was being tipped in, I saw the shape and put my hand over it to protect it. I knew straightaway what it was. I had just seen the ones on display at Fort Raleigh."

Knowles had picked out a token made in Nuremberg like the ones Harrington found in 1950 at Fort Raleigh. Though later specialists pegged those tokens as dating to later than 1586—and therefore more likely of Jamestown than Roanoke vintage—Horton maintained the artifact was strong evidence for Elizabethans. "The only time that Roanoke and Hatteras are linked was in the late sixteenth century," Horton stubbornly insisted. "The art historians are simply wrong."

The same day Knowles found the German token, the team also uncovered a chunk of smelted copper with traces of lead, tin, and antimony, suggesting that metalworking similar to that conducted by Gans on Roanoke was taking place here as well. The metal proved to be European in origin. While the token might have been passed along in trade, the chunk of smelted copper, Horton argued, showed that Europeans were not just passing through; they were conducting metallurgical work beyond the abilities of Native Americans in that day.

In 2015, after years of patient negotiations, Dawson finally won access to the site that Phelps excavated. The hilly patch of dune was covered in twisted live oaks and lay between a marsh and the Pamlico Sound, one of the last undeveloped lots on the road.

"It was the mother lode," Horton told me one morning as he showed me around the site. The extensive shell deposits from the left-overs of Indian meals seemed to show continuous occupation in the sixteenth and seventeenth centuries. Phelps believed there was a gap in occupation in the decades around the time of the Roanoke voyages, but Horton's unpublished results strongly suggest the continued Native American presence, a finding backed up by the village noted at the site on the de Bry map.

One afternoon Horton's dig director, Charlotte Gouge, came across a hunk of iron as big as an orange while working with her trowel in a trench not far from where the ring was found. "There was a cylindrical ball shape on the end that caught my eye," she said. With Horton's approval, Dawson took it back to his garage. "I fried it." More precisely, he applied electricity to the lump in order to reverse

University of Bristol archaeologist Mark Horton, right, ponders a new trench on the Cape Creek site on Hatteras. The dig is operated and funded by the local Croatoan Archaeological Society.

the oxidation that took place while it lay for four centuries or so in the damp ground. The conservation process, called electrolysis, shed the rust and revealed a distinct shape.

"I picked a cold night because you immerse the object into a liquid that evaporates in warm air," Dawson explained. After zapping it, "I knew immediately what it was." He then applied museum-quality wax to protect the surfaces from air that might trigger further rusting. Dawson recalled showing the cleaned artifact the next morning to Horton, who was dumbfounded. "Scott!" the archaeologist cried. "That's a rapier!"

The full weapon is a slender straight blade with two edges and an elaborate hilt, and it grew in popularity after its invention early in the sixteenth century. French, Spanish, and Italian soldiers or gentlemen of the era called it an épée, as modern fencers still do. By the 1570s it appeared in England under the term "rapier," which may derive from the Spanish word for elegant clothes. It was what today we call a dress sword.

Dawson's electrolysis revealed part of the rapier's handle, complete with a sweeping ring that curved down to protect the hand of its wielder. Somehow a gentleman's dress sword found its way to an old Native American trash dump. The style, Horton concluded, fit late-sixteenth-century models. And because a gentleman was unlikely to part with his rapier, and less likely to sell it, it seemed an unusual trade item to turn up on a remote barrier island decades after its manufacture in England.

Like the ring, the rapier was a tantalizing clue pointing to Elizabethans living on Croatoan. One breezy April evening, I drove to the dig house, a beach cottage that doubled as bunk room and laboratory for the annual excavation season. I waited as a herd of deer trotted across the road as the lighthouse beam swiveled above the dune grass. Horton was on a sofa drinking beer as his students bustled about, cataloging turtle bones and washing pottery on the porch while others cooked pasta. He was suffering from his first bout of poison ivy, after refusing advice to wash immediately, and one eye was red and puffy. He paused periodically between swigs to scratch his bottom, which apparently was likewise affected. ("When he uses my phone, I want to wash it off immediately," one of his assistants told me.) "Right!" he said ebulliently by way of greeting, and hauled himself up to rummage through a plastic box as his trousers fell to alarming levels. "Mark!" exclaimed several exasperated students simultaneously.

"Aha!" He handed me the bit of sword hilt, ignoring their outrage. It was a small curving piece of metal designed to protect the wielder's hand. "You could argue that this is Manteo's. After all, he was made a lord and likely given a rapier in the ceremony."

The image was seductive: Manteo returning to his Indian village as an English lord in velvet and taffeta finery with a gentleman's dress sword. Alternatively, the object might have belonged to one of the Lost Colonists, perhaps a Cittie of Raleigh assistant who had purchased the status item before the voyage after receiving his coat of arms. It also could have been exchanged for food by a hungry Lane settler in the hard days of 1586, or even been given, traded, or stolen from one of the men left on the island at Grenville's 1585 arrival.

Horton believed these and other artifacts, like the ring, copper bun, and evidence that people were making lead balls to shoot guns, were proof of Elizabethans among the people of Croatoan. Metalworking certainly suggested Europeans were here for a long period of time, not just on a brief visit. And if the items were made and used by Native Americans, they had to obtain the technology as well as the materials.

The lives of the Croatoan clearly underwent dramatic changes between 1600 and 1700, before a new wave of English began to settle the Outer Banks. For example, the protein of choice switched from surf to turf. Through painstaking analysis of thousands of bits of bone and shell, Horton's team members discovered that the locals began to leave behind far fewer fish and turtle remains and many more deer and bird bones. The simplest explanation for this shift was the introduction of firearms. The people of Cape Creek were making lead shot and also using dress pins, a sign that the Indians had adopted Western clothes along with weapons. One scholar says, "The fashionable Elizabethan woman was a walking pincushion." But pins are notoriously difficult to date, because their shape did not change much over the centuries.

"They are living as Native Americans, but we're finding material culture to suggest they are wearing clothes and living a partly European lifestyle," Horton added, then paused reflectively as he explored his left nostril and rubbed his reddened eye.

For Horton, the Cape Creek finds revealed the pivotal moment when Old World met the New World as the Elizabethans shared their technical knowledge with the Croatoan, who in turn trained them in the ways of surviving in a strange environment. They became a hybrid culture even before the second wave of English colonists arrived. As far as Horton was concerned, he had all but resolved the four-century-plus mystery.

Taking a last swig from his bottle, however, he acknowledged a serious gap in his carefully constructed theory. Much of what seemed Elizabethan was mixed together with other artifacts dating to the second half of the seventeenth century, at least six decades after White's 1590 voyage. "It's deeply problematic that this stuff turns up two generations later," he had admitted earlier that day. "Can I have another beer?" he called out plaintively to no one in particular. The students did not interrupt their tasks to reply, much less comply.

All the possible goods that Horton claimed were owned by Raleigh's settlers, in other words, might be trade items pawned off on Indians from the English settlements sprouting along Chesapeake Bay in the seventeenth century. The rapier might be an old-model sword traded south from Jamestown decades later. An antiquated gun might end up in the hold of a ship bound for the Chesapeake and then be sold for deerskin or corn. Even a chunk of European copper might simply be a sign that a passing trader or a castaway showed a local Indian how to melt down and hammer out a pleasing shape.

Native American trade networks stretched hundreds and even thousands of miles long before Europeans arrived; the copper worn by Carolina and Virginia Algonquian chiefs and the stones of their axes came from distant mines and outcrops, and their shell beads were traded far to the west. Native Americans also were adept at making any object useful. Horton's team found a tiny piece of glass shaped into an arrowhead. Everything that Horton found could have made its way to Croatoan without the involvement of a Roanoke colonist.

I fingered the earliest clearly dated object found by Horton's team, a metal disk made in Antwerp and stamped with the year 1644. Called a coin weight, it verified that a gold or silver coin actually weighed the amount specified by the government producing it. Others retrieved, including one measuring the weight of Hungarian ducats, were made in 1648. But Horton had an answer for why what he insisted were sixteenth-century artifacts were mixed with such later objects.

"We've excavated other bits across Hatteras Island, and this Elizabethan material doesn't turn up; it is just here," he said. There was something special about Cape Creek. "What if the rapier was an heirloom, until it became too worn and broken that they threw it away? Oh, there's Granddad's old sword in the corner rusting away, why are we keeping that!"

The Lost Colonists, he went on, would have held on to their precious reminders of home—a sword, a cloak, a Nuremberg token emblazoned with a cross—until the objects were too worn or lost their meaning. In the meantime, they began to obtain trade items as the European presence to the north increased. "If you can explain the social context, then it suddenly makes sense. The things we are finding are not those they would be trading from Jamestown anyway!"

While it is true that selling guns and swords and even bottles to Indians was forbidden in the early years of the Virginia colony, there is little doubt that hungry settlers were willing to part with whatever they had for food. Powhatan, for example, acquired hundreds of swords, despite the ban. As compelling as Horton's vision was—Natives and Lost Colonists peacefully learning from each other—it wasn't the only explanation for how European material ended up in the Cape Creek village.

Horton smiled indulgently at my skepticism and then poked around in another plastic box. He triumphantly pulled out a plastic bag containing an object he was sure clinched his case. It was a sliver of dark stone no bigger than a half dollar found in 2015 next to what resembled a lead pencil. "I immediately thought of Jamestown," he said with satisfaction.

Several years earlier, archaeologists working there uncovered a similar, though larger, piece of slate, incised with faint marks. A combination of high-tech NASA analysis and drugstore talcum powder revealed that it was the oldest European drawing pad known in North America. The Jamestown slate was crammed with pictures of birds, lions, and a man in a ruff smoking a pipe, as well as two symbols, possibly copied from Harriot's long-vanished Algonquian dictionary. "Slate and chalk are easily found in England, and you could make a note or a list or sketch anything," Sloan from the British Museum told me later. Sometimes a lead pencil was used to cut an image so that it would be indelible.

Horton's slate was even smaller and the incisions fainter than the one at Jamestown. He photographed the surface and magnified it back in Bristol. "I saw it and said, egads!" he recalled as I examined the tiny bit of rock. "What it is actually showing is quite clearly the murder of Wingina!"

He could make out a soldier in an Elizabethan-style outfit shooting a gun at the neck of a Native American dressed with a headband and two feathers. And the only person who might have drawn this scene of Lane's men assassinating the Indian leader, he believed, was the artist on the 1585 expedition: John White. This, therefore, was the governor's personal writing tablet portraying a European soldier firing point blank at an indigenous man.

He grabbed his laptop and flopped back on the sofa. After opening a file with a magnified image, he handed the computer to me. I could make out two lines that might be a gun barrel and the outline of what was conceivably an Indian head resembling the one on the old nickel. There were dots suggesting bullets in between, but I felt like I was gazing at the summer sky with a friend who imagines a rabbit in a cloud. "Can anyone see the soldier here?" Horton called out to the room. "It is very obvious when you see it." Reactions were mixed. "I'm dubious," said one team member who bent over my shoulder. "If you squint," said another. The scratches, I said, all seemed so impossibly small, though Horton gleefully parried that White was a talented miniaturist. In this he was right; the artist's drawing of the fort Lane had built in Puerto Rico includes the minuscule image of the flagship *Tiger* painted in such detail that the awning over the stern deck is clearly visible.

If the archaeologist was correct, then the slate depicted one of the most important moments in American colonial history, the first murder of an Indian leader by the English, and one that sealed the fate of the Roanoke voyages. The event served as a grim harbinger of subsequent violence perpetrated by European Americans.

I tagged along a few days later when he took the object to the same NASA center that examined the Jamestown artifact. Technicians put it in a chamber to obtain high-precision three-dimensional X-ray images—3,142 to be exact. Gathering all that data took less than an hour, but that would be just the start; the information then required extensive and expert tweaking to provide anything like a better close-up. Busy with other projects, Horton had not quite gotten to it a year later. When I tried to reach him, I was told he was in Zanzibar or, no, was it Madagascar? Months later he emailed me that his slate analysis was not yet complete. "I am still not totally happy with it," he wrote, "but as you know I think this remains our best evidence. I still think there is clearly an image of a soldier, but I am sure you must think its looking into clouds."

I felt frustrated by the slow pace of research. Horton was juggling too many projects to bring his full attention to bear on his Cape Creek finds. But there was, I realized, one artifact outside his control that might yield fresh results, the one that ignited the search for Roanoke settlers on Hatteras in the first place.

The ring that Phelps found at Cape Creek in 1998, hailed as a potential major breakthrough, still rests in the library vault at East Carolina University. Amid all the muddy potsherds and bits of copper, this glamorous object seemed the only personal link to Raleigh's colony. But because Phelps published no scholarly reports on the artifact, the only information I could find was in old news clips.

A local historian in Manteo filled in some of the gaps. She studied the ring shortly after its discovery and had asked a friend, John Brooke-Little from London's College of Arms, to take a look. The college granted White and his assistants coats of arms four centuries earlier.

Recently retired, Brooke-Little had served at Queen Elizabeth II's coronation and was known for sporting a long cape while commuting on the subway. He named one of his sons Merlin.

When I visited the Manteo researcher, who requested anonymity, in her windowless office at Fort Raleigh, she dug out of a crammed file cabinet a handwritten response that she received from the heraldry expert after sending him photographs of the ring. "The seal and drawing is quite clear," he wrote on October 27, 1998. "It is a lion passant; the tail is not erect and shown in the way in which it is usually drawn." Brooke-Little added, "I have done a couple of hours research at home in my library and I find that a family of Kendall of Devon and Cornwall are credited with a lion passant crest, although preliminary research seems to indicate that this was not officially recorded."

His response excited the Manteo historian, who has devoted a large portion of the past several decades to unraveling Roanoke's innumerable historical knots (she found, for instance, the record of Eleanor Dare's birth in London). She knew two Kendalls were associated with the Roanoke voyages. A Master Kendall was part of Lane's 1585 expedition, while Abraham Kendall was aboard Francis Drake's 1586 fleet that rescued the colony leader and his men. Either man might have traded or lost his ring while on Croatoan, though neither was linked to the Lost Colony.

"So we had a strong suggestion of the presence of a man with the right name to a crest of a ring that was found," she told me. "Reasonable enough. But that needed in-depth research." She informed Phelps that Brooke-Little's results were preliminary, and proposed a ten-thousand-dollar project focused on a study of the ring. "The College of Arms is notorious for burning up money. Of course [Phelps] never got the money, so I have not pursued it beyond the original research," the researcher added. "And Brooke-Little"—who died in 2006—"did not follow up."

It seemed a promising thread to follow. So while in London, I made an appointment with a herald at the imposing seventeenth-century compound that houses the college, in the heart of the capital. A gold crown surmounted the iron gate leading into a broad courtyard. The top of St. Paul's cathedral dome peeked out above the dormered roof.

Inside, the lobby seemed more an altar of a wealthy nature cult than a memorial to English genealogy. Behind an elaborate polished balustrade sat a wooden throne empty save for a purple cushion. On the step below the throne was a golden lion the size of a Chihuahua and the miniature head of a black elephant embracing a small sword with its trunk.

A balding man with a ruddy face and checked shirt and tie popped out from behind a thick oak door. Christopher John Fletcher-Vane, son of a baron and the current Portcullis Pursuivant of Arms in Ordinary, ushered me briskly through the same door and bounded up several flights of stairs. "I haven't been a herald long," he explained apologetically as I tried to keep up. "I was a barrister for forty years, but I studied archaeology at Cambridge and excavated an Anglo-Saxon palace." His office was heavy with bookcases and oil portraits of men with white wigs. One particularly forbidding face was that of his ancestor who served as royal governor of Massachusetts and helped found Harvard College, where George Bancroft would later resurrect Virginia Dare and recast the Roanoke story as a romantic tale.

Heralds began as sports announcers. They kept score at medieval jousts. To call out the correct names of combatants, they had to know the shields and crests used by the contestants encased in armor. That expertise made them useful to the crown. In 1484, King Richard III set up the College of Arms to corral the growing menagerie of supporting dragons and jumping unicorns and to grant new ones for up-and-coming families favored by the monarch. The college still oversees royal ceremonies like the opening of Parliament, while doing pay-the-bills genealogical work and producing fresh coats of arms for those who want a little more toff in their tree.

I showed Fletcher-Vane a high-resolution picture of the ring but didn't mention the name Kendall.

"The lion looks to me to be the crest, since it is not shown on a shield." He explained that the crest is what rests on top of a shield that contains the coat of arms, a nod to its use on jousting helmets. He frowned. "But there are an awful lot of lions in heraldry. I can show you a published book on crests and everyone has a lion passant. It is quite difficult to find a list of crests in circulation then. Many people just made them up, and we had no way to stop them. There are lots of self-assumed lions rampant or passant. I'll show you this book, and you will be horrified at the number of lions passant. It's a tragedy, that's what this is."

He explained that a "beast rampant" is an animal rearing into the air with three paws raised, while a "beast passant" stands with only one paw off the ground. Then he dashed down the stairs and led me to a small corner room dominated by an ancient copy machine and crammed with books from floor to ceiling. He pulled a thick leather-bound book from the shelves containing countless family names associated with the lion passant crest. I mentioned Brooke-Little's theory about Kendall. "I find that pretty far-fetched," he said, flipping through pages. "Kendall is not listed in any of these books." He was also skeptical that a colonist would have had the status to wear a gold signet ring. Fletcher-Vane looked up Ralph Lane's family crest, which is a lion rampant rather than passant.

"Let's look for John White, shall we?" he exclaimed suddenly. He led me across the lobby and into a hushed hall filled with oversized leather-bound books. Two elderly men bent silently over large volumes. Though it was a bright spring day outside, the dark wood and profound silence gave the main library a tomb-like air. After some discussions with the librarian and a phone call to a nearby office, a young archivist in a pink sweater appeared with a long blue box.

She unrolled a scroll-like document and spread it across a long table. Dated January 7, 1587, and titled "Grant of Arms for the City of Raleigh in Virginia, and for Its Governor and Assistants," the document notes the "expedient and ancient custom" of honoring men "employed in the most honorable service of God, their prince, or country in peace or war."

This was one of three copies of the only known document associated with the Cittie of Raleigh corporation, the one that mentions White and his twelve assistants. I spotted the name of George Howe, the colonist killed just a week after his arrival in the New World. "He was clubbed to death," I said a little too loudly, pointing at the name. The archivist looked at me with ill-concealed alarm.

Fletcher-Vane concluded that neither White nor any of his Lost Colonists were likely to have owned a gold signet ring. "If you were granted a coat of arms and you were leaving for America in ten days' time, you don't rush off and get a ring with a crest," he said as the archivist rolled the charter back up. "That's just common sense." He paused for a moment. "Are you sure this ring is gold?" he asked.

All I knew was what I had read in Phelps's unpublished notes. As I left, he suggested I contact the nearby Victoria and Albert Museum, which houses the world's largest collection of decorative arts and might be able to offer further insight.

"Lions seem to have been a popular choice," Rachel Church told me after looking over pictures of the Cape Creek ring. She was the museum curator who specialized in signet rings. "We have examples in our collection made in gold, silver, bronze, and brass and of varying degrees of quality." Church showed me a picture of a gold ring from the early seventeenth century in the collection that was owned by Sir Walter Raleigh's brother-in-law. The deeply etched eagle opening its wings was striking, far more detailed and carefully carved than the rougher outlines on Phelps's ring.

Even as a layperson, I could see its quality and sheen were of a far higher caliber than the Cape Creek artifact. "I would have guessed that yours was more likely to be brass than gold," she added.

If the ring were brass, then it was unlikely to be a special possession worn by an Elizabethan noble. "It would be the kind of thing you could have walked into a London stationer's shop and get off the shelf," archaeologist Bly Straube told me when I got back to the United States. "It is not specially made for you or your family." Yet for Native Americans, the cheap alloy was at the time highly desirable. Brass signet rings from the late seventeenth century turn up in Indian graves in Quebec, Rhode Island, and Jamestown.

I visited the Manteo historian again at Fort Raleigh, and she fished a notecard out of her battered file cabinet written by Phelps on January 19, 1999, that accompanied a photograph of the ring. "The jeweler who cleaned it remarked on its hardness, which indicates a carat-count between 10 and 14 carats—goodly content of silver and copper in the alloy. The ring is a size 10 (just my size!). More later."

Then I searched out Frank Riddick, the jeweler whom Phelps said he consulted in his unpublished report. He no longer owns a jewelry shop but has a charter company called Fishy Bizness. Riddick readily recalled the archaeologist's visit nearly two decades before. "He showed up one day at my shop and wanted to know if it was gold or not," he said. "There weren't many jewelers on the Outer Banks then."

Jewelers, he explained, typically scratch the surface of a gold ring to make sure it is not just plated, and they can determine the karat using an acid. "But since this wasn't about buying or selling, we didn't do that. I just told him that I thought it was gold." Riddick said he hadn't conducted any tests on the ring. His offhand opinion, like Brooke-Little's "preliminary research," had morphed into accepted fact.

Next I called Charles Ewen, an archaeologist at East Carolina University who had known Phelps. He agreed to take the ring from the vault to subject it to X-ray fluorescence to determine its precise elemental composition. We met early one afternoon at a student hangout on the fringe of campus. Ewen is a genial academic who inherited Phelps's position but has tried, with mixed success, to steer clear of the Roanoke vortex. "I don't have any theories about the settlers," he told me and then proceeded to give me his. "Except that they probably tried to sail home in the pinnace and drowned."

He told me that he was interviewed about the ring by the Russian website *Pravda*, which was unable to obtain an image of the object; instead it used a picture of Tolkien's ring of Mordor. "Do you want to see my precious?" he asked, his voice sinking into a Gollum-like croak.

Ewen reached for his worn leather satchel and pulled out a small white box. He opened the lid and handed it to me like an engagement ring. The object was chunkier than in the photographs, a little bigger than a fraternity ring. The stylized lion that roared within its round setting looked blurry. The metal had a muted sheen that gave off a dull greenish-yellow luster.

We drove to a nearby facility where archaeologists are conserving remains from Blackbeard's flagship. Erik Farrell, a scruffy young man in a T-shirt, greeted us in a small lab with a large white table flanked by black file cabinets. He extracted what looked like a cross between a ray gun and a hair dryer from a black case and set the instrument upright on a Lucite stand. "The X-rays hit the thing and bounce back, and the results show up here," he said with a nod to a laptop screen as he pulled green latex gloves over his hands. "Each element has its own distinct signal."

Farrell seated the artifact on top of a small metal disk above the snout of the device and flipped a switch. As Ewen and I leaned over the screen, a series of peaks, like those on a heart monitor, appeared from left to right. "Yep," Farrell said. "See these blue lines? They should peak here if this was gold. And they don't. There's no gold. Only copper."

Ewen smacked the side of his head. "Wow, wow, wow!" he exclaimed, his academic detachment suddenly out the window. "It's a brass ring! *MythBusters* here!" Farrell confirmed that the ring was made of a brass alloy; small amounts of zinc and lead were mixed in with copper and a trace of silver. "In this period, you get trace silver in copper," he added. There was no sign that it was even gilded.

"The ring is just the latest modern myth about the Lost Colony," said Ewen as we drove away from the lab to return the ring to the library vault. "It's not gold and it is not likely to be related to the Kendalls." A passing storm over the snow-white cotton fields left behind a bright rainbow that seemed to mock my efforts. We looked at the dramatic sight in silence for a moment. Then Ewen spoke. "Pot of brass."

I was starting to feel like John White trying to return to Roanoke. Every time it seemed I was well on the way to confirming a new clue—the pottery at Site X, Cape Creek's rapier, and now the ring—the rug felt pulled from underneath my feet. So when I heard the rumor about Simão Fernandes, I was primed to be skeptical but could not resist pursuing the intriguing tip.

CHAPTER NINE

Rejoicing in Things Stark Naughty

Few people besides Quinn have thought so long and hard about the Roanoke voyages as Karen Kupperman, now a professor emerita at New York University and a leading authority on the venture. On a bitter winter afternoon in Manhattan, we met for the first time at a café, moving in silent agreement to find a table as far from the chill blasts emanating from the front door as possible. Kupperman wore green-framed glasses and short gray hair, and at first she seemed reserved. She patiently endured an hour or so of my questions about sources, Quinn, and her own theories about Roanoke. By the time we had ordered coffee, she appeared convinced that I was serious about the quest and also not seriously disturbed. "You can't be too careful," she explained later. As I would learn, the Lost Colony mystery draws more than its share of obsessives.

"Have you heard about the woman in Portugal who claimed to have found Simão Fernandes's papers?" Kupperman asked me, leaning forward and slightly lowering her voice. "The whole story is crazy. I can send you her name."

Fernandes was the Portuguese pilot on all three major Roanoke expeditions, as well as White's archnemesis. More than any single person, he is blamed for the failure of the governor's colony after refusing to carry the settlers north to the Chesapeake. But as far as I knew, he had left nothing behind in writing. In the late sixteenth century, very few seamen could read and write, and fewer still could do so in a foreign language. The idea that this pirate could put pen to paper—much less put together his memoirs—seemed a stretch. But I was excited by the prospect of an alternative view.

With the historian's lead, I pieced together what was known about Fernandes's alleged papers. In the spring of 2012, a person who identified herself as Marie Carvalho phoned Doug Stover, the park historian at Fort Raleigh National Historic Site on Roanoke Island. As he recalls it, she said in broken English that she was an engineering student in Portugal who had come across two storage cartons in an archive. Inside were old ship's logs. A friend had told her they were written by a Portuguese pilot named Simão Fernandes, who she had heard was involved in the first English settlement attempt in North America. Carvalho wanted to know if Stover was interested in seeing the documents.

The news electrified the small community of Roanoke scholars. If true, the discovery could shed light on everything from the venture's financial details to his thoughts on the missing colonists. Because Fernandes spent months on transatlantic crossings with all the players and knew Raleigh and Walsingham, any of his observations could provide a breakthrough in our understanding of the Roanoke voyages, which depends so heavily on White's accounts.

Stover invited Carvalho to Fort Raleigh for a conference that October to commemorate the seventy-fifth anniversary of the first performance of the outdoor drama *The Lost Colony*. Historians, archaeologists, literary scholars, and other researchers were slated to descend on Roanoke Island for the meeting titled "Roanoke Conundrum—Fact & Fiction." Carvalho said that she had to be in New York on business around that time and agreed to come to the meeting. They discussed logistics. He suggested that she take the train to Norfolk; he could have her picked up for the two-hour drive south.

Stover then wrote up a memo for a project designed to organize, analyze, and publish the Carvalho papers, which he said were twenty-five linear inches in size and located in Portugal's national archives.

The brief document included Carvalho's e-mail address and a summation of Fernandes's historical importance.

As the October meeting kicked off, word flashed among the participants that the Portuguese engineer had texted Stover that she was on her way. It wasn't true. She never showed up, nor was she heard from again. Carvalho disappeared as utterly and completely as the 1587 settlers.

"It was bizarre," recalled Kupperman, who had been eagerly awaiting her arrival at the meeting. "We contacted archivists in Portugal, but they didn't know what we were talking about. And it turned out 'Carvalho' is the 'Jones' of the Portuguese world."

Two scholars, including James Horn of the Jamestown Rediscovery Foundation, flew to Lisbon but failed to find Carvalho or the documents in Lisbon's main archive. "There was a great archivist who spoke English, but we weren't able to find anything on Simão Fernandes, and she had no recollection of this young woman named Carvalho," he told me. "It's like she vanished off the face of the earth." Even Gabriel Rocha, a Portuguese-speaking historian now at Drexel University, had no luck finding her during a long stint in the Lisbon archives.

By the time I spoke with him, Stover had retired from the park service, and his memory of the conversation with the Portuguese engineer was spotty; he said that her first name might have been Maria rather than Marie, which was a French name. Even a Freedom of Information Act request I filed resulted in no new leads. The only clue to Carvalho's identity was the e-mail that she gave the park ranger. She had never responded to him, nor could I get a reply.

The address was linked to the University of Coimbra, one of the world's oldest continuously operating learning institutions. Founded in 1290, the university lay in the central part of the country in a city that was Portugal's medieval capital. Neither Horn nor any other American historian had looked for Carvalho or the documents in Coimbra. "I would go there," advised Horn. Rocha agreed. The possibility that Fernandes's papers were somewhere out there haunted them, but they were too busy to follow up.

Because finding those documents could rewrite the entire history of the Roanoke voyages, I decided to take on the task myself. I flew to Lisbon and headed north, picking up the trail where the historians had left off. I arrived in Coimbra at sunset amid a heavy spring downpour. Students scurried down the streets, their black academic robes pulled like burkas over their heads. The old town's red roofs, domes, spires, and golden crosses rose up on a steep hill above the Mondego River, glittering as the low sun shot through the lifting clouds. A double rainbow suddenly arched over the university buildings clustered along the hilltop.

"I can check the e-mail to see if it existed," said José Pedro Paiva, the head of the faculty of letters, when I met with him the following morning. "It's an old e-mail, so maybe she was enrolled a long time ago. But it is a very common name." Two days later, he left a curt response that his tech administrators were unable to trace the address. In the meantime, I shuttled from department to department but found no Carvalho—and there were many—familiar with the documents. On the last day, I made one last-ditch effort to unearth the pilot's logs in the university archives but came up empty-handed. When I did check the student rolls from the mid-sixteenth century, Fernandes was not listed; it seemed unlikely that the crusty buccaneer was college material. Discouraged, I went back to my hotel and read through everything known about the pilot. There was no sleeping anyway, because a wild graduation party featuring a series of heavy-metal bands blared from a park across the river until dawn.

To my surprise, I realized that we have more detail about Fernandes's life and exploits than White's and Lane's combined. In fact, he was better traveled and more cosmopolitan than Raleigh, Hakluyt, or Harriot. He also worked for or knew many of the most powerful courtiers of Elizabethan England. And he could write. Though there is no known portrait, we have a fleeting glimpse of the villain of Roanoke. He wasn't the tall, dark, and unabashedly sinister figure of the *Lost Colony* drama, where he struts about the stage kicking dogs and frightening children. A Spanish sailor described him as "bald of the head, blond, of medium thick body."

I wondered what else history had gotten wrong about this intriguing man and what bearing that might have on what unfolded on the North Carolina coast in the summer of 1587. Perhaps the glaring inaccuracies in our understanding of Fernandes could point me to just-as-glaring omissions in the historical record of the Lost Colony. So I set out to investigate more carefully this mysterious figure who played such a critical role in the Roanoke voyages. What I found turned my understanding of the entire effort on its head.

Fernandes was born around 1538 on the island of Terceira in the island chain of the Azores. If you drained the oceans, each would mark the summit of some of the world's highest mountains. Portuguese explorers encountered the islands in the early fifteenth century a thousand miles west of Lisbon. Settlement of this chain, long before Columbus's time, marked the real start of the European march to the New World.

"When your Simão Fernandes was born here, this was a fresh new capital city for the Portuguese empire," said Francisco Maduro-Dias, a local historian who lives outside the main town of Angra do Heroísmo on Terceira, which is about the size of Long Island. With its stone walls and deep-green fields, the island looks more like Ireland than Portugal, while Angra could be a Caribbean town, with its pastel-colored houses clustered around a tiny harbor overlooked by a massive Spanish fort. "Try to see it as a refueling station on a major highway, a place for repairs and to get fresh food and water. This was really the first international service city in the world. You can't speak about Angra without talking about the New World and Asia. Everything crossing the Atlantic stopped here. The world passed before his eyes."

Columbus anchored in the archipelago on his return from his first voyage to the Americas. I knew from reading about the Roanoke voyages that nearly every expedition halted in the Azores for provisions, as did Spanish treasure ships returning from the New World. Slavers from West Africa and vessels with Indonesian spices and Chinese

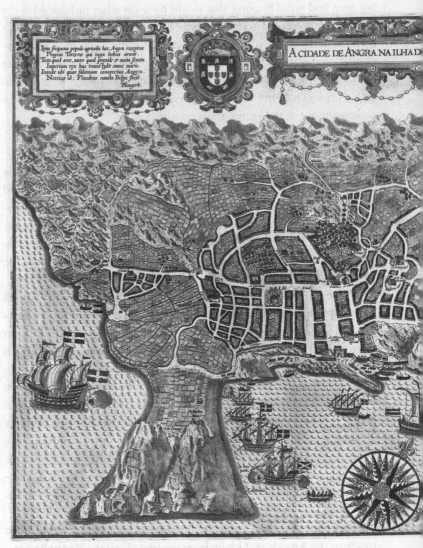

Terceira Island, with its prosperous port of Angra, was a bustling international crossroads in the sixteenth century and early home to Roanoke pilot Simão Fernandes.

silks also crowded the little harbor of Angra. The new global economy sparked by European domination of the oceans in the sixteenth
century led right to Fernandes's door.

He inherited the straw-colored hair of his father, a prominent
Catholic merchant nicknamed el Ruivo, or "the fair." Recent archival sleuthing by Rocha, the Drexel historian, uncovered evidence that
the father had extensive business connections with Lisbon but fell on
financial hard times just as his son came of age. Simão set off to work
on Spanish ships plying the North and South Atlantic, where Portuguese pilots, considered the best in the world, were in high demand.
"They knew the world's waters when no one else did," East Carolina University historian Larry Tise told me later. "They were like
NFL football players—'What kind of contract can you give me this
year?'" Technically, only citizens of the Spanish province of Castile
could be licensed as pilots on vessels of the empire, but shipowners
frequently ignored this requirement out of sheer necessity. Ferdinand
Magellan, for example, was born outside Coimbra but was chosen to
guide a Spanish ship on the first circumnavigation of the globe.

Spain's expanding control of much of the world's oceans depended
on accurate maps. As a pilot working for Spain, Fernandes would
almost certainly have sworn the required oath "not to give or sell or
lend the sea chart to a foreigner from outside of this kingdom." The
world of sixteenth-century charts was filled with intrigue, bribery,
and spies. At Seville's Casa de Contratación, or the House of Trade,
a legendary master map called the Padrón Real was said to rest in a
chest that could only be opened with two different keys held by two
officials, both of whom had to be present to reveal its contents. These
were the encrypted databases of their day.

Fernandes might have taken part in a 1566 Spanish voyage to the
Outer Banks piloted by Domingo and Baltasar Fernandes, two Portuguese pilots who were possibly older relatives. His common name
makes his early voyages difficult to pin down, but he seems to have
sailed along the coast of Brazil and in the Caribbean as well as along
North America. Yet the young man abandoned Spanish service by
1570 to seek a new life and fortune, working the Bristol Channel that
separates Wales from England. England had absorbed the smaller

country half a century earlier, but London exerted little power over a land that lay 150 miles to the west. The channel served as one of Europe's most notorious pirate havens. A stiff import tax imposed on French wine spurred a major smuggling ring. Merchants would secretly drop off casks in the Welsh port of Cardiff and then ship them across to Bristol, thereby avoiding the tax. The under-the-table business drew pirates, who built up networks that involved sheriffs, mayors, and even senior members of Elizabeth's court.

Fernandes might also have chosen this area because he had family ties with local merchants. Portugal and England boast Europe's oldest alliance, and Bristol and the Azores were closely linked. In 1501, King Henry VII granted exploration patents to three Portuguese subjects, two of whom had the last name Fernandes. They made at least one successful voyage to the New World and seem to have returned with three Inuit who spent time in Westminster Palace. The Portuguese won pensions from the English king in thanks for their service. Though the name is common, the men might well have been our pilot's ancestors, and his merchant family could easily have had long-standing English contacts.

The Portuguese pirate settled across the channel from Bristol, in Cardiff, and found a patron in William Herbert, who was at the center of the Cardiff piracy ring and the brother of a powerful member of Elizabeth I's Privy Council. Herbert bought quality goods from pirate merchants at bargain prices, and few locals had the interest or nerve to blow the whistle on his illegal activities. "He would do deals with them on ships, drink with them, invite them to his house, and assure them of safe-conduct," said James Cowan, an amateur historian in Cardiff who has studied the era. "Imagine a sort of Sicilian mafia," he told me as we stood next to Herbert's tomb in a medieval church in the middle of town. "People were terrified of him. It was this wild and prosperous Barbary Coast sort of place."

Fernandes initially served as pilot on a vessel owned in part by the son of a wealthy Elizabethan courtier. He learned to handle the world's second-largest tides that sweep in and out of the frequently stormy channel and make the area more challenging for sailors than even the Outer Banks. After I spent a harrowing day sailing as crew with Mark Horton from the English side to Cardiff and back—and on a fine May day with a motor as a backup—my respect for Fernandes's skills as a seaman deepened.

He quickly turned his profits as a pilot into a ship of his own, and he made friends with John Callice, one of Tudor England's most notorious pirates. The two seized a Portuguese caravel and sold its cargo for the fantastic sum of twelve hundred pounds. The outraged Portuguese ambassador in London complained that Fernandes killed seven men on the ship with his bare hands. He was briefly thrown in a Cardiff jail, but Herbert managed to have him released on bail and the charges reduced to "suspicion of piracy."

The queen came under pressure from Portugal and other foreign governments to rein in the piratical trade in the rowdy world that was Wales. In March 1577, Fernandes was sent to London under guard and again jailed. The Portuguese ambassador wrote with satisfaction that there was evidence "enough to hang him." Pirates in that day were executed from a London dock at low tide, their bodies left to dangle in the water for three successive tides. Callice, already imprisoned in the Tower of London, made a pathetic plea to Walsingham, undercutting his fearsome reputation. "I do bewail and lament my former woeful and wicked life." He offered to inform on his former colleagues "to clear the coasts of other wicked pirates, as he knows their haunts, roads and creeks."

By November, both men were free. The queen pardoned Callice, though he had to repay the owners of the vessels he confiscated. A member of Middle Temple agreed to be responsible for Callice's debts. Despite the outraged protests of the Portuguese ambassador, Fernandes was likewise released. Both pirates were too valuable to hang. Instead, they were given posts as senior officers on an English voyage to the New World.

Fernandes seized the opportunity to climb England's social ladder and was soon described by one contemporary as "Walsingham's man." The queen's secretary of state was one of the realm's most powerful men and the leader of an extensive spy ring. The Portuguese pilot was no doubt a walking gold mine of cartographic information, as well as intelligence about the routes and ports favored by Spain's treasure fleets, information that King Philip II attempted at all times and by many means to conceal.

Callice, meanwhile, slipped back into freelance pirating. Years later, as Fernandes was leading Grenville's large fleet to Virginia, Walsingham tried to placate the furious French ambassador after Callice captured three French ships in a single week "and ransomed and tortured the men and mariners with extraordinary cruelties." The last heard of the pirate comes in a letter to Walsingham, reporting that the inveterate pirate sold a cargo of linen—no doubt stolen—in North Africa. "He is gone back again to sea, whither God knoweth."

Fernandes converted from Catholicism to the Church of England and married an Englishwoman. He became, despite his criminal past, a respectable gentleman. One document describes him as a London merchant. He likely became a naturalized citizen, which made it possible to acquire real estate. This was an era in which the line between entrepreneurs and pirates was blurry. A privateer was simply a pirate with a license from the government to steal the cargoes belonging to other nations.

His rise in the ranks of English explorers was noted with alarm by the Spanish ambassador in London, who decried him to Philip II as "a thorough-paced scoundrel" but acknowledged him as deeply knowledgeable about Spain's New World empire. The ambassador knew Fernandes was trading on state secrets learned while in the Spanish service. The navigator continued to take on a series of increasingly demanding and important missions for his adopted country, including his 1578–79 voyage with Raleigh and the quick reconnaissance of the North American coast for his half brother Gilbert the following year.

On November 20, 1580, Fernandes met John Dee in his study on London's outskirts, an area that held one of England's largest libraries as well as a large collection of globes, charts, and navigational instruments. The gaunt and white-bearded scholar was England's great Renaissance man. An accomplished legal expert, mathematician, and astrologer who determined the most auspicious date for Queen Elizabeth I's coronation, he served as her informal science adviser. His Aztec obsidian mirror—"the black stone into which Dr. Dee used to call his spirits," states its inscription—is in the British Museum, not far from White's watercolors. In addition to regularly speaking with angels, he was obsessed with obtaining the most accurate maps possible. If he had had his way, America would have been named Atlantis.

Raleigh, Walsingham, and the queen all spent time in his study. The Portuguese pilot presented Dee with a detailed map of the world that must have thrilled him. Weeks before, the scientist had made his case to the queen as to why the English had the legal right to settle North America (an ancient Welshman and King Arthur were cited as previous New World explorers). Dee, who was close to Adrian Gilbert and later corresponded with Harriot, was an eager investor in the search for a passage to Asia and is credited with being the first to make the case for a British empire.

An inscription on the table-sized chart, which is now kept in the British Library, notes that "Fernando Simon" of Terceira lent Dee the map that shows the coastlines of Europe, the Amazon River snaking through South America, and the outline of what would later be called Russia's Kamchatka Peninsula. Compared with other maps from the era, it is remarkably detailed and accurate and includes a curious mix of Spanish, English, and Portuguese nomenclature. The mix makes it highly likely that Fernandes drew it himself or oversaw its production. The chart, a copy made by Dee's servant, gave one of the most learned men in England vital geographic information that Spain desperately wanted to keep secret. Some historians believe Raleigh used the map in planning the 1584 reconnaissance mission to the Outer Banks.

Soon after, Fernandes was tasked with piloting the first English trade mission to the spice islands of Indonesia led by Captain Edward Fenton and organized by the Earl of Leicester, a rival of Raleigh's for the queen's affections. It was a sign of the Portuguese pilot's growing ties with leading courtiers. The Spanish ambassador in London, Bernardino de Mendoza, reported to Philip in April 1582, "The pilot of the principal ship is a Terceira Portuguese, called Simon Fernandez, a heretic who has lived here for some years, and is considered one of the best pilots in the country." (By "heretic," Mendoza meant Fernandes had converted to Protestantism.)

Richard Madox, the Anglican chaplain on the voyage, left a wickedly gossipy journal detailing the 1582 mission that never made it out of the Atlantic because of the vicious shipboard disputes, bad weather, and inadequate provisions that plagued so many Tudor expeditions. Through the pastor, we get a fascinating glimpse of the Portuguese pilot in the close quarters. Like John White, he detested Fernandes, nicknaming him "the swine" and cursing him as "a ravenous thief with talons more rapacious than any vulture" who stands out as the "head and origin of all evil." But then, Madox doesn't seem to have liked anyone on board. He called the ship's captain "the deceiver" and another senior officer "the buffoon." Others were parasites, swell-heads, or simply stupid.

The pilot also offended a chaplain on a second vessel, who complains that he "rejoiced in things stark naughty"—a word then meaning "insolent"—"bragging in his sundry piracies." He calls Fernandes's sailor tongue "offensive to God, and nothing Christian-like."

Madox reports that Fernandes was far more than just a rough seaman. He claimed to have "a free pardon from five Privy Councilors"—referring to the queen's leading advisers—"for carrying on war with Spain." This stunned the cleric, who insisted naively that England and Spain were at peace. Fernandes's home island was, in fact, at that moment under siege by Philip II, who had claimed the Portuguese throne; Elizabeth quietly supported a rival who was then in exile in London. This was a proxy war that led to the direct conflict between Spain and England. Fernandes's boast suggests he was part of the growing anti-Spanish faction in England that included his patrons Raleigh and Walsingham. An undated Spanish deposition from the era mentions that during a visit to Brazil, Fernandes tried to drum up local support for Philip II's challenger.

Madox also reports that the pilot spoke "a swill of many languages." Fernandes was no doubt fluent in Portuguese, Spanish, and Latin, as well as in English and Welsh. "Only a merchant with permanent trade connections with England would be able to do that," said Pedro Cardim, a historian at Lisbon's New University, when I met him in his concrete high-rise office. "Portuguese at that period were usually bilingual. They could speak Portuguese and Castilian, and if they had to learn a third language, they would turn to French or Italian, not to mention Latin. English would almost never be an option. That makes the case of your Fernandes unusual."

He explained that the pilot would have been well aware that his New World experience gave him extremely valuable knowledge that could be shared for profit and social advancement. Pirating, he added, was an ordinary activity in that era that meshed well with his family's merchant background. And Portuguese pilots were far more than just hired drivers. They were also known for their ability to serve as mediators with Native Americans in the New World.

"They had been doing it for eight decades or so," Cardim said. "They knew how to communicate, and this kind of expertise ended up being important. It is not just about navigation. When you get there, you have to know how to establish contact with peoples from a different world."

Fernandes, I recalled, was present at the first meeting with the Native Americans on the Outer Banks beach in 1584, coaxing along Amadas and Barlowe, his juniors.

The idea that this interesting character left behind his personal record of events began to seem plausible, even likely. After all, Madox recorded that the pilot "boasts of himself as a notable author." The pastor scoffs at the idea, claiming that the Portuguese would better be called "a perverter of books." He adds that "in these books nothing else is contained but trivialities and vulgarities and what the wit of a sailor would know." His claim that Fernandes had written salty tales of his roving life, which might, perhaps, still survive, was exciting. We have, however, only a single letter in his hand, a dry request for supplies prior to the 1583 voyage. His English is solid, his hand confident, and his signature has flair.

Fernandes was clearly an ambitious self-made man who skipped among faiths, countries, and cultures, from the Old World to the New, and was not beneath looting and murdering, all the while working his way up the treacherous Tudor social ladder. Why, I began to wonder, would he sabotage his patron's colony and jeopardize everything? When I returned to the United States, I contacted a retired nurse practitioner in Pittsburgh for the answer.

It is one of the Lost Colony's most persistent myths. As early as 1812, an American historian declared that "the projects of a great man"—Raleigh—"the hopes of a nation, and the lives of many innocent people, were blasted together by the perfidy of that contemptible mariner . . . Every step he took, on that expedition, was marked with a design to defeat the colony." Fernandes didn't fare much better with Quinn, who criticized the pilot as "violent, quarrelsome and unattractive" and cursed with "instability of character." Paul Green, author of *The Lost Colony* still performed at Fort Raleigh National Historic Site, makes good use of him as a snarling cad impatient to give up the dull work of colonizing for plunder on the high seas. He is the bad egg in black, a suspected Spanish spy and fall guy for White's colony.

This colorful if extreme character drew the attention of Olivia Isil when she did a stint as a nurse on Roanoke Island in the 1990s. An opera lover far from the nearest professional company, she made do with the outdoor drama.

"As a devotee of opera, I think villains are much more interesting and complex," she said. While volunteering at the local historical association, Isil began to read up on the shadowy Fernandes. "I approach historical research somewhat cynically," she added. "Like Voltaire, I believe that most history is the lie that people choose to believe."

During the voyage from England to Roanoke with the Lost Colonists in 1587, White continually blames Fernandes for undermining the mission. The governor accused him of "lewdly forsaking" the fly boat during a storm off Portugal as well as for failing to secure adequate supplies during their sojourn through the Caribbean. He even implies that while the colonists were busy gathering provisions on a Caribbean island, Fernandes went off to enjoy sex with a colonist or fellow sailor.

When the flagship arrived off Port Ferdinando on July 22, 1587, White and his assistants prepared to go ashore to check on the small company of men Grenville had left behind. Then they would sail on to the Chesapeake to found the Cittie of Raleigh. As we've seen, the governor reports that as they settled into the boat, "a gentleman by the means of Fernandes called to the sailors in the pinnace" and told them all the colonists would have to disembark on Roanoke. There would be no voyage to the Chesapeake. The sole excuse given was that "the summer was far spent."

It is perhaps the most dramatic moment in the 1587 voyage, a Judas-like betrayal of Raleigh's orders by a foreign mercenary that would doom the settlers to death among vengeful Indians. Rather than argue, White turned the other cheek. "Wherefore it booted not the governor to contend with them, but passed to Roanoke."

Isil's curiosity settled on the mysterious "gentleman by the means of Fernandes" who announced the decision. She suspected that this person was the real decision maker rather than a go-between simply conveying the message. "The gentleman in question was obviously so influential that 'it booted not the governor' to contend with him," she says. "White apparently lacked the authority or the means to dissuade him." In that day, "gentleman" was not today's polite if fusty term. It applied solely to someone of rank. White noted that this person did not plan to stay in Virginia. Isil believes he could have been Raleigh's representative, who outranked both the governor and the pilot and was sent to ensure the voyage's success.

The mysterious man and Fernandes might have had any number of reasons not to proceed to the Chesapeake. They might have picked up intelligence in the Caribbean that the Spanish expected them to settle in the great bay, demanding a change of plans. (Fernandes was fluent in Spanish; it is unlikely that White was.) The pilot might have counseled against sailing into its unknown waters with women and children in hurricane season. There is even an elegantly simple possibility proffered by Warren McMaster, a former sailor who works on the *Elizabeth II* at Roanoke Island Festival Park. "Fernandes wanted the two pregnant women off his ship before they gave birth," he told me over beers one night at a local bar. Mariners, he explained, feared such a disruptive event. It's also possible the two women, including White's daughter, Eleanor, demanded to go ashore after their horrendous journey, and the governor chose to credit Fernandes and the obscure gentleman with the decision, to cover up that embarrassing detail.

Whatever his reasoning, Fernandes had no obvious motive to sabotage the colony, given that he was an assistant in the Cittie of Raleigh corporation and therefore almost certainly an investor. This status gave him his own coat of arms, a major milestone for any social climber in Elizabethan England. "He had as much—if not more—to lose than anyone if the colony failed," Isil noted. And if the Jane Pierce who was among the colonists was, in fact, Fernandes's sister or niece, then he had an additional incentive to ensure the colony's safety and survival. Nor is there evidence that Raleigh censured him on his return to England in late 1587. In fact, he fought with distinction against the Spanish Armada aboard the queen's galleon the following year. No one suspected of treason, particularly not a foreigner in xenophobic England, would have gained such a commission.

Isil also examined the old assumption by historians that the pirate yearned to abandon the settlers in order to attack Spain's treasure fleet before it reached the Azores, prompting the excuse that "the summer was far spent." Those ships would typically travel up the Gulf Stream and across the Atlantic before late summer, when hurricane season commenced. Yet Isil points out that the three vessels remained anchored off Port Ferdinando for more than a month; when a storm forced them to put to sea in August, they dutifully returned. "Such a delay hardly reflects an over eagerness to get on about the business of privateering," she added in a 2012 paper—one submitted for the same conference that Marie Carvalho was to attend.

Isil concludes that Fernandes was "no better or worse a man than Raleigh or Hawkins or Drake . . . They were pirates all, ambitious and self-serving," she says. "But being foreign born, Fernandes had a lot more to prove." That overseas origin made him a suspicious figure in later centuries as well, when British and American scholars were only too happy to make the Azorean pilot a villain; his name alone sounded Spanish enough to convict him in the court of Anglo-American history. The irony, of course, is that Fernandes hated the Spanish more than most English did. They had conquered his homeland and made it impossible for him to return long before Spain attacked England.

Her creative research exposes the fact that Fernandes has served as a scapegoat for centuries, blamed for Roanoke's failure. But I discovered there was more to the story than rehabilitating a villain.

When I left Portugal after my fruitless quest for his missing logs, I stopped in Seville to visit the General Archive of the Indies, home to the largest collections of documents relating to the Spanish Empire. I also wanted to see the metropolis that Fernandes almost certainly visited when it was the wealthiest and most cosmopolitan city of Europe. Every ship of the Spanish crown arriving from the New World was required to unload here so the government could keep careful tabs on Philip's revenues.

It was only April but already hot. The archive sits between the extravagantly crenellated cathedral, the world's largest, and the lavish Moorish palace where the empire's maps were kept under lock and key. I wanted to see a document—of course, Quinn long ago beat me to it—containing a curious deposition made by an experienced Spanish pilot named Pedro Diaz. Captured by the English, he sailed with Grenville's 1586 resupply mission. Carefully interrogated by Spanish officials after his release, much of his information is corroborated in English reports. No common sailor, he seems an educated and reliable source who gathered valuable intelligence.

Diaz relates that Fernandes was not simply "a skillful pilot" but "the author and promoter" of the Roanoke venture. He seemed to be saying that Fernandes, rather than Raleigh, was the mastermind behind the effort, or at least the person who helped conceive and launch it. His intriguing use of the word "author" reminded me of what Madox mentioned about his literary pretensions. In an echo of Diaz, the cleric calls Fernandes the "persuader and originator" of a campaign to persuade Captain Fenton to abandon the long mission to East Asia in favor of Atlantic pirating.

Quinn is quick to dismiss Diaz's claim as exaggeration; he even relegates the information to a footnote. I was about to do the same when I met David Wheat, a young historian from Michigan State

University. He was working at the archive on the early Atlantic slave trade, and he suggested we cross the river to eat dinner in the quarter once frequented by mariners like Fernandes. Over tapas, I mentioned Diaz's claim and asked whether it was plausible that a Portuguese pilot might exert considerable influence on an English endeavor.

"For the last couple of weeks I've been looking at documents relating to this little tiny town near Cartagena," said Wheat, after thinking for a moment. The port on the Caribbean coast of Colombia was the one Drake burned and looted in 1586, carrying off the hundreds of slaves who might have ended up on Roanoke.

"Ships would go 'off course' and end up in this town instead of Cartagena," he continued. "The records show captains claiming that the town officials forced them to unload their cargoes and paid less than they would have received at the bigger port. But we think there is something else going on." The captains' claims, he explained, appeared to be a ruse to sell illegal goods or avoid customs duties by landing in a smaller town eager to participate in trade at the expense of its bigger rival. I told Wheat that Fernandes and his fellow pirates used Cardiff in precisely this way, as a small port largely free from government control, to fence their stolen merchandise. The historian suggested that Roanoke offered a similar opportunity, and it lay just off the route that led from the Caribbean to the Azores, a strategic location.

"Setting up a little port town in an out-of-the-way place would be a great way to turn a profit," he added. "And he had connections to make this happen. So Roanoke would be another Azores. It would create regional commerce and provide a chance to subvert the Spanish." Fernandes, in other words, could have envisioned the Cittie of Raleigh as a new Azores. After all, he could never go home again, because it was under Spanish control and he was an avowed enemy of the king of Spain.

I recalled that Walsingham, Fernandes's first patron, had long backed a network of English trading centers abroad. The pilot was in a position to persuade Raleigh and Walsingham, two of England's most powerful figures, to turn a mere privateering base into a lucrative entrepôt. He grasped that real wealth in the new world order was to be had not in the occasional grand theft but in controlling a port where merchandise could be turned into cash.

I walked back to my hotel through the empty streets, past the cathedral where Christopher Columbus—the son of a wool merchant—lay in his tomb. I began to see Fernandes and the entire Roanoke venture in a new light. He had introduced the young Raleigh to the wider world of privateering and was an instrumental player in Sir Humphrey Gilbert's plan to settle America. He passed on critical intelligence to John Dee and worked directly for—and therefore, at some level, knew—other key stars in the Elizabethan firmament. More than any of them, he had valuable firsthand experience on how the new global economy, driven by ruthless pirate-merchants, worked in practice.

Neither saboteur nor just another sea dog, Fernandes was just the man to pull England out of its self-contained stupor and fashion a kind of metaphorical grappling hook to link England with North America—all with an eye, of course, to his own personal gain. He made the right contacts and got the right jobs, and at sea he ruled supreme over navigational matters. Without his expertise, it is questionable whether Raleigh could have launched his colonization scheme in the first place. Of course the pilot vetoed, or was part of a team that vetoed, moving to the Chesapeake. Yet William Strachey saw an old chart in 1611 drawn by an unnamed Portuguese that marked the James River as the region's choicest settlement spot. Long after he vanished off the Azores aboard an English fleet in 1590, Fernandes may have played a critical role in founding Jamestown and ensuring his adopted country's foothold in the New World.

If Raleigh was "perhaps the supreme example in England of a gentleman not born, but made," as one historian put it, then the pilot was a precursor to those later New World immigrants who mastered a strange tongue and navigated a sometimes hostile culture to become successful Americans. Consider how he arrived as a foreigner in a piratical gang, barely escaped execution, and rose to win the trust of the queen's inner circle. He switched religions, found an English wife, and quickly became indispensable. Two azure waves emblazon his coat of arms granted just before he left for Roanoke in 1587, recalling his Azorean heritage while underscoring just how far he had come up the social ladder.

When I confided my thoughts to Isil, she thought I was going too far in giving Fernandes a leading role in Raleigh's venture. But in some archival folder or attic missed by Quinn, we both still hope, is the literary work of this self-described "notable author" waiting to set the record straight. "What did Simon write?" she mused. "A ship's log? An account of the 1587 voyage? Perhaps a will? It's all out there!"

By now, however, I had exhausted my most promising leads. The excavations at Site X and Cape Creek seemed, like the 1590 account penned by White, full of frustrating discrepancies and contradictions. "Because so much archaeology is rooted in trying to prove what one wants to prove, we frequently are guilty of clinging to untenable flotsam as though our reputations were in danger of drowning," Noël Hume once wrote.

One summer afternoon, I maneuvered Horton and Luccketti into Noël Hume's elegant living room in a tony suburb of Williamsburg to sort out flotsam from solid proof. Nearly ninety, the archaeologist sat ramrod straight in a chintz wing chair with a view of the broad James River. He listened closely as the two younger archaeologists took turns deferentially laying out their findings. Horton and Luccketti had only met the day before. Beneath their veneer of polite academic detachment, I sensed mutual disdain.

It was as though two lawyers stood before a judge, each making his case. Noël Hume asked the occasional question, his palms pressed together. When they were done, the only man to have successfully broken the Roanoke curse shook his head, unconvinced that either of the excavators had nailed the case of the Lost Colony. "You both have a lot of work to do," he said.

The possibility remained open that both Luccketti and Horton were right. Governor White seemed convinced the settlers went to Croatoan, but made a point of mentioning twice the plan to move fifty miles inland. Luccketti didn't claim that *all* the settlers went to Site X, only some fraction of the group, perhaps a half dozen colonists. On that, he and Horton agreed.

"There are arguments about where to go and what to do," Horton speculated, after we left. "The council condemns someone; another is exiled. I think internal discipline broke down. Some were starving. The clever ones say, 'Bugger this! We're going to move in with the local Indians here.' They took wives and had a lot of skills and material culture to share with Manteo's people. But this is where they would be welcomed and supported. Even if you were going inland, you would want to have someone who stayed here on Croatoan. I suspect they would have sent the women and children here; it's almost certainly where Virginia Dare turns up."

Just as Lane split up his group in order to forage for food, the White settlers might have headed off in at least two different directions. One might have moved inland to live with the Indians at the head of the Albemarle Sound, while the other went south to keep watch for the governor's return amid their allies the Croatoan. Settlers in both places could have initially built English-style cottages and insisted on English-style burials before eventually assimilating with the Indians, though they may have merged with the locals so quickly that they had left few distinguishing European traces behind.

Neither research team could claim indisputable physical evidence of the colonists' fate. "We do not have the proverbial smoking gun," Luccketti later acknowledged. When pressed, Horton also admitted his finds were, at best, ambiguous. Though he has uncovered a long-lost Portuguese church on the East African island of Zanzibar and recovered tiny grains of thousand-year-old rice in the jungle of Madagascar, the conclusive answer to the Roanoke puzzle eluded him as much as it had Talcott Williams more than a century before.

There is one artifact, however, that says *precisely* what happened after White's departure. It presents a far darker picture of the colonists' fate than the tale of gentle assimilation assumed by Horton and Luccketti. If authentic, it is nothing less than a mother's piercing cry of woe echoing down the centuries, pointing to an appalling massacre, to the colony's luckless and violent end.

"Don't go there!" Luccketti told me bluntly when I asked his opinion about this controversial object. He warned that straying into this particular slice of the Roanoke vortex would destroy my credibility. Several historians rolled their eyes when I brought up the subject. Yet Samuel Eliot Morison, the Harvard scholar who did for early American history in the twentieth century what George Bancroft did in the nineteenth, proclaimed it "either one of the most stupendous discoveries or stupendous hoaxes in American history." Either way, what's known as the Dare Stone was too enticing a clue to be ignored.

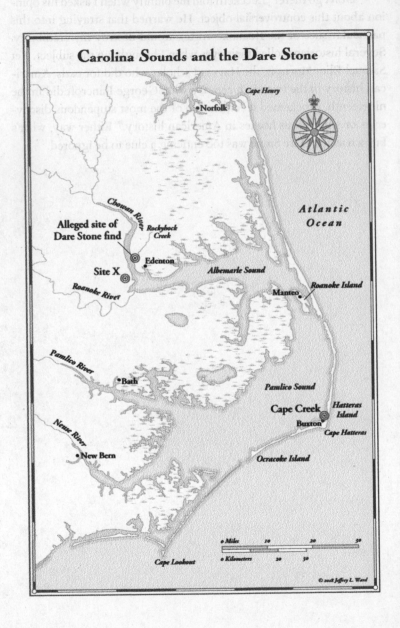

Carolina Sounds and the Dare Stone

Cape Henry

●Norfolk

Chowan River

Alleged site of
Dare Stone find

*Rockyhock
Creek*

●Edenton

Site X

Roanoke River

Albemarle Sound

Manteo●

*Atlantic
Ocean*

Roanoke Island

Pamlico River

●Bath

Pamlico Sound

Cape Creek

*Hatteras
Island*

Buxton

Cape Hatteras

Neuse River

●New Bern

Ocracoke Island

Cape Lookout

o Miles   10   20   30

o Kilometers   20   30

© 2018 Jeffrey L. Ward

CHAPTER TEN

We Dare Anything

At 11:00 on the morning of Monday, November 8, 1937, Emory University geologist James Lester went to the school's alumni building to make a phone call. When he hung up, he saw a middle-aged man cradling a bundle. The alumni secretary explained that the man, who introduced himself as Louis Hammond, wanted someone to examine markings on a rock.

"We went out in the hall with Mr. Hammond, the finder, where he removed the stone from within a large piece of coarse cloth and showed it to us," Lester said later. The geologist set the irregular dark gray stone, which was a little more than a foot long and a little less than a foot wide and two inches thick, on a nearby radiator to get a better look. There were incisions, but they were difficult to make out.

Hammond explained that he had found the twenty-one-pound stone near the Virginia–North Carolina border, about six hundred miles northeast of the Atlanta college. An English professor and a physics professor walking down the hall were drawn into the examination. The academics could make out a rough cross and the word "Ananias." Soon a crowd of students gathered "and pushed forward, snatching at phrases spoken concerning the Lost Colony," the geologist recalled.

At that moment, Lost Colony fever pervaded the country. That spring, President Franklin Roosevelt sketched out on a piece of White

House stationery the design for a commemorative stamp featuring Eleanor Dare cradling her baby among tall trees. The caption read, "In Memory of Virginia Dare." Below the sketch and above his signature, Roosevelt wrote, "Square stamp, 5 cents, Baby Blue." The final design commemorating her 350th birthday followed his directions.

In August, on the day marking Virginia Dare's birthday, Roosevelt attended a performance of the *Lost Colony* production that had just opened on Roanoke Island and gave a stirring speech before several thousand people on the rising threats to democracy at home and abroad. "Perhaps even it is not too much to hope," he mused, "that documents in the old country and excavations in the new may throw some further light, however dim, on the fate of the Lost Colony and Roanoke and Virginia Dare."

Here, in the professors' hands, was an artifact that might do just what the president had wished three months earlier. The professors retreated with Hammond and the stone into the alumni office, which quickly filled with the curious. Lester and his colleagues then took the finder and the stone to the relative privacy of the biophysics lab in the basement to decipher the inscription. Lester and J. Harris Purks, the physics professor, took the lead.

The news traveled fast across campus, and a young history professor named Haywood Jefferson Pearce Jr. rushed to the lab to assist in the translation. At five feet six inches, Pearce resembled a scholarly Charlie Chaplin with his small frame, thick hair, and small mustache. He had served during World War I and studied at the Sorbonne in Paris. Pearce had recently published a well-received biography on a Confederate general and was one of the university's rising stars. Lester and the others welcomed him, given his extensive knowledge of southern history.

The team continued to work until nearly eleven that night, with only brief breaks for lunch and dinner, and secured the rock overnight within a physics apparatus case. The next morning another dozen professors appeared, hoping for a chance at seeing the stone and assisting in its analysis. "On account of the crowd and confusion, very little progress was made on the inscription," a summary of events in the Emory archives notes. One can imagine the polite jostling as each tried to get a closer glimpse of the lettering and offer advice on its decipherment.

Hammond explained to the academics that soon after finding the stone, he had gone over the inscription with an indelible pencil, a steel brush, and a nail in his unsuccessful attempts to read the hard-to-see words. It was soon clear to everyone in the biophysics lab that the stone contained a heartrending message: a grieving daughter abandoned in the New World writing to the father who had tried and failed to find her.

By Tuesday afternoon, the professors agreed that the next step was to visit the site where Hammond said he found the rock. Securing additional archaeological evidence was a key to authenticating the inscription. The decision was also a way to cool the charged atmosphere on campus.

That day, L. E. Hammond of Alameda, California, signed an agreement with Emory giving him one dollar in exchange for the university's assuming temporary custody of the stone. It was to be

Haywood Pearce, center, examines the Dare Stone shortly after Louis Hammond brought it to Emory University in 1937. James Lester is on the left with Ben Gibson, a Georgia Tech geologist, on the right. *Brenau University*

kept locked in the treasurer's vault at night. The contract gave Emory "exclusive rights to conduct research studies in the history and origin of said stone" and to publish the results.

Early on Wednesday morning, Lester, Purks, and Pearce, along with two others, set off from Atlanta with Hammond as their guide. Hammond described himself as a former produce dealer from California and said that he and his wife were touring the country. He told the professors that he had found the stone that summer, the very season that the Lost Colony drama began fifty miles to the east and drew nationwide publicity. None of the Emory staff recorded whether Hammond said he went to the play or knew about the president's visit to celebrate Virginia Dare's birthday, though it was national news at the time.

Hammond said that he and his wife were riding on the newly opened Ocean Highway linking Virginia with Florida and stopped just shy of the bridge crossing the Chowan River to pick up hickory nuts. The bridge passed just west of North Carolina's old colonial capital of Edenton, a sleepy town that looks over the waters where the Chowan and Roanoke empty to form the head of the wide Albemarle Sound. Fifty miles to the east is Roanoke Island and, just beyond, the Atlantic Ocean.

Hammond had only a rough drawing he had made on a paper bag to serve as a map. He told the Emory professors that he had noticed a rock with odd markings while walking in the woods. Then he dragged it to a nearby sand spit on the river to wash off the dirt. He remembered that just offshore he had noticed a sunken barge. He later put the stone in the trunk of his car and while passing through Atlanta in November thought to seek professional help.

When the team arrived in Edenton, Hammond had trouble pinpointing the place where he first saw the rock. They wandered in the swamp until he pointed out "the approximate spot where he stumbled upon the stone," Pearce wrote later, though—like many involved with the Lost Colony before and since—the historian kept the precise location secret. Lester noted that the spongy land was slowly being submerged by rising water and that there was no native rock in the vicinity.

The men also found a sandy shoal that Hammond recognized as the place where he cleaned the rock. They noted the presence of the sunken barge offshore. No other stones or any other artifacts were found. After two nights, twelve hundred miles, and one tire puncture, the men were back at Emory.

The team resumed the transcription of the rock the next day, Friday, and worked through the weekend. By late Sunday night, the decipherment was complete. The result stunned the Georgia professors.

Ananias Dare & Virginia Went Hence unto Heaven 1591" and "Anye Englishman Shew John White Govr Via" was written on one side. There was also a cross, reminiscent of the agreement White said he made with the colonists on his 1587 departure: "I willed them, that if they should happen to be distressed in any of those places, that then they should carve over the letters or name, a cross in this form," indicating on the page a Greek cross. The inscription intimated that Eleanor Dare's husband and her young child died not long after White's August 1590 rescue mission.

How they died and what Eleanor suffered were the subjects of side two. "Father Soone After You Goe for England Wee Cam Hither," the tale begins, placing Eleanor herself as the storyteller, speaking directly to the governor from a refuge somewhere off Roanoke Island. The colonists suffered two years of "Onlie Misarie & Warre" that led to the death of more than half the settlers.

At some point, an Indian appeared with news that a ship had arrived off the coast, but he told her that the Native Americans had fled because they feared the arriving Europeans would exact revenge, though for what reason is not stated. Because the ship quickly departed—presumably a reference to White's aborted 1590 search effort—the stone records that the surviving colonists assumed the governor was not aboard the vessel.

Tragedy struck soon after, according to the inscription, when Indian shamans warned that the spirits were angry and all the remaining English, save seven, were abruptly killed. Apparently, the appearance of White spooked the Native Americans. Among the dead were

"Mine Childe" and "Ananias to Slaine wth Much Misarie." The dead were buried four miles east of "This River," with their names "Writ Al There on Rocke."

The inscription states "Put This Ther Also," a confusing phrase given that the message mentions that an Indian would take the stone to White—presumably, then, to Roanoke or Croatoan on the coast—in exchange for "Plentie Presents." The story ends with the writer's initials—"EWD"—obviously for Eleanor White Dare.

The day after the work deciphering the wording on the stone was complete, Hammond signed a new contract, this one with four Emory professors, including Lester and Pearce. The unusual agreement created a partnership that gave Hammond title to the stone, which they all agreed "seems to be of historical and monetary value." If he sold it, the four academics—who would continue to study the rock on campus—would split 10 percent of the profits. But the Emory men also had the chance to meet any competitive bid.

After putting his name to the document, which was notarized that Monday, Hammond left Atlanta, leaving only a post office box in California as contact information. At that point, Hammond had only received a single dollar. None of the Emory men ever saw him again, nor could a series of investigators track him down. Hammond disappeared as thoroughly as the Lost Colonists.

Fearful that the news of the stone's sensational message would leak before they were prepared to face the press, the Emory team apparently resorted to secret code in communicating with one another. A November 19 Western Union telegram sent from Edenton by Jeff Davis McCord, one of the Emory men who accompanied Hammond on the trip north the previous week, to a colleague back in Atlanta was written in Latin. It says, cryptically, "carrying shields cannot make them reveal their secrets."

A week later, North Carolina's leading newspaper, Raleigh's *News and Observer*, got wind of the discovery and headlined its article "Grave of Virginia Dare Believed Found in the State." The garbled story quoted Pearce—whose name was misspelled—confirming discovery of the tombstone and breathlessly added that he was seeking evidence of "an ancient and highly cultured, but long ago extinct civilization," rivaling that of the Aztecs and Incas, that flourished in northeastern North Carolina.

The team was forced to respond. "The report that any member of the Emory University faculty has found the grave of Virginia Dare is false," a hurriedly drafted statement read. "A stone bearing an inscription relating to the Dare family has been placed in our custody for investigation." A university team was still deciphering the message, "but until certain questions have been cleared up it obviously would be unwise for their translation to be made public." Emory, however, refused to deny or confirm the inscription's authenticity. The news went out on the Associated Press wire and was reprinted across the country.

The professors had in their possession an artifact like no other found in colonial America and one that put them under an intense media spotlight in what Lester recalled as "the hysterical days of November." Academics and the public alike were riveted by each new report on the find. The inscription's discovery on the heels of the Virginia Dare celebration ensured the message would receive maximum publicity and those involved in its analysis could reap national renown. For a small university in a southern city of fewer than 300,000 people, the Dare Stone was big news.

Before releasing any more information, the Emory team embarked on an innovative effort to study several separate aspects of the stone to determine if it was indeed carved in 1591. Lester determined the stone was vein quartz, common to central and western North Carolina. Using similar rock, the professors tried without success to replicate the look of the letters using acid. They consulted stonemasons, but without finding consensus on whether the letters were chiseled by hand or made using contemporary machinery such as a sandblaster. Others examined the wording to determine if it was indeed Elizabethan usage. Pearce, meanwhile, considered whether the tale told by the stone was plausible.

After weeks of effort, they found nothing to persuade them that the inscription was a modern forgery. On January 30, 1938, nearly three months after Hammond appeared at Emory and six months after he claimed to find the stone, Eleanor Dare's awful story was made public. Newspaper readers couldn't get enough of the tragic tale—a mother lost in the wilderness among Indians, her husband and baby brutally murdered, a doomed plea to her distant father.

In May, Pearce published a scholarly article in the *Journal of Southern History* called "New Light on the Roanoke Colony" that summed up the work of the Emory group. He found only minor instances in word usage that might be unusual in Elizabethan times and concluded that a mallet and chisel were likely the instruments used to carve the message and that "such tools must have been available to the Roanoke colonists." Pearce all but pronounced the stone to be genuine. He also declined to name Hammond, at the finder's request.

The three-day November excursion to Edenton, while fruitless, had convinced the Emory team that Hammond was a man of "persistence and fidelity," with a character "beyond the reach of the most perfect actor," as Lester told faculty members in April 1938. "If he is a crook or confidence man, he has no business carrying a piece of stone around showing it to college men. He should be selling gold bricks to the hard-boiled bankers of America." The geologist said Hammond made no slipups on the long car trip. "Every one with whom he came into contact was favorably impressed with his simplicity and his naturalness. Frankly, I believe that man was what he said he was."

Lester added that Purks "had in his possession a statement from him, which he asked be kept confidential, that clarifies many of the minor points of obscurity surrounding him." That document has not been found. But Lester added, "Conversation and correspondence with Mr. Hammond indicate that he is utterly incapable of writing such a message." A forger, he added, would have to master history, Elizabethan language, cartography, geology, and stone carving to pull off such a convincing fake.

University administrators, however, were suspicious. Days after Hammond left Atlanta, Emory contracted with Pinkerton's National Detective Agency to investigate his background. Although he clearly stated that he lived in Alameda, in the San Francisco Bay Area, the detectives inexplicably looked for him among produce dealers in Pasadena, far to the south. Not surprisingly, they failed to find him. A December contract with the Retail Credit Company led to a search of

Alameda police records, banks, and post office employees. That effort uncovered no sign of an L. E. or Louis Hammond in the area. The one contact that Hammond had provided was a Mr. Dove, a thirty-eight-year-old small-time jeweler in east Oakland. Dove had done occasional business with Hammond, the investigators reported, but recalled only that he was "a regular fellow" with a pension and a wife. He didn't even know Hammond's address.

Herbert Milton Dove—also spelled Done in some records—is listed in the U.S. Census and in military files as a jeweler who lived with his father and later served in World War II. By contrast, there is no record of a Louis or L. E. Hammond in the immediate area. It is one thing to lose a colony in the sixteenth century, but it seemed another matter entirely to lose a twentieth-century Californian who claimed a pension and a wife.

Nonetheless, Purks and Lester said they corresponded with Hammond via his post office box or a general delivery address—a not uncommon method in those days when millions were moving around in search of jobs. There is, however, no record that any investigator staked out the box or extracted the home address of the box owner, and no letters written by Hammond have shown up in Emory's archives.

While the professors involved in the study of the stone remained convinced that Hammond was on the up-and-up, the doubts of university administrators grew. Three days after the university went public with the inscription, a senior university administrator named R. C. Mizell warned in a letter that "the rock is probably a fraud" and that "by giving publicity, Emory is allowing itself to be used to further a fraud." He suggested that the university wash its hands of the object by giving it to a historical society.

This was, after all, a golden age for clever crooks and confidence men. Forgery thrived during the Great Depression, when honest work was hard to find. Fake Indian relics were sold across the country. In New York, Edward Mueller passed off counterfeited dollar bills for years. In the Netherlands, a Dutch painter fooled art historians with forged paintings that he said were unknown Vermeer originals.

Most famously, a clerk found a brass plate in California in 1936 that recorded the landing of Sir Francis Drake north of San Francisco on his round-the-world voyage, seven years before he arrived at Roanoke with supplies for Ralph Lane and his men. A famous historian at the University of California at Berkeley declared the plate authentic and displayed it proudly at the campus library, but debate about its legitimacy continued to rage among scholars.

"The Dare Stone has much more in its favor so far as authenticity goes than the Drake brass plate," Lester insisted in his April address to the faculty. But he added that the inscription's age could only be proven by archaeological finds corroborating the claims made by the message—namely the graves of Ananias and Virginia Dare. "Only upon these findings will the truth of the inscription be established."

Emory's president sided with Mizell, and the university administrators pressed its faculty to divest itself of the questionable artifact. On March 18, the Emory team warned in a memo to Pearce that Hammond likely would demand the stone back within a month and urged cooperation with North Carolina archaeologists who were demanding to see the rock. That a Georgia university was keeping a tight hold on an artifact that might be central to their history irked Carolinians. Pearce balked.

His refusal to share the rock with North Carolina academics only increased suspicions among them about the inscription's authenticity. The press attention threatened a public relations disaster for their state. First, it was embarrassing that an object of such potential importance to North Carolina was in the possession of Georgians. Second, the message of the rock clashed with the air of mystery around the colony's fate created by the outdoor drama that had just opened on Roanoke Island. The play and the new state park were key to the economic success of the poverty-stricken coast. The Dare Stone threatened to unravel this carefully constructed plan built on state and federal funds.

Losing support from Emory, Pearce turned the academic quest into a family affair. The young historian's enthusiasm spread to his father, Haywood Pearce Sr., the president of a small women's college outside Atlanta called Brenau. His progressive stepmother, Lucile, known for driving her own car long before it was considered proper for a southern lady to do so, was also drawn into the effort. The cry of an early pioneer woman, deprived of a child and husband who died in agony, appalled and fascinated the three Pearces.

In 1938, to the relief of anxious Emory administrators, Pearce junior purchased the rock from Hammond with funds sent to the finder's post office box through an Oakland bank. Whether he used his father's or Brenau College funds, or whether five hundred or a thousand dollars was paid, is unclear. A 1966 letter from a successor to Pearce senior states that the college paid five hundred dollars, but officials at Brenau today, where the stone remains, say no receipt has yet surfaced.

The Pearces made at least one cast of the famous rock and had it displayed at the Georgia exhibit at the 1939 World's Fair. It proved one of the most popular items on view at the fairgrounds in Flushing. This was more than just irritating to many North Carolinians. Another state was baldly usurping their identity as the home of the first English settlers in the Americas, and it was doing so in front of the entire world. A British diplomat who saw the Dare Stone at the fair requested a cast for the British Museum to reside in proximity to White's watercolors.

Pearce senior complained about "considerable skepticism" and "some ridicule" emanating from North Carolina regarding the stone. He and his son dismissed this criticism as sour grapes. Hammond had brought the stone of his own free will to a Georgia institution, not to Duke or the University of North Carolina.

Pearce then set out to find the *other* mysterious rock—the one mentioned on Hammond's stone—and to do so without interference from jealous North Carolina rivals or skeptical Emory bureaucrats. He took a leave of absence from Emory and devoted all his time to researching the rock. Father, stepmother, and son embarked on several expeditions to Edenton to survey and excavate during 1938 and 1939. "With the second stone in hand, competent scientists may be enlisted who can proceed with confidence toward the search for the remains of the first Americans, Raleigh's Lost Colony of Roanoke," father and son wrote in a 1939 Brenau newsletter.

The excavations in the Edenton area, done with the help of local

African Americans, came to nothing. "I believe our best chance to find it and also to find the burial place of the Lost Colonists is to give the matter as wide publicity as possible," Pearce senior explained in a 1939 letter to a friend, adding, "I personally have little doubt that they are in Chowan County," where Edenton was located. Desperate, the Pearces offered a five-hundred-dollar reward for a clue, a small fortune in the Depression-era South.

A cottage industry in Lost Colony rocks immediately sprang up. Men appeared out of the Carolina swamps with inscribed stones related to the Roanoke voyages. The Pearces and the North Carolina state historian, Charles Crittenden, vied to obtain these objects, fearful that the other side would get the jump on the historical sensation of the decade.

When a crudely carved stone with Virginia Dare's name scratched on its surface appeared in the small town of Columbia, between Roanoke Island and Edenton, Crittenden made the long journey, only to be rebuffed by the rock's owner. Finally he cajoled the man into allowing the rock to be taken to the state museum in Raleigh for study.

A distinguished panel of more than a dozen historians, archaeologists, and English scholars gathered to consider the new find. The rock was determined to be ballast stone brought from England. But the panel concluded, "Every mark seems as fresh as if made yesterday." The rock was quickly returned to its owner, who was harshly criticized in the local press for his deception. So when a stonecutter named Bill Eberhardt showed up at Brenau in May 1939 carrying a rock with shallow chisel marks and the date 1589, the Pearces sent him packing.

Eberhardt, a gaunt man in his thirties who lived on the nearby Chattahoochee River, was persistent. He returned with yet another stone a few weeks later that had a list of fifteen Lost Colonists—presumably those massacred at the instigation of the shamans—and a date of 1591.

The Pearces agreed to accompany Eberhardt to the place where he said he found the rocks on a hill outside Greenville, South Carolina, in the rolling uplands of the state and nearly four hundred miles south-west of Edenton. They were, for reasons that remain obscure, quickly convinced of the stone's legitimacy and promptly bought several acres around the site for eight hundred dollars.

"We now have the grave stone which was placed on the graves of the seventeen massacred colonists," Pearce senior wrote in triumph to the North Carolina Historical Commission on July 11, 1939. The rock, he added, "contains the names of Ananias and Virginia Dare and fifteen others." He noted that the object was found three hundred miles from Roanoke Island before bluntly refusing the commission's request for a cast of the first Dare Stone.

The Pearces set to work digging for the colonists' remains in the midsummer heat. A month later, Pearce senior admitted privately that after a month of hard work they had again found nothing. "Our excavations where the stones were found have thus far been fruitless," he wrote to the president of Wesleyan College in Macon, Georgia. "However, the soil there is red clay and parties who have experience in this area report that nothing is left after fifty to seventy-five years. So I have almost abandoned hope of finding any skeletons."

Eberhardt, however, retained his magic touch for finding carved stones with a strange circular writing that differed markedly from the first Dare Stone. He never left them in place, as the Pearces demanded, but always carried them to the door of their Victorian home at Brenau or their trenches in South Carolina. That summer he presented more than a dozen stones telling a harrowing sequel to the Hammond inscription.

In them, Eleanor described dozens of surviving colonists trekking inland to the Appalachians, gradually picked off one by one by hostile Native Americans. It was too good a story to keep secret, and Brenau College made an official announcement on July 25, 1939. "If the authenticity of these stones is established, some commonly accepted facts in American history must be discarded," noted the *Atlanta Constitution* on its front page. The Lost Colonists had apparently trekked deep into the South long before the English were thought to have explored the region.

To win the backing of the skeptical scholarly community, Pearce junior organized an academic conference for September, inviting historians from around the country. The meeting was abruptly canceled when a new wave of stones appeared at the Pearces' door. This set of ten stones, a few found by people other than Eberhardt, recorded an increasingly frantic Eleanor encouraging her father to continue his search as her dwindling band sought a safe refuge in what was now northeastern Georgia. One was said by a local man to have been picked up within six miles of the college. The trail that began on Roanoke Island passed nearly to Pearce's doorstep.

Caught up in the excitement of the hunt, they didn't stop to question this peculiar coincidence.

More carved stones followed in 1940, including eight that led to an Atlanta suburb and completed the horrifying gothic tale with an uplifting end. Eleanor birthed another child, Agnes, with her new husband, an Indian king, and settled down in a Cherokee village. A ledge over a cave that Eberhardt found on the Chattahoochee River was carved with "Eleanor Dare heyr sit hence 1593." Another stone revealed she was buried in 1599 "on a great hill" but not before pleading with her father to take her daughter back to England.

By the time thirty-four scientists arrived at Brenau on October 19, 1940, for the long-postponed academic meeting, the nation had been following the latest Dare Stone finds in the newspapers like a popular serial. Reporters swarmed a meeting that included some of the most famous names in academia, including the presiding scholar, Harvard's Samuel Eliot Morison.

Morison, who that year published a seminal volume on American history, was a famous skeptic of fraudulent artifacts. He had publicly dismissed the Drake brass plate as a hoax, infuriating its Berkeley backer. He noted with disapproval that this professor, who had long sought the artifact, had "provided an irresistible temptation for some joker to have fun at the expense of the distinguished professor." Morison's word carried enormous weight among his colleagues and with the public.

The crowd of reporters was shut out of the three-hour evening session in which the assembled historians, geologists, and archaeologists debated the authenticity of the stones and heard testimony from some of the finders, including a man who said he found one stone embedded in a wall of an old gristmill that had stood longer than anyone could remember. All those connected with the stones were rural Georgians of varying degrees of literacy who seemed unlikely perpetrators of an elaborate Elizabethan hoax. After examining the stones and all the available evidence, a committee of the leading experts chaired by Morison declared, "The story told by the stones is in perfect harmony with facts related by history," adding, "The preponderance of evidence points to the authenticity of the stones."

At a crowded press conference, however, Morison hedged his bets, telling reporters that the stones were either astonishing discoveries or colossal hoaxes.

Most journalists ignored the hedging, telling their readers that top American academics believed the stones' lurid tale—of a young woman trying to hold together a lost band of Elizabethans among savage Indians—was now historical fact. "Dare Stones Appear Authentic to Experts," read the headline of Raleigh's News and Observer, which had broken the first story in 1938 but had remained skeptical of Pearce's claims. "Atlanta (only ten miles from where the stone trail ends) has undisputed possession of Scarlett O'Hara. It looks like now she has a Half Nelson on Eleanor Dare," the newspaper concluded.

The Lost Colony was no longer lost, and its story was now a respectable part of American history. Revelations made at the meeting that the principal discoverer, Eberhardt, had a history himself of faking Indian relics received little attention. Everyone, it seemed, wanted to believe the carved messages.

A month later, Morison's committee set out a research plan in order to certify the stones' authenticity. This called for further analysis of the stones' makeup, excavations to find graves or other relics of the colonists, and an intense study of the words and phrases to ensure their Elizabethan usage. The panel also recommended that the writing be compared with graffiti from the era as well as a thorough investigation of Eberhardt's past and rumors that a man in the 1930s hawked fake stones on Roanoke Island. The committee urged Pearce to cooperate with other academics, particularly North Carolinians.

The historian, with the backing of his father and stepmother, ignored the recommendations. Instead of pursuing the scientific analyses, Pearce junior helped a local playwright produce a script based on the dramatic tale told by the rocks, which was designed to compete directly with North Carolina's *Lost Colony*. He even contacted Cecil B. DeMille when he heard the famous Hollywood director—whose father was born not far from Roanoke Island—was considering a movie version of the Roanoke settlers. "We would be glad to receive you or your accredited representative at Brenau College and provide any further help in our power," Pearce wrote.

DeMille replied politely that the Dare Stones were "extremely interesting" and added that their story was "one of the most fascinating" in American history. He acknowledged that he was considering a film on the Lost Colony but added that he was still "studying the subject." Pearce wrote again but never heard back.

Meanwhile, the Georgia stonecutter continued to find stones with regularity, including one that told of two remaining colonists, including the young Agnes, imprisoned in 1603.

Eager to bring this remarkable tale to the American public, Pearce wrote up a lengthy piece about the Dare Stones and sent it to one of the nation's oldest and most circulated magazines, the *Saturday Evening Post*. The editors contacted Morison after looking over the manuscript. This time, the Harvard professor did not hedge. "I personally went to Gainesville to investigate the Eleanor Dare Stones and believe them to be genuine, as did the other professors present," the historian replied.

The *Post* asked a staff writer, Boyden Sparkes, to fact-check the piece. Sparkes was an imposing man and enterprising writer who had taken a bullet through the leg and scalp in 1921 while covering a miners' conflict in West Virginia. He worked for newspapers around the nation and ghostwrote autobiographies of wealthy Americans such as automotive magnate Walter Chrysler. He had married into a well-connected North Carolina family, spent time on the Carolina coast, and was no doubt aware of the controversy when he took on the assignment.

Sparkes visited Pearce at Brenau. "I'm still open-minded," he told the reporter. "I never say they are authentic. It's too early." Yet Sparkes found that he "becomes resentful when his stones are challenged."

In speaking with Pearce's Emory colleagues from the original study team, Sparkes found them doubtful of the stones' authenticity, despite the imprimatur from Morison. Lester, the geologist who was the first to encounter Hammond, said that one of the Eberhardt stones—number 25—appeared freshly carved. In a report, he wrote, "It makes me believe it has been doctored . . . the lack of lichenous material in the grooves seems to be the first glaring drawback to any of the stones that I have seen." He told Sparkes that this particular object was a fake.

Lester and Purks, eager to protect their professional reputations, quietly helped Sparkes assemble his case. At his request they checked the books that Pearce, their longtime colleague, took out of the Emory library prior to the find of the first stone. They found no evidence that he had been researching Elizabethan history before Hammond's arrival or that he might be part of a larger conspiracy.

But the reporter latched onto news of Eberhardt's past—his faked Indian relics, including stones with Mayan and Aztec designs. He discovered that the stonecutter had ties with the other two Georgians who had presented Dare Stones to Pearce. He also found that Eberhardt's main source of income was selling moonshine.

One night Sparkes confronted him in his cabin on the Chattahoochee. "Bill was in bed," Sparkes wrote with a reporter's eye for detail. "On his head was a khaki deer-stalker hat. He was wearing the jumper of his overall. The overalls were hanging stiffly on a nail in the wall. He is a disorderly hermit. He was reading the picture section of an Atlanta paper." He found the man "a sly, cagey fellow with a streak of humor." Eberhardt was too smart to confess, but Sparkes concluded that he had given Pearce "42 stones, all forgeries, for which he was paid a total of about $2000. A few others were provided by Eberhardt's cohorts." (Those forty-two did not, however, include the first Dare Stone found by Hammond.)

Sparkes's April 1941 magazine article, "Writ on Rocke: Has America's First Murder Mystery Been Solved?," was an investigative tour de force. Sparkes laid out Pearce's delusions—and hinted at possible collusion—with devastating thoroughness and a tough sarcastic edge. He ended the piece noting that the words "Emory," "Atlanta," and "Fake" could be read in some of the Eberhardt stones as acrostics, like in a crossword puzzle. A Georgia hillbilly had outwitted not just Pearce but some of the nation's finest minds.

"I am sure," Sparkes concluded dryly, "that Eleanor Dare had nothing to do with it."

Soon after the article appeared, Eberhardt met with Lucile Pearce to hand over a new inscription. This one read, "Pearce and Dare Historical Hoaxes. We Dare Anything." His streak of humor had taken a dark turn to blackmail, and he threatened to expose the Pearces if they didn't pay him off.

Pearce junior confronted Eberhardt, who refused to sign a document admitting he had faked the stones. The historian went to the *Atlanta Journal*. The May 15, 1941, story laid out the sordid saga in a banner headline on its front page titled "Hoax Claimed by 'Dare Stones' Finder in Extortion Scheme, Dr. Pearce Charges." The news topped the day's reports on Hitler's invasion of Iraq and Rudolf Hess's flight from Nazi Germany to Britain. Other newspapers quickly jumped on the story. "Eleanor Dare Stones Are Branded Fraudulent," said the headline in the *New York Herald Tribune*. A liquor company took advantage of the publicity to print an advertisement showing the faked rocks headed "Easy to Be Fooled!" decrying "Thousands Spent for 'Rocks of Roanoke.'"

Pearce's reputation as a serious scholar was ruined. The others involved in the authentication effort distanced themselves from the scandal. Lester said later that he had known all along the letters were sandblasted, and Morison disingenuously insisted that he had declared the stones fake while presiding at the Brenau meeting.

An unhappy silence descended on the Pearce home. The historian's niece, Sissy Lawson, said that the family never discussed the Dare Stone embarrassment. ("All I remember is that Pearce senior, my grandfather, gave me a thrashing when I knocked over his chess table," she told me when I tracked her down in Gainesville.)

The European war and the Japanese bombing of Pearl Harbor in December pushed the Dare Stones out of the headlines and the public mind. Pearce junior joined the U.S. Army in 1942, and his father died the following year. His stepmother, Lucile, took over the school briefly and then died when she drove her car into an oak tree in 1946. That year, Pearce junior moved to distant East Michigan University in Ypsilanti, where he remained until his retirement in 1963. He never published again, save for a brief 1947 paper on Spanish friars in Georgia. Lawson said her uncle rarely visited his hometown after the war, preferring to spend his summers at a boys' camp in the mountains of Georgia that his father had founded.

"He was an affable gentleman with a shock of white hair and sense of humor," recalled Reinhard Wittke, an East Michigan historian who shared an office with Pearce in the 1950s until Pearce's retirement. He recalled an absentminded man well respected by his students. But when I asked Wittke about the Dare Stones, he was baffled. "Never heard of them," he said. "[Pearce] never talked about his past." It was a strange comment to make about a historian. Pearce died in 1971 in Florida and returned to Brenau only to be buried in the family plot next to his father and stepmother.

In a folder in Emory University's archives, several pages of undated scrawl reveal an attempt to sort out the acrostics that Sparkes spotted in the inscriptions of the stones. It's not clear who authored the painful effort or when, though it was likely done in the days following the publication of Sparkes's article. "Only two letters used more than once," reads one note. Then there is "Pearce" and "Fake" marked among the words. At the bottom of the last page are three devastating words, each given its own line. "Pearce is sad."

This could have been the end of the tale of the Dare Stones, a saga of discovery, credulousness, fraud, and disappointment. Sparkes demolished the authenticity of the rocks that Eberhardt and his cohorts produced, as well as Pearce's promising career. But there was one lingering detail that nagged at the reporter. Eberhardt had been shown to be responsible for all the stones but one—the one that Hammond carried into Emory that November morning and which incited all the frenzy that followed. Its successors were frauds, but could the first have been authentic?

After his article was published, Sparkes continued his hunt. The fatal obsession that gripped Pearce had passed to him.

CHAPTER ELEVEN

Heap Plenty Wampum

Sparkes discredited all the rocks, but his evidence against the first stone's authenticity was circumstantial. The reporter complained that Pearce "could tell me less about Hammond than about Eleanor Dare." But he had no better luck. He could only offer rumors by North Carolinians, who said that an unnamed tourist once tried to hawk an inscribed stone on Roanoke Island. No one, however, could provide any substantive details.

Sparkes also tried to link Hammond with Eberhardt. He stated confidently that a mysterious "L. E. Martin," who offered money to a friend of Eberhardt's in exchange for a rock inscribed with the word "Yahoo," was Hammond. But he cited no evidence for this claim, other than the implication of the two identical initials. There is no sign he interviewed the man. The best that Sparkes could do was to taint Hammond's stone by linking it to the clear forgeries. That effort was successful. Academics and the public accepted his conclusion.

Yet his failure to nail down Hammond's identity and motive gnawed at him. After the article hit newsstands in April 1941, Sparkes wrote to the Emory physicist Purks that he was hot on the trail of a "Mr. X" whom he believed to be Hammond and intimated that he was close to unmasking the culprit. Purks wrote back, asking for more details, but Sparkes replied in June, "I want to keep the identity of Mr. X a secret for a little while longer because I am pursuing the investigation." Busy during the war years, Sparkes spotted "a cigar-smoking captain" resembling Pearce in a War Department corridor in Washington, but the officer vanished without a word. The reporter, however, did not forget his quarry when peace returned, though even Pearce had moved on to self-imposed exile in Ypsilanti.

"A delayed action fuse on what might have been a bomb a few years ago has finally functioned," he wrote to Purks in 1946. Sparkes had finally procured a photograph of a man who made fake Indian relics in Massachusetts. He was sure it was Hammond, and he wanted everyone at Emory who had met the stone's finder to examine the image. Purks agreed and passed it around the team to see if it matched the man who appeared at Emory nearly a decade before. Purks took a scientist's approach to the request. He showed the picture to some of the men who had met Hammond without mentioning the stone or Sparkes, in order not to influence their response. None guessed outright. He wrote up a detailed account of the results. Some saw a similarity, while others did not; Purks could not say with certainty that the man in the image was Hammond. "No attempt was made to make contact with Dr. Pearce," he added.

The reporter, however, read this scholarly ambiguity as likely confirmation. He replied to Purks that while "the thing isn't conclusive . . . there is a resemblance between your Hammond and this other." Perhaps, Sparkes wrote, the man was a relative, "a dumber brother." His obsession seemed to overwhelm his journalistic instincts. When Sparkes died in 1954, in a North Carolina hospital less than one hundred miles from where Hammond claimed to find the object, he was no closer to proving that the first stone was a forgery.

The original Dare Stone, Hammond's singular discovery, was eventually placed in a case in the Brenau library, more as a warning than a challenge to scholars.

There were occasional attempts by archaeologists in the years that followed to determine its authenticity. South Carolina's state archaeologist, Robert Stephenson, examined the rock in 1983 at the request of Brenau officials. Placing the stone under a microscope to study the inscription provided no new clues, other than underscoring the fact that it was a type of rock not found naturally around Edenton. He could offer no suggestions for chemical or physical analysis that might be useful and doesn't mention using paleography—the study of old scripts—as a line of evidence.

"I doubt if it will ever be possible to conclusively resolve this enigma," he wrote to the Brenau staff. "I am, though, reasonably convinced that the whole matter was a well conceived hoax." He based that conviction on the logical incentives for finding such a stone in 1937, ranging from promotion of the newly opened Ocean Highway that passed by Edenton to an attempt at nabbing a Hollywood movie deal. Pearce, he believed, was an innocent victim of a well-produced deception. "I myself have been taken in by hoaxes (such as a gold-bearing Spanish shipwreck that never existed) and I do not consider myself a gullible person. This can happen to any of us." Stephenson suggested the Brenau keep the stone "as a memento of a hoax and a symbol of what might have been." If it were authenticated, however, he added that it would immediately become "one of the major national treasures" in the Smithsonian Institution.

Instead, the rock became a perennial subject of conspiracy and mystery, appearing in pseudodocumentaries, such as the *In Search Of . . .* series narrated by *Star Trek* actor Leonard Nimoy. "Hoax springs eternal," quipped one Brenau administrator in the 1970s. No scholar in his right mind would risk his reputation on the Dare Stone, which by now was academically radioactive. Fortunately, I was no scholar.

In 2010, a historian at the University of North Carolina at Wilmington named David La Vere published a book called *The Lost Rocks*. It was a brief but meticulously researched history of the whole Pearce affair from start to finish. He concluded that the authenticity of the first stone had yet to be proved or disproved. "Here is something that, if it is a hoax, it is one of the best ever," he told me when I met him in downtown Raleigh one afternoon. "Here we are still talking about a stone found in 1937, and we still can't say if it was real or not!"

His book attracted the attention of a young film producer named Brandon McCormick who was casting about for a fresh angle for a cable show about the Lost Colony. Because McCormick lived in Atlanta, he paid a visit to nearby Brenau. "I took at face value that it was a hoax," he said. McCormick brought in a pair of stonemasons (one of their previous credits was *Search for the Lost Giants*) who showed that the Eberhardt rocks were filled with modern drill marks that proved them forged. Because Sparkes had already proved this beyond any doubt, the results made for good television but didn't contribute any new revelations. McCormick said he could dig no deeper. "The History Channel likes its mysteries solved within an hour," he told me with chagrin.

After the show aired in 2015, McCormick—like Sparkes—couldn't let go of the subject. "It's been an obsession," he admitted. Though he hadn't trained as a researcher, he trolled the microfiche at Emory and was stunned by the number of American newspaper headlines just prior to World War II that covered the rocks. "I could go mad over this," he admitted. "We love mysteries. And this is a letter from a girl to her dad—her first word is 'Father! Come find me!'"

The media attention spawned by La Vere's book and the television program put the Dare Stone again in the limelight, prompting Brenau's president, Ed Schrader, to remove it from the library to his personal office, which is protected by a better alarm system. Schrader, a geologist, also took the stone (with irony that the Pearces might not have appreciated) to a North Carolina lab in order to slice off the bottom section, below the lettering. McCormick filmed the diamond saw cutting through the stone for a second History Channel documentary, which aired in 2017. "We wanted to look at the chemistry and geomorphology," said Schrader, a silver-haired scientist who has run the university since 2005.

The results of the destructive test were compared with ballast stones, including one from Roanoke Island that likely came from England. The Hammond stone proved to be of a type common to central North Carolina and Virginia, as Lester had concluded in 1937, rather than a stone carried across the Atlantic in an English ship. More important, the test revealed an exposed interior as bright as the white meat of a well-done turkey breast contrasting sharply with the worn gray on the outside.

Brenau president Ed Schrader holds the Dare Stone during a 2016 test at UNC Asheville in which part of the rock was sliced for analysis. *Brenau University*

Whenever the original inscription was made, the white letters must have stood out sharply against the dark exterior. This made just such a stone a logical choice for a Roanoke colonist but a poor one for a forger, who would have to age the markings so that they appeared as weathered as the stone's natural surface. This can be done through chemicals, but that would have required considerable expertise.

Schrader asked an English professor named Kevin Quarmby at Oxford College of Emory University, a nearby rural feeder school for Emory (with no connection to the British school), to examine the stone's wording. A former Shakespearean actor from England, he found it convincingly Elizabethan. "I've seen nothing that says it might not be 1580s," he told me.

Quarmby noted that the writer used a superscript *e* to write the word "ye," which today would read as "the." He said that particular lettering was used only briefly and would therefore be less likely for a hoaxer to be aware of and to imitate. He freely admitted, however, that he was no expert in Elizabethan paleography, the study of deciphering and dating writings from the second half of the sixteenth century. All the stone's early detractors, he added, were 1930s men likely to be skeptical that a woman like Eleanor Dare could write, or even show enough initiative to record her story. But he admitted there was not enough solid evidence to confirm the stone's authenticity. "All I can go on is my gut feeling," said Quarmby.

Given the charged history of the rock, gut feeling and strong opinion felt woefully inadequate. The attempts to prove or disprove the Dare Stone's authenticity seemed more designed to keep television viewers from switching channels during commercial breaks than producing serious data. I was sure more serious analysis could be done. That should have been a clue that I was captive to the Roanoke vortex.

On a bright November day in 2016, I paid a visit to Brenau in Gainesville, on the far fringe of Atlanta's sprawl. Most of the rocks that once beguiled America are now stowed in the attic of a Victorian house on campus. Kathryn Amos, a university administrator, is the keeper of the objects. She met me at the door, and I followed her up three flights of stairs.

"The article in the *Saturday Evening Post* was such an embarrassment that the president said it would ruin the reputation of the college, so they were hidden away," she said as she searched for the right key on a jangling ring. "World War II was a good diversion." She opened the door into the low gabled space.

The floor was covered with dozens of ragged flat stones, all filled with the same strange swirly and shallow incisions. "These are fakes," she said. I imagined Sparkes examining the same stones in 1940 with a skeptical air as Pearce hovered nervously behind him. "But it does make for an interesting story. We still don't know how Eberhardt did it. He was a country boy who found out we had a president crazy enough to cough up a couple of hundred bucks every time he brought in a rock."

After the humiliating revelations, no one had the courage to lose or the heart to destroy the stones. Instead, they were hidden under the school auditorium and then in a boiler room under the amphitheater before they were brought here a decade ago. They passed into local legend. Amos said students spun tales of the ghost of Eleanor's lost daughter Agnes, the child imagined by Eberhardt and said to haunt the campus. But save for the occasional newspaper article reviving the story, the saga of the Dare Stones was swept under Brenau's rug.

"When I got here twelve years ago, I thought the stones were interesting but probably a hoax," Schrader told me. It seemed fitting that a man dedicated to rocks would be a successor to Pearce senior. "But I had a very strong feeling about the original stone." Hammond's rock sat on a side table in the president's office next to a bottle of Virginia Dare Wine, with a label featuring a cheerful curly-haired blonde.

The arrangement felt like a shrine. I slid on the white cotton gloves laid out next to the stone and picked up the rock that Pearce had first seen in the alumni office at Emory eight decades ago. The letters proved surprisingly hard to make out, even after I had looked at online images that highlighted the words. I understood why it took the Emory team so long to decipher the message.

Later, I leafed through the 1940 Morison committee recommendations ignored by Pearce. My idea was to use the panel's road map to match up experts who could offer their views and, if Schrader were game, allow extensive analysis using modern methods. By building up several lines of evidence distinct from one another, it might be possible to resolve the controversy of the stone's authenticity once and for all. The Brenau president had already conducted geological research on the stone's composition, as the committee suggested.

Morison's panel also told Pearce to closely examine the forms of letters on the stones. The inscription, after all, wasn't in the form of a letter written on paper. Carving rock requires a different approach from penning parchment. The scientists urged a focus on stone graffiti from the period, such as those in the Tower of London, where prisoners carved their names, dates, prayers, and sufferings into the bare stone walls. "Close prisoner 32 weeks, 224 days, 5376 hours," wrote a T. Salmon in 1622.

I tracked down Matthew Champion, a medieval graffiti expert who leads the Norfolk Medieval Graffiti Survey in Britain and the undisputed expert in the arcane world of old English stone carving. He started the project when he visited a small church in eastern England in 2010. The churchwarden assured him there was nothing much to see. When he shone his flashlight at an angle to the stone, however, the walls came alive with shallow carvings and drawings of demons, dates, and even the outlines of hands. Champion and his colleagues have since recorded more than twenty-eight thousand inscriptions in nearly seven hundred churches, and that is only in a single English county.

Champion's work puts the Dare Stone in a new light. He discovered that churches were the medieval equivalent of New York subway cars and overpasses, canvases for the masses. Stone carving was as much public pastime as a specialty craft. He agreed to take a look at high-resolution images of the Hammond stone, which he had not heard about and had never seen before. I waited with a measure of dread, suspecting he would report back that it was an obvious fake and I was a foolish dupe. His reply, which came within hours, made me stand bolt upright from my chair.

"To be honest, I find myself in slightly uncomfortable circumstances this evening," he wrote. "When faced with such historical myths and legends as the Dare Stone my usual role is that of debunking them. However, on this occasion I am finding that rather difficult to do. Given the evidence of the inscription, within the wider context of informal sixteenth century graffiti inscriptions, I would be very reticent of simply passing this away as a forgery." Were the inscription on an English church wall—leaving aside the contents—"I would have no hesitation in accepting it at face value."

He was particularly struck by the weathered nature of the incisions that closely matched the stone. "Such surface patination takes many years to achieve naturally," he explained. "When an inscription is first cut it would appear bright white on the stone, particularly so on this type of stone, and it takes a great deal of time for that whiteness to fade." To back this up, he included pictures of similar stone carved in the 1980s in which the pale letters still stood out starkly from the darker stone despite more than three decades of weathering. Though chemicals could be used to mask the age, he added that these typically leave behind telltale blotches that are easy for the trained eye to spot.

Champion then swept away an argument made in 1940 that the stone carver's use of Roman text rather than the Gothic or black-type form of lettering signaled a fake. "The use of Roman text at this period is really very common," he explained. "The Roman italic type-face was first used in England in 1559 and by the 1580s was the norm," including in graffiti. He attached photographs of similar letters dating to the era.

He also examined suspicious figures on the Dare Stone, such as what he called "a rather modern looking 5," but offered convincing contemporary examples. "There is nothing here that strikes me as obviously anomalous in any way, shape or form, at least in regard to the style and mechanics of the inscription," he concluded. "My only hesitation would perhaps come from the use of the abbreviation 'VIA' for Virginia." Given that the term "Virginia" was only created in 1584, there were no known carvings of the word from the era to say for sure.

While Champion couldn't vouch for the stone's content, he was skeptical that a 1930s forger would have had the savvy to age the let-ters artificially and also be expert in late-sixteenth-century English inscriptions. "From my study of the graffiti and documents of the period I see no glaring problems with what is on the stone."

With that surprising judgment in hand, I turned back to the Mori-son panel and its next recommendation. The academics had called for specialists in the use of specific words and phrases used on the stone.

"There is nothing that jumps out as a forgery," said Heather Wolfe at the Folger Shakespeare Library in Washington, D.C., one of the world's leading research institutions on Shakespeare and his times, after examining high-resolution images of the Brenau stone. Her one doubt regarded the use of the three initials—"EWD"—because this was not a standard way to sign one's name in that era. When I checked with another Elizabethan literature scholar, Jean Wilson of Cambridge University, she found the phrase "greate plentie presents" peculiar but added "there's nothing in the inscription that couldn't be of its purported date."

I had fully expected these skeptical scholars, with no previous knowledge of the stone's history, to make short work of Hammond's rock and its melodramatic story. Instead, as my excitement grew, they seemed to line up in favor of its authenticity. Then I contacted the

Reverend Professor Diarmaid N. J. MacCulloch, a knighted Oxford don and Church of England deacon. MacCulloch's PhD was in Tudor history, and he also holds an advanced degree in theology. When not writing award-winning books on the Reformation, this polymath is a television personality who presents series such as *How God Made the English* and *Sex and the Church*. He quickly extinguished my excitement with one droll and devastating sentence.

"It has all the plausibility of Dick Van Dyke's Cockney accent in *Mary Poppins*," he responded after viewing the stone's images. "You can rest assured that it is a risible forgery," he added. "Even before I got to the second side with its cod-Elizabethan language, the nature of the orthography and the phrase 'went hence unto heaven' gave it away. In more than half a century of looking at Elizabethan tombstones, I have never seen a similar phrase. It sounds like something a Victorian stained-glass window might contain."

MacCulloch proceeded to swat down Quarmby's superscript theory involving the word "ye." Then he noted the lack of contraction marks commonly used at the time. The carver's decision to spell out Arabic numbers rather than use the more common Roman numerals was laughable. "Why write 'seaven' when you could write 'vii'?" he asked. He dismissed "misarie" as "an odd spelling even by Tudor standards." The initials that bothered the Folger's Wolfe left him incredulous. And the carver's use of the name "Ananias" was absurd, he added. "You simply wouldn't call your husband by his Christian name in any circumstances; you'd call him husband or, in this case, my husband."

As for Eleanor's plea that her father give the Indian messenger "greate plentie presents," the phrase to him seemed right out of a bad Western. "Just in case some Native American can read Tudor English, and then they will get Heap Plenty Wampum." MacCulloch's derision left me deflated. I had a sinking feeling that this was yet another instance of a Lost Colony clue that was an illusion.

Wolfe at the Folger, however, quickly parried the Oxford don's criticisms. She found a reference to "went unto heaven" dating to 1616 as well as an Oxford English Dictionary mention of "misarie." The

American scholar explained that numbers in that day were written out or expressed in Roman or Arabic numbers. And, she added, "some people used contraction marks; others didn't." She didn't take Mac-Culloch's view that Eleanor Dare's Tonto-esque use of the phrase about presents was necessarily anachronistic.

Nor did she share MacCulloch's scorn about the unlikelihood of Eleanor's naming Ananias. "Yes, an Elizabethan woman would refer to her husband by his Christian name in a situation like this," she said. The only point on which Wolfe and MacCulloch agreed was that the use of three initials—"EWD"—was odd. Most people of the day would have used only the initials for their first and last names. Given that Dare might have wanted to underscore her maiden name in a letter to her father, however, that hardly seemed strong enough evidence to render the stone a forgery on its own.

MacCulloch dismissed Wolfe's response. It provided "far too many benefits to far too many doubts." The stone was, he declared with no caveat, "a fake." When I pressed him again, I received this curt reply that brooked no follow-up: "Enough already."

Who was right? Unsure what to make of this academic deadlock, I went back to Champion, the graffiti expert, for his opinion. "The authenticity of this stone can never be fully and finally established without further corroborative evidence," he responded. "They really have to address the matter as a serious archaeological project," said Champion. "This would be a major, and controversial, reassessment of the stone, which would rewrite early colonial history, so any argument needs to be as fully watertight as possible."

That means a high-tech study of its patina to go along with geological, graffiti, and linguistic lines of evidence. Eric Doehne, a geologist and art conservator in Los Angeles, wrote a book on stone conservation and analyzed the Dead Sea Scrolls and the Sistine Chapel. Though he had not heard of the Dare Stone, his family visited the Outer Banks when he was a child, and he dimly remembered seeing the outdoor drama. "There are geochemical methods to look for trace

elements and isotopes that could support one or the other interpretation," he told me. "Ultraviolet or multispectral photography can be
useful in guiding where to sample."

But when I called Schrader at Brenau to see if he wanted to pursue
a multidisciplinary approach with these experts to resolve the matter once and for all, his response was lukewarm. His spokesperson
later told me, "Our plan is to move forward as quickly as is prudent."
A year passed, and a friend of the president's explained to me that
Schrader feared losing control of what could become a major historical
breakthrough. I thought of Pearce's possessiveness that kept him from
collaborating with others as the Morison panel urged.

The rock's engaging mystery had put Brenau on the map, first as
a triumph, then as humiliation. The stones had been discredited once.
If the one with a shred of potential legitimacy were proved unequivocally a fake, then the college might have to endure a national spotlight of ignominy all over again. And if it proved the real thing, then
Schrader might be compelled to remove it from its shrine in his office
and hand it over to a major museum.

Even the most thorough research results, however, may not convince longtime skeptics like Evans from the First Colony Foundation.
White's final visit to Roanoke was long thought to have taken place
in 1591 rather than 1590. A legal suit related to the mission surfaced
in a British archive after World War II confirming that the governor
arrived on Roanoke Island in August 1590. The stone's message, however, cites a 1591 date. "You don't need a scientific test," said Evans.
"This was a 911 call to John White to come quick, but the date is
wrong. It's a hoax."

There was, however, one Morison recommendation that didn't
require in-depth analysis of the stone. "The search for graves, skeletal remains, and other possible relics should be resumed as soon and
pursued as thoroughly as possible," the report stated. By then, the
Pearces had already sought in vain the second stone mentioned in the
Hammond inscription, the rock said to mark the murdered colonists'
resting place, including that of Virginia and Ananias Dare.

In the aftermath of Sparkes's article and Pearce's ruined career,
professional archaeologists steered well clear of the publicly discred-

ited rock. For three-quarters of a century, no one bothered to follow up the Pearces' excavations around Edenton.

But I knew someone who cared even less about scholarly respectability than I did. He was the human equivalent of the Dare Stone, a divisive figure whose name was a kind of trigger word for many of those involved in Roanoke studies. (The historian in Manteo refused to let me use her name in this book if it contained his.) Fred Willard, the same man who badgered Phelps into digging at Cape Creek, was firmly convinced that he could find the second stone and solve the mystery that had daunted so many credentialed scholars for so long. When he invited me on one of his expeditions, I happily agreed.

Willard has been the Zelig of Lost Colony television, invariably popping up on the perennial cable shows that promise to resolve America's oldest cold case in an hour, including commercials. He lures producers into mosquito-ridden swamps with promises of old buried coffins and carved stones that never quite pan out. They love him anyway, because ratings show that viewers love him too. He never earned an advanced degree, and his title is often given as "maverick archaeologist."

When I finally met him one cold winter morning in a Manteo diner, he was not hard to spot among the crowded booths. His bald pate, scraggly beard, and piercing eyes gave him the look of a vengeful marsh prophet. "We think the main colony went inland to harvest sassafras," he told me as he finished his eggs. Their vanishing act was, he is convinced, an elaborate ruse to protect Raleigh's valuable monopoly from competitors. I found it hard to imagine more than a hundred people and scores of sailors working on dozens of ships agreeing to a vast conspiracy of silence. For more than a decade, however, Willard and a band of followers tramped through the dense wetlands west of Roanoke Island, seeking in vain the physical evidence necessary to back up the novel, if unlikely, theory.

The 2012 discovery of what lay under the patch on the White map and the revival of Dare Stone publicity at almost exactly the same time drew Willard out of the swamps. It's an odd fact that Hammond said he found his stone near the mouth of the Chowan River, just a few miles from where, eight decades later, Luccketti and the First Colony Foundation began to dig at Site X. Willard quickly picked up on this apparent coincidence.

Parsing old maps, photographs, and Pearce's accounts, Willard believes he has pinpointed the site of the Dare Stone discovery. I followed his battered blue Suburban as we drove out of Manteo, across the Virginia Dare Memorial Bridge, and onto the narrow road that straddles two drainage canals filled with dark water and bordered by shadowy marsh. On the way we stopped at his headquarters, the Lost Colony Center for Science and Research, a ramshackle house that smelled alarmingly of mold from a recent flood, to pore over satellite photographs as if we were preparing a military campaign. Willard was even wearing camouflage. Finally we continued our drive west and halted at a parking lot next to an abandoned marina just upstream from where the Chowan River meets the Albemarle Sound, just outside Edenton. The place had a desolate air; a sunken boat was still tied to the rotting pilings. Just beyond, through the trees, where a small creek meets the Chowan, Willard says Hammond picked up the famous rock.

With his wife, Kathryn, we walked gingerly through cold mud toward the water. The two met in an archaeology course at East Carolina. Though she's half his age, they shared a common fascination with the Roanoke story. A self-described autistic, Kathryn also is a peanut heiress. "When my father passed away, and I came into my inheritance, I didn't know what the heck to do with my money," she said as we trudged through the mud. "Then I met Fred."

The muck eventually grew too deep, and the January sun was already dropping swiftly behind the trees, so we retreated.

The following summer, Willard made a more concerted effort to investigate the area, hiring an archaeology team to excavate as the History Channel filmed. Though they found extensive Indian pottery, their holes filled up too quickly with water for the search to bear much fruit. Undeterred, Willard then turned his attention to the stone marker referred to in the Hammond rock. The inscription states that those colonists killed during the massacre, including Virginia Dare and her father, Ananias, were buried on a hill four miles east of the river, their names "Writ Al There on Rocke."

On a cool and clear fall day, I came along on one of his frequent weekend expeditions seeking the missing tombstones. Willard's screen fame attracts a loyal cadre of volunteers for weekend assaults on America's oldest mystery. The current target was a farm on a low hill four miles from the Hammond site on the Chowan. Our convoy of three vehicles bumped across the furrows and halted at the pine trees lining the bottom of the sloping field. The team immediately divvied up a bulky screened box as well as a GPS device, shovels, and a metal detector and moved quietly into the forest's deep shadows in single file.

Leading the way was a freelance astronomy teacher and guitarist with a droopy mustache named Frank Jones who wore a camouflage cap with matching high boots. I envied his waterproof trousers made of some high-tech wicking material, as well as the plastic straw along his neck that was connected to a concealed water supply. Behind him was a lean and taciturn farmer in thick work gloves named Gaston Pinner and a certified clinical aromatherapy practitioner named Wendy Corcoran, in a red sweater with long gray hair. A middle-aged stocky man named George, wearing bulky metal-detecting headphones, vanished into the woods before I could get his last name. Bringing up the rear were Kathryn, sucking sullenly on a giant candy cane, and a limping Fred Willard. "I'm sore," he explained, pointing to his right shoulder. "I shot a 180-pound deer yesterday and had to haul it out. I can barely walk today."

I asked him why, if the inscription said the second stone was east, we were four miles to the north of the river. He brushed off this directional discrepancy with a swipe of his thick hand. "After thirty years of research, I think they moved northeast," Willard said, adding that the colonists would have followed the meandering creek as they moved inland.

"Indian sites are always along the water," he explained. "If murder took place, then it would have been a raid at an Indian village." The burials, he said, would be on a hill above a Native American settlement. "I know we're attempting to find the proverbial needle in the haystack," he said, wheezing and pausing to grab a tree for support. "But I have four farmers under contract with about five hundred to eight hundred acres in that four-mile zone. We've eliminated two and we have two to go." The permissions allowed him to dig.

The 1586 account by Lane suggested that this inland region, with its richer soil and more plentiful wildlife, was a more prosperous and populous area than the fringes of the coast such as Roanoke or Croatoan. This prosperity, however, drew Iroquois or Susquehanna raiders from the west and north. "We think these Indians came down for a raid and got very, very lucky and captured twenty-four English," he said, referring to the stone's assertion that two dozen settlers died in the two years following White's 1587 departure. "They ritualistically tortured and murdered all of them until the chief stepped in." The Indian leader, he said, allowed seven to live, including Eleanor Dare.

Clay Swindell, the archaeologist at the Museum of the Albemarle who has worked at Site X, said that a combination of raids and European disease left this area largely depopulated by the time the second wave of English settlers arrived in the second half of the seventeenth century. The Iroquoian speakers called Tuscarora—Mangoaks in Carolina Algonquian—dominated the area by then. But he added that there is no evidence to back up Willard's specific claim that colonists were kidnapped.

Soon the gentle slope disappeared into a full cypress swamp. A small finger of land extended into green-tinged goo, amid the flared trunks of ghostly-looking trees. Even though it was late fall, mosquitoes lazily circled. "Set it up here!" Willard barked. Without further instruction, the obedient crew placed the screen on top of short wooden posts. Frank dug a hole nearby, tossing thick masses of earth into the box. The clumpy soil smelled musty. Pinner and Corcoran took turns shaking the sifter for a minute or so before feeling with their hands through the clay for signs of broken pots or other artifacts.

Willard carefully eyed their progress as he leaned on a cane, occasionally reaching in to spread the damp dirt. "Nothing," he said after a few minutes with a note of disgust. He abruptly directed the team to move in a straight line back up the hill. The volunteers reassembled the screen box and dug a fresh hole. "What I want to be is systematic!"

declared Willard. George, the man with the metal detector, wandered back holding an iron spike and an old bottle of the fortified flavored wine called Mad Dog 20/20. He gave Willard the spike. "That's from logging machinery," Willard said, handing it back to George, who promptly vanished again.

Willard brusquely ordered the crew to move back up the slope to dig another test trench. After half a dozen holes that revealed no artifacts, he abruptly called it a day, saying the next time they would dig at another farm. The eager volunteers were crestfallen. On the way back up the slope to the trucks, Corcoran quietly expressed her dismay. A gregarious woman, she had helped organize a charity event for the dig at the local country club, with backing from the owner of a McDonald's, while devoting countless weekends to working under Willard's supervision.

"I got tick bites, poison ivy, and I killed a snake in the process," she told me. She was happy with the work but frustrated by Willard's tendency to bounce from one place to another without finishing an investigation. Her disappointment with leaving this particular site was based on a recent find that she and other volunteers had made the week before, when they met on their own initiative to poke around the farm. "We've already found stones here," she said as we emerged from the woods. She pointed at a large old pin oak at the top of the rise, where the team found a pile of rocks hidden in the tall grass. One appeared to have letters. They called Willard, insisting that he come right away.

"Yes, I got a call three days ago that they'd found a stone with writing," Willard confirmed while the crew packed up their equipment. "You gotta remember these are novices, not professionals," he added, without a hint of irony. "It is totally inconclusive. I've got the stone in my truck. You can see it for yourself."

He rummaged around in the back of his worn blue Suburban crammed with plastic boxes and wood scraps. Finally he pulled out an irregular flat brown stone about a foot long and half as wide. "On the front side of the stone they said was the word 'DARE.' On the back side was carved a *V* and an *A*." I couldn't see any markings until Willard splashed it with water from a plastic jug. Then I could make out dark splotches on the rock. Two of the markings were somewhat

Volunteers working with Fred Willard in 2016 found a stone near Edenton, North Carolina, that they speculated could mark Virginia Dare's grave.

V- and A-shaped but seemed more likely to be natural because they were not carved incisions. No matter what angle I looked at the other side, however, I couldn't make out the word "DARE," or any word at all. Willard was similarly skeptical.

After the volunteers dispersed, I joined Kathryn and Fred for a meal in Edenton. I asked him why he felt so sure that the rock Hammond brought to Emory was real. "We know that the stone was found sitting on top of a major Indian site," Willard replied. "How would the guy have known to put a forged stone there? And he put all the information on the stone about seven people being saved." He also noted the Jamestown account mentioning seven Roanoke colonists—including a young woman—enslaved following a massacre.

Hammond could have read about the seven slaves mentioned by Machumps and recorded by Strachey. And Indian sites along rivers in eastern North Carolina are common. What he could not have known was what lay under the patch on the White map that directed archaeologists to the area just across the Chowan River. Based on what was known in the 1930s, it made little sense for a forger to pretend to find a stone at that spot. Croatoan or Roanoke would have been better choices, because they were close to the coast and accessible to White, for whom the letter was allegedly written. Yet this fact did nothing to prove the Dare Stone authentic.

When dessert came, I asked Willard why he had spent so many years searching for the Lost Colony. "People will kill to solve this!" he told me. "It's the most exciting unsolved mystery in American history." Then he listed those who got in his way, starting with his mentor Phelps. "I fired them all," he declared, *Apprentice*-style.

Suddenly he leaned forward menacingly, his beard grazing the apple cobbler on his plate. "Look me in the eye! You know who you are looking at! Get in my way and I will fucking run over you!" He leaned back into his chair, his counterfeit fury spent and his attention now on the cobbler. "It's about having fun," he added mildly, "and the moment anyone causes me not to have fun, they are gone."

Fed up with Willard's bullying and disorganization, Corcoran severed her ties with him a few months later. He kept the stone that she and the others found. When I saw him the following spring, he took me aside to tell me about "a significant find" that might be a Lost Colony game changer. He had forgotten that he had shown me the rock already, in a considerably more skeptical mood. Willard bristled when I asked him why he changed his mind. Later I heard he was trying to sell the rights to use the stone in a cable channel special. There were also rumors among his followers of a mass grave with Indian copper. Somehow nothing solid ever came to light, but there was always just enough of a hook to keep you from changing the station at the commercial break.

Willard, however, never sold the rights to the newly found stone. In October 2017, while deer hunting on his property, he lost his balance and fell from a tree. "Hold me up," he told Kathryn when she rushed to his aid. "Let me look at the farm." He died in her arms, gazing over the fields. Before he passed away, the seventy-seven-year-old asked her to spread some of his ashes where Hammond claimed to have found the Dare Stone outside Edenton and at Cape Creek on Hatteras, where a quarter of a century earlier he had first noticed the Native American artifacts unearthed by Hurricane Emily.

Have you ever heard of *The Treasure of the Sierra Madre*?" a historian friend of mine asked when we were having dinner one night, referring to the 1948 John Huston film about three American gold prospectors in Mexico. "That's what the Lost Colony is—guys looking for treasure, and when they find it, they kill each other. Nobody survives."

I had spent much of the meal grousing about the lack of solid data and the endless theorizing. If the geologists were right, then the archaeologists on Roanoke Island had been chasing ghosts for well over a century in their search for a settlement. Meanwhile, Luccketti and his team had yet to determine if the colonists lived at the spot suggested by what lay under the patch on the White map. After years of work, he concluded Site X was "an enigma." And while Horton told a good story of Lost Colony descendants treasuring heirlooms at Cape Creek, he had yet to do the hard-core scientific analysis necessary to support his claims. The Dare Stone remained in a kind of academic limbo, unexamined by the bevy of experts necessary to show whether it was real or fake. And Willard had never discovered the graves of Ananias and Virginia Dare that he sought with such doggedness.

"But," I protested to my friend, "there's no gold involved. Even the ring is brass."

"Why do people search for Noah's ark?" he replied. "Why do people search for Amelia Earhart? What is going to come out of it? You can't own it. You get fifteen minutes of fame. But anybody could be that person. There is a mental illness involved with searching for something that can hardly be found. I've seen so many people go over the deep end. It's a disease. That is why the Lost Colony is such a great story."

That explained why the atmosphere among those searching for clues was so oddly charged. Willard's dramatic outburst—"I will fucking run over you!"—seemed to sum up relations among the researchers, professional as well as amateur. Luccketti and Horton were quick to criticize each other's research, while Noël Hume and the National Park Service had fought to a bitter standstill about the earthwork. Evans's First Colony Foundation refused to participate in a public panel that included Horton and Prentice, and organized their own competing symposium. The Lost Colony Research Group denounced the Lost Colony Center for Science and Research. The Croatoan Archaeological Society was locked in an ongoing battle with a splinter group that threatened legal action over credit for the Cape Creek excavations. Accusations of sloppy science, bad faith, and even fraud flew. And there was no love lost between Willard and everyone else. Ewen from East Carolina University was the only archaeologist to attend his funeral.

No one seemed to want to talk to anyone beyond the confines of their group, much less collaborate. I had covered lots of archaeology digs throughout my journalistic career, including in the fractious Middle East, but had never encountered such hostility and suspicion among people essentially seeking the same thing. "You are an evil and cruel person," read an e-mail from one to another copied to my in-box. There was some disturbing power that Roanoke seemed to hold over those who tried to solve a mystery that probably was unsolvable.

My dinner companion parted with a warning: "You better watch it yourself."

When I got home, I looked at my stacks of books and piles of papers. I told myself that I was just a writer following a story, doing a job. True, I had trouble changing the subject from the 1580s when I was with friends and family. I would wake up in the morning puzzling over the strange smoke signals that John White saw. I was impatient with geologists like Schrader and archaeologists like Horton, pestering them with e-mails and phone calls to see if they had completed their long-promised analyses.

I had to admit then that this went beyond professional diligence and into the very obsession that I had observed in so many others.

Maybe, I thought, I was asking the wrong questions. What made the Roanoke story so interesting, as my historian friend had said, was not necessarily what happened to the colonists but why we care so much and so deeply. How could a few long-dead Elizabethans hold me, and so many others, in such a strangely tenacious grip?

Brent Lane had said that the real story of Roanoke "had nothing to do with Virginia Dare and the poor lost white people—the lost cause of the sixteenth century and all that southern gothic shit." I wondered if he was wrong. I recalled the label of the wine bottle in Schrader's office shrine at Brenau, with its imagined blond-haired and blue-eyed Virginia Dare. The real power exerted by the Lost Colonists was not in archives or archaeological trenches but in the stories they spawned.

If I couldn't pinpoint exactly where White's settlers went after he departed in 1587, or how they ended their days, then at least I could explore how their story had morphed into a legend so enduring that it remains—even now—a reliable source for American pop culture. At the time, turning away from my quest for a solid scientific answer to the colonists' fate felt like a diversion—or even a retreat. But tracing the rise of the subsequent Roanoke myths led me where archaeologists and historians could not: to the Lost Colony's likeliest descendants and their extraordinary four-hundred-year journey.

PART THREE

The Revelation

I GOT LOST BUT LOOK WHAT I FOUND.

—Irving Berlin, *Annie Get Your Gun*

CHAPTER TWELVE

Who's Afraid of Virginia Dare?

She is the most famous American about whom so little is known. Her grandfather, John White, mentions her only once and then just in passing. Her sole biographical details are the dates of her birth and baptism. Like nearly a quarter of the babies of that era, she may well have perished before her third birthday, when White waded ashore after his long struggle to return to Roanoke.

Yet as I plowed through papers, books, and websites, a teenaged Virginia Dare kept turning up on old tobacco tins, in fantasy novels and horror movies, and even as the name of a San Francisco rock band ("songs for runaways, alcoholics, and deep sleepers").

Most alarmingly, I learned that the daughter of Eleanor and Ananias Dare had become a rallying cry for white supremacists who envision her plight—an innocent blond girl surrounded by dark and dangerous savages—as analogous to the immigration crisis they believe threatens the United States today. Discovering how the babe of Roanoke became an icon of racial purity, and part of an ongoing national struggle to define what it means to be an American, seemed a good place to start my search for the source of our perennial fascination with the Lost Colony.

The first reference that I could find to Virginia Dare after White's brief note came a full two-and-a-half centuries later. It was George Bancroft, the Harvard historian who had studied in Germany and was later hailed as the father of American history, who resurrected the child in 1834 as "the first offspring of English parents on the soil of the United States."

Bancroft published the first volume in his seminal work at an opportune moment. The 1830s were a volatile and violent time for Americans. The nation's founders were dead, and the 1829 to 1837 populist presidency of Andrew Jackson—nicknamed King Mob—threatened to tear the country apart. The Irish and Germans, many Catholic, flooding into the country alarmed Americans of English and Scottish origin. A massive Protestant evangelical revival was under way. Meanwhile, an 1830 act of Congress drove tens of thousands of Native Americans west of the Mississippi so that white planters and their black slaves could colonize the Deep South. Yet the rising numbers of enslaved African Americans posed their own threat; Nat Turner's 1831 rebellion in Virginia, just across the border from Roanoke Island, sparked white fears of massive insurrection. In subsequent years, southern states severely curtailed the rights of blacks, whether enslaved or free.

Protestant whites descended from British settlers felt the country's dominant heritage and their control over the nation's direction slipping away. Eleanor's daughter quickly became the emotional focus of the vanished settlers' tale, the innocent infant abandoned in a dangerous land amid dark savages capable of brutal murder. Within a year after publication of Bancroft's bestseller, she was being referred to in newspapers as "the first Anglo-American, Miss Virginia Dare."

Dare was particularly appealing to white women. The 1830s also marked the appearance of periodicals for women and writers who could attract this growing readership. Journalist Margaret Fuller and author Harriet Beecher Stowe launched their careers in this period. Eliza Lanesford Cushing, an American born in Massachusetts, was part of this vanguard of female authors. Her mother and sister were also authors. She married a doctor and moved to Montreal in 1833. From her Canadian home she transformed the infant of Roanoke from a historical footnote into a legend, coining the term "Lost Colony" in the process.

Cushing specialized in patriotic historical romances such as *Sara-*

toga and *Yorktown* and published frequently in women's magazines. The dearth of female figures in early American history, however, frustrated her. She remedied the problem in a December 1837 article published in the *Ladies' Companion* called "Virginia Dare; or, The Lost Colony." For the next century John White's resurrected granddaughter would play the starring role in the legends of Roanoke.

Just how and why Cushing latched onto the final Roanoke voyage isn't clear, although Bancroft's history likely provided a spur. "This is when we start saying that the colony was lost as opposed to it simply failed," said Tom Shields, a literature professor at East Carolina University who rediscovered the long-forgotten piece. Cushing pioneered an approach copied ever since. She drew on the historical record until the point of White's departure and then moved into romantic fiction.

In her story, a massacre wipes out almost everyone but the vulnerable baby, who survives with the help of the loyal Manteo. She grows into a fair-haired beauty who dazzles the swarthy Indians. "The fairy-like proportions of her form, the delicate hue of her skin, the soft ringlets of her hair, and eyes of heavenly blue, were their delight and admiration." The girl is lily-white both inside and out. "She seemed to be invested with a halo of brightness and purity, which lent a touching charm to her beauty," Cushing writes.

As a young woman, however, she's betrothed to a vindictive Indian with "uncontrolled passions." Fortunately, a Spanish soldier materializes to rescue her. They end up with Manteo and his son on a ship bound for Spain. Manteo dies, but the happy couple raises his child in the shadow of the Pyrenees. Time and European civilization ensure that "every trace of his savage origin was eradicated from his character and almost from his memory."

It is a chilling epilogue that reveals more about mid-nineteenth-century America than about sixteenth-century Roanoke. This was an era when children were often removed from their Indian parents for acculturation, a process now widely considered a form of cultural genocide, a process inflicted in this same era on the remaining Native Americans in eastern North Carolina.

Fantastic tales of Virginia Dare—and, through them, the once-obscure story of Roanoke—proliferated. In 1840, the *Southern Lit-*

VIRGINIA DARE.

"Though her attire was that of an Indian princess, her skin was of dazzling whiteness." In this 1857 woodcut from *Harper's New Monthly Magazine*, Virginia Dare lives incongruously among Carolina Algonquians in Great Plains–style tepees.

erary Messenger, which regularly published darkly romantic stories by Edgar Allan Poe and other well-known writers, printed an article by Cornelia Tuthill, a Connecticut author who drew directly on Bancroft's history for her version. "It is a wonder that no one has before paid a tribute to the memory of Virginia Dare," she wrote in her letter to the editor, apparently unaware of Cushing's earlier piece.

Her story portrays Eleanor Dare as a stalwart pioneer and proto-feminist who persuades Raleigh to include women on the mission. Virginia later matures into a New World Diana, "chaste and fair," who wears a white doeskin off one shoulder. The beautiful young white girl, a capable huntress who holds herself aloof from the adoring Indians, became the signature theme of Virginia Dare stories in the decades that followed.

A remarkable sculptor named Maria Louisa Lander likely read some of these tales as a youth in Massachusetts in the 1840s. When not quite thirty, she moved by herself to Rome. There she met Nathaniel Hawthorne, who hailed from her hometown of Salem, site of that other shadowy piece of early American history, the 1692 witch trials. Impressed by her talent, and possibly in love with this unusual expat, the famous author commissioned Lander to sculpt his bust.

Hawthorne was taken with the attractive artist, who was "living here quite alone, in delightful freedom" with "genuine talent, and spirit and independence enough to give it fair play." He describes her as a young woman who wore a plain pea jacket in her studio, "thousands of miles from her New England home," and "going fearlessly about these mysterious streets, by night as well as by day; with no household ties, nor rule or law but that within her."

No doubt drawn to the story of an independent woman living a solo existence thousands of miles from family and friends, Lander seized on Dare as the subject for a new kind of American-themed sculpture that went beyond tired Greek and Roman mythological themes. In 1858, she completed a small-scale model of a young European woman dressed as an Indian.

"We have recently seen a photograph of an exquisite statuette, executed in marble by Miss Lander at Rome," that "represents Virginia Dare, the first offspring of English parents born on the soil of the United States," noted the *New-York Tribune*. "The figure is semi-nude—the drapery, which is charmingly conceived and executed, being worn like an Indian blanket—and the ornaments are wampum beads."

A talented and single young American female in Rome, however, drew suspicion and envy in the tight-knit expat community. Hawthorne eventually refused to see her when rumors of scandal—she might have posed for a colleague as a model, thus soiling her reputation—dogged Lander. She continued work on the final and nearly life-sized Dare statue in white Carrara marble, completing it in 1860. But living in Rome as an outcast became unbearable, so she returned to the United States just as the Civil War began.

Before departing, Lander placed the statue on another ship bound for America that sank in the Mediterranean Sea off the Spanish coast. Unfazed, she paid salvagers to haul it from the water two years later. She had the statue boxed up again and put on another ship that arrived in Boston by 1863, in the middle of the bloody conflict. By then, Lander had lost her own brother, a poet and explorer, to pneumonia while he fought rebels in Virginia. As Confederate and Union forces battled at Gettysburg, she boldly placed the sculpture on exhibit in her Boston studio as "the National Statue."

Critics declared it "essentially and entirely American" and a "fresh example" of a new kind of American art. One wrote that the image "blended characteristics of both races . . . into one harmonious physique." It was a contentious subject in an era when many states in the North as well as the South forbade racial mixing. The Indian theme of her sculpture suggested that to be American meant to acknowledge and incorporate aspects of the indigenous people then so feared and despised.

Lander elaborated in an interview: "This design shows that we have in our own country rich subjects for sculpture without resorting to the old heathen mythology." Virginia Dare promised a forward-looking American art unencumbered by Old World conventions.

A New York collector bought the statue for the huge sum of five thousand dollars and had it installed in his apartment. Before he had paid for it, a fire broke out that killed the collector but didn't damage the statue. His heirs refused to honor the purchase, and the marble Virginia Dare went to live again with Lander, now in her new home in Washington. She kept it in her sitting room until her death in 1923, when it was willed to the State of North Carolina.

A week before the Civil War began, virtuous Virginia Dare took on a menacing aspect. The wife of a North Carolina Episcopal minister, Mary Mason, published a three-part serial in the *Raleigh Register* that drew on a popular William Wordsworth poem. In her version, an evil shaman turns the girl into a white doe. When a party of English hunters wounds the deer years later, she reverts to her human form long enough to thank her killers for freeing her from the spell and cursing the "red men of America." They were, the expiring Virginia said, unworthy to continue "possession of this noble and beautiful land." It was no wonder that God "has suffered a superior and advancing race of his creatures to supplant them in their rich and noble birthright."

The author notes approvingly that the dying girl "lives to witness their extinction and the wide occupation of their forfeited patrimony by that superior Race, the Anglo Saxon, with their bondsmen, the sable African, the red man's inferior."

The final serial appeared as Virginia and North Carolina wavered on leaving the Union; the article next to the story was titled "Secession

Practically Considered." One week later, rebel forces bombed Fort Sumter in Charleston Harbor, sparking the Civil War. As the nation violently clashed over slavery and the status of African Americans, Virginia Dare began to assume a new role. No longer an innocent figure sprinting through the woods of Roanoke Island, she emerged in postwar America as a potent symbol of the inevitable dominance of white Anglo-Saxon Protestants from the Atlantic to the Pacific.

Her star rose in tandem with growing fears in the 1890s that America's founding culture was under siege. Italians and eastern European Jews crowded into New York, Chicago, and other northern cities by the millions, bringing unfamiliar traditions derided by many northern European whites as barbaric. Simultaneously in the South, the newly achieved rights of African Americans led to a violent backlash in the form of vigilante justice and harsh Jim Crow laws designed to limit their power. Under her romantic gloss, Virginia Dare reminded former Confederates of their own failure and loss and the threat posed by dark savages now identified as the freed slaves rather than vengeful Indians. For the fast-expanding nation as a whole, she became "the patron saint of manifest destiny" and a kind of "Protestant Madonna" who could "exert a pervasive moral influence over the savage pagans," historian Robert Arner writes.

Virginia Dare sounded an alarm and promised the ultimate triumph of Anglo-Saxon civilization over the barbarians, and she did so with sex appeal. White's granddaughter, Arner adds, mutated into a "forbidding threatening goddess" capable of killing with ease, as well as "the all American girl dressed up in revealingly scanty doeskins."

No one made better use of this disturbing figure than Sallie Southall Cotten, later hailed as a leading southerner in the women's movement. An inveterate organizer and writer, Cotten lived much of her adult life on a remote thousand-acre farm in northeastern North Carolina raising nine children, three of whom died in childhood. She fought a long personal crusade to give Virginia Dare a more prominent place in the American pantheon, a crusade deeply tied to the era's expanding movements for white supremacy and women's rights.

Appointed to a committee planning her state's participation in the 1893 World's Columbian Exposition in Chicago, the forty-six-year-old Cotten went to Roanoke Island to choose white holly wood trees to be cut near "Old Fort Raleigh," to fashion a desk displaying scenes from the Roanoke voyages for display in Chicago. A local newspaper reported her tramping through the woods, "stirring the ashes of historic memories, and cultivating patriotic sentiments on the spot where the first white American child was born."

She hoped memorializing the events on the island "will moisten the eye with the sad memory of the lost colony and awaken heartfelt pride that the first birth of that great race that now rules the continent was the product of North Carolina soil, and feminine pride that was the birth of a girl child." This was, she wrote, the American "Bethlehem story." (She wasn't alone in using biblical terms; one contemporary historian called Roanoke "that inevitable John the Baptist," preparing the way for Jamestown.)

With six other women, Cotten chartered the Virginia Dare Columbian Memorial Association on August 18, 1892, Dare's birthday, with the goal of publicizing "the first white child born on American soil." Though it seems strange today, the numerous earlier births and baptisms of Spanish children in what became Florida, Georgia, and South Carolina did not count, because they and their southern European mothers were not considered white. North Carolina was, she wrote later, where "the history of America, and the history of white women in America, began." That year marked the opening of Ellis Island as well as the national peak in African American lynchings.

Cotten printed up a tract on Virginia Dare, a biographer says, that she "foisted on just about everyone she met" at the World's Fair that opened the following May. She failed to garner much enthusiasm amid belly-dancing exhibitions and the turning of the first Ferris wheel. She took heart, however, when the nickel she put in a Midway slot machine noted her weight—141 pounds—and predicted, "For you I see a heroic effort and handsome reward."

Cotten then encouraged a group of businessmen to create the Roanoke Colony Memorial Association in 1894 and became its only female board member. The association bought and protected the Fort Raleigh site; it was the same group that gave archaeologist Talcott Williams permission to excavate. The association president declared

Roanoke of "supreme importance in the history of the Anglo-Saxon race in America."

The same year the association was formed, prominent citizens on Roanoke Island founded another organization—the Manteo White Supremacy Club. At one meeting, the club considered celebrating Virginia Dare's upcoming birthday "with a grand white supremacy rally" to celebrate "the first white child born upon American soil," according to Raleigh's *Morning Post*. The event would underscore the group's "determination to protect at all hazards the pure womanhood of North Carolina and perpetuate white supremacy to our latest posterity." They hoped for a speaker "on fire with a deathless love for the defenseless women and helpless children of the dear old State and for good government administered by white men."

Memorializing Virginia Dare was not simply a patriotic way to mark the nation's founding, then, but part of a concerted effort to ensure whites remained in firm control. Honoring the Raleigh voyages was a way to reinforce the ruling race's domination. In 1896, the Supreme Court backed strict segregation laws in the South; shortly after, North Carolina lawmakers "at last disenfranchised the Negro," Cotten noted approvingly. In 1902 Carter Glass, a Virginia politician and later United States Secretary of the Treasury, backed his state's plan to limit black voters and thereby ensure "complete supremacy of the white race in the affairs of government." The following year, W. E. B. Du Bois, the African American activist and historian, proclaimed that he only wished it possible "for a man to be both a Negro and an American, without being cursed or spit upon by his fellows."

In this charged Jim Crow environment, Cotten wrote a "Hiawatha"-like poem called "The White Doe" in which an evil shaman turns Virginia Dare into a deer. "She, the heir of civilization, they, the slaves of superstition," summed up Cotten's view of Anglo whites versus other ethnicities. Later, the innocent creature is fatally wounded by the wicked Wanchese with an enchanted silver arrow and dies in the arms of an adoring Indian brave at a sacred spring, which at her tragic demise dries up and produces scuppernong grapes. He turns the white grapes into juice; Virginia Dare's transformation into a Jesus-like American savior is complete.

The silver arrow, Cotten's poem explains pedantically, "was the gleaming light of Progress, speeding from across the sea," that produced "the vine of Civilization in the wilderness of strife." It's an interpretation, the historian Arner notes, "that would have done credit to George Bancroft." Both the poet and the historian saw white progress as the broom to sweep away backward Native American culture—and, by extension, African American culture as well. Dare sacrificed herself in this noble cause.

Cotten set off on an eccentric national tour in the late 1890s to read her lengthy and turgid work in halls usually given to vaudeville and other popular entertainments. To make the recitals more dramatic, the southern matron, then in her fifties, traded her severe black Victorian dresses and hats for a supple pale doeskin. In Washington, she performed in the elderly Lander's sitting room solely for the benefit of the sculptor and her famous statue.

She maintained the common view among southern whites of her day that segregation was critical for genetic as well as cultural reasons. Most states, North and South, forbade interracial marriages. During a visit to Cuba, Cotten was horrified to discover "its people are a hopelessly mixed race," adding, "To this I seriously object forever." The result was "to degrade a superior race." At an 1897 meeting of the National Congress of Mothers, she called for "scientific motherhood" to create "a grander, nobler race." Such ideas presaged the rise of eugenics, the belief and practices aimed at improving the genetics of a group, which became popular in both the United States and Nazi Germany in subsequent decades.

In this climate, any suggestion that the Lost Colonists assimilated with Native Americans, who were seen by many whites as genetically inferior, was strictly taboo. Virginia Dare might dress like an Indian, but she had to die before she could produce a hybrid degenerate. Nor was this view held solely below the Mason-Dixon line. Under the headline "Virginia Dare Made Symbol of Earliest U.S. Womanhood," the Providence *Bulletin* concluded, "The ancient Greeks would doubtless have regarded her untimely taking as an ordained sacrifice to the gods."

In 1907, immigration into the United States peaked at 1.3 million. Cotten's campaign prompted North Carolina artist and poet Mary Hilliard Hinton, a Colonial Dame and Daughter of the Confederacy, to make Virginia Dare the centerpiece of her state's contribution to the exposition that year, celebrating the three hundredth anniversary of the founding of Jamestown, considered the first permanent English settlement in the New World. Signs in the exhibit proudly proclaimed White's granddaughter the first "infant child of pure Caucasian blood" who launched "the birth of the white race in the Western Hemisphere" and the "advent of the white woman in America."

When President Theodore Roosevelt visited the exposition held in nearby Norfolk, he didn't tour Hinton's exhibit. But in a speech attended by thousands, he rejected growing talk of what many were calling "race suicide" amid fears that the refugees would dilute Anglo-American blood and destroy the country's moral fabric. The newcomers, the president told the crowd, would quickly assimilate. The current tide of immigration was an extension of the past three centuries that produced "a new and distinct ethnic type" that "has never been fixed in blood."

Roanoke Island emerged in this era as a pilgrimage site for Anglo-Americans seeking to reaffirm their racial dominance at the annual celebration of Virginia Dare's birth and baptism. "White civilization is triumphant because it is best," North Carolina lieutenant governor Francis Winston declared categorically in a 1908 speech there. "The Indian is gone; there is no room on earth today for vicious, incompetent, and immoral races. White civilization is triumphant because it is best." It would have been obvious to his audience that he was speaking of contemporary white power over African Americans. At the 1910 picnic, North Carolina's Episcopal bishop, Joseph Blount Cheshire Jr., admonished the assembled crowd to "not degrade the memory of these early pioneers in the settlement of America by supposing that they at once forgot their Christian nature, and voluntarily and promptly sunk into heathen barbarism, within less than one genera-

Virginia Dare gave her name and blond locks to a series of sweet wines popular during the first half of the twentieth century and revived by Francis Ford Coppola in the early twenty-first century. *Francis Ford Coppola Winery*

tion." The bishop insisted that the settlers instead endured "a nobler fate"—that is, heroic deaths at the hands of the Indians akin to martyrdom. Better to die than assimilate.

Hinton, an Anglican and niece to a governor, was so taken with the speech that she had it published. "To be white and of Anglo-Saxon descent and a member of the Episcopal Church was, in their view, to be living at the very pinnacle of civilization," explained the Reverend Donald Lowery, rector of the Church of the Holy Innocents in the town of Henderson west of Roanoke Island. "The amazing thing is that as racist as his views sound, Cheshire was considered a progressive on race issues in his day."

In the meantime, Cotten's poem, published in 1901, proved popular enough to win a commercial sponsor. A winemaker mailed a copy to any interested reader. "Compliments of Garrett and Co. Pioneer American wine growers, Norfolk, VA, producers of the famous Virginia Dare brand of Scuppernong wine," read a flyer that the company inserted into each copy. An early label called her "The First Lady of the Land."

It wasn't the first or last time the infant of Roanoke, now invariably portrayed as a beautiful young woman, was a vehicle for commerce. As early as 1871, Virginia Dare Tobacco was a popular brand, featuring a blonde with exposed breasts standing beside a lake in a forest surrounded by swans. Virginia Dare Wine, however, proved more enduring than her tobacco. (One uncharitable reviewer suggested its success rested on the fact that Cotten's long and tedious work was best appreciated drunk.) The label featured a smiling white teenager with blond curls. One of the advertisements urged customers to "touch the lips to Virginia Dare Wine." The purity and whiteness extended even to the color of the beverage. "Virginia Dare will appeal to every lover of a clean, sound, wholesome wine," notes Paul Garrett in his 1905 *The Art of Serving Wine*. "The original scuppernong has a white skin and makes a white wine." The company's Pocahontas wine was naturally made with red grapes; there was no blending of reds and whites. The more romantically inclined believed that the white wine came from grapes harvested from Roanoke Island's Mother Vineyard that grew from the sacred spring washed with Virginia Dare's blood.

In the immediate aftermath of World War I, as a new generation of women fought to win the right to vote, Virginia Dare remained a mascot of Anglo-Saxon dominance. Politicians in the South, all white males, feared that black women might use the ballot box to upset white dominance. In 1920, state legislators in Raleigh gathered to consider the nineteenth constitutional amendment, which would grant women the franchise. Suffragette Gertrude Weil, a progressive Jewish activist in eastern North Carolina and a protégé of Cotten's, dismissed "the menace of the negro woman's vote" as a red herring. "Equal suffrage does not necessarily imply universal suffrage," she insisted, assuring nervous legislators that gender equality would not threaten white supremacy.

Weil confronted an entrenched opposition led by Bishop Cheshire and Hinton that warned of "your country's danger from Feminism, Woman Suffrage, and Socialism," according to a broadside published at the time. "We Plead in the Name of Virginia Dare that North Carolina Remain White," read the headline. The legislature narrowly failed to support the amendment. Neighboring Tennessee did, how-

We Plead in the Name of Virginia Dare, that North Carolina Remain White.

Our Foreign Born Citizens

Taken from *The National Geographic Magazine* of February, 1917.

Page 105: "Only ONE-FIFTH of the population of New York and Chicago is of NATIVE WHITE ANCESTRY. LESS THAN A THIRD of the population of Boston, Cleveland, Pittsburgh, Detroit, Buffalo, San Francisco, Milwaukee, Newark, Minneapolis, Jersey City, Providence, St. Paul, Worcester, Scranton, Paterson, Fall River, Lowell, Cambridge and Bridgeport, are of NATIVE ANCESTRY. More than two-thirds of the Germans live between the Hudson and the Mississippi, and north of the Ohio."

Compare this map with the boasted Woman Suffrage Map and see your country's danger from Feminism, Woman Suffrage and Socialism.

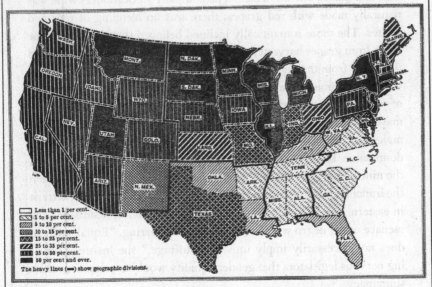

Less than 1 per cent.
1 to 5 per cent.
5 to 10 per cent.
10 to 15 per cent.
15 to 25 per cent.
25 to 35 per cent.
35 to 50 per cent.
50 per cent and over.
The heavy lines (━━) show geographic divisions.

MAP SHOWING THE FOREIGN STOCK IN THE POPULATION OF THE UNITED STATES—BY FOREIGN STOCK IS MEANT FOREIGN BORN AND CHILDREN OF A FOREIGN-BORN FATHER OR MOTHER

The States in black have more people who are either immigrants or the sons and daughters of immigrant parents than they have of native stock. The immigrants of the United States and their children would populate to its present density all of the United States west of the Mississippi, with Alabama and Mississippi added.

(Brown Printing Co., Montgomery, Ala.)

This broadside warned against "Feminism, Women Suffrage, and Socialism" in a time of rapid immigration that had largely passed North Carolina by. *North Carolina Department of Natural and Cultural Resources* ever, and national suffrage was assured women on August 18, 1920—the birthday of Virginia Dare.

Bishop Cheshire went on to lead the Roanoke Colony Memorial Association. In 1926, a state lawmaker at the annual Virginia Dare birthday celebration that he oversaw praised her "purest Anglo-Saxon blood" and read a message from President Calvin Coolidge commending the early settlers' "indomitable and fearless spirit." The British ambassador strayed off message in his talk, warning against that "most fallacious of all modern premises in politics, the general superiority of the Nordic races." Adolf Hitler had just published *Mein Kampf*, in which he predicted the "Germanic" people of North America would remain masters of the continent so long as they do "not yield to blood pollution by mixing with lesser races."

In the middle of the Roaring Twenties, women could buy Virginia Dare dresses made of crepe de chine silk with a scarf collar and rows of shoulder buttons—"as beautiful and refined as their name." Virginia Dare clubs organized by society women sprang up around the country, including in Brooklyn. The Virginia Dare Duo played in clubs, while children, ferries, steamers, and schooners were christened in her name. This was, not coincidentally, also the decade when the Ku Klux Klan membership peaked at six million.

The Virginia Dare craze was primarily but not completely a white phenomenon. "Blackberry cordial, / Virginia Dare wine— / All those sweet colors / Flavor Harlem of mine!" wrote African American poet Langston Hughes in a 1927 paean to the beauty of black women's skin. Cotten would not have been amused.

Virginia Dare Wine, however, suffered from Prohibition, which came into force the same year women got the vote. "De-alcoholized," it quickly lost its profitable luster, but the fermented sugary beverage bounced back after 1933 repeal. The Garrett Company created one of the first advertising radio jingles ("Virginia Dare—say it again") that made the spirit once again a hit.

One of the children who heard the snappy tune was a young Italian American named Francis Ford Coppola. "My parents wouldn't drink it, since it wasn't to the taste of Italians—it was too sweet," recalled the film director. "But as a kid I was attracted to this beautiful blond Cinderella-type girl on the label," he told me. "She seemed like she was from a fairy tale."

By then, deep in the Depression, the spiteful Anglo-Saxon huntress had lost her hard racial edge. At Virginia Dare's 350th birthday celebration on Roanoke Island on August 18, 1937, President Franklin Roosevelt made no mention of a full-grown white woman stalking the forest with her trusty bow. Instead, he criticized England for its aristocratic ways and rejected domestic worries that either dictatorship or anarchy threatened the United States.

The Protestant Madonna once again became an infant; when Roosevelt himself designed her commemorative stamp, she was swaddled in Eleanor's arms. He even signed her birth certificate, belatedly issued that day by the State of North Carolina. Her father's occupation was listed as "Assistant to Governor John White," while her mother was a "Housekeeper."

Virginia Dare after World War II provided either a titillating tale for adults or a child's fantasy. The 1954 novel *Roanoke Renegade* is, one historian says, "a hair's breadth this side of pornography," with the *other* Roanoke babe, the Harvie child born just after her, having all the fun. Dare also softened into a charming story for teenage girls in illustrated books: a pretty child lost in the woods who learns to survive and has many adventures (*Virginia Dare: Mystery Girl* was popular in the late 1950s). Her wine soon vanished from the shelves even as her story receded from popular culture. Her name, however, retains a talismanic power. "It represents a challenge, a new start, and a mysterious destination," explained Virginia Dare lead guitarist Brad Johnson, when I asked why his San Francisco band chose that moniker.

In 2013, Coppola was casting about for a new name for a Sonoma winery that he had purchased. On a tour of Italian Swiss Colony, another classic old label, he wondered what happened to Virginia Dare Wine. His fascination revived, he bought the rights to revive the trademark. "It was part of America that was gone," he told me. "The notion that I could bring something back intrigued me. Being a young country, we don't have many myths. And I like to put things back together." Given that the Roanoke voyages got their start thanks to the wine licenses doled out by Raleigh, there is historical justice in this beverage carrying on the legacy of John White's granddaughter.

The vintages from his reinvigorated Virginia Dare Winery include the White Doe—Chenin Blanc and Viognier. There is also a red blend called Manteo. Though the grapes today are Californian and the wine more in tune with modern American taste buds, it is the same smiling blonde with blue eyes on the label.

The child of Ananias and Eleanor Dare has made another, less innocent comeback in recent years. Weeks before the 2016 election of President Donald Trump, she appeared in national news stories following a Washington meeting sponsored by the National Policy Institute, dedicated to "the heritage, identity, and future of people of European descent in the United States."

One of the speakers, Peter Brimelow, runs a website called VDARE.com, named for John White's famous granddaughter, that uses the image of a white doe as its logo. The website, "America's voice on patriotic immigration reform," urges tight restrictions on those from non-European countries. It has been widely denounced by hate-tracking groups for providing a platform for white nationalists and supremacists.

In a November 16 letter to the president-elect, 169 members of Congress urged Trump to reconsider his appointment of Steve Bannon as White House chief strategist. They noted that "leading white nationalists," including VDARE's Brimelow, backed Bannon, who resigned in August 2017 amid an outcry following a white nationalist rally in Charlottesville, Virginia, that led to violence. News reports cited links between Brimelow and White House political adviser Stephen Miller. As an undergraduate at Duke University in North Carolina, Miller organized an antiterrorist group "for the defense of America and the civilization of the West" and warned in meetings that non-Europeans were not assimilating.

Brimelow is himself an immigrant. A former financial journalist, he was born in Britain and settled in Canada before moving to the

United States. After publishing his 1995 book, *Alien Nation*, which lambasted American immigration policy, he launched the website "dedicated to preserving our historical unity as Americans into the 21st Century." In 2007, he created the VDARE Foundation to support its efforts. Trump's election brought him into the national spotlight as a spokesman for the alt-right movement. At a conference prior to the Republican's victory, he told the audience, "You need to have everybody in the country voting the way that Southern whites vote."

He told me that he had been fascinated with Virginia Dare since studying American history in Britain in the 1960s. Brimelow, who declined to meet with me in person, chose her as the inspiration for his website after the birth of his daughter, which came late in his life, during a second marriage. "I empathized with John White," he wrote in an e-mail. "I picked the name because I wanted to focus attention on the very specific cultural origins of America, at a time when mass non-traditional immigration is threatening to swamp it."

For Brimelow, the most important lesson of Roanoke and its aftermath is that the Native Americans allowed themselves to be overwhelmed by outsiders with devastating consequences. "They simply found themselves out-voted, which is going to happen to us if we are not careful," he noted in a website post. When an Iowa congressman in 2017 said "we can't restore our civilization with someone else's babies," Brimelow tweeted, "This shouldn't even be debatable, let alone controversial. It's just a truism." When Virginia Dare's birthday approached in August, the website recommended a donation to the VDARE Foundation as a birthday present, "to enable us to continue to defend American national identity and fight for patriotic immigration reform."

The VDARE founder's views would have been familiar to Cotten and members of the Manteo White Supremacy Club a century earlier, who perceived the nation as locked in a battle between European civilization and foreign barbarism. That view is as old as the legend of the Roanoke settlers. "It is in the name of Virginia Dare herself that we defend the traditional American community and give it voice," Brimelow writes. "We cannot allow the Lost Colony to prove analogous to America itself."

But Virginia Dare is agile enough to span both sides of the nation's contemporary political and cultural divide. While Brimelow echoes the triumphal march of white progress in "The White Doe," modern feminists like writer Marjorie Hudson emphasize the poet's vision of a brave woman who adapts to a harsh reality.

As Cotten did, Hudson lives in rural North Carolina. After losing an unborn child, she struggled with depression in the tragedy's aftermath and first encountered Cotten's poem while working on an essay for an anthology. She knew dimly of the Lost Colony but quickly immersed herself in the tale. Interest turned to passion and a two-decade-long personal journey, summed up in her book *Searching for Virginia Dare*.

Hudson is tall with brown bangs and black glasses. When I visited her at her home in the woods, the dining room table was cluttered with children's books from the 1950s and 1960s about Virginia Dare, along with old bottles of wine, brandy, and crème de menthe bearing the name of the infant of Roanoke. At the time when she was growing up in Washington, D.C., "history was large marble buildings." But John White's story hit her hard. The artist-governor's anguished and fruitless hunt for his family and the other colonists enchanted and appalled her.

She found the stories surrounding Virginia Dare even more intriguing. "She is the archetypal mother, a source, like a great river, of strength and blood for descendants of a convergence of two great peoples," Hudson writes in her book, part travelogue and part memoir. "I begin to see that for some, especially the 'just folks' I talk to, Virginia is an emblem of grace—a blood sacrifice to atone for European sins against Native peoples. If we are all one, all descended from her image as English and Native American, then whatever divides us is inconsequential." Once a sacrifice to ensure Anglo-American dominance, the Roanoke child had now transformed into an amends for the wrongs done by generations of whites against Indians.

I asked her why the story has had such an enduring appeal to female audiences, at least white ones. "Women took on this story looking for inner strength," Hudson said. "That was certainly the case with Sallie Cotten. Virginia Dare was a symbol of a young woman surviving difficult circumstances. She tells us that we can be brave." The legend also puts Native Americans in a central role while underscoring how immigrants adapt and prosper. "A truism hiding in the story is that new Americans step up to become the most American. My sister-in-law is from Brazil, and she loves this country."

Hudson is uncomfortable with the more racist aspects of Cotten's poem, and she frowned when I mentioned Brimelow's website. "It is time to let go of some of the childish thoughts about how this country was formed," she told me. "Our minds are drawn to the shiny—the gold signet ring, the pretty side of things—but our country's past is no more pretty than any other country's wayward history."

I asked her how a child who vanished one week after her birth could have played so many conflicting roles in service of the deep-est hopes and trepidations of Americans. "Virginia Dare is a blank slate that people can project on," she responded. In her book, Hudson says that the Roanoke babe, "born and baptized then lost to history, has been reinvented by the imagination for centuries, taking the form most congruent with the imaginer's vision."

It dawned on me that Virginia Dare legends weave together the American desire to assimilate and our anxiety about doing just that. Despite the racism woven into the story, Hudson isn't willing to jettison her; she is unwilling to concede the field to Brimelow and his views of racial superiority. And like Cushing, who invented the Virginia Dare romantic genre long ago, Hudson is frustrated by the dearth of female characters in early American history. "Eleanor got on a ship four to five months pregnant on a cockamamy scheme to live in a new world," she said. "Maybe she's the one we should honor."

At least since the 1880s, the people of Roanoke Island have cel-ebrated Virginia Dare's birthday with speeches and a picnic. These days, the National Park Service and the Roanoke Island Historical Association throw a family-friendly party with help from the cos-tumed cast in the outdoor drama *The Lost Colony*. The event takes place at Fort Raleigh, in the vicinity of where she was born.

Curious as to how this icon of early America is commemorated in the twenty-first century, I arrived at the park one steamy late August morning. Minivans and SUVs already crowded the few shady parking spots. On the lawn next to the park's low-slung administration building, a few dozen children darted through clusters of slower-moving adults. Among them were women in long skirts and white ruffs and men in leather loincloths. I left the car's air-conditioning reluctantly, opening my door to a bath of humid air and the piercing sound of cicadas.

A small round Indian-style dwelling—made of what looked more like fiberglass than reeds—stood on the lawn next to a white folding table. A large block of dark clay sat on the middle of the table, melting in a plastic bag. "Would you like to make a pot, sir?" said a freckled blue-eyed young woman in a fringed deerskin. A single white feather dangled from her ear, and a sliver of white across her one visible shoulder revealed a tan line. I formed a badly lumpy clay vessel and then moved on past a man making balloon animals and a woman painting faces. The hula hoops and sacks for races lay untouched in the rising heat and glare. The one line was to shoot arrows. A curly-haired young man with black painted lines around his biceps and calves and wearing what looked like a fox-fur loincloth showed children how to aim at the homemade target. The only people of color seemed to be actors wearing makeup.

Several sharp claps pierced the thick air. "Gather round, gather round, and learn how to bow to the queen!" said a foppish figure in a feathered white hat. He wore a heavily embroidered puffy white doublet and white hose and spoke in a high-pitched and imperious imitation English accent. "When the queen comes forth we shall all bow," he ordered. The children turned to stare. "And we shall say, 'Long live the queen!' We are also going to wave—go on, put it in the air and wave thus." His right hand imitated the flapping wing of a small bird.

We dutifully practiced the cry and the wave. The children seemed dubious of the queen's shrill master of ceremonies, and the adults looked uncomfortable at the idea of cheering a monarch. A gusty hot breeze swept across the lawn. "I believe the queen is approaching!" announced the fop. I turned to see a golf cart discreetly parked around the side of the building. A young woman wearing a heavy black-and-gold dress and an unnaturally red wig adorned with an elaborate crown swept into view. She also wore a wide smile and miles of pearls as a black-T-shirt-wearing attendant carried her lengthy train.

Elizabeth I fluttered her blue-silk gloves at the milling crowd. The master of ceremonies prompted our cry and wave, to which we half-heartedly responded. "You did such a smashing job, thank you!" he said as the queen continued to smile and wave, an impressive feat given the temperature was well over ninety and she was wearing an outfit that weighed nearly sixty pounds. A tall man with a beard and white ruff stepped up to a waiting microphone. "I am Sir Walter Raleigh! Thank you for coming! I'm glad my colony was so successful!"

There was an awkward pause, and the children drifted back to the games, and the adults retreated to the shade of the pine trees. There were no more speeches, no message from the president or exhortations by a bishop. No governor was in attendance. Park rangers loaded sheet cake and ice cream onto a nearby table as parents maneuvered their children close to the queen and her retinue for pictures. The commemoration of Virginia Dare's birthday, an event that once drew crowds and famous speakers and even a president, was now an anodyne children's event, a welcome alternative to another hot day on a local beach.

I ducked out of the party and walked across the parking lot to the entrance of the Elizabethan Gardens. Carved out of the national park in the 1950s by the Garden Club of North Carolina, the ten-acre site mimics a sixteenth-century pleasure garden. At its dedication on Virginia Dare's birthday in 1955, dignitaries planted a magnolia tree representing Mother England and another representing her daughter, the United States. Queen Elizabeth II sent a rosebush from Windsor Castle. The garden has lately struggled to survive and recently sold its rare portrait of Queen Elizabeth I at Sotheby's to pay for a new garden shop roof.

"Today is Virginia Dare's birthday!" said the woman at the cash register. The shop smelled of potpourri and soap. "The entrance fee is only $4.29," she added. I must have looked blank. "That's how old she is—429! And we always have a fried chicken southern lunch; it's a tradition with us. There's cake after."

I entered the shade and quiet of the garden with relief. Camellias and lilies lined the walks. A towering bronze statue of Queen Elizabeth I—according to the brochure, the largest ever made of the Englishwoman who gave her name to Virginia—dominated a squat round brick plinth at the intersection of two paths. The hulking shape with a too-large head resembled more the nightmarish Queen of Hearts in *Alice's Adventures in Wonderland* than the Elizabethan ruler.

Nearly hidden at the edge of the thick woods was a slightly sunken garden with a narrow pine-straw-strewn avenue lined with leafed-out azaleas. Water oaks, twisted by the relentless winds, stood as a backdrop to a cylindrical stone column at the end of the path. Perched on top was none other than Lander's faithful companion, the statue she carved on the eve of the Civil War.

Like the mythical Virginia Dare, the statue led a restless existence. Its peculiar journey from Rome to the bottom of the sea and then to Salem, Boston, New York, and Washington didn't end with the death of the artist, who bequeathed it to North Carolina. Placed in Raleigh's Hall of History under the portraits of uniformed Confederate generals, the statue's state of undress provoked a public scandal. A newspaper later noted "a Marble Lady, clad only in fish net," that had done time "in the dingy basement of the Supreme Court." It was said to have suffered from vandals who smeared lipstick on her stone mouth.

Carved in Rome, lost in the Mediterranean, recovered, and displayed up and down the U.S. East Coast, Maria Louisa Lander's statue of Virginia Dare now stands in the Elizabethan Gardens on Roanoke Island. *Tania Gail*

State officials finally sent Lander's sculpture to Roanoke Island for display at the new Fort Raleigh National Historic Site.

Park rangers, however, blanched at displaying the statue of an adult who in fact might have died in infancy, so it was again sent into storage, where it was again submerged in a deluge. No one seemed to know what to do with this full-grown woman in her revealing outfit who wasn't quite a real historical figure.

Eventually, Lander's creation was pawned off on playwright Paul Green, who wrote the outdoor drama *The Lost Colony* that is performed just down the path and through the woods. Shipped west to his estate outside Chapel Hill, the sculpture remained for years in its box. He finally donated it to the newly created gardens.

She might have been a Grecian nymph, except for the shell necklace pulled close against her throat and a similar bracelet around her upper arm, in the style that John White pictured Carolina Algonquian women wearing. Her fine features were purely European, but she wore a fringed and beaded dress made of tightly woven fishnet. A marble heron sat contentedly at her feet. Dare's hollow eyes looked north to the Albemarle Sound, which was so close I could hear the light thump of waves against the sand. A hundred yards east, invisible through a patch of dense woods, stood the Fort Raleigh earthwork.

After surviving fire, water, abuse, and neglect, she seemed at ease on the forest's edge. There wasn't another soul in sight, but someone had paid Virginia Dare a visit on the morning of her birthday. In her pale marble arms, Lander's statue held a large green-and-white spray of *Hosta plantaginea*, also known as August lily, which demurely covered her bare breasts. The plant, with its sweet fragrant late summer bloom, is a favorite food of roving deer.

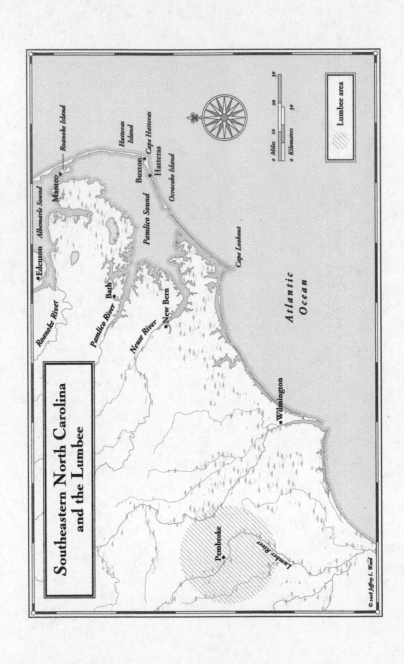

Southeastern North Carolina and the Lumbee

Lumbee area

Atlantic Ocean

Roanoke Island

Hatteras Island

Cape Hatteras

Buxton

Hatteras

Manteo

Albemarle Sound

Ocracoke Island

Edenton

Pamlico Sound

Roanoke River

Bath

Pamlico River

New Bern

Neuse River

Cape Lookout

Wilmington

Pembroke

Lumber River

0 Miles 10 20 30

0 Kilometers 30

© 2018 Jeffrey L. Ward

CHAPTER THIRTEEN

Swamp Saints and Renegades

Virginia Dare's lonely travails in the dark forests of Roanoke still mirror whites' anxieties amid the growing numbers of black and brown people with whom they share a country. They inspire women yearning for independence. But I was surprised to discover that there are also Native Americans who lay claim to the virginal huntress.

I stumbled on this odd fact while chatting with Lowery, the Episcopal priest. He was instrumental in a recent campaign to elevate the status of Virginia Dare and Manteo, the first Anglicans baptized in North America. These two players in the Roanoke drama are now not just wines. They are saints.

He told me that the push to place the English baby and the Carolina Algonquian man on the list of Episcopal "saints and worthies" in 2015 was for him deeply personal. "I grew up with the story that we were partially descended from the Lost Colony," he added. "My father was a Lumbee Indian." As a child, he was told that the Raleigh settlers wandered inland and joined this Native American tribe on the North Carolina mainland about two hundred miles southwest of Roanoke Island.

"These were the 'broken tribes,'" Lowery explained. Documents are few, but anthropologists suspect that in order to survive, bands of Algonquian, Iroquoian, and Siouan speakers from across the region, decimated by war and disease, retreated to this swampy sanctuary in the seventeenth and early eighteenth centuries. English became the lingua franca as their ancient traditions faded amid repeated calamities. This loose collection of peoples even lost their old tribal designations; Lumbee, which means "dark water" in Siouan, is only the latest of half a dozen names applied to the thirty-five thousand people enrolled in the state-recognized tribe; another thirty thousand claim Lumbee identity. That makes it the largest Indian group east of the Mississippi, and yet it remains one of the least known as well as one of the most impoverished.

Early English settlers avoided this part of North Carolina with its marshy soil that was difficult to farm, prone to frequent flooding, and plagued by rampant malaria. One of the earliest mentions of the area's inhabitants is in 1754, when an English visitor noted "a mixed crew, a lawless people" living in "vacant lands being inclosed in great swamps." The swamps afforded protection from the invaders as well as rich sources of game and fish.

Gaelic-speaking Scottish Highlanders eventually arrived, bringing their slaves to help drain the marshes and lay out fields. West Africans were soon speaking in the Celtic tongue of their masters while harvesting tobacco. Huguenots, Protestant refugees from France, also drifted into the area two centuries after their ancestors' ill-fated attempt to settle just south of here in the 1560s. Spanish castaways might have flavored the unusual mix, and escaped slaves found here a safe haven from white owners. Though deeply rural, the area was more diverse than even some American cities of the day.

Just before the Revolution, the last North Carolina royal governor complained of "a number of free negroes and mulattoes who infest the country and annoy its inhabitants." Mulattoes referred to any persons lacking "pure" blood—that is, those from mixed backgrounds. There was no mention of Indians, but mulattoes could be the product of Native American and African American, as well as European, unions. Many of the inhabitants fought on the American side in the Revolution; in the early years of the new nation they could own land and vote, though they could not testify against a white person in court.

Those policies changed dramatically in 1835, just as Virginia Dare and the Lost Colony first assumed prominence. While the scattered bands of Indians in eastern North Carolina escaped the grim fate of their Cherokee cousins to the west who suffered the Trail of Tears to Oklahoma, their rights were severely curtailed. They were lumped in with the group generically called "free persons of color." North Carolina's new constitution denied them access to the ballot box and made it illegal for them to carry guns without a license, an onerous regulation for a people who hunted for a living. They were even forbidden to serve in the military. Resentment at their second-class status simmered.

During the Civil War, the Confederate Home Guard killed a Lumbee father and son who refused to dig battle trenches with black slaves. The victims' son and brother Henry Berry Lowrie witnessed the brutal murders and launched a violent rampage that lasted for nearly a decade. "In a sense, Henry Berry Lowrie was the making of the Indians," wrote sociologist Guy Johnson, who researched the tribe in the 1930s. "He was their martyr and hero, and he focused attention on their grievances in a dramatic way."

Seen as a Robin Hood to locals and as a dangerous thug by the state, Lowrie led an armed band of blacks and poverty-stricken whites, as well as Lumbee, that robbed and killed wealthy whites throughout Robeson County, the Indians' heartland. An undated photograph shows a handsome and dark-haired young man with eyebrows that nearly meet over a piercing gaze, a broad nose, and a beard as thick as a beaver's pelt; he was said to have striking gray-blue eyes. Lowrie told one reporter that "we don't kill anybody but the Ku Klux," referring to the white supremacist group that targeted people of color. The *New York Herald* noted "his roving propensities" came from his Scottish background, his "cunning and fortitude" from his Indian ancestors, and his "docility and ferocity" from his Negro roots. This multiracial background combined with his capacity for organization and violence sparked panic among the region's whites.

A regiment of federal troops and a hefty reward failed to secure his capture. Lowrie even blew up the county safe and stole the twenty-eight thousand dollars set aside as reward money for his capture. "If you will pardon my language, he had real big hairy balls," said the

Reverend Lowery, who added that he is the renegade's fourth cousin four times removed. "It was put out that he shot himself while cleaning his gun, but in my family they say he went to California and died in 1925."

A major source of Lumbee ire was the state's refusal to let their children attend white schools. Instead, they were forced to depend on the underfunded and substandard schools for blacks, dooming their children to an impoverished future. In the 1880s, as the push to roll back minority rights obtained in the wake of the Civil War gained strength, the state legislator representing Robeson County, Hamilton McMillan, came up with a clever solution to address the crisis while weakening his political opponents.

Lumbee Indians were solid Republicans in their day, as were other minorities who favored the party of Lincoln. McMillan was a white Democrat. He began to research an old story—one he said he had heard told among the Indians—that the Lost Colonists settled with the

Lumbee Henry Berry Lowrie launched a rebellion in southeastern North Carolina after the Civil War. In the aftermath, the tribal claim to have taken in the vanished Roanoke colonists was thrust into the limelight.

Croatoan Indians, who in turn wandered southwest to join other refugees in the swamps. The list of settlers with the John White expedition includes a Henry Berrye, and McMillan claimed that Henry Berry Lowrie was his direct descendant, three hundred years later. He argued that the Indians of Robeson County had rescued the abandoned English colonists from starvation and therefore deserved the gratitude of whites.

The Democratic-controlled legislature, eager to avoid further rebellion in the troublesome county, agreed with McMillan's assessment. The Indians were given the new name of Croatan and granted their own school system. They were forbidden to marry "a person of negro descent to the third generation inclusive," a restriction identical to that applied to whites. This was a gift rather than a punishment, because it raised the legal status of the Croatan above that of African Americans.

The strategy worked; many of the Indians switched their allegiance to the Democratic Party, weakening the already marginalized Republicans. "It was all tied up with race," Lowery told me. "The deal was that if we voted Democratic then, we could have our own schools. The whites got the cream, the Lumbee got the milk, and the African Americans got the broken bottle."

When the tribe asked the U.S. Congress to grant them full federal recognition, however, the claim that "your petitioners are a remnant of White's lost colony" fell on deaf ears. Congress declined, as it has ever since, despite numerous attempts.

McMillan's successful campaign, however, was not simply a cynical political maneuver. Even after his 1885 legislative victory, he grew ever more fixated on proving the Lost Colony connection. Three years later he compiled a small book with the prodigious title of *Sir Walter Raleigh's Lost Colony: An Historical Sketch of the Attempts of Sir Walter Raleigh to Establish a Colony in Virginia, with the Traditions of an Indian Tribe in North Carolina, Indicating the Fate of the Colony of Englishmen Left on Roanoke Island in 1587.*

Extracting information from the taciturn Croatan proved no easy task. "After the year 1835"—the year they were denied fundamental rights—"these Indians who murmured greatly at the injustice done them in being classed as 'mulattoes' or 'free persons of color' became suspicious of white men and at first we found difficulty in eliciting any facts relating to their past history," McMillan notes. Much of his argument centers on their oral tradition. His most moving passage is a speech that he reports an elderly Indian gave at the inquest investigating the Lowrie murders during the Civil War.

"We have always been friends of white men," the Native American is said to have told the court. "We were a free people long before the white men came to our land. Our tribe was always free. They lived in Roanoke . . . One of our tribe went to England in an English ship and saw that great country," an apparent reference to Manteo. "We took the English to live with us. There is the white man's blood in these veins as well as that of the Indian . . . We moved to this land and fought for liberty for white men, yet white men have treated us as negroes. Here are our young men shot down by a white man and we get no justice, and that in a land where our people were always free." Aside from the name Berry, McMillan noted numerous other surnames similar or identical to those of the final Roanoke settlers. He also claimed that when white settlers finally penetrated the area in the mid-eighteenth century, they found a large tribe "tilling the soil, owning slaves and practicing many of the arts of civilized life," and speaking an "almost pure Anglo Saxon English."

His claims take a more bizarre turn, however, when he adds that the Native Americans had communication not just with the Lost Colonists but also with other "more civilized races" such as Persians who "established a colony in the West Indies a thousand years ago" and twelfth-century Welsh settlers who explored the forests of North Carolina.

While he convinced a majority of North Carolina legislators, McMillan won few converts to his theory in academia. Historians dismissed his more eccentric notions and complained that his claims about the Roanoke voyagers lacked documentary evidence or clear sources. Even his assertions about Indians "practicing many of the arts of civilized life" had little obvious basis. There were no court records of the eloquent inquest speech. Ethnologist James Mooney, the reigning late-nineteenth-century white expert on Native Americans, wrote the description of the Croatan Indians for the 1907 *Hand Book of American Indians North of Mexico*. He dismissed the Lost Colony connection as "baseless." The Croatan, he concluded, were a mix of Indians, early white settlers, runaway slaves, "and probably also of stray seamen of the Latin races." While not wholly discredited, McMillan's assertion failed to gain traction in the following decades.

A reporter for *Appleton's Magazine* visited several Croatan households on a 1907 tour with McMillan. Normally reluctant to speak with white strangers, the Indians welcomed the former legislator and his guest. One Jim Diel "spoke in a high, almost falsetto voice, peculiar to all these descendants of the Lost Colony, who still use the old Saxon English."

When the reporter asked about Virginia Dare, he received blank looks. "But say Virginia Darr, and there will be an eager 'Yes, yes—we know Virginia Darr, she is our mother way back.'" They also claimed her transformation into a white doe was an ancient Indian legend told by their ancestors. (That seems unlikely, because the story of the white doe mimicked much of a Wordsworth poem written in England a century before.)

The Croatan, however, soon turned against their new tribal name. Local whites shortened "Croatan" to "Cro" and used it as a nasty epithet. "They pronounced it with a sort of sneer," writes Johnson. "It soon became a fighting term, and for many years it has been virtually taboo in the presence of Indians." Today it remains an insult that can lead to bloodshed. In 1911, the tribe successfully petitioned the legislature to change their name from Croatan to "the Indians of Robeson County." They were, notes the sociologist, willing to give up their Lost Colony roots "for the removal of the curse of 'Croatan.'"

After two more name changes, the tribe settled on Lumbee, and in 1956 Congress acknowledged the group as descended from "the earliest white settlements" in Robeson County, noting the similarities in Lost Colony surnames, but stopped short of confirming them as Lost Colony descendants. The legislation granted it a measure of national recognition as an Indian people, but not as a tribe, which would have provided extensive federal aid.

The claim that their ancestors aided the Roanoke settlers no longer seems to bolster their cause among whites. The tribe is centered within one of the nation's poorest counties, with alarming levels of unemployment, violence, and addiction. Other Indians often view Lumbee with suspicion. "They are infiltrators," confided a Cherokee friend of mine. "They are not 'factual' Indians." Some African Americans dismiss the Lumbee claim to Native American identity as a convenient way to avoid the societal burden of being black. U.S. Senator Sam Ervin, the North Carolina lawmaker later famous for his role in the Watergate scandal, called the tribe "the most neglected minority group in the history of the nations."

The heart of the Lumbee community is the little town of Pembroke, set in a landscape of marsh and forest laced with canals and creeks and dotted with small farms. Though it lies between the busy beaches of the Outer Banks and the crowded highways of Charlotte, Pembroke feels far removed from the modern Sunbelt. Driving into town one fall morning, I passed the Lost Colony Trading Post, a gas station hawking Chinese-made moccasins, its sign fading and cracked. Then I crossed the iced-tea-colored Lumber River—the Anglicized version of the Siouan name—still swollen from a recent tropical storm that inundated much of the county and forced thousands from their homes.

Nine out of ten Pembroke residents call themselves Lumbee. The community, originally named Raleigh, grew up around the Croatan Normal School, founded in 1887 to train teachers in a single modest brick building. Now it is the vibrant campus of the University of North Carolina at Pembroke. Parking beside the entrance to Old Main, I saw a statue of a diminutive and bearded white man in a dashing cape, Hamilton McMillan. Inside the administration building is a museum as well as a conference room, where, on the morning I visited, a Lumbee youth group shook rattles, banged on drums, and sang Native songs to launch the annual Southeast Indian Studies Conference.

Because their traditional forms of dress and ritual dimmed as they mixed with a variety of tribes and then with whites and blacks, the young men in the group drew on the clothing and sounds from the peoples of the Great Plains to reclaim their heritage. Lumbee became devout Protestants centuries ago, and many remain deeply attached to their Christian faith.

Chief Harvey Godwin opened the gathering. Speakers discussed indigenous spirituality in North Carolina prisons as well as a violent 1958 conflict between Lumbee and white supremacists (the unwelcome outsiders were sent packing). During a coffee break, I told Godwin the wide range of hair and skin colors in the conference room surprised me. "All the tribes were mixed, and everyone here is racially mixed as well," said the chief, a burly man with a broad nose and a graying ponytail.

Like the Reverend Donald Lowery, Godwin grew up hearing the story that the Lost Colonists joined the tribe. "Some believe it and some don't," he said with a politician's tact. When he visited the Outer Banks years ago, he recalled feeling "a connection to the place, and it could be a thread back to then," referring to the sixteenth century. But he remained agnostic on the matter.

One of his late relatives, a UNC Pembroke historian named Adolph Dial, had revived McMillan's theory in the second half of the twentieth century. "The survival of colonists' names, the uniqueness of the Lumbee dialect in the past, the oral traditions, the demography of sixteenth century North Carolina, the mobility of the Indian people, human adaptability and the isolation of Robeson County, all prove the 'Lost Colony' theory," he wrote. Dial believed that his unusual last name derived from Dare and that he was descended from Virginia. Yet as with McMillan, he failed to convince many of his academic colleagues of his theory.

Dial died in 1995, and the alleged link with the Roanoke settlers has since fallen out of favor. "It is so improbable," Mary Ann Jacobs, chair of the American Indian Studies department at the university, told me as we walked to lunch in the college cafeteria. "How in the world would all of those white people have made it all the way here?" she asked. "Why would they stay here with us? Why would they come to this area in the first place? This was swamp then—not like now," Jacobs added, gesturing at the manicured lawns, "and there were no ditches and canals."

McMillan was vague about his sources in the Lumbee community and overstated how many tribal families share surnames of Lost Colonists, she said. Most of those names are common in Britain in any case. She added that later masters likely passed on their surnames to slaves, as was common in the South. Jacobs concluded that the link with Roanoke was more about nineteenth-century politics than Elizabethan history. "It made us look better in white eyes," she said. "It tied us to what amounts to North Carolina royalty."

At lunch I chatted with Vibrina Coronado, a Lumbee independent scholar. "My maternal grandmother told us we were descendants of Manteo, the Indian leader, but we never discussed what that meant," she said. "This grandmother had an uncle named Manteo." Though the link with the Lost Colony fascinated her, she was skeptical. "I've never doubted that Lumbees in general and my family in particular were mixed racially and ethnically, but the story told about the tree carved with the word 'Croatan' seemed like the Disney version," she said.

In the nineteenth-century South, Lumbees must have been a disturbing reminder that the region's strict racial categories were arbitrary distinctions imposed by an anxious white majority. "Remember, there was no such thing legally as an Indian; you were white or colored," said Jay Vest, an American Indian Studies professor at the college. The 1835 law attempted to build a wall between those who were white and those who were not, but the boundaries were too permeable. "Our bodies were evidence," added Jacobs, a tall and light-colored woman with long brown hair. "Some of us have blue eyes and white skin, and there is a gradation of tone."

I glanced around the campus sidewalks crowded with students as we strolled back to Old Main. No one seemed to fit into the usual checkerboard categories of the rural South, which tends to the extremes of dark and light. Skin shades varied from ivory to copper to dark chocolate, and hair ranged from straight to curly to kinky. "The Croatan today are undoubtedly one of the most heterogeneous groups ever brought together under one name," concludes the sociologist Johnson.

The scene reminded me of an experience that flummoxed African American educator Booker T. Washington on a visit to Oklahoma: "The whole situation out here is complicated and puzzling, and if one attempts to understand it he is very deep into the intricacies of a social and political history so full of surprises that it reminds him of *Alice in Wonderland*."

The Lost Colony link was a neat way for white legislators in Jim Crow North Carolina to accept the diversity of traits among Lumbee. They were seen as the result of a mixing of Native Americans and

Europeans driven by utter necessity. For them, it was comforting to imagine that the colonists remained English enough to keep their surnames and language and taught Indians their European ways. That was more palatable than the image of colonists completely subsumed in the indigenous culture.

More than a century later, however, a new and controversial tool unavailable in McMillan's day emerged that offered an opportunity to make sense of that *Alice in Wonderland* quality I encountered in Pembroke and, perhaps, resolve the Lost Colony mystery in an unexpected way.

Historians hunt for long-forgotten documents in archives, while archaeologists seek the objects that people left behind. A new generation of Roanoke searchers is turning to the human genome as an entirely new line of evidence to track the colonists' fate.

Gene sequencing recently moved out of scientific laboratories and into the world of genealogy. This effort is a particular preoccupation for Roberta Estes, a computer scientist from Michigan. After working in the tech industry for three decades, she grew intrigued by the new field of genetic genealogy around 2000. Suddenly people could sample their genes to determine their family heritage at a reasonable cost.

Estes eventually quit her high-tech consulting job to start a business designed to help individuals grasp the meaning locked within their DNA. "My goal was to put it all in terms people could understand," she said.

In 2005, Estes read some chatter on a genealogy website about the Lost Colony and the possibility that genetic data could provide insight into the settlers' fate. Her father is from northeastern North Carolina, and she has Native American genes on both sides of her family. The mystery of the Roanoke colony had long fascinated her. "I thought, well, can DNA solve this?"

Soon after, she helped found several Lost Colony–related genetic projects to collect data related to the vanished settlers, including one focused on today's population on Hatteras, as well as among Lumbee. She also gathered genetic data on the Melungeons, an Appalachian ethnic group, some of whom claim descent from Lost Colonists. Those qualified to join the projects only needed a surname on the list of Lost Colonists as well as evidence of early settlement in eastern North Carolina.

She anticipated gathering enough data to find a link "relatively quickly and painlessly." As historians and archaeologists already know, however, the Roanoke mystery does not give up its secrets so easily.

When I spoke with Estes, she first insisted on explaining the three primary forms of DNA genealogical tests. Each has its limitations. One test samples your autosomal DNA, the genetic material that you inherit, half from your mother and half from your father. Which half of your parents' genetic material you receive is random. The further back you go in your ancestry, the fuzzier the data becomes. Individuals inherit an average of 6.25 percent of the genetic material from each great-great-grandparent. "Less than 1 percent is generally considered noise," she said. "That happens between five and six generations. By then, DNA gets divided into pieces too small to associate with specific ancestors." As a result, autosomal DNA results can't accurately capture ancestors from Elizabethan times.

Two other approaches can get around this limitation. You can test the Y chromosome in a man, the chromosome inherited father to son along with the surname, or the mitochondrial DNA (mtDNA) inherited mother to daughter (both genders get it, but only women can pass it on). Unlike autosomal DNA, these tests provide far more accurate information on the paternal and maternal lines, respectively, stretching back much further in history. "Y and mtDNA does not wash out over time," explained Estes. "You can use it to look through a periscope that goes far back in history." These tests are more effective in determining individual origins, she explained. But these tests also provide an incomplete picture, because they reveal a line through the father or through the mother but not both. If you are female, then your mtDNA won't confirm your father's story that you are directly descended from ancient Samoan royalty.

Estes's initial task was to build up a database of potential Lost Colony descendants using as much DNA data as possible—autosomal,

Y, and mtDNA. Yet even a massive database of likely candidates, no matter how complete, is not enough to point the historical compass to a Roanoke settler. Her primary challenge, then, is to find someone—living or dead—with whom to compare their genetic data. That means either pinpointing existing descendants of the Lost Colonists in Britain or uncovering bones reliably identified as those belonging to one of the settlers. The latter path would be the most direct, but it requires successfully sequencing (after first *finding*) DNA from old remains.

In the best cases, that is a difficult, expensive, and time-consuming process that only a few labs in the world can accomplish. But the technology is rapidly evolving. Just a few years ago, extracting genetic-material DNA from bones left in warm and wet environments like that of the Outer Banks was unthinkable. New techniques can now amplify tiny fragments and recover the genetic map of those long dead. Scientists recently sequenced the DNA of individuals buried in colonial Cuba and in a Bahamian cave. So what was once scientifically impossible is now conceivable.

That would, of course, still require bones confirmed to be those of Lost Colonists. No dig at Fort Raleigh or at Site X has uncovered human remains from the period. Mark Horton's team did encounter a burial while digging at Cape Creek on Hatteras. It appeared just as a tropical storm bore down on the island. "We were finding pottery and other interesting stuff, and suddenly someone said, 'This looks human,'" one of the team members told me, requesting anonymity because of the sensitivity surrounding Native American remains. "We found a mandible upside down that was definitely human." A sudden storm forced a halt to the dig. Later, once it had passed, the team found the bones to be an intact single burial in a flexed position that is typical of Algonquian cemeteries. The excavators immediately alerted the state archaeologist, who in turn contacted Greg Richardson, the chair of the North Carolina Commission of Indian Affairs. "He said, 'Rebury it,'" the team member said, and the excavators complied.

In 1990, Congress passed a law protecting Indian and Eskimo graves and cultural goods on state and federal land. The legislation sought to end the widespread practice of exhuming Indian remains for scientific study without the permission of their descendants. If archaeologists find Native American skeletons on state or federal land today, they must contact the likely next of kin before removing or analyzing them. In recent years, scientists and Native Americans have ended up in lengthy and acrimonious court battles over the use of scientific data gleaned from Indian bones.

The most famous case involved the bones of a nine-thousand-year-old skeleton dubbed Kennewick Man after the site of its 1996 find on the Columbia River in Washington State. After a bitter fight lasting more than two decades, his remains were returned to the Colville tribe and reburied when DNA analysis determined he was an ancestor of that people. Even if the remains are on private land, as was the case with Cape Creek, archaeologists today are increasingly reluctant to disturb Native American dead. And if bones of a colonist were somehow obtained, accurate dating would then be critical to ensure that the buried English man or woman was Elizabethan, rather than a later Jamestown trader. To determine if the person had living relatives today, an existing British relative would still have to be found in order to make a comparison.

The second approach is to match the Y DNA sequence of someone with a Roanoke surname in the United States with both early ties to North Carolina and a Native American background to that of a living Lost Colony descendant in Britain. No such living descendant, however, has yet been identified. There are only two known children of White's settlers who were left behind in England, both siblings of Virginia Dare. The first was the daughter of Eleanor and Ananias Dare, Thomasine Dare, who died as a child within a year of her parents' departure for Roanoke. The second was John Dare. He was the son of Ananias, and Eleanor was likely his mother, though it is possible he was from a previous marriage or was illegitimate. We know that he inherited his father's property after a 1594 court decision declaring Ananias legally dead.

"So far, we have not found one family we can identify in England that is a colonist family," Estes said. The week before we spoke, she had gathered DNA from a member of a Berry family who lives near Bristol. Richard and Henry Berrye from the 1587 voyage—the ones McMillan believed were related to the Lumbee Berrys—likely came from the area, though there is no definitive historical record linking them to this particular modern family. "We are left with uncomfortable speculations and leaps of faith," she added ruefully.

Estes is hopeful, however, that old records from parish registers could still pop up to link Lost Colony relatives such as the Berry brothers with present-day individuals. If she can show a genetic link between the Berrys of Britain and the Lumbee Berrys, that might provide a clue backing up McMillan's claims. Estes noted that the Robeson County Berrys trace their ancestry within the region to at least the early eighteenth century.

Gathering and analyzing Lumbee DNA, however, has proved another formidable complication in her quest. Some Native Americans see mining genetic data as the latest form of grave robbery by white people. That's why the legislation passed by Congress and signed into law restricting archaeological work was put into place and hailed by Indians as an important victory. Native peoples also point out that they were more likely than Europeans to absorb outsiders—particularly women and children—in their traditional cultures, thereby mixing their genes while retaining tribal identity. Genetic tests, therefore, may offer skewed results.

For many Lumbee, the issue of DNA is particularly fraught. When I mentioned genetic testing to the Reverend Donald Lowery, he warned me away. "If you choose to wade into this one, you are entering a racial and sociopolitical minefield," he said. "Good luck." The results, Lowery added, can upset traditional ideas of identity and divide the community.

"It is one thing for Indians to discuss among themselves their varied ancestry, but they resent any outsiders doing so," writes Karen Blu in her book *The Lumbee Problem*. "This is partly because, in the South, the terms 'mixed-blood' and 'mulatto' have usually meant a combination of Black and non-Black ancestry."

Chief Godwin told me that genetic testing is not part of the admission test for the Lumbee tribe, which is based instead on cultural knowledge and ties to the local community. The tribe is still fighting for full federal recognition, and some Lumbee fear that DNA could be used to delay further or even reject this request. Others said they are troubled by the focus on genetics as a solution to identity. "I don't have the desire to get my DNA tested—I probably have some African American blood—and I am sure many people do, many who identify as white," Coronado said. "It just seems like a small bit of someone that is expanded to mean things it may not mean."

Estes found herself treading through this minefield when she helped create the Lumbee DNA Project. "They wouldn't even talk to me," she said of the tribe's members, sounding both puzzled and annoyed. She did collect a modest number of samples from a few willing individuals who "feel they have Lumbee heritage" but "generally" are not members of the tribe. Her results revealed an unusually high percentage of European genes compared with other Native American groups—as much as 96 percent. She also uncovered a significant percentage of African genes among her subjects. In fact there was little sign of Native American genes at all. This may be a result of sample size, and Estes said she believes that a larger study would reveal further Indian DNA. "I don't doubt that the Lumbee have some Native, someplace," she said. The Indian genes would be in a line not tested. "The Berry line is the best bet for that," she added.

In a 2009 paper, Estes wrote that the high percentage of European genes in her subjects could signal "either earlier European contact or a significant infusion of European Y-DNA, perhaps from the Lost Colony." Because most of the Roanoke settlers were men, there's a greater chance that they passed on their Y chromosomes to a line of male Native Americans. But, again, without a Roanoke colonist's bones or a British family member to compare the data with, the link to the Lost Colony remains wishful thinking rather than a scientific conclusion.

The Reverend Donald Lowery, who is pale with a touch of red in his thinning hair, told me that he sent off a swab for an autosomal as well as a Y DNA test and shared the results with Estes's project. Because his father was a full Lumbee, he anticipated a substantial percentage of Native American genes. Instead, in line with what Estes found overall, the data showed that approximately 85 percent of his genetic makeup is northern European, mostly centered on northwest Ireland. Most of the remainder was of West African origin. About 2 percent of his genes were Siberian, which may point to ancestors who began to migrate across the Bering land bridge at the end of the last Ice Age some fifteen thousand years ago.

While his DNA said nothing of a link to the Lost Colony, it did provide Lowery with a fresh perspective on his rich and complicated heritage. "I am proudly Lumbee," he said, "but recognize that is an identity constructed by my ancestors to secure a better deal for themselves in the Jim Crow South."

Not all feel that way. When Lowery presided over a funeral for one of his father's brothers at an Indian church in Robeson County a week before, "one of the locals at the service commented on how proud he was we no longer pretended to be white," he recalled. "I didn't get into the African DNA thing. It just wasn't worth it."

Estes, meanwhile, continues to build the databases that might someday provide clues to the Lost Colony's fate. "I don't want people to come away with the idea that DNA is a magic bullet," she said. "But it could solve some of this mystery by inferring that the colonists survived."

New pieces of the puzzle, both English records and more precise genetic data, could emerge in time. Though it is fraught with technical challenges and ethical implications, Estes is confident that this fresh line of evidence could complement historical and archaeological finds. But as with archival searches and excavations, genetic testing is not likely to resolve the mystery of the settlers anytime soon. "We will never be able to say positively that we have traced the Lost Colonists," she added. "The best we will be able to say is 'we think' or 'probably.' There is no genie to wave a wand and give us the answer. This is a waiting game."

One day in the 1940s, Margaret Locklear was picking cotton in the flat farmland a few miles outside Pembroke. "Some people from New York came up to the field and dug up a casket and took the boards and bones," she recalled one crisp fall afternoon as she sat in her nephew's pickup truck near the same spot. "We knew it was Virginia Dare's grave."

Locklear, who is ninety-three, is a slight woman who wore a Carolina blue beret over her lean nut-brown face. She grew up the child of Lumbee sharecroppers who turned over half of every harvest to the white landowner. The family home was gone, swallowed by pines and underbrush, but her memory of the gravesite under a tall hickory tree just beyond her father's mule barn remained vivid. An old black man born into slavery told her of Union General William Tecumseh Sherman marching through and raiding white smokehouses to distribute meat to the hard-pressed Indians in the area. He also told her about Virginia Dare. "She was the first white person born in America. And this was her grave," Locklear recalled him saying, and she pointed out the truck window at a bare patch of sandy soil. That was all she knew. "The white people then didn't let you know *nothing*," she added.

A 1938 local newspaper account, written when Locklear was thirteen, mentions "a gnarled hickory tree" standing sentinel over what was rumored to be Virginia Dare's grave, "surrounded by a sea of waving white cotton." Lush grass grew in an area six feet long and two feet wide. Indians left the place alone, the article reported, because of a legend that "the Great Spirit will frown upon those who dare to molest this sacred soil." Where the hickory tree once stood was now the edge of a field. I asked Locklear what had become of the wooden boards and human bones taken by the New Yorkers. "We never heard nothing more about it," she said.

Her nephew, Raymond Cummings, a county commissioner, recently decided it was time to commemorate the oral tradition while the older generation still survives. "Be sure to see the sign—we just put it up," he told me as he stood beside the pickup. Locklear rapped hard on the window to signal that she was ready to go, and he was quick to comply. "It's just down the way."

I waved goodbye, wondering about this strange story of the white child passed down for generations by Native and African Americans. The tale's validity seemed less important than its tenacity. Long after the alleged link with the Lost Colony ceased to offer political advantage, the legend persisted. The inhabitants of this remote rural region, despite centuries of social taboos and laws designed to ensure racial purity, had quietly mixed their traditions and genes, blending Indian,

European, and African into one people. The infant of Roanoke seemed to serve as a kind of mythic token of their unusual heritage.

In the fading autumn light, I drove a few hundred yards down the nearby two-lane road without seeing the gray-and-black state historical marker I had expected to find. I turned around in the parking lot of an old clapboard church—Henry Berry Lowrie is said to have used its steeple as a sniper post—and cruised slowly back. And then I spotted what looked like a street sign facing the bare field. I rolled to a stop as the sun slipped behind a distant line of trees. It read, simply: VIRGINIA DARE BURIAL SITE.

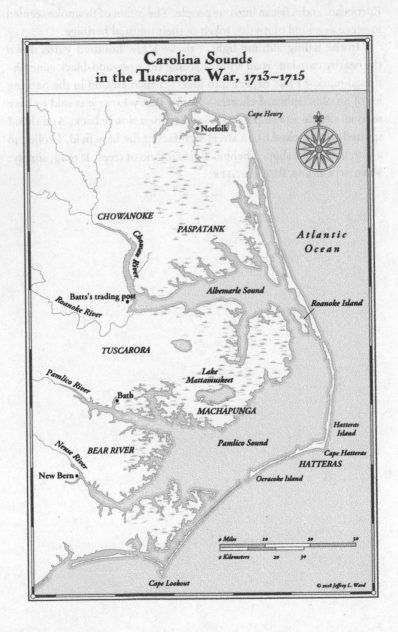

Carolina Sounds
in the Tuscarora War, 1713–1715

Cape Henry

• Norfolk

CHOWANOKE

PASPATANK

Chowan River

Atlantic
Ocean

Albemarle Sound

Batts's trading post •

Roanoke River

Roanoke Island

TUSCARORA

Pamlico River

Lake
Mattamuskeet

• Bath

MACHAPUNGA

Neuse River

BEAR RIVER

Pamlico Sound

Hatteras
Island

Cape Hatteras

HATTERAS

New Bern •

Ocracoke Island

0 Miles   10   20   30

0 Kilometers   20   30

Cape Lookout

© 2018 Jeffrey L. Ward

CHAPTER FOURTEEN

Return to Roanoke

"It is an odd fact that many Americans who arrive at Jerusalem are either lunatics or lose their mind thereafter," a visiting Anglican vicar observed in 1870. Protestants from the United States seem particularly susceptible even today to the temporary religious psychosis called the Jerusalem syndrome. A mild case leads to an obsession with ritual purity or the need to deliver an impromptu sermon in a sacred place while wearing a hotel bedsheet. In its most famous variety, the victim believes he or she is an important figure like Jesus or Mary. The city's Kfar Shaul Mental Health Center treats dozens of people for the condition annually, though officials say those affected likely number far more.

But the affliction, which can affect those with no previous history of mental disturbance, is not unique to this tinderbox of monotheistic religion. In Florence, visitors can be overcome with what is called Stendhal syndrome, named after the French author, when viewing the city's dazzling artistic treasures. Dizziness and disorientation can result. Something similar afflicts some Japanese tourists confronted for the first time with Paris.

What I had begun to call Lost Colony syndrome seemed to take the form of an urgent and overwhelming need to resolve the question of what happened to the colonists. The victim is compelled to set out his case like a prosecuting attorney, no matter how conjectural the

conclusion. It has many variants, from a fixation on the hunt for artifacts to a mania for genealogy, but it metastasizes to dominate a person's waking life. This obsession was what Brent Lane had described
to me—and which held him, despite his claims otherwise, in its grip. I
myself evidence a mild form. Historians like Quinn and archaeologists
like Horton were caught up in it to varying degrees. Phillip Evans and
Fred Willard fell further down on the spectrum, having each devoted
decades and a small fortune to the exclusion of much else. Then I met
Clyde Miller.

The first annual Lost Colony Festival took place in the little
town of Windsor in Bertie County, about sixty miles west of Roanoke Island. It was a cloudless and shimmering April day, like the
one Verrazano described half a millennium ago. There was standing
room only in the local nature center as an archaeologist with the First
Colony Foundation outlined recent findings from the nearby Site X
excavations. After he finished his presentation, a tall older man with
disheveled white hair suddenly stood up and waved a three-foot-long
cylinder of paper above our heads.

"I would love to present this list of people who say they are Lost
Colony descendants," he announced in a loud and sonorous voice.
The archaeologist smiled wanly from the podium as the man went on
for several minutes about his genealogical research. People seemed to
know him; they quickly jostled to the exit. Curious, I intercepted him
later, and we walked out of the dark room into the blinding sunshine.

"This is not legend!" Miller exclaimed, as if I had challenged him.
He had smudged black-framed glasses and a distracted air. "This is
all done with wills." The last word sounded like "wheels," but more
drawn out in the middle. With a flick of his thick wrists, he unrolled
the paper he was carrying on a nearby picnic bench. It opened like an
ancient scroll. It was large enough to serve as a tablecloth. The entire
surface of the paper was covered with twisting family trees stretching
in loops and curves, folding in over themselves before branching back
out, like kudzu on the side of a southern barn. The tiny script of the
names was nearly too small for me to read.

"I have been working on this tree for forty-six years," he said
proudly in his slow and booming delivery. "That's my entire family

tree—over 133,000 names. Daddy's line goes back to Joseph of Arimathea. And Mama's goes back to the Mandeville family in the Tower of London. But I didn't put my great-grandfather in out of respect for the queen." The queen was Queen Elizabeth II. He explained that he would not publish the full story while she was alive, given certain sensitivities that better remained secret but that I took to be some sort of interracial scandal involving the House of Windsor. As he pointed at a series of names on the chart explaining his relation to the colonists, I quickly found myself lost. But while Miller's detailed family tree seemed difficult to understand, his insistence that the Roanoke settlers lived on in the genetic and social fabric of North Carolina did not.

The stories of the colonists that still pervade eastern North Carolina serve a variety of purposes, just as Virginia Dare does for feminists and white supremacists. For Lumbee, the link helped ensure better schools and a measure of respect from the dominant culture. Among whites, the lineage provided a noble past to rival the wealthier and imperious planter aristocracy of Virginia and South Carolina. (An old southern saying has it that North Carolina is a "vale of humility between two mountains of conceit.") These are practical ways to put distant history to use.

Miller looked as white as almost everyone else at the festival, apart from a few Native American vendors, though the town of about thirty-five hundred people was half African American. "My grandmother told me about being part Croatan," he was saying. "She said if they had known I was Croatan Indian, they'd have forced me to go to Central, the black school. Of course she didn't tell me about her father. That would have torn the family apart."

My head was still spinning from a family tree that went back to Joseph of Arimathea, the man credited with burying Jesus. But from what I could make out, Miller was using the mystery of the Lost Colony to make sense of a shadowy past. That history embraced not just the initial conflict between Europeans and Native Americans but the shadowy legacy of a slave culture that brought Africans to this region—likely as early as 1586. The succeeding centuries were often unimaginably violent, from the devastating war fought between English and Indians that ended in the creation of a Tuscarora reservation near Windsor in 1717 to the brutal lynching two centuries later of a black man named Peter Bazemore a few miles outside town.

Miller was being literal, trying to build a link between an American today and a Lost Colonist from 1587. Of course, being lost means, by definition, lacking records of births and marriages and deaths. DNA, for the time being, is no help. Between the time of White's departure and the second wave of the English is an unbridgeable gap that even the most upgraded version of Ancestry.com cannot span.

Yet it struck me that Miller was, in some way that he could not quite articulate, engaged in something more than a quixotic effort to trace his relations back to ancient Judaea via Tudor England. It was as if, using his convoluted and tangled family tree, he were attempting to stitch together the black, red, and white parts of his splintered past, the "mongrel remnants" that so many Americans share to some degree, a reality largely lost amid the nation's long-standing racial divides.

It was getting late, and the festival was winding down. I made my excuses and edged toward my car. As I rolled out of the gravel parking lot, he was still chatting with me through my open window, talking about his plans to study at Oxford. During the long trip home, I pondered my next step. Eliza Cushing, who first coined the term "Lost Colony," warned that when it comes to the Roanoke story, it is unavoidable to go forth "into a world of conjecture." Even Quinn could not resist making that leap, though he dressed it up in scholarly language. I decided to follow Miller's example and succumb fully to the Lost Colony vortex to see where it led me, but in my own way. I began with Occam's razor.

If the best hypothesis is the one with the least number of assumptions, then which applies to the vanished Roanoke settlers?

After returning from Windsor, I walked through the possibilities. First, there is no evidence in Spanish archives that England's European enemy destroyed the colony. Second, the settlers might have used a pinnace left behind or built a boat to sail to Newfoundland or England, or moved to Chesapeake Bay. Either option required complex logistics, and in any case some might have stayed behind.

Third, massacre, starvation, and illness resulting in death were all possible outcomes. But if they occurred while the English were still on Roanoke, at least, John White reported no evidence such as graves or skeletons on his brief return to the settlement in 1590. Fourth, Wingina's people or another tribe might have enslaved them; the strong palisade the governor found suggests the settlers felt endangered. But he found no Greek cross, the secret token to be carved into a tree if the settlers left in distress. Of course, White might have made this all up, to hide his failings or protect Raleigh, but this meant accepting a successful cover-up.

At Jamestown, the stories that emerged about Powhatan's culpability in killing the colonists, and of English slaves made to work copper, seemed tied up with the London Company's public relations problems. They were in any event based heavily on the testimony of Machumps, who might have had his own agenda. Later, the colonists' needed to justify Indian extermination in the wake of the 1622 rebellion, so painting their enemies as murderers made Powhatan's perfidy politically valuable. That didn't make these claims true.

Even John Smith's intelligence about a few scattered people in European clothes and stone houses seemed at best ambiguous. It could just as well point to distant Spanish towns or shipwreck victims. Besides, would an English woolen coat or dress even survive intact if worn for more than two decades? And was a stone house necessary or even desirable in a land where wood was so readily available?

That left the fifth possibility: the settlers joined nearby Indians, either "fifty miles into the main" or on Croatoan—or both. The fort symbol White hid on his map pointed to the head of the Albemarle Sound. This was a strategic spot for trading and exploring the Carolina hinterland while keeping an eye out for arriving ships. Such a move also might have reflected an annual Native American migration from the coast to the interior during the winter. In the wake of Wingina's murder, however, moving in that direction would have posed dangers, because it is not clear the English or Croatoan had any remaining allies in that direction.

Scott Dawson's analogy was hard to dispute. "Imagine a time before texting," the Hatteras native said. "You ask your wife in the morning to leave a note at home naming the restaurant where you will meet for dinner. You come home from work to change clothes and find a note that says, 'We're going to the Shipwreck Grill.' What do you do? Will you head on over to the Shipwreck Grill, or Café 12?" To him, it was self-evident that at least some of the colonists did what their message for the governor said (if White reported his find accurately). They went to Croatoan. As Horton suggested, this might have been the best place for many of the women and children, far from Wanchese and his people and where they could keep an eye out for the governor's return.

Yet even if White made up the "secret token" or misread it for some reason, the Croatoan were without a doubt the single most important allies for the English, and quite probably the only ones. This alliance was crucial for the settlers' survival. The colonists were primarily middle-class city people, like the ones criticized by Harriot on the Lane expedition for their lack of survival skills. As John Smith wryly noted at Jamestown, "Although there be deer in the woods, fish in the rivers, and fowls in abundance in their seasons," yet "we [be] so unskillful to catch them, we little troubled them nor they us."

For the Croatoan, an alliance with the unpredictable foreigners made eminent sense. With a small population likely not much larger than the English on Roanoke, they faced a daunting confederation of enemies on the mainland. Backing the English could offer a constant flow of weapons, tools, and commercial goods that would provide a critical advantage over their more numerous rivals. After all, they expected the governor to return with more settlers and supplies.

White even leaves us with a moving image of the Indians and Europeans working together in the aftermath of the botched mainland raid that killed or injured some Croatoan busy looting Wingina's abandoned town of Dasemunkepeuc. As the sun rose, they joined awkwardly together to gather "all the corn, peas, pumpkins, and tobacco that we found ripe, leaving the rest unspoiled." The fact that they didn't destroy the unripe crops is a sign that both groups felt confident they could hold on to this territory. English guns and Croatoan local knowledge made the two small and vulnerable bands a formidable local power.

Manteo was the critical link between the two cultures. At Raleigh's orders—and, almost certainly, with the blessing of the queen—he was made lord of both Roanoke and Dasemunkepeuc, "in reward of his faithful services." Most historians mention the honorific in passing, as if it were a gold star given to a good student. In Tudor England, however, titles were serious business, translating into power and wealth. As a member of the peerage, Lord Manteo was technically even higher in rank than Raleigh, a mere knight. No other Native American has since been granted the title. He was, in fact, the obvious choice to lead the colony after White's 1587 departure; as far as we know, none of the assistants had been to Virginia before or spoke Carolina Algonquian. He also knew, better than anyone, the principal foe of the English: Wanchese.

Yet Manteo is traditionally seen as merely a dutiful and loyal adviser, while some indigenous people label him a traitor or lackey. As with Fernandes, the complex and interesting non-Anglo character has been reduced to a one-dimensional portrait. Though he dressed as an Englishman and spent a total of fifteen months in London, his people greeted him with joy on his 1587 return. He might have calculated that throwing in his lot with the English would give both himself and his tribe a far more powerful position than under Wingina's reign.

By 1588, if they were still alive and living with the Croatoan, the colonists would have learned the rhythm of the seasons, breaking into smaller groups in the winter and spring to hunt and forage. They may well have moved back and forth across Pamlico Sound. "The Indians from the back country came regularly in the early springtime to the coast of the Cape Fear for the seawater fish and oysters which were abundant," early-twentieth-century author James Sprunt wrote of a tribe that lived on the southern end of the Outer Banks. First they would imbibe yaupon tea and purge. Then they would "gorge themselves to repletion with the fish and oysters." Turkeys and squirrels supplemented the spring diet. By May and June, there were acorns and walnuts, as well as blue crab and land tortoise, easy to catch and highly nutritious. After planting corn, beans, and squash, the settlers would have learned to find berries and dig up tuckahoe roots. Sunflowers provided oil as well as bread. The harvest began in late summer, and fall was devoted to gathering fruits and nuts and drying and smoking deer and other game for the coming winter. Throughout the year, there were always more fish and oysters.

As time passed and White failed to return, the Europeans would have changed more than their diet. They would have traded out their culture. Without resupply from England, woolen dresses and leather shoes would have rapidly worn out, to be replaced by soft deerskin. Corn bread quickly substituted for biscuits, and Indian coil-made ceramics replaced broken English pots made on a wheel. Once gunpowder stores were used up or a gun jammed, bows and arrows and nets would have been the only way to hunt game. A reed-poled hut covered with adjustable grass mats might have felt better suited to the climate than a stuffy thatched cottage. Local herbs flavored their stews and healed their illnesses. With a working knowledge of Carolina Algonquian so necessary for survival, spoken English would have fallen away.

As David Phelps noted, the class structure of royal family and commoners, though practiced on a smaller scale, would have felt familiar to Elizabethans. They would have found some common religious ground; both groups, after all, believed in a version of heaven and hell and an overarching deity. Eventually, rather than lay the heads of their dead facing east, toward Christian resurrection, they would have adopted the Algonquian practice of folding their deceased loved ones' arms and legs to mimic the body's position before birth. Some English songs and dances as well as technological know-how might have entered the Croatoan repertoire, but the Lost Colonists would have found not just a New World home but a new way to live.

It was not an easy life, even before the advent of European diseases; arthritis often set in while Carolina Algonquians were barely out of their twenties, and life expectancy hovered around age thirty-five. Women could expect to lose every fourth child before it reached the age of five. But these grim statistics were not so different from those in Elizabethan England.

Archaeological finds in the past few decades demonstrate the Native Americans and early European settlers already lived virtually cheek by jowl. A 1560s Spanish fort in western North Carolina was built adjacent to a Native American town—the locals even helped the soldiers build their encampment—and Jamestown's streets were often filled with Virginia Algonquians trading deerskins for tools and Venetian beads. Indians routinely visited settlements like Plymouth and New Amsterdam to trade and share a meal and even spend the night. The Roanoke settlement, wherever it was located, was almost certainly close to Granganimeo's village.

Most historians now accept that the Lost Colonists, if they survived, merged with indigenous society. "It is probable that some of the Roanoke colonists did live on and melt into the native population," writes NYU's Kupperman. "This could have been true of the several hundred enslaved Africans and Indians from the Caribbean left by Drake, the three men abandoned by Lane's colony in their haste to leave, or the fifteen men left by Grenville." The colonists might even have encountered the Africans and South Americans left behind by Drake who would have blended in as well with the locals.

Michael Oberg, a historian at the State University of New York at Geneseo, adds, "Ralegh's colonists were lost only to those Europeans who searched and failed to find them. Indian people knew what happened to them." He concludes that "they became Algonquians and were no longer English men and women."

Why, then, the mystery? If assimilation is the simplest and most logical answer that fits the few facts we have, then why do we invoke aliens and zombies to explain what happened to the Lost Colonists? What is the nature of the "horror within" that still lurks on Roanoke Island?

I went back over the centuries of theorizing and discovered a single thread that runs unbroken from today back to the very beginning. In his 1605 play, Ben Jonson and his co-author celebrated the settlers mixing with the Indians to make beautiful babies, but that bawdy Elizabethan tolerance (tempered by the assertion that the beauty came only from the English genes) soon gave way to strictly corseted Puritan morality.

The one famous exception proves the rule. When John Rolfe wed

Pocahontas in 1614 after she was taken captive, the bond proved not the start of a merging of two peoples but a one-of-a-kind diplomatic marriage. Unlike the Spanish and French, the English firmly rejected mixing with Native Americans. By the end of the seventeenth century, Virginia enacted the first laws prohibiting marriage between Europeans and either Africans or Native Americans. "Intermarriage had been indeed the method proposed very often by the Indians in the beginning" to secure a peaceful coexistence, noted Virginia-born Robert Beverley almost wistfully in 1705. "And I can't but think it would have been happy for that country, had they embraced this proposal."

Instead, the inevitable ties were illicit and harshly punished. Spanish spies at early Jamestown reported that forty or fifty English abandoned their countrymen to live with Indian wives. In 1612, the Virginia governor had those settlers living among Powhatan's Virginia Algonquian people captured and then "hanged, sunburned, some broken up on wheels, others to be staked and some shot to death" to discourage others from following suit. "All this extreme and cruel torture [the governor] used and inflicted upon them to terrify the rest for attempting the like," one eyewitness reported. Despite these extreme measures, men continued to desert, whether for food or female companionship or to escape the severe discipline at the fort.

Englishwomen also became part of Virginia Algonquian society. A decade later, Indians captured Anne Jackson during the bloody Native American uprising. Her brother thought she was dead, and when he learned three years later that she survived, he set off with another colonist to retrieve her. He found her among the Pamunkey Indians, but she refused to go back with him. So did his traveling partner. When Anne returned in 1629, apparently against her will, she was locked up in a house until a ship could take her back to England.

During his 1701 travels through Carolina, John Lawson met English traders who "find these Indian girls very serviceable to them" because they could learn more quickly the Indian tongue while enjoying "the satisfaction of a she-bed-fellow" who cooks and instructs them on the "customs of the country." The explorer even proffered racial mixing as the most likely outcome of Raleigh's vanished settlers. "In process of time, they conformed themselves to the manners of their Indian relations," he writes. Yet Lawson instinctively recoiled from the very idea, perhaps because this suggested white women found Indian husbands. "And thus we see how apt human nature is to degenerate," he concluded with disgust.

Contemporary commentators played down the fact that most whites, even those taken captive, preferred their new families to their old homes. Though we don't have any reliable numbers, the decision by many Europeans to join and stay in Indian society was colonial America's dirty secret. In 1747 New York's surveyor general reported to the king's council that "no arguments, entreaties, no tears of their friends and relations, could persuade many of them to leave their new Indian friends." The few who did "in a little time grew tired of our manner of living, and run away again to the Indians and ended their days with them." Benjamin Franklin, with only some exaggeration, remarked that "no European who has tasted savage life can afterwards bear to live in our societies."

Whites and blacks could expect a high degree of acceptance in Native American society, although warrior-age men might be deemed too unreliable and be killed. Newcomers might be enslaved for a time, but they often took up life with a family of a recently deceased person, sometimes literally filling the shoes of the lost one. They could even rise in the ranks and become political leaders. This is, in part, why Lumbee and other Native Americans are reluctant to accept DNA as a true marker of tribal identity; it is cultural affiliation more than blood that determined if a person belonged.

If this desire to remain Native American was the result of Stockholm syndrome, in which hostages develop a close bond with their captors, it didn't work both ways. Even an Indian child reared among the colonists would slip away, Franklin noted, and "there is no persuading him ever to return." The taint of a darker skin color and a Native background kept them apart. "We have no examples of even one of these Aborigines having from choice become Europeans," one New Yorker wrote in 1782.

For white Americans—and particularly women—"going native" became a disturbing yet thrilling popular genre in the late eighteenth and early nineteenth centuries that highlighted Indian subjugation and rape. As the frontier vanished in the east, however, the very notion of the two peoples mixing became taboo. That is why, in nearly all the Virginia Dare romances of the mid- and late nineteenth century, the young maid keeps herself apart from the lusty Indian braves. Every other colonist, at least those of childbearing years, has to die. She has to be rescued by a European or be turned into a white doe to avoid her partnering with an Indian warrior.

No one expressed the taboo against racial mixing more clearly than Bishop Cheshire in 1910. "Never let anyone persuade you to believe for one moment" that the colonists were "swallowed up and amalgamated with half-naked heathen Indian savages, so that no remnant was left which could be recognized by their white brethren of Virginia," he warned his listeners at the annual Virginia Dare birthday celebration. "The descendants of those first Christian inhabitants of our land are not to be sought in the mongrel remnants, part Indian, part white, and part negro, of a decaying tribe of American savages." His blatant warning to not even consider the possibility of "mongrel remnants" struck me as a clear case of a man locking the barn door after the horse has bolted.

Even the respected historian Quinn—an Irishman!—was not wholly comfortable with the idea of English settlers casting off their Anglo heritage. He argued that most of the colonists created a proper English village near the Chesapeake, and fretted about those left behind to the south. "We are forced to accept as a fact that they became Indians themselves, and their children and grandchildren wholly so," he writes with a tone of obvious reluctance. He only grudgingly admitted "a handful of them may have contributed some genes to the Hatteras Indians."

This abiding unwillingness to embrace the idea that the colonists assimilated with the Croatoan, like the stories around the virginal Virginia Dare, reflects centuries of deep anxiety about sex between the races—particularly between European women and non-European men. Unlike the Spanish, Portuguese, and French, who tolerated interracial mixing to varying degrees, the English in the New World moved quickly to punish those who strayed. (Virginia had a loophole called the "Pocahontas exception" that allowed members of the white upper classes to retain their status while claiming the Powhatan princess as their ancestor.) Those laws remained in effect as late as 1967, when the U.S. Supreme Court ruled against Virginia's statute banning interracial marriages. The woman in that famous case, *Loving v. Virginia*, was of mixed African-Algonquian ancestry.

This old unease, running so quiet and deep through our history, is reason enough to fill Roanoke Island with scary supernatural beings and turn Croatoan into a blood-borne virus, "a demon of plague and pestilence" that incites a murderous rage. The fascination that the Lost Colony inspires is, in the end, not about settlers getting lost in the woods; it is about our primal fear of losing our identity in a land constantly reshaped by new arrivals. I remembered the Secotan prophecy recorded by Harriot, that "there were more of our generations yet to come, to kill theirs and take their places." Having done just that, later Americans, it seems, inherited the fear that the same fate would befall them.

The Lost Colonists, after all, weren't described as lost until the 1830s, when Nat Turner's rebellion and the forced removal of indigenous tribes hardened racial boundaries. That was the decade when a song-and-dance routine called the "Jim Crow," involving white performers wearing black face and ragged clothes, first became popular. The Roanoke settlers didn't vanish; they were lost in order to veil the likely but inconvenient truth that the survivors simply ceased to be white.

When Governor White returned in August 1590, it was the prime season for harvesting corn, fishing, and gathering shellfish from the warm Pamlico Sound. While he visited Croatoan before moving on to Roanoke, he reports seeing no one on either island. The three fires and footprints he subsequently mentions show that there were people there, just none who wanted to make contact.

The Indians might have feared his ship was Spanish, intent on killing the settlers and their allies. Alternatively, Wanchese and his tribe might have been back in control and worried the English would seek revenge if the colonists were dead or enslaved. They had reason to worry: two decades before, a Spanish captain in Chesapeake Bay hanged Virginia Algonquians to avenge the deaths of several Jesuits, though only after baptizing the victims as Christians.

Recent tree-ring data from bald cypress in the Great Dismal Swamp between Roanoke and Jamestown shows that the Southeast underwent an extended drought that was particularly severe in northeastern North Carolina between 1587 and 1589. This doesn't mean they starved; the crisis might have pushed the Croatoan and colonists to the mainland, where bodies of freshwater and carbohydrate-rich roots might have allowed them to survive the lean years.

The surviving colonists also might have seen White's ships with fear rather than joy. Three years is a long time; by then they might have chosen Carolina Algonquian spouses and had children. A homecoming with family back in England would be awkward. In later cases, many Europeans living among Native Americans for far less time refused to return or hid from their former friends and family. The Lost Colonists, in other words, may have wanted to remain lost.

Curiously, the name Croatoan itself appears to have migrated by the time English explorers returned in the following century. While it clearly denotes the tribe as well as the island between Hatteras and Ocracoke in the Elizabethan era, several seventeenth-century English maps place the word instead on the mainland opposite Roanoke Island, at the former site of Wingina's town; this is also when the waterway separating Roanoke from the mainland began to be called Croatan Sound, its current name. Other maps place the word "Croatoan" to the south, on the mainland opposite Hatteras. This is where White drew most of his images of Algonquians and their way of life, and also where Smith's 1608 map referred to the home of four mysterious clothed men.

When the second wave of English began to move south of the Albemarle Sound around 1700, they made no reference to the Secotan, Roanoke, or Croatoan people. Instead, they mention a small Algonquian tribe called the Mattamuskeet or Machapunga, who numbered about one hundred members and could field thirty warriors. The newcomers, along with seizing lands, captured Indians and sold them as slaves to the West Indies and even Pennsylvania. In the resulting Tuscarora War, one of the first victims was John Lawson, who was tortured and killed in 1711 as a spy. The Machapunga, allied with the Tuscarora, launched raids and captured English settlers as far away as Roanoke and Hatteras. Acting governor Thomas Pollock calls them "expert watermen" with the advantage "of such dismal swamps to fly into . . . where it is almost impossible for white men to follow them." Like the Lumbee's ancestors to the southwest, they retreated into an area that provided them with a measure of protection. If there were Croatoan—and Lost Colony—descendants among the Machapunga, they made their home in the very area visited by the Lane and Grenville expedition in 1585.

The Tuscarora eventually surrendered, but "a handful of Indians who would not come into the treaty with the rest have spilt more innocent blood than all the rest," complained the Reverend John Urmstone in Bath, referring to the nearby Machapunga. "They are like deer, there's no finding them." Later, he added, "we are forced to sue for peace."

The bloody uprising prompted North Carolina's legislators in 1715 to impose a fifty-pound penalty for whites who married anyone black, mulatto, or Indian. The same year, the colony created its first Indian reservation along Lake Mattamuskeet's shores for the tribe. Though short-lived, it drew some of the remaining indigenous people from the Outer Banks. A visiting pastor half a century later described "the few remains of the Altamuskeet [Mattamuskeet], Hatteras, and Roanoke tribes" living "mostly along that [Pamlico Sound] coast, mixed with the white inhabitants." According to David La Vere, they kept a low profile: "Eastern North Carolina Indians learned to lay low, become invisible, being seen by the surrounding white population only when they wanted to be seen."

In the following century, escaped and free African Americans arrived as well. Historian Arwin Smallwood at North Carolina A&T State University even posits that the Africans likely dropped off by Drake in 1586 might have been the direct ancestors of those Machapunga so adept in war. "They were, after all, soldiers accustomed to the swamps," he told me. "Both Africans and whites from the Roanoke voyages merged with the coastal Indians to create some of the first mixed-race people in North America long before the 1619 arrival of enslaved Africans at Jamestown," he added.

According to a social history of the Mattamuskeet published in 1975 by Patrick Garrow, the tribe's descendants in the eighteenth and nineteenth centuries "enjoyed a social status only slightly higher than slaves." As their refuge shrank as Europeans proliferated, the indigenous children were regularly removed for "apprenticeships" designed to place them under the care of whites that erased their culture. "The trend among these families since the Civil War towards increased mixture with black families, as well as the apprenticeship policy in the early nineteenth century, has effectively destroyed all but a dim awareness of their 'Indianess,'" writes Garrow.

When anthropologist Frank Speck visited the area in 1916 with a Mohawk graduate student, he found the Machapunga "are of the Algonquian stock and have intermarried with negroes and whites." He writes that "persistent inquiry among the settlers of Albemarle and Pamlico sounds" brought to his attention "a few individuals who are descended from Indians" who appeared to be a mix of Indian, African, and European features. He concludes that "the living descendants of the Machapunga, by a liberal estimate, can hardly number more than one hundred."

Though these people did not speak a word of Carolina Algonquian, Speck noticed they made nets with different-sized meshes to capture specific species, using fibers from a local variety of milkweed, just like Algonquians far to the north. "Until recently," he adds, "native baskets were made of hickory and oak splints, in the manner prevailing among all the Iroquoian and Algonquian bands of the east."

Seven years later, Speck mentioned in another academic paper that many of the remaining Machapunga had since left the mainland. "In North Carolina there are a number of uninvestigated bands of mixed Indians," he writes. "For example, the Machapunga are represented by about one hundred survivors on Roanoke Island."

Roanoke Island? When I read Speck's throwaway line late one night, I yelped out loud.

If Lost Colonists joined the Croatoan and moved with the tribe to the mainland and became part of the Machapunga, then their descendants, more than three centuries later, would have returned to precisely where they began. They would have come full circle—back to Roanoke Island. In that Jim Crow era, however, they would have been classified as colored. The putative descendants of Virginia Dare, that paragon of whiteness and symbol of the nation's Anglo-American heritage, would have been considered black.

Bishop Cheshire, with his loathing of "mongrel remnants," would no doubt have been vexed. So would the members of the Manteo White Supremacy Club. Because they are no longer available for comment, I asked Peter Brimelow from VDARE.com if he shared my delight at the irony. "Not particularly," he replied, before launching into a diatribe against the fantasy of the "coming racial nirvana" predicted by immigration enthusiasts.

On a cold and rainy February night in 1862, a small and dangerously overcrowded boat beached near the old earthwork on Roanoke Island. Some twenty men, women, and children scrambled up the sandy bank, 275 years after the Lost Colonists had done the same. The new arrivals were the first of more than three thousand enslaved people to flee their eastern North Carolina masters for the protection of President Lincoln's troops. What came to be called the Freedmen's Colony spawned hundreds of tents and houses, including a church and school, along a dusty grid of streets on the island's middle and north end.

A Union Army minister named Horace James, who was put in charge of organizing the settlement, envisioned the colony as pioneering the next step in the American experiment, what he called "a new social order." While Raleigh's people sought gold only to find "starvation and an early grave," the "magic touch of freedom" now would make the "wave-kissed shores" of Roanoke Island "the abode of a prosperous and virtuous people, of varying blood but of one destiny." Nearly three centuries after the failure of the Elizabethan effort, Roanoke would spawn "a happy commonwealth."

As the English had learned long before, however, the new settlers found that the island lacked the resources, like good soil and fresh water, necessary to build a large and thriving community. Nor were the local whites eager to be a minority in James's "happy commonwealth." After the conflict, property owners sued to get their land back, and most of the residents of the colony left the island. A few, however, remained to join those already living here to build a small but thriving African American community on the outskirts of Roanoke's largest settlement. In the 1870s the growing town was dubbed Manteo and made the seat of a county named in honor of Virginia Dare. Known as excellent watermen, the men of color took up fishing and oversaw operation of a lifesaving station on nearby Pea Island (near the site of the long-vanished Port Ferdinando), the only U.S. station staffed solely by blacks.

Arsonists burned the station in 1880. In the 1890s the Manteo White Supremacy Club lobbied for white supremacist candidates, and in 1901 Dare County approved a state measure to disenfranchise blacks. Although subject to the same harsh laws and prejudice as elsewhere in the region, blacks had a larger degree of independence here, where plantation culture had never taken root and government control was weak. While several lynchings took place in the counties immediately to the west, no mob murders of African Americans are documented on the Outer Banks. Greater liberty and economic opportunity drew other Negroes, a category that since 1835 had included everyone of mixed blood, living in the subsistence economy that long characterized much of the state's eastern mainland.

The Machapunga, as a consequence, were considered black when they moved the fifty miles or so northeast to Roanoke Island from their more isolated mainland villages. "Today, the ancestry of these people is so predominately Negroid that any Indian blood is thoroughly disguised," another anthropologist wrote about Manteo's Machapunga in 1960.

On a quiet and unusually warm Sunday morning in spring, I cruised through Manteo's quaint downtown, with its restaurants named 1587 and the Lost Colony Brewery and Cafe. Most of the tourist action clusters on the east side by the picturesque harbor, where the *Elizabeth II,* the sixteenth-century reproduction vessel, is docked at Roanoke Island Festival Park.

Across the main highway to the west is the predominantly black neighborhood. Since I was a child, I had passed through Manteo without even suspecting its existence. The houses were older and smaller than those on the whiter side of town, and the streets quieter. I pulled up outside a plain brick church with a small white steeple and a side parking lot crammed with cars. The Church of Three Ships on Sir Walter Raleigh Street is also called Haven Creek Missionary Baptist Church.

If slaves could cross the creek—the Croatan Sound—then they could find haven on Roanoke. Founded in the Freedmen's Colony during the Civil War, the church's first official minister was Zion Hall Berry, who claimed full-blooded Cherokee descent (in North Carolina, the term "Cherokee" is often a generic designation for Indian). I could hear a choir in full swing through the half-open windows. Late and underdressed, I loitered outside in the shade until the service ended. It lasted three hours. The pastor, sweating heavily from preaching in the heat, invited me into his tiny office. He was not from the island, and he told me that the community's main source of knowledge had recently died. The other, a 102-year-old woman, was too ill to chat.

Later I met with Joan Collins and Darrell Collins at a café down the street. The cousins are light-skinned professionals in the twilight of their busy careers; Darrell is Manteo mayor pro tem and a former park ranger well known for his talks on the Wright brothers, while Joan is retired from the federal government and deeply involved in community activities. Their great-grandfather was in the lifesaving service, and they share a great-great-grandfather in Zion Hall Berry.

"They say he was full-blown Cherokee," said Joan. She pulled a copy of an old photograph out of her purse. The black-and-white image revealed a large man with a broad face and an intense dark-

Zion Hall Berry, a nineteenth-century preacher, claimed Indian descent and founded numerous Baptist churches across northeastern North Carolina.

eyed stare. "We have a side of our family that is very heavy into our Indian heritage," continued Joan. "They do powwows. The chief of the Roanoke-Hatteras tribe is my cousin."

By the tone of her voice and arch of her brow, I sensed she was skeptical of the Native American connection, so I asked if she had had her DNA tested. "My father did, and there was hardly any Indian at all," she said. "Same for my brother and sister—in fact, our balance was a little more white than black, which makes me chuckle. For my powwow cousins, this is their life. But we have heard the stories about Indians since we were young."

Darrell said that his grandfather had Indian features as well as an uncompromising Native American outlook on survival. "We are descendants of the Skyco tribe," he said. Skyco is the Roanoke Island community between Manteo and Wanchese, named for the son of the Chowan Indian chief held hostage by Ralph Lane in 1586. Also spelled Skiko, it was his grandfather's middle name. He would take Darrell and a cousin camping in the swamp to set traps for rabbits and squirrels. "One day we had a campfire going, and we got water on the campfire. My grandfather said that young Indian braves don't spill water on a campfire, and he tied us up with briars," Darrell recalled with a laugh. "After that my mother didn't let us go out in the swamp with him."

I asked them if they were raised with the story of the Lost Colony and Virginia Dare. Darrell looked at me with a level gaze. "I was raised on stories of Harriet Tubman," he said.

Before leaving Manteo, I stopped by Roanoke Island Festival

Park to say hello to Warren McMaster, the sailor who spends his days in wool stockings and pantaloons aboard the *Elizabeth II* answering tourists' questions about the Roanoke voyages. Leaning comfortably against the rigging, with his spare frame and jaunty goatee, he looked very much the Elizabethan pirate. "I tell them this was the first permanent English settlement in America," he said during a break between visitors. "But that was Jamestown," I responded, confused. He smiled. "What, are you prejudiced against Indians?" he answered. "That's what I say. After all, what is more permanent than one hundred and fifteen settlers arriving and staying in the New World?"

On my way out of the park, I sought out an unusual historical marker someone had mentioned to me. After asking around, I finally found the 1994 bronze plaque from the North Carolina Society of the National Society Colonial Dames XVII Century, surrounded by low bushes in the parking lot. The marker was placed "in grateful recognition of the gifts of food, friendship, and assistance with which the native inhabitants greeted the first Europeans to Roanoke Island in 1584." Though the thank-you came more than four centuries late, it seemed a start at addressing the ghosts of Roanoke.

As I drove north heading toward the Virginia line, I smiled at the idea that the one group in eastern North Carolina with the least interest in being linked with Virginia Dare—African Americans—may in fact be the very ones with the strongest claim to her lineage. Darrell Collins was too polite to say it, but for those who counted themselves black, Virginia Dare was not *their* history. She was, after all, still an avenging angel of white supremacy for some. That helped explain why I encountered so few blacks at the Fort Raleigh and Windsor festivities.

My destination now was a suburb in the city of Chesapeake named for the Chesapian tribe that gave the bay its name. The Collinses' cousin and chief of the Roanoke-Hatteras tribe, Marilyn Berry Morrison, lives in a two-story brick house in a tidy development of mowed yards beside a cul-de-sac. She was a statuesque middle-aged woman with light brown skin and two ponytails braided in long leather strands. Two starfish-and-pearl earrings dangled above her bright Indian-print dress.

Zion Hall Berry was her ancestor as well. "He had one wife and nine mistresses," she said with an easy laugh, retrieving from another room a large framed blown-up photograph that matched the one Joan had in her purse. "That's truly a Cherokee! Our identity was kept from us," she added, her voice suddenly serious. "Everyone was afraid that if it was revealed, we would be carted off."

To be an Indian, she explained, meant that you could lose your land and be sent to a reservation or, worse, sold to work on a Caribbean sugar plantation. Some descendants of the Lost Colony—or lost colonies—might have ended their days tending cane in a Hispaniola field. While the indigenous people quickly adopted English and Christianity, ancient traditions like night fishing survived. Morrison said that her uncles held a light to draw fish they called "nanny shad" that would leap into the boat. I thought of John White's drawing of Algonquians fishing with a low fire inexplicably burning in their log canoe.

Medicinal herb remedies were also part of that legacy, such as sassafras to purify your blood or fight measles and chicken pox—European diseases that, along with smallpox, cholera, bubonic plague, malaria, influenza, and the common cold, killed untold numbers of New World Indians. In addition, she was taught to cook with bay, sage, and other local plants; herbs were growing in large pots in the backyard.

Morrison spoke about the sixteenth century as if describing an event from her childhood. "We stood on the shore when Sir Walter Raleigh's people came, and we treated them friendly. We taught them everything we knew. Then they ran out of supplies and began to steal our food. That's the hurting thing."

She leads a group of about two hundred registered members in their uphill struggle to win state and federal recognition as an official tribe. "We are the only race that has to go through so much to prove who we are," she said, indignation in her voice. She had a point. Still the majority, whites ultimately determine the legal identity of people of color and who can and cannot be classed as an Indian by state and federal authorities.

For several years Morrison organized annual powwows on Roanoke Island as a way to keep alive the tradition of their Native

This White watercolor of Algonquian fishing reveals the immense variety of aquatic and bird life in the Carolina sounds and the skill with which the indigenous people collected seafood, skills that may have been transmitted to the twentieth century.
British Museum

Chief Marilyn Berry Morrison speaks at a powwow of the Roanoke-Hatteras tribe. Morrison calls the Lost Colonists and her tribe, which includes European and African American ancestors, "all one people."
Marvin T. Jones

American lineage. Her family's origins were based on Roanoke Island and Hatteras. She said that a century ago the anthropologist Speck interviewed her great-grandmother, who identified as a Hatteras Indian. "We also have roots with the Mattamuskeet," she added, using the other name for Machapunga. "When they killed our chief Wingina, some of us migrated to the mainland."

I asked about DNA, and she said that her father was tested and told her he had traces of Native American genes, but she wasn't concerned with the details. "I claim Native American based on tradition," Morrison said, adding that she doesn't deny her white and black parts.

"We *were* the Lost Colony," she responded, when I brought up the Raleigh settlers. "Our surnames, like Berry, appear on the colonists' list. We are the original melting pot. We are all one people." But when I pressed, her story wasn't one of gentle assimilation. "We used them for fish bait," she said of the colonists. "We enslaved and traded some of them, just as Europeans did to us. We killed the men and took the women and children." As warriors or soldiers, grown men were more difficult to acculturate.

Morrison opened a hefty binder with the results of years of genealogical work. She collected as many dates and pictures as she could. The faces were a heady mix of kinky hair and straight, dark skin and light. "My dad had gray eyes," she said. "You just have so many different hues." My eyes lit on one name that lacked a photograph or birth or death date. "She was my great-great-grandmother," Morrison said. "She was from Roanoke Island."

Later I found her tombstone in an overgrown cemetery outside Manteo, a couple of hundred yards from Croatan Sound. A slender column topped by an elegant stone finial recorded her birth in 1876, the end of Reconstruction and the start of the Jim Crow era, and her passing in 1921, the year that the worst race riot in American history left hundreds of African Americans in Tulsa dead. Her name was Virginia Dare Bowser Tillett.

There are people in eastern Europe who were born in the Austro-Hungarian Empire, grew up in Czechoslovakia, spent their teenage years in the Third Reich, lived out middle age in the Soviet Union, and died in an independent Ukraine—all without leaving their village. Abandoned in a strange land, the Lost Colonists and their descendants might have undergone similar wrenching changes.

If they avoided massacre, starvation, and enslavement, the settlers abandoned many of their familiar laws, foods, traditions, and beliefs as well as their native language. Decimated by disease, the Carolina Algonquians in the early seventeenth century appear to have come under the sway of the Tuscarora to the west. Their children and grandchildren might have fought the second wave of English invaders a century later. In the early nineteenth century, they would have been decreed people of color and assigned a status "only slightly higher than slaves."

Without moving beyond a radius of fifty miles, the descendants of Raleigh's voyages would have been labeled as originating on three different continents—Europe, North America, and then Africa—in as many centuries; truly an *Alice in Wonderland* journey that no DNA test could ever fully untangle. Their journey seemed as extraordinary as Miller's genealogical scroll.

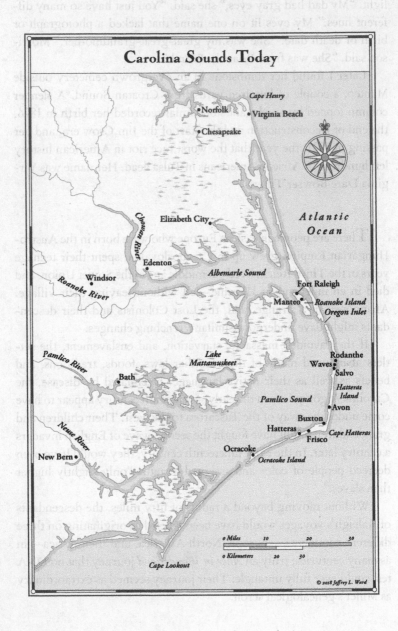

Carolina Sounds Today

Cape Henry

Norfolk • Virginia Beach

Chesapeake

Atlantic Ocean

Chowan River

Elizabeth City

Edenton

Albemarle Sound

Roanoke River

Windsor

Fort Raleigh

Manteo — Roanoke Island
Oregon Inlet

Pamlico River

Lake
Mattamuskeet

Rodanthe

Waves

Salvo

*Hatteras
Island*

Bath

Pamlico Sound

Avon

Buxton

Neuse River

Hatteras

Frisco

Cape Hatteras

Ocracoke

New Bern

Ocracoke Island

0 Miles   10   20   30

0 Kilometers   20   30

Cape Lookout

© 2018 Jeffrey L. Ward

CHAPTER FIFTEEN

An Old Buck Christmas

"You look lost," said the young woman behind the bar, her long blond hair pulled back in a practical ponytail. She poured beer into a mug. Through the restaurant's glass windows, I could see tourists swarming the decks of the *Elizabeth II* across from the Manteo marina. On this scorching August afternoon, I was enjoying the air-conditioning while poring over Google maps of the area on my laptop. I told her I was a writer doing research. "Oh, I'll be speaking with you later!" she said brightly. I looked at her, perplexed. "I'm Eleanor Dare," she explained and headed off with the beer on a tray.

I had arranged with the manager of the *Lost Colony* outdoor drama to speak with the key actors before their performance that evening at Fort Raleigh. Given that they had spent an entire season in character, I was curious if their experience gave them insights inaccessible to historians, archaeologists, and genealogists.

America's oldest mystery is the subject of one of America's longest-running plays. Just a short stroll from the fort, Depression-era workers carved an amphitheater out of the sloping dunes leading to the Albemarle Sound to house the production written by playwright Paul Green. It was slated for one season, but since opening night in 1937 more than four million people have seen what he called a "symphonic drama" that uses music, song, dance, and historical characters to entertain and inform.

No one since John White and George Bancroft has had a bigger impact on how Americans see the Roanoke voyages. Even for those who have not seen the production, its version of the story permeates the field. "You just can't get away from that damn play," one historian told me. "It impacts everything we think about the colony."

When he began work on the script, the North Carolina playwright had already won a Pulitzer Prize for his depiction of a southern hero of mixed-race ancestry facing the insurmountable odds posed by segregation, a daring subject for that day. The 1927 award committee noted that *In Abraham's Bosom* "brings us face to face with one of the most serious of the social problems of this country." Green subsequently wrote a sympathetic drama about another mixed-race hero, Lumbee renegade Henry Berry Lowrie.

Green's fascination with the Roanoke venture began early. As a college student, he watched the 1921 filming of the silent movie at Fort Raleigh dramatizing the colony and returned to school to write a sugary tale about a grown Virginia Dare. He toyed with a story about a Lumbee attempting to prove his Lost Colony connection. "I want to take a representative of the Croatan race who is determined to prove that he is a white man, a descendant of Sir Walter Raleigh's lost colony," he wrote in his diary. "He goes to all lengths to prove it."

Green's awareness of ethnic tensions permeates *The Lost Colony*, which begins with Amadas and Barlowe arriving in the midst of a Native American harvest ceremony and concludes with the hungry White colonists abandoning their fort to march off into the dark woods. In an early version of the third act, as the abandoned colonists grow increasingly sick and desperate, the feverish Anglican reverend cries out, "Evil has been wrought here, the spilling of blood, the murder of innocent ones! Shall we ever thrive here?" The call echoes through American history.

John Herbert Roper, Green's biographer, notes that the play is "all about races mixing together." In a pointed slap at Bishop Cheshire, the playwright has one settler who was a lonely beggar in England find love in the arms of a local Algonquian woman. "Come to your bed, old lady," he calls to her one cold winter night. The two peoples, Green suggests, would create something new and better by mingling.

The playwright went against the grain of most of his fellow southern whites in his support of civil rights and by insisting on "the integration of all things." In 1940, he collaborated with black author Richard Wright to adapt his best-selling *Native Son* for Broadway. Though their brief alliance unraveled, Green took Wright to the annual "Negro Day" performance of *The Lost Colony*, open to African Americans from around the region.

Yet Green was still a product of his time, and his script has its share of cringe-producing moments. Simão Fernandes—played by his Tudor name, Simon Fernando—is a dastardly pirate contrasted with the simple but virtuous Devon farmers who make up the White colony. A middle-aged Indian woman plays a giggling squaw for comic relief. And though there is no evidence that a clergyman was among the colonists, the pious priest is given to frequent prayer.

Later that afternoon, I drove to Fort Raleigh and walked through

In a 1952 production of *The Lost Colony*, Wanchese (played by Carl Kasell, future NPR host) watches as Queen Elizabeth I, Lillian Prince, takes her first puff of tobacco, the "potable gold" that would tie England irrevocably to North America. *North Carolina Collection, University of North Carolina at Chapel Hill Library*

the woods leading past the earthwork. *The Lost Colony* is performed in the stockade-enclosed amphitheater that is all that remains of the 1930s Wild West–style state park that so irritated the archaeologist Harrington. On the main stage, several young men in T-shirts kicked up sand in a pitched sword-and-club battle. "There's a fight call at 5:30 p.m. every night," explained Lance Culpepper, the associate producer. "We do a full run-through of all the fight scenes."

He showed me to the production's greenroom, a wooden boardwalk along the Albemarle Sound. As I waited while Culpepper went off to round up Manteo and Wanchese, I noticed some of the benches lined up behind the stage were marked in block letters with the words "Indians only." Two buff young men arrived. They weren't yet dressed for their parts, which mostly involved applying thick body paint to give their tanned but still pale skins a convincing Native American look. "That's why we have to sit on those benches," explained Joseph Cassala, who played Manteo. "Our makeup could ruin the colonists' clothes."

I asked him why they imagine two Indians might have developed such diametrically opposed views of the English.

"Manteo felt that the coming of the English was inevitable and thought that if he helped them, it would better his people," said Cassala, a tall college student wearing a black Nirvana T-shirt. "They had big ships and armor." At school, he had long conversations with Native American friends pushing for Indian rights. Those discussions gave him insight into Manteo's behavior toward the whites. "I think he tried to see the good in these people and trusted them—you could say to a fault. You could trace what has happened to Native peoples since by going back to this one person."

Zachary Scott, who played Wanchese, said that both he and Manteo crossed the Atlantic to see what the English were all about. "After a year, I'm fully burnt out," he said, in character, "and pretty convinced that I'm not willing to be a part of this." Scott, who sported a baseball cap and a sleeveless Batman tank top over his stocky torso, said that the indigenous were doing just fine before the English came. He found the newcomers caught up in greed and control.

"Wanchese was really frustrated with how these people were so obsessed with material objects rather than just enjoying life. When he finds out about Wingina's death at the hands of the white men, that pushes him over the edge." Scott added that Manteo's decision to convert to Christianity and abandon his people's gods also likely played a role in the two men's rivalry.

That rivalry is a central theme of the play, the tension over whether to accept or reject the Europeans and their ways. Green cast Manteo as the loyal ally and Wanchese as an angry Indian brave who ultimately rejects the English and resorts to violence. Both speak in staccato Tonto-esque language.

"That's changed some this year," said Scott. "We each get a monologue so that we can explain our perspective. But what frustrates me is that Wanchese is still painted as the bad guy. He's the one kids are scared of. But he is just trying to protect his people."

He paused, looking out over the Albemarle, where a thunderstorm was rapidly building. It was just the sort of powerful August storm that prompted White to leave the island in 1590 after his brief search. "There are two villains in the play, Wanchese and Simon Fernando. I've heard it said that these are the two who actually speak the truth. Wanchese fears the English, and Fernando warns the colonists not to go to the New World, that they will face hunger and death. They are both proved right." A popular T-shirt among cast members is emblazoned with the phrase "Wanchese Was Right."

With curtain time approaching, the two left to dress as thick drops began to splatter on the wooden planking. I retreated to the shelter of the costume shop. The cramped space was bustling with colonists lacing up bodices. Wingina stood calmly in the middle of the room as a makeup artist carefully drew intricate white designs over his body paint. The patterns mimicked images of tattoos drawn by John White that were pinned on the walls of the shop.

The play's dialogue might date to the 1930s, but the outfits, designed by award-winning Broadway costume designer William Ivey Long—whose mother acted as Queen Elizabeth I in the production—are strictly Elizabethan. Long carefully researched and designed the clothes worn by both Indians and colonists following a devastating 2007 fire that destroyed the building. He examined Tudor woodcuts and Dutch and Flemish paintings as well as John White watercolors and made clothes that reflected the middle-class status of the majority of the colonists. The European men sport cloaks over doublets and puffy sleeves, while the women wear bodices and long skirts; both sexes placed the starched and pleated adornments called ruffs around their necks. Thanks to White's drawings, the Algonquian outfits were simpler to reconstruct, though Long made some concessions to the twenty-first century. "We use leather bras that are skin color for the women," he told me later.

I found Simon Fernando in an open black shirt and black hip-length pirate boots. He had curly black hair and swarthy skin and looked the part of a rough pirate. "I think he was misunderstood," said the actor Topher Embrey, in a surprisingly earnest and gentle voice. "I feel like he was with the colony from the start, but gets no credit. Everyone praises Sir Walter Raleigh, but when Simon has something to say, no one's listening."

I asked him why. "First off, he's not like them," Embrey explained. Did his status as a foreigner, presumably one with darker skin, make him a target of suspicion? "You think?" said Embrey, with a laugh presumably born of experience. I asked him if he wanted to play one of the more virtuous characters in the play, like Sir Walter. He smiled and laughed again before leaving to finish his makeup. "If I were a few shades lighter!"

A familiar face, that of my lunchtime bartender, appeared. Shannon Uphold, her blond hair now demurely braided, was in her second year playing John White's daughter, a fearless pioneer woman in Green's telling. "Eleanor is kind of like the girl on the farm who could run around in her sundress and have a great time," she said. "She doesn't need to be in finery, but she also knows how to live that life."

I asked her why, in her opinion, the historical Eleanor, who left a young daughter behind in England, would choose to come to the New World.

"I love to think of her as a sixteenth-century feminist and that this was her choice, but in that time it may simply have been that her dad wanted her to go. Who wants to leave their own children behind? But you do what you have to do." Uphold said that the stark message on the Dare Stone, whether it was authentic or not, moved her. "Eleanor hoped and prayed to see the masts of her father's ship returning," she said, pausing. "I think about it every day. Now I am getting all emotional."

She paused again, her eyes wet. "There is something about donning that costume and holding a fake baby. There are nights onstage when I'm looking at the moon with this doll in my arms, and I think to myself that this could be a real baby and my dad is gone. I see her getting on a ship three months pregnant, in a ship filled mostly with men. I can't imagine those conditions."

Uphold said that Eleanor Dare has become her personal inspiration. "I was born and raised in West Virginia, and after my summer here last year I went to New York. Living the dream! These people went to a new world, and I'm trying to do that in my own way."

Thunder boomed and lightning flashed through the windows. When I stepped out the door a few minutes later, sheets of rain hid the Albemarle. I retreated back inside to wait it out. Culpepper, the associate producer, stood nearby, peering with a scowl at a radar weather map on his phone. Bands of green, blue, and red covered the screen. "It's been like this all week," he said with a sigh, before making the call to cancel the performance. (After the premiere of the play on July 4, 1937, Green wrote in his diary, "Agony of rain in first act.")

I returned the next night, when the skies were clear. Green's drama balances primary sources like White's account and Harriot's descriptions with dramatic battles and a Falstaffian drunkard who falls in love with a happy-go-lucky Indian.

In Green's final scene, he invokes a Spanish ship off Port Ferdinando to motivate the hungry settlers to abandon their Cittie of Raleigh after a long and fruitless wait for White's return. The ragged band of men, women, and children set off, accompanied by Manteo's nuclear family, bravely singing, downstage right, into a copse of gnarled live oak. As they disappear, the music swells and a spotlight shines on the frayed flag with a Cross of Saint George fluttering atop the fort's stout palisade; another illuminates a post carved with the word "Croatoan."

An experienced dramatist, Green doesn't say what took place

next; he leaves that for the audience to ponder as it shuffles out of the stockade. He understood the power of an unsolved mystery.

Just as I remembered as a child, we walked out of the theater and onto the dimly lit path winding through the woods. The earthwork was hidden in shadow, and the forest still felt by turns enigmatic and sinister. The crowd, mostly beach tourists with their sleepy kids in arm or tow, remained strikingly silent.

On a gray and raw morning in early January, I drove east across the causeway linking Roanoke Island to the beach town of Nags Head. Turning south into Cape Hatteras National Seashore, I crossed Oregon Inlet on a high bridge arching over the waters whipped by wind and current. At the top of the span, as I always do, I turned left to take in the Atlantic Ocean and then swiveled to the right to see the Pamlico Sound—Verrazano's Sea.

Each body of water seemed as vast as the other; there was no other land in sight but the perilously narrow strip of sand that is the north end of Hatteras Island. It looked like a long runway set in the sea as my car descended steeply down the south side of the bridge toward land.

Exposed to the fury of northeasters and hurricanes, this three-dozen-mile stretch of island, which ends near Cape Creek, where the island makes a sharp turn to the southwest, likely never supported full-time Native American communities. Ralph Lane sent a group of men here to subsist on oysters and fish in the hungry spring of 1586. English settlers and shipwreck victims were living here by the early eighteenth century in a village called Kinnakeet, thought by some to be a Carolina Algonquian term meaning "land of the mixed," though it also might refer to a sumac-and-tobacco preparation. The daughter of Chief Kinnakeet was said to have married the castaway English-man Thomas Hooper here in the late seventeenth century.

Long after the indigenous people had vanished as a distinct culture, and the U.S. Postal Service gave the town the prosaic name of Avon, the people here continued to drink yaupon, the local caffein-ated beverage Harriot encountered on his 1585 mission, longer than others on the Outer Banks. "The last yaupon gatherers on Hatteras Island were Negroes," wrote historian Gary Dunbar in his 1956 doctoral thesis. What's clear is that this community, like so many remote areas in eastern North Carolina, was a place where Native Americans, Europeans, and Africans quietly intersected. "This was an isolated area," Darrell Collins had said. "You are related to everyone, whether you are white or black."

Avon today, with its sister towns of Salvo, Waves, and Rodanthe, consists mainly of rows of mammoth oceanfront rentals hunkered behind the protective walls of sand dunes, with more modest houses on the sound side. Blowing sand and water frequently cover the two-lane road that is the only link to the mainland; the occasional northeaster or hurricane severs the highway completely.

I passed beeping backhoes pushing sand from the shoulders. A few miles on, I pulled in to the parking lot of the community center in Rodanthe that was long the common school for the villages. It also marked the halfway point between Fort Raleigh and Cape Creek. Stepping out into the brisk air, I could simultaneously see the Pamlico and hear the roar of the North Atlantic behind the line of dunes. Geologists call this "a perennial erosional hotspot"; on White's 1585 map it is a large cape poking like a sharp barb into the ocean. Today it exists only as a set of treacherous offshore shoals. More ships have wrecked on this section of coast than on any other stretch of the Eastern Seaboard.

Scott Dawson was waiting in his truck. The Hatteras native had invited me to a local Christmas celebration. The rest of America had turned off the carols, put the tree on the curb, and stored the strings of lights in the attic, but the islanders were just gearing up for their Yuletide festival. They called it Old Christmas or, alternatively, Buck Christmas.

The people of Hatteras, along with North African Berbers and conservative Greek Orthodox monks, still keep to a calendar introduced by Julius Caesar. In 1582, two years before the first Roanoke voyage, Catholic Europe adopted the calendar created under Pope Gregory XIII to update the increasingly inaccurate Julian version. John Dee, the English mystic and scientist with whom Fernandes shared his cartographic knowledge, urged Queen Elizabeth I to back the more precise system, with a few caveats, but she declined under pressure from Anglican clerics opposed to adopting popish time. Not until 1752 did the British Empire, including its American colonies, accept the change. The new calendar chopped out eleven days for accuracy's sake, but the independent-minded people of the Outer Banks resisted this innovation. That's why Christmas came late on Hatteras.

I was curious, given the age of this peculiar tradition, if there might be a whiff of the Elizabethan to the celebration. This was, I knew, likely just a romantic notion, more Bancroft than Quinn, but I had learned not to dismiss out of hand any clue, no matter how improbable.

"You won't be a tourist, since you are with me; you will be a visitor," Dawson assured me as we walked to the back of the building. It wasn't quite noon, and the inaugural event of the day, the oyster shoot, was about to begin on the basketball court behind the center. "Please don't load your gun until after your name is called," shouted a man sitting behind a card table. "And guns on the table can be shared."

A burly man in a black biker T-shirt strode up grasping a shotgun, his hand adorned with a large Confederate flag ring. "I don't share my Harley, my woman, or my gun!" he declared loudly. A few people guffawed as men, women, and children lined up to shoot. The target attached to the basketball pole was a standard round bull's-eye.

"The winner gets a half bushel of oysters," Dawson explained. Bits of shot ricocheted off the metal pole and rained onto the crowd. No one seemed to mind. I wedged my body behind a pickup truck to avoid the shrapnel. A man nearby introduced himself as Dewey Edwards Jr.

"How long has there been an oyster shoot?" I asked.

"Let me ask my daddy," said Edwards, a large man in a baseball cap. Dewey Edwards Sr., seventy-two, ambled over.

"This is a new thing at Old Christmas," he told me. "We only started doing this forty-five or fifty years ago."

"What else happens besides shooting?" I asked.

"Oh, there's a little music, a little dancing, a little fighting, and then there's Old Buck," Edwards replied.

"What—or who—is that?" I asked.

"Old Buck comes out of Trent Woods every Christmas, and it's good luck to see him," Edwards said. "It's two guys under a cowhide."

From others I heard similar versions of the same tale. Long ago, a Spanish bull shipwrecked during a hurricane and busily began impregnating the cows and raising general havoc. A hunter eventually shot what was by then called Old Buck in Trent Woods, the forested area at the southern end of Hatteras, where the last Indian village was said to have been. Every Christmas, Old Buck returns. "Maybe not this year," Edwards told me in a confidential tone. "I heard the guy that does it is in Florida, and he's sick."

The winner of the shooting contest was seventeen-year-old Andrew Midgett. The Midgetts and Midgettes are the omnipresent family here, and descendants of the people who bought a parcel of land from the last recorded Hatteras Indian in the late eighteenth century. It was a Midgette who, with Willard, first spotted the Cape Creek artifacts washed up from the 1993 hurricane, and it was a Midgette who owned the Cape Creek lot where Phelps and, later, Horton dug. "I brought my own bucket," the young man told me as he lugged his half bushel to the parking lot and set it in the bed of a battered truck.

Old Christmas was a community reunion, when children and grandchildren make the trek back to the Outer Banks to see their families and hang out with old friends. What was increasingly a busy and generic beach town reverted for a few hours to the traditional village of centuries past. The men drank beer and the children darted around on the playground, alarmingly close to the shooting range. A cold wind blew hard off the Pamlico, but the boisterous crowd, now totaling seventy or eighty people, didn't seem to notice.

Dawson walked up. "People are complaining that there are so many tourists now at Old Christmas," he said.

"Which ones are tourists?" I asked, looking around, unable to guess who might not be a local.

"Oh, somebody saw a couple of Virginians. But they left."

A group of men in rubber coveralls poured bushels of oysters into a giant pot in the side yard. The team hovered around the cauldron. Every now and then, they would dump a pile of steamed shellfish on a long board littered with short knives necessary to pry open the tough covering. I went inside into the warmth of the community building, where a dozen women were preparing the traditional chicken-and-pastry supper.

A drum set dominated the stage, and a slightly askew Christmas tree stood to one side. At the foot of the stairs leading to the stage, a thoroughly modern Santa Claus was giving delighted children stockings filled with oranges and candy. When I asked around about the origin of Old Christmas, several people deferred to Maggie Midgette. She was a trim woman in a black sweater.

"There's always been an oyster roast, a supper, and a dance," said the seventy-three-year-old, who grew up here. "We used to have skits in blackface," she added. "But then some people up in Virginia gave us trouble about that, so we stopped." The critics didn't know that this version of blackface was more likely a holdover from a medieval English tradition than from the racist shows popular among whites a century ago. A visitor in 1938 referred to the "Olde Christmas Masque" demonstrating "the persisting traditions of their colonial ancestors."

Midgette said that at the end of the evening Old Buck invariably came. "The kids loved that. And the men would duke it out."

I wasn't sure that I heard her correctly. "Duke it out?" I asked.

"Sure," Midgette responded. "My brother liked to fight; he enjoyed it. It was just something we did. Afterwards you would say, 'It's all good.' It cleared the air," she explained, smiling sweetly.

"Did this happen late in the evening, when the women and children have gone home?"

She shook her head. "Oh no. We would egg them on!" she said, relishing the memory. "And some women fought too."

"They did?" I said in surprise.

She paused and looked at me fixedly. "I fought." Her quiet voice and steely gaze left me with no doubts. "Now some women here wouldn't admit it. But I don't mind saying."

Four white-haired men then took the stage at the far end of the room to play "Johnny B. Goode," followed by a rockabilly version of "White Christmas." A drunken young fisherman in rubber boots hauled a very elderly woman onto the dance floor, to the crowd's delight. A woman joined us at the table and told me she knew something about local traditions. "We put marsh grass under our beds to get toys at Christmas," she said loudly over the amplified music. "My mother did it, and my kids do it too."

Only the very young and the very old seemed to be inside. Most of the adults were outside, despite the onset of a cold drizzle that accompanied the gusty winds. A few minutes later a young woman came through the door. "They're not fighting out there after all," she announced with evident disappointment. She said that a man threw a beer at one of the guys cooking oysters, who promptly punched him in the jaw. But that was the end of it.

"The police stopped coming years ago," Dawson told me as he ate a plate of chicken and pastry while eyeing a long table devoted entirely to pie. "They got tired of breaking up the fights."

The casual violence reflects a fierce autonomy with deep roots on the Outer Banks. While residents were "industrious and self-sustaining," the authors of a book on local history report they were also "unruly and ungovernable." Despite the recent influx of outsiders, that remains the case. Many view formal authority, such as the National Park Service, with deep suspicion if not outright hostility.

Dawson pointed me to two older women sitting at one of the long white tables. Olive Patrick was eighty-nine, and her sister Lovie Midgett was ninety-four. They were both lean with coiffed hair. I asked Midgett, who was elegant in a dark-blue blouse and pearls, about island life when she was a child. "I grew up on Rodanthe when there were no cars," she said. "We walked. Not that there was any place to walk to," she added with a laugh.

Once, during World War II, she recalled that the family house shook with the force of a ship torpedoed by a German U-boat just offshore. For a time, she patrolled the beach at night to keep an eye out for spies from German ships trying to infiltrate the United States. I asked her about Old Buck. A lone drummer had always accompanied the animal's presence, Midgett said, but he had recently died.

"Maybe Old Buck won't show up tonight," I said, recalling what the man outside had told me.

"He's coming," she said firmly. "We don't give up easy on our traditions."

An hour or two later, the front door opened with a gust of wind. A young guy in camouflage entered holding the reins of a creature with a makeshift black-and-white head and horns. Behind was a body colored more like that of a zebra than a bull. "Here's Old Buck!" the man chanted loudly and rhythmically as he led the rambunctious four-legged beast around the room.

As the creature lunged at squealing children and laughing adults, I noticed Old Buck wore one set of black boots and one pair of loafers. Parents crowded as close as they dared to snap pictures with their iPhones. Old Buck charged Midgett and her sister, but they ducked with glee and practiced agility. After a few circles around the room, the bull sauntered out into the darkness, presumably to his hideaway in the Trent Woods.

I couldn't say if the strange ritual was an echo of anything that the Roanoke colonists might have performed. As part of the ancient central European tradition of Krampus still practiced in Austria and Germany, young men dress as fearsome horned animals at Christmas to terrify misbehaving children, a kind of anti–Santa Claus. Other than Joachim Gans from Prague (who was Jewish), however, there are no records of central Europeans on the Outer Banks in colonial days.

Old Buck seemed more closely related to Old Tup, an effigy of a ram paraded by young men through medieval streets of northern England at Christmas. The event survives in England only in an old folk song that goes, "The horns that grew on his head, sir, they grew so mighty high, that every time he nodded his head he nodded against the sky." Old Tup was part of a medieval tradition of Christmas skits called mummings to solicit money. Performers blackened their faces or wore masks to avoid being identified as beggars. Father Christmas and some representation of Beelzebub might show up, and, though comic, the skits often had the sober themes of death and resurrection. The name Old Tup certainly sounded close to Old Buck, though I knew that this link was just one more bit of conjecture.

As the evening wore on, Dawson told me that there might be more fights, but not until long after midnight, when people were really drunk. "It's much calmer now than it used to be," he added with a note of regret. "It used to be a few-hundred-man fistfight, village versus village. My grandfather was a Golden Gloves boxer who would lay people out."

I had a long drive ahead of me that night and the weather was worsening, so I decided not to linger. I paused to say good-bye to Maggie Midgette. "Do people here talk about being descended from Native Americans?" I asked her spontaneously.

"Most everyone here would say they have Indian blood," she said. With her dark hair and eyes, and the faint olive hue of her skin—traits she shared with Dawson—she certainly looked as if she did. Estes, the DNA genealogist, had told me that genetic testing on a few old Hatteras families revealed more African American traits than Indian. Before I began my Lost Colony search, I would have said everyone in the room was white. Now I knew there was no such thing as "white," much less "pure Anglo-Saxon blood," particularly not in a corner of America like this, where the genes of Native Americans, Africans, and Europeans were jumbled through the centuries, despite the harsh laws imposed by distant legislators. The Roanoke voyagers themselves were a mélange of Welsh, Scottish, French, Portuguese, Danish, and other European groups besides English. In the land that is mixed, everyone in the room was a mongrel in different proportions.

"And what about the Lost Colonists?" I asked.

She narrowed her eyes. "Well, those colonists did settle this island," she said slowly. "Of course, no one would say they were descended from them, but . . ." Her words trailed off. Then she winked.

Of course, the blackface, brawls, and Old Buck didn't point conclusively to some lingering tradition of long-ago Elizabethans stranded on this faraway shore. The refusal to give up a quirky medieval ritual or the Julian calendar might just as well be a remnant of the English who arrived in the early eighteenth century. Like much else in the search for the Lost Colony—Horton's rapier, Luccketti's pottery fragments, the Dare Stone—Old Christmas offered beguiling but inconclusive evidence. Yet I liked the idea that despite assimilation with Carolina Algonquians some quirky Yuletide custom brought by the English survived the centuries, like the Machapunga's proclivity to make nets the same way their ancestors did. This was history in peripheral vision, hard to capture, not quite myth and not quite fact.

Outside, a cold and steady rain blew as the ocean thrummed hard against the beach. I was soaked before reaching my car. Waiting for the heater to warm me up, I remembered the line from George Bancroft's 1834 history: "Imagination received no help in its attempts to trace the fate of the colony of Roanoke."

As I drove north over Oregon Inlet, fierce gusts blew my car across the yellow lines above the dark waters. On the opposite shore a couple of miles later, a historical marker flashed by. The highway was deserted, so I reversed the car and shone my headlights onto the gray-and-black sign canted at an angle from the relentless gales. "Roanoke voyages, 1585–1590, based operations at inlet near here. Long closed, it was named for pilot Simon Fernandes." His surname was the Portuguese version, and his given name the English one, but the mix-up seemed appropriate.

The windshield wipers beat their fast rhythm as blasts of wind gently rocked the car. I hadn't unequivocally found the Lost Colony, but in my fever dream of obsession I did glimpse why this story exerts such a powerful grip on our imaginations and haunts us still. We weren't really looking for long-dead Elizabethans. We were, instead, wrestling with what it meant to be American amid our national mashup of genes and traditions. We still are. That's the wisdom the vanished colonists can still impart, the real secret token they left behind. Through them, we get to remake ourselves with the changing times, as is always the case with any good myth.

That drama, as with Green's play, has no inevitable outcome. It does, however, grant us the courage to do what they likely did, to step into the dark woods in an unfamiliar place and trust that, eventually, we will emerge in some new and unexpected form.

Coda: A Brave Kingdom

On a late July afternoon in 1609, almost two decades after White's final Roanoke visit, a sturdy Spanish ship sailed north along Hatteras Island's sandy coast on a mission to seek out a rumored English colony. Spanish spies reported that the trespassers had recently sailed into Chesapeake Bay and built a fort staffed by one hundred men at a place called Jamestown. Philip III's advisers counseled swift action. Spain's council of war for the Indies urged, "An armada should be assembled, with all possible speed, to go hunt them and drive them out from wherever they may be, punishing them exemplarily."

The king did not want to risk reigniting the costly war with England so recently concluded. After the death of Elizabeth I and his father, Philip II, he and James I navigated a fragile peace. The young Spanish monarch bet that the settlement would fail of its own accord. Instead of sending an armada, he ordered the naval commander Francisco Ferdinando de Ecija to sail from St. Augustine to the Chesapeake to gather intelligence. The captain also had secret orders to scout out possible sites for Spanish forts that could be built up and down the coast of eastern North America. Once the little English settlement collapsed, Spain would sweep in to assert its control from Florida to Maine and ward off any future interlopers.

To keep his cover, Ecija hoisted a Dutch flag as he moved north from St. Augustine. When the ship rounded a sandy cape, likely along the north end of Hatteras, the crew spotted a large plume of smoke rising into the hazy summer sky as the sun descended over the Pamlico Sound. He ordered his men to drop anchor at a convenient cove nearby so that they could investigate the apparent signal on the following morning.

As the next day dawned, Ecija realized that the anchorage he had chosen was "where the said English were settled earlier, and where they had been in times past." The Spanish captain, like his predecessor in 1588, had stumbled on the decaying remains of Port Ferdinando. The rotting slipway and barrels left by the Roanoke voyagers must still have been visible. At least one of his crew recognized the place, because he had sailed with the earlier mission.

Then Ecija saw another large plume of smoke rising nearby. "And thus we went sailing along the shoals" to find the source of what he presumed to be a signal fire. He sent two men into the rigging as lookouts and posted crew with muskets and readied the cannon in case this was a trap. The ship passed an inlet that appeared too dangerous to enter. For a time, the sailors could see no evidence of people as it cruised up the long and straight line of beach.

Then, an hour before sunset, seven Native Americans suddenly appeared on the beach and began to wave and shout. Ecija brought his vessel "as close to land as a stone's throw from the surf" and hailed the Indians, presumably in Spanish, as the ship rode just beyond the light surf. "But it appeared that they were fearful," he reports. "And they climbed a hill and began to play on some flutes." He ordered the anchor dropped, and the crew called out again, "but they made no move of any sort to come to the beach."

With darkness fast approaching, the perplexed crew gave up their attempts to make contact and moved the ship offshore to anchor for the night. They made little progress sailing up the coast the next two days amid heavy rains and contrary winds. "And all during this period they"—the Indians—"never left off making smoke signals to us," he adds.

Brisk winds forced the ship back to the same spot where they had seen the flute-playing Indians previously, apparently just north of Port Ferdinando. Two new smoke plumes rose into the sky, and Ecija made for the nearest one. "And as we came abreast of it, six Indians appeared just as [the others] had before, drumming to us and shouting." The captain again enjoined the crew to skirt the shore. "But we were not able to speak to them as they took off and climbed up through the ravines. And we were anchored, awaiting them."

It was a strange cat-and-mouse game, the Spanish coasting close to the long strip of barrier island, the urgent shouting, and then the Indians' retreat into the sand dunes. Frustrated by this odd behavior, Ecija ordered his men to haul up the anchor and head north to the Chesapeake to seek out the English at Jamestown.

"And as we were turning away from them, a great number of them who [were] in ambush within the ravines with some bows and quivers came out into sight."

If it were an ambush that had lost the essence of surprise, the Native Americans didn't give up their efforts to attract the attention of the European vessel. Half a dozen of the men took off in a sprint, shadowing the ship as the crew unfurled the sails and began to move north, "following us at a full run along the beach for a great stretch until we left them behind by sailing. And as they went along, they were continually blowing on some pipes and shouting to us."

The shouts were indecipherable as the sails caught the July breeze and sped the vessel ahead, leaving the sprinting Indians behind. Above the sounds of the surging surf and creak of the ship, Ecija could make out what he called tunes "made by foreigners," by which he seems to mean Europeans. It is an extraordinary and eerie scene: Native Americans playing what were apparently Old World melodies as they raced desperately along the beach, shouting at the departing ship.

Ecija and his crew later entered Chesapeake Bay, only to be chased away by an English ship guarding the entrance. Standing out to sea, the captain revealed to his officers the secret orders directing him to continue far up the coast to look for candidate sites for Spanish forts. No one liked the look of the weather, however. The ocean swells grew longer and higher, and a stiff breeze sprang up; there was an ominous cast to the sky in the south. The men agreed that "the season is much advanced" and that "this coast is so dangerous in the season that begins with August," meaning that this was the period when hurricanes swept up the Eastern Seaboard. The decision to abandon the mission and return to St. Augustine was unanimous. The retreat likely saved their lives, because a massive hurricane moved through three days later.

It was arguably the most significant storm ever to pass up the Atlantic coast. Had Ecija succeeded in his secret mission, the future of any English designs in the region might have been imperiled. The same hurricane also caught the flagship of an English fleet carrying a new Virginia governor and supplies destined for the starving settlers at Jamestown. These were the men shipwrecked on Bermuda, six hundred miles to the east, and forced to build a new ship to complete their journey.

William Strachey, the governor's secretary, was on board the ship. Once safely in Jamestown the following spring, he relayed the adventure back to England, spurring Shakespeare's *Tempest*, which was first performed in 1611. The bard's famous play opens in the midst of the wild storm that shipwrecks passengers and crew on a remote island ruled by Prospero, the magician-scientist modeled on John Dee, and inhabited by the wild Caliban, possibly based on the Virginia Algonquian Machumps, who claimed that the Indians had enslaved or massacred the Lost Colonists.

Back in St. Augustine, Ecija wrote a report for the king detailing his expedition. The captain speculated that the haunting music he heard on the Carolina beach "was a signal that they had for the ships that passed by, judging from the diligence with which they did it."

It apparently never occurred to him that the combination of a Dutch flag and his crew's shouts in Spanish might have confused those onshore. The Netherlands was still allied to the English, and the peace with Spain was a new development. These peculiar Indians might have sought contact with those they perceived as friends, only to be frightened when they realized they were face-to-face with potential enemies.

It's possible that Ecija and his men had just encountered Roanoke colonists or their kin. Perhaps the locals were eager to be rescued. Maybe they simply sought to exchange news or goods. Europeans might have found the Lost Colonists after all. But because they were dressed in deerskins rather than woolen jerkins, and speaking Carolina Algonquian rather than English, their original identity would have been too obscure to recognize. The melodies that so perplexed Ecija might have been a clever way to alert the passing ship to their English origins, without giving away their identity to a potential foe.

Yet like so much in the search for the Lost Colony, this is a story that can never be confirmed; the final leap has to be one of imagination.

Perhaps the men who ran at full speed along the beach in their leather loincloths, blowing furiously on their pipes, played the same English tunes that John White ordered sung on the eve of his granddaughter's third birthday in 1590, off the northern end of Roanoke Island. "Be not afeard; the isle is full of noises," Caliban tells the arriving Europeans in *The Tempest*. "Sounds and sweet airs, that give delight and hurt not."

Acknowledgments

In searching for the Lost Colony, I found an extraordinary number of people willing to lend their time and expertise. Along with those mentioned in the book, special thanks are due David Amber, Nathan Boniske, Asma Bouhrass, Marta Cavaco, Edward Collins, Vibrina Coronado, Joao Costa, Paul Farago, Mark Fleming, Glenn Fox, Josephine Hookway, Juliet Kaczmarczyk, Alexandra Merrill, Pedro Pinto, Tyson Sampson, Kim Sawyer, Fred Schwab, Aisling Tierney, and the crew of the *Elizabeth II* as well as Ann Lawler's crab cakes. I feel particular gratitude for Mahan Kalpa Khalsa's understanding and patience.

National Geographic supported countless research trips with the firm advocacy of my editor there, Glenn Oeland. The Hodson Trust–John Carter Brown Fellowship, directed by Adam Goodheart, graciously provided access to the John Carter Brown Library at Brown University as well as its remarkable staff and international community of scholars, along with eighteenth-century accommodations near Washington College to complete the writing—and with funding to boot. Such fortunate backing made, I hope, for a much better book. Thanks, finally, to my editor at Doubleday, Yaniv Soha, and my agent, Ethan Bassoff, a dynamic duo that so calmly and ably guided this long voyage.

Notes

Elizabethans are notorious for creative spelling; Walter Raleigh recorded his own name in dozens of variations. To ensure ease of reading, I have rendered most sixteenth- and seventeenth-century quotations in modern English and names in their current popular forms. For events described by English accounts in those centuries, time has been counted according to the Julian calendar, while Spanish and Portuguese dates from the era have been converted from Gregorian into Julian time.

PRELUDE

xv   "put us in good hope": David B. Quinn, *Roanoke Voyages*, 2:610.
xvii   "to the place at Roanoke": Ibid.
xvii   "with a reasonable space": Ibid.
xvii   "It was much further from the harbor": Ibid., 611.
xviii   "we had a sea break into our boat": Ibid.
xviii   "beat them down": Ibid., 612.
xviii   "until they sunk": Ibid.
xviii   "Before we could get to the place": Ibid.
xviii   "the light of a great fire": Ibid., 613.
xviii   "many familiar English tunes": Ibid.
xix   "a secret token agreed upon": Ibid.
xix   "a high palisade": Ibid.
xix   "I greatly joyed that I had safely found": Ibid., 616.
xix   "fifty miles into the main": Ibid., 613.
xx   "where our planters are": Ibid., 617.
xx   "to visit our countrymen": Ibid., 618.

xx   "as luckless to many": Ibid., 715.

xx   "Would to God my wealth": Ibid.

INTRODUCTION: THE TERROR WITHIN

5   "make plans to brave": "It's Baaaackk! Psychopath Is Spooktacular!" HiddenOuterbanks.com, Oct. 18, 2015.

5   "creatures, maniacs, zombies": "Frightening Halloween Festivities on the Outer Banks," Blog.kittyhawk.com, Oct. 6, 2015.

6   "massacres, murders, and other bloody scenes": Seaworthy, *Nag's Head*, 126.

6   "the barbarous years": Bailyn, *Barbarous Years*, title.

7   "there could be something sinister": "Zombie Colony of Roanoke": Zombie Research Society. Last modified Oct. 22, 2009. zombieresearchsociety.com.

7   "Wander off the stage of history": Charles Frazier, *Thirteen Moons*, 414.

8   "This venture had little": Jenkins, *History of the United States*, 8.

8   "The fate of the 'Lost Colony'": Chitwood, *History of Colonial America*, 44.

8   "Raleigh's missing settlers still haunt": Arner, "Romance of Roanoke," 45.

10   "The profound significance": Sloan and Chaplin, *New World*, 7.

10   "is full of grinning, unappeased": Lawrence, *Studies in Classic American Literature*, 60.

CHAPTER 1: SOME DELICATE GARDEN

17   "great fires because of the numerous": Wroth, *Voyages of Giovanni da Verrazzano*, 13.

17   "seashore completely covered": Ibid., 13.

17   "clothed with palms, laurel, and cypress": Ibid., 137.

17   "The sky is clear and cloudless": Ibid., 135.

17   "making various friendly signs": Ibid.

18   "was seized with terror": Ibid., 136.

18   "an isthmus one mile wide": Ibid.

19   "As for the Indians": Herbert Bolton, foreword to *Barcia's Chronological History of the Continent of Florida*, by Barcía Carballido y Zúñiga, 5.

19   "attract them to our service": Pickett and Pickett, *European Struggle to Settle North America*, 18.

20   "The entire Spanish nation": Ibid.

20   "Many persons died of hunger": Sauer, *Sixteenth Century North America*, 75.

24   "a weak, and poor state": Great Britain Public Record Office, *Calendar of State Papers*, 4, xvii.

24   "They care little for foreigners": Sharpe, *London Review of Politics, Society, Literature, Art, & Science* 11 (1865): 45.

26   "Books wherein appeared angles": Fauvel, Flood, and Wilson, *Oxford Figures*, 62.

26   "obstinate ignorance, pedantry": Shirley, *Thomas Harriot: A Biography*, 42.

26   "Pity the poverty": Ibid., 43.

26　"These enclosures be the causes": Lipson, *Economic History of England*, 1:162.

26　"There are more than two hundred": Strickland, *Letters of Mary, Queen of Scots*, 2:77.

27　"great terror to the people": Andrews, *Trade, Plunder, and Settlement*, 185.

28　"not actually possessed": David B. Quinn, *Set Fair for Roanoke*, 18.

28　"riotous, lascivious, and incontinent": Trevelyan, *Sir Walter Raleigh*, 18.

28　"a thorough-paced scoundrel": David B. Quinn, "A Portuguese Pilot in the English Service," in *England and the Discovery of America*, 250.

28　"frustrated by the usual Elizabethan blend": Nicholls and Williams, *Sir Walter Raleigh*, 12.

29　"Desirous to do somewhat": Ibid.

29　"Man may not expect the ease": Birch and Oldys, *Life of Sir Walter Raleigh*, 254.

29　"He that commands the sea": Sir Walter Raleigh, "A Discourse of the Invention of Ships," *The Works of Sir Walter Ralegh KT* 8, 325.

30　"was a man noted": Nicholls and Williams, *Sir Walter Raleigh*, 45.

30　"Gilbert's scheme was wrecked": J. B. Black, *Reign of Elizabeth*, 805.

30　"the language and logic": Mancall, *Hakluyt's Promise*, 129.

31　"There is a mighty large old map": Maine Historical Society, *Documentary History of the State of Maine*, 2:216.

31　Hakluyt's 1582 book: Hakluyt, *Divers Voyages Touching the Discovery of America and the Islands Adjacent*, xc.

31　"five or six of the best captains": Hakluyt, *Principal Navigations, Voyages, Traffiques, and Discoveries of the English Nation*, 12:76.

31　"wax cold and fall": Great Britain Public Record Office, *Calendar of State Papers: Colonial Series, America and West Indies, 1574–*, no. 4.

31　"stay the Spanish king from flowing": Hakluyt, *Discourse Concerning Western Planting*, no. 1, 154.

32　"I am most willing": Great Britain Public Record Office, *Calendar of State Papers: Colonial Series, America and West Indies, 1574–*, no. 4.

32　"the souls of millions": Hakluyt, *Discourse Concerning Western Planting*, no. 1, 10.

33　"shall be of the allegiance": David B. Quinn, *Roanoke Voyages*, 82.

34　"so sweet, and so strong": Ibid., 94.

CHAPTER 2: ALL SIGNS OF JOY

35　"never making any show": David B. Quinn, *Roanoke Voyages*, 98.

35　"After he had spoken of many things": Ibid.

36　"In less than half an hour": Ibid.

37　"When he came to the place": Ibid., 99.

37　"all signs of joy": Ibid.

37　"very handsome and goodly people": Ibid., 98.

37　"clap it before his breast": Ibid., 101.

38　"fat bucks": Ibid., 105.

38   "You wear great clothes": Ibid., 99.
39   "Their towns are but small": Harriot, *Briefe and True Report*, 24.
39   "to an island which they call Roanoke": David B. Quinn, *Roanoke Voyages*, 106.
39   "At the north end thereof": Ibid.
39   "to meet us very cheerfully": Ibid., 107.
39   "caused us to sit down": Ibid.
40   "other wholesome, and medicinal herbs": Ibid., 108.
40   "and with all beat the poor fellows": Ibid., 109.
40   "the land produces little to eat": Ibid., 790.
41   "after the manner": Ibid., 108.
41   "We brought home": Ibid., 116.
41   "Fain would I climb": Trevelyan, *Sir Walter Raleigh*, 49.
43   "The members had to be restrained": J. B. Black, *Reign of Elizabeth*, 322.
44   "mantle of rudely tanned skins": David B. Quinn, *Roanoke Voyages*, 116.
44   "well proportioned in their limbs": David B. Quinn, *Set Fair for Roanoke*, 50.
44   "No one was able to understand them": David B. Quinn, *Roanoke Voyages*, 116.
44   "some of the people": Great Britain Public Record Office, *Calendar of State Papers: Colonial Series*, 26:33.
45   "Pointing with a finger": Trevelyan, *Sir Walter Raleigh*, 77.
45   "Arms of Walter Raleigh": Ibid., 78.
47   Some scholars believe: Gullberg, *Mathematics*, 109.
48   "invocations or conjurations": Sharpe, *Witchcraft in Early Modern England*, app.
48   "intolerable pride and insatiable ambition": David B. Quinn, *Set Fair for Roanoke*, 66.
49   "glasses between his teeth": Bushnell, *Sir Richard Grenville*, 30.
49   "you will wrest the keys": Bent, *Short Sayings of Great Men*, 455.
49   "because on the mainland there is much gold": David B. Quinn, *Roanoke Voyages*, 328.
50   "Betwixt the decks": Middleton, *Tobacco Coast*, xxiv.
51   "they said the Indians": David B. Quinn, *Roanoke Voyages*, 184.

CHAPTER 3: FIRING INVISIBLE BULLETS
54   "We were all in extreme hazard": David B. Quinn, *Set Fair for Roanoke*, 63.
54   "the ship was so bruised": David B. Quinn, *Roanoke Voyages*, 177.
54   accused Fernandes of "unskillfulness": Ibid., 189.
56   "of the age of 8": White, "A Wife of an Indian 'Werowance' or Chief of Pomeiooc," British Museum, 1906,0509.1.13.
57   "were well entertained there": David B. Quinn, *Roanoke Voyages*, 191.
57   "a ceremony in their prayers": David B. Quinn, *Set Fair for Roanoke*, 187.
57   "to demand a silver cup": David B. Quinn, *Roanoke Voyages*, 191.
57   "we burnt, and spoiled their corn": Ibid.

59   "enemies of those of Port Fernando": David B. Quinn, *Set Fair for Roanoke*, 142.

59   "You can do nothing": Anderson, *Honorable Burden of Public Office*, 88.

59   "the new fort in Virginia": David B. Quinn, *Roanoke Voyages*, 210.

59   "one of the wives of Wingina": White, "One of the Wyues of Wyngyno," British Museum, 1906,0509.1.17.

59   His watercolor of a werowance: White, "An Indian 'Werowance', or Chief," British Museum, 1906,0509.1.12.

60   "to possess Philip's purse": Cell, *English Enterprise in Newfoundland*, 46.

60   "predatory drive of armed traders": Andrews, *Trade, Plunder, and Settlement*, 356.

60   "the King's Isle": David B. Quinn, *Roanoke Voyages*, 215.

61   "the goodliest and most pleasing territory": Ibid., 208.

61   "If Virginia had but horses": Ibid.

61   "being savages that possess the land": Ibid., 209.

61   "The savage people rule": Peterson, *American Trinity*, 53.

62   "for they count this": More, Bacon, and Neville, *Three Early Modern Utopias*, 63.

62   "If the title of occupiers": Raleigh, *Works of Sir Walter Raleigh*, 2:23.

62   "a modern fable": Seed, *American Pentimento*, 30.

62   "Possession is nine-tenths": Ibid., 15.

62   "For a copper kettle": Smith, *Journals*, 175.

62   "The people naturally": David B. Quinn, *Roanoke Voyages*, 209.

63   "in the presence of the Indian": Kupperman, *Roanoke*, 65.

63   "seeking revenge on every injury": Lenman, *England's Colonial Wars*, 220.

63   "a botanical philosopher's stone": Ralph Bauer, "A New World of Secrets: Occult Philosophy and Local Knowledge in the Sixteenth-Century Atlantic," in Delbourgo and Dew, *Science and Empire in the Atlantic World*, 110.

64   "the true and only God": Harriot, *Briefe and True Report*, 27.

64   "may be in a short time": Ibid., 25.

64   "spring-clocks that seem to go of themselves": Ibid., 27.

64   "conjurers" who could predict: Ibid., 54.

64   "because we sought": Ibid., 28.

65   "Within a few days": Ibid.

65   "by shooting invisible bullets": Ibid., 29.

65   "St. Mary's Bay": David B. Quinn, *Roanoke Voyages*, 215.

66   the "wild men": Ibid., 204.

67   "for a savage, a very grave": Ibid., 259.

67   "whilst there was left": Ibid., 267.

67   "We heard certain savages call": Ibid., 271.

68   "which was fasted": Ibid., 272.

68   "We be dead men returned": Ibid., 278.

68   "the only friend to our nation": Ibid., 275.

68   "seem to prophesy": Harriot, *Briefe and True Report*, 29.

68   "one who watches": Oberg, *Dominion and Civility*, 39.
68   "Because there were not to be found": Harriot, *Briefe and True Report*, 6.
69   "to live upon shellfish": David B. Quinn, *Roanoke Voyages*, 283.
69   "Christ our Victory": Ibid., 287.
70   "thwart his buttocks": Ibid.
70   "with all love and kindness": Ibid., 108.
70   "not only victuals, munitions": Ibid., 289.
72   for the "unrighteous intercourse": Irene A. Wright, *Further English Voyages to Spanish America*, 197.
72   "we had many Turks": Corbett, *Papers Relating to the Navy During the Spanish War*, 21.
72   "Most of the slaves": Irene A. Wright, *Further English Voyages to Spanish America*, 159.
72   "as did the black slaves": Ibid., 54.
73   "meant to leave all the negroes": Ibid., 204.
73   "who do menial service": Oberg, *Head in Edward Nugent's Hand*, 99.
73   "a great storm": David B. Quinn, *Set Fair for Roanoke*, 137.
74   "Considering the case": David B. Quinn, *Roanoke Voyages*, 292.
74   "left all things so confusedly": Hakluyt, *Principal Navigations, Voyages, Traffiques, and Discoveries of the English Nation*, 12:347.
74   "showed themselves too fierce": Harriot, *Briefe and True Report*, 30.
74   "their long and dangerous abode": David B. Quinn, *Roanoke Voyages*, 293.
75   "an astonishing feat": Kupperman, *Roanoke*, 81.
76   "100 Turks brought by Sir Francis Drake": David B. Quinn, "Turks, Moors, Blacks, and Others in Drake's West Indian Voyage," 101.
76   "he would be glad to hear": Ibid., 104.
76   "the saddest part of the story": Morgan, *American Slavery, American Freedom*, 34.
76   "The only reasonable explanation": David B. Quinn, *England and the Discovery of America*, 432.

CHAPTER 4: SMALL THINGS FLOURISH BY CONCORD
79   "one whole year and more": David B. Quinn, *Roanoke Voyages*, 233.
79   "slanderous and shameful speeches": Harriot, *Briefe and True Report*, 5.
80   "The discovery of a good mine": David B. Quinn, *Roanoke Voyages*, 273.
80   "for pleasantness of seat": Ibid., 257.
80   "This brilliant, ruthless, and sardonic creature": Wallace, *Sir Walter Raleigh*, 4.
81   "you freely swore that no terrors": David B. Quinn, *Roanoke Voyages*, 514.
81   "If you proceed": Ibid., 493.
81   "I am fully persuaded": Ibid.
85   sister of "Fornando Simon": William S. Powell, "Who Were the Roanoke Colonists?," 51.
85   "This city of London": Harkness, *Jewel House*, 1.

85   "great multitude of people": Charles Knight, *London* 1–2, 254.

86   "Military outposts always failed": H.G. Jones, *Raleigh and Quinn*, 125.

86   "The whole 1587 project": David B. Quinn, *Set Fair for Roanoke*, 231.

88   "It is to be feared": David B. Quinn, *Roanoke Voyages*, 768.

89   "the state of the country and savages": Ibid., 523.

90   "where Master Ralph Lane": Ibid., 524.

90   "and the disposition of the people": Ibid., 526.

91   "token or badge": Ibid., 527.

91   while a "fire arrow": Ibid., 529.

92   "it being so dark": Ibid., 530.

93   "Because this child": Ibid., 532.

93   "some controversies rose": Ibid., 533.

95   "I myself was wounded": Ibid., 567.

95   "the reason why the English": Ibid., 791.

96   "other debris indicating": Ibid., 811.

96   "Pressed as I am": Padfield, *Maritime Supremacy and the Opening of the Western Mind*, 32.

99   "much rain, thundering and great spouts": David B. Quinn, *Roanoke Voyages*, 608.

99   found the "secret token": Ibid., 613.

99   spotted another "great smoke": Ibid., 610.

100   "the light of a great fire": Ibid., 613.

100   houses were "taken down": Ibid., 614.

101   "and about the place": Ibid., 615.

101   "the savages our enemies": Ibid., 616.

101   "The whole existence of the colony": Margaret F. and Dwayne W. Pickett, *The European Struggle to Settle North America*, 27.

102   "where our planters were": Ibid., 617.

103   "Thus you may plainly perceive": Ibid., 715.

CHAPTER 5: A WHOLE COUNTRY OF ENGLISH

109   "They were the best portrayals": Kupperman, *Roanoke*, 129.

109   concepts about the "noble savage": West, *Changing Presentation of the American Indian*, 16.

110   "I greatly joyed": David B. Quinn, *Roanoke Voyages*, 616.

110   "untimely death by murdering": Knapp, *Empire Nowhere*, 170.

111   "bound only for the relief": Ibid., 94.

111   "extremity of weather": Trevelyan, *Sir Walter Raleigh*, 348.

111   "It is the sinfulest thing": Bacon, *Essays*, 110.

112   "rare virtues in medicine": Harriot, *Briefe and True Report*, 9.

112   "All ships and goods are confiscate": David B. Quinn, *Raleigh and the British Empire*, 215.

112   "I shall yet live to see": Trevelyan, *Sir Walter Raleigh*, 348.

113   "forced and feared them": Quinn and Quinn, *English New England Voyages*, 166.

113 "gold is more plentiful": Jonson, Chapman, Marston, *Eastward Hoe!* (A&C Black), 61.

114 "Why, is she inhabited already": Ibid., 60.

114 "A whole country of English": Ibid.

115 "They shall have all the lands": "First Charter of Virginia, April 10, 1606."

116 "a savage boy": Percy, "Jamestown," 4.

116 Among today's Hopi: Hedrick, "Hopi Indians, 'Cultural' Selection, and Albinism."

117 "a man of large stature": Beverley and Campbell, *History of Virginia*, 48.

117 "certain men clothed at a place": Smith, "True Relation of Such Occurrences and Accidents of Note as Hath Happened in Virginia," 9.

117 "short coats, and sleeves to the elbows": Ibid.

117 "where they have abundance of brass": Ibid.

117 "We had agreed with the king": Ibid.

118 "southward we went to some parts": Smith, *Travels and Works*, 55.

118 "Here Pasaphege and 2 of our own men": General Archive of Simancas, *Dept. of State*, no. 2588, fol. 22.

119 "Here the King of Pasapahegh": Ibid.

119 "the south sea, a mine of gold": Smith, *Journals*, 102.

119 "I am very hungry": John Smith, *The General Historie of Virginia*, 302.

119 "by throwing them overboard": Mark Nicholls, "George Percy," EncyclopediaVirginia.org.

120 "made a hole to bury him": Smith, *Works, 1608–1631*, 638.

121 "You shall find a brave and fruitful seat": U.S. Library of Congress, *Records of the Virginia Company of London*, 17.

121 "true and sincere declaration": Congressional Serial Set, 63.

122 "men, women, and children": Strachey, *Historie of Travaile into Virginia Britannia*, 85.

122 "these unfortunate and betrayed people": Strachey, *Historie of Travaile*.

124 "have great care not to offend": "Instructions for the Virginia Colony, 1606."

124 for "devilish treachery": Purchas, *Hakluytus Posthumus*, 22.

124 "this our earth is truly English": Ibid., 228.

124 "to search of the lost company": Ashton, *Adventures and Discourses of Captain John Smith*, 178.

124 "little hope and less certainty": Ibid., 223.

125 "a man full of all vanity": Christopher M. Armitage, *Literary and Visual Ralegh*, 11.

125 "the greatest Lucifer": Burns, *The Smoke of the Gods*, 50.

125 "Our situation is such": Shirley, *Thomas Harriot: Renaissance Scientist*, 4.

125 "I was never ambitious": Ibid., 29.

126 "the sovereign remedy": Burton, *Anatomy of Melancholy*, 399.

126 "emperor of Roanoke": Trebellas, *Fort Raleigh National Historic Site*, 61.

127 "These tell us, that several of their ancestors": Lawson, *New Voyage to Carolina*, 66.

127   "The smallpox and rum": Ibid., 234.

127   "perished miserably by famine": Robertson, *History of America: Books IX and X*, no. 59, 31.

128   "no trace was ever found": Hinton, *History and Topography of the United States*, 1:22.

128   "the germ of our institutions": Bancroft, *A History of the United States*, vii.

128   "disasters thickened" and "a tribe of savages": Ibid., 119.

128   "The further history of this neglected plantation": Ibid., 121.

129   "Imagination received no help": Ibid., 123.

129   "the first offspring": Bancroft, *A History of the United States*, 106.

129   "that paradise of the new world": *Weekly Raleigh Register*, Nov. 9, 1835.

130   "The fate of this last colony": Cass, *Speeches, Etc.*, 40.

130   "I have thought of myself": Clough and Hair, *European Outthrust and Encounter*, 3.

131   "The attempts to knit together": David B. Quinn, *Set Fair for Roanoke*, 231.

131   "restrict himself to what is exactly": Ibid., xv.

131   "clouded by sentiment": Ibid., 345.

132   "enclosures for breeding rabbits": Ibid., 351.

132   "limitations, ambiguities, and omissions": Ibid., xvii.

133   "The story of the colonies": Ibid., 399.

CHAPTER 6: CHILD OF SCIENCE AND SLOW TIME

136   "Medicine jar pottery": Richard Gray, "Did Disease Drive Off Colonists on Roanoke Island?," *Daily Mail Online*, June 22, 2016, www.dailymail.co.uk.

136   "As soon as they had disembarked": David B. Quinn, *Roanoke Voyages*, 835.

138   "some old English coins": Lawson, *New Voyage to Carolina*, 65.

138   "to view the remains": William S. Powell, *Paradise Preserved*, 23.

138   "are but scanty": Seaworthy, *Nag's Head*, 126.

138   "dense copses of live-oak": Edward Bruce, "Loungings in the Footprints of the Pioneers," *Harper's New Monthly Magazine*, May 1860, 733.

139   "Earth-work Built by Sir Walter Raleigh's": Johnson, *Long Roll*, 156.

139   "but with little success": "Roanoke Island," *Continental Monthly*, May 1862, 551.

139   "My early memories": Elizabeth Dunbar, *Talcott Williams*, 82.

140   "By little short of a miracle": Williams, "Surroundings and Site of Raleigh's Colony," 61.

140   "Today half of the old entrenchment": William S. Powell, *Paradise Preserved*, 37.

142   "These little objects have a unique": J. C. Harrington, "Evidence of Manual Reckoning in the Cittie of Ralegh," *North Carolina Historical Review* 33, no. 1 (1956): 10.

142   "No physical remains of the settlers' homes": Ibid.

145   "Every archaeologist dreams": Stick, *Outer Banks Reader*, 255.

147   "that the poison which the crucible": Georg Agricola, *De Re Metallica*, 474.

147   "sucking it through clay pipes": Harriot, *Briefe and True Report*, 3.

151   "That is to say, I hold an object": McMullen, *One White Crow*, 23.

152   "unknown whether fallen bodies": Sumner, "Remote Sensing of the McMullen Site," 20.

152   "Since no mention is made": Prentice, *Fort Raleigh National Historic Site Archaeological Overview and Assessment*, 176.

152   "structures or some features": Ibid., 182.

155   "This harbor is the natural site": Williams, "Surroundings and Site of Raleigh's Colony," 54.

155   "of little strength": David B. Quinn, *Roanoke Voyages*, 790.

155   "no discernible pattern": Prentice, *Fort Raleigh National Historic Site Archaeological Overview and Assessment*, 191.

CHAPTER 7: A FOUR-HUNDRED-YEAR-OLD COVER-UP

171   "It appears to have a central cross": Ambers et al., "Examination of Patches on a Map of the East Coast of North America by John White," British Museum Department of Conservation and Scientific Research, CSR Analytical Request No. AR2012021, 6, www.britishmuseum.org.

172   "are difficult to interpret": Ibid., 8.

172   "the lines give the impression": Ibid.

172   "One other possible": Ibid.

173   "If your honor rub this powder": Cooper, *Queen's Agent*, 137.

173   "The paper must be dipped": Ibid.

174   "The search for the colonists": "Ancient Map Gives Clue to Fate of 'Lost Colony,'" *Telegraph*, May 4, 2012, www.telegraph.co.uk.

179   "Evidence of an early colonial presence": Klingelhofer, "Progress Report on 2012–13 Multidisciplinary Research at Salmon Creek," 12.

179   "The possibility exists that it is Elizabethan": Ibid.

181   "It cannot be a coincidence": Evans, Klingelhofer, and Luccketti, *Archaeological Brief for Site X*, 8.

CHAPTER 8: POT OF BRASS

187   "Everybody who lives here has a theory": Gray, "Unearthing Clues to Lost Worlds."

188   "Dr. Phelps just went": Catherine Kozak, "Signet Ring Crowned N.C. Archaeologist's Career," *Virginian-Pilot*, March 8, 2009, pilotonline.com.

188   "a broad smile": Catherine Kozak, "Buxton Crew Digs Up Possible Lost Colony Link: Gold Signet Ring Could Support Theory of a Trek to Hatteras," *Virginian-Pilot*, Oct. 14, 1998, pilotonline.com.

188   The Cape Creek ring: Charles Heath, "Postcontact Period European Trade Goods and Native Modified Objects from the Cape Creek Site (31Dr1)," app. 4. Unpublished manuscript.

188   "is the first direct tie-in": Pittman, "Myth in the Memory," 158.

189   "Signet Ring Crowned": Kozak, "Signet Ring Crowned N.C. Archaeologist's Career."

190   "a clattering bag of madness": Leigh Holmwood, "First Night: BBC1's Bonekickers," *Guardian*, July 9, 2008, www.theguardian.com.

190   "I googled Manteo": DailyMail.com, "Town's Shock as Residents from Mystery US 'Twin' Turn Up Bearing Gifts."

195   "The fashionable Elizabethan woman": Picard, *Elizabeth's London: Everyday Life in Elizabethan London*, 133.

CHAPTER 9: REJOICING IN THINGS STARK NAUGHTY

210   "bald of the head": Patronato 265, R.60, General Archive of the Indies, Seville.

214   "not to give or sell or lend": Delbourgo and Dew, *Science and Empire in the Atlantic World*, 34.

216   "suspicion of piracy": David B. Quinn, *England and the Discovery of America*, 249.

216   "enough to hang him": Ibid.

216   "I do bewail and lament": Ewen, *Golden Chalice*, 10.

216   "to clear the coasts": Claire Jowitt, *Pirates?*, 34.

216   as "Walsingham's man": David B. Quinn, *England and the Discovery of America*, 249.

217   "and ransomed and tortured the men": Ewen, *Golden Chalice*, 16.

217   "He is gone back again to sea": Ibid., 17.

217   "a thorough-paced scoundrel": David B. Quinn, *England and the Discovery of America*, 250.

217   "the black stone": Granger, *A Biographical History of England*, 324.

218   "Fernando Simon": Cotton Collection, Cotton Roll XIII.48, British Library.

218   "The pilot of the principal ship": D. Bernardino de Mendoza to Philip II (April 1582), 340–42, General Archive of Simancas.

219   "the swine": E. G. R. Taylor, *Troublesome Voyage*, xxvi.

219   "a ravenous thief": Ibid., 193.

219   "rejoiced in things stark naughty": Ibid., 202.

219   "a free pardon from five": Ibid., 197.

219   "a swill of many languages": Donno, *An Elizabethan in 1582*, 234.

220   "boasts of himself": Ibid.

220   His English is solid: Simon Ferdinando to Frobisher (1581), Cotton MS Otho E. VIII, f. 103.

221   "the projects of a great man": Williamson, *History of North Carolina*, 53–54.

221   "violent, quarrelsome and unattractive": David B. Quinn, *England and the Discovery of America*, 262.

221   "lewdly forsaking" the fly boat: David B. Quinn, *Roanoke Voyages*, 517.

222   "a gentleman by the means": Ibid., 523.

222   "Wherefore it booted not the governor": Ibid.

223   "He had as much": Olivia A. Isil, "Simon Fernandez, Master Mariner and Roanoke Assistant: A New Look at an Old Villain," in Shields and Ewen, *Searching for the Roanoke Colonies*, 76.

223 "Such a delay hardly reflects": Ibid.

224 "a skillful pilot": David B. Quinn, *England and the Discovery of America*, 259.

224 "persuader and originator": E. G. R. Taylor, *Troublesome Voyage*, 54.

226 "perhaps the supreme example": Malcolmson, *Renaissance Poetry*, 62.

227 "Because so much archaeology": Noël Hume, *Virginia Adventure*, 85.

229 "either one of the most stupendous discoveries": "Dare Stones Appear Authentic to Experts," *Raleigh News and Observer*, 1940.

CHAPTER 10: WE DARE ANYTHING

231 "and pushed forward, snatching": James Lester, "The Virginia Dare Stone 1938," box 1, folder 9, Rose Library, Emory University.

232 "In Memory of Virginia Dare": "Mail to the Chief: Franklin D. Roosevelt's Stamp Designs," Smithsonian National Postal Museum, postalmuseum .si.edu.

232 "Perhaps even it is not too much": Franklin Roosevelt, *The Constitution Prevails* (New York: Macmillan, 1941), 327.

232 "On account of the crowd": "Summary of Events Relating to the Hammond Stone," IWA 71, box 1, folder 9, Rose Library.

234 "exclusive rights to conduct": Hammond and Emory contract, Collection IWA, box 1, folder 7, Rose Library.

234 "the approximate spot": Pearce, "New Light on the Roanoke Colony," 150.

235 "Ananias Dare & Virginia Went": Pearce, "New Light on the Roanoke Colony," 149.

235 "I willed them, that if they": David B. Quinn, *Roanoke Voyages*, 614.

235 "Father Soone After You Goe": Pearce, "New Light on the Roanoke Colony," 149.

235 Among the dead were "Mine Childe": Ibid.

236 "Put This Ther Also": Ibid.

236 "seems to be of historical": Hammond and Emory contract, Collection IWA, box 1, folder 7, Rose Library.

236 "carrying shields cannot": McCord to Robert F. Whittaker, telegram, series 071, box 1, folder 6, Rose Library.

236 "an ancient and highly cultured": "Grave of Virginia Dare Believed Found in the State," *Raleigh News and Observer*, Nov. 22, 1937.

237 "The report that any member": Emory University statement, Collection IWA 71, box 1, folder 8, Rose Library.

237 "the hysterical days": Lester, "Virginia Dare Stone."

238 "such tools must have been": Pearce, "New Light on the Roanoke Colony," 163.

238 "persistence and fidelity": James G. Lester and J. Harris Perks, Jr., "The Virginia Dare Stone," Address to the Faculty Club of Emory University, Dare Stone Collection, box 1, folder 9, Robert W. Woodruff Library.

238 "had in his possession": Ibid.

239 "the rock is probably a fraud": Mizell to Legare Davis (February 2, 1938), Collection IWA 71, box 1, folder 6, Rose Library.

241 "considerable skepticism": Pearce senior to C.D.M. Stringfield, May 17, 1939. Dare Stone Collection, box 3, Correspondence folder, Brenau University.

241 "With the second stone in hand": *Brenau Bulletin*, March 1, 1939.

242 "I believe our best chance": Pearce senior to Jasper Wiggins, Dare Stones Collection, box 3, Correspondence folder, Brenau University.

242 "Every mark seems as fresh": A Meeting, box 126, Roanoke Island folder, North Carolina Archives.

243 "We now have the grave stone": Pearce senior to Stringfield, July 11, 1939, box 3, Correspondence folder, Brenau University.

243 "Our excavations where the stones": Pearce senior to Dice Anderson (August 4, 1939), box 3, Correspondence folder, Brenau University.

243 "If the authenticity of these stones": *Atlanta Constitution*, July 26, 1939, 1.

244 "provided an irresistible temptation": Gitzen, *Francis Drake in Nehalem Bay 1579*, 23.

245 "The story told by the stones": *Brenau Bulletin*, Nov. 15, 1940.

245 "Dare Stones Appear Authentic": *Raleigh News and Observer*, "Dare Stones Appear Authentic to Experts," Oct. 21, 1940.

246 "We would be glad to receive you": Boyden Sparkes, "Writ on Rocke: Has America's First Murder Mystery Been Solved?," *Saturday Evening Post*, April 26, 1941.

246 "extremely interesting": Ibid.

246 "I personally went to Gainesville": Ibid.

246 "I'm still open-minded": Ibid.

247 "It makes me believe": Ibid.

247 "Bill was in bed": Ibid.

248 "Pearce and Dare Historical Hoaxes": "Hoax Claimed by 'Dare Stones' Finder in Extortion Scheme, Dr. Pearce Charges," *Atlanta Journal*, May 15, 1941.

248 "Easy to Be Fooled": T. W. Samuels Bourbon advertisement, box 1, folder 6, Rose Library.

249 "Only two letters used": Handwritten note, series 071, box 1, folder 6, Rose Library.

CHAPTER 11: HEAP PLENTY WAMPUM

251 "could tell me less about Hammond": Sparkes, "Writ on Rocke."

251 "I want to keep the identity": Sparkes to Purks, January 26, 1946, series 071, box 1, folder 6, Rose Library.

252 "A delayed action fuse": Ibid.

252 "No attempt was made": Purks to Sparkes, date unknown, series 071, box 1, folder 6, Rose Library.

252 "the thing isn't conclusive": Sparkes to Purks, series 071, box 1, folder 6, Rose Library.

253 "I doubt if it will ever be possible": "Letter and Report from Robert Stephenson to John Sites," April 15, 1983, box 3, Correspondence folder, Brenau University.

253 "Hoax springs eternal": John Sites to Betsy Reitz (Nov. 12, 1985), box 3, Correspondence folder, Brenau University.

257 "Close prisoner 32 weeks": Knight, *London*, 246.

262 "The search for graves": Advisory Committee Recommendations, Thomas English to Crittenden, box 135, Roanoke Island folder, North Carolina Archives.

CHAPTER 12: WHO'S AFRAID OF VIRGINIA DARE?

277 "The fairy-like proportions": Cushing, "Virginia Dare," 80.

278 "It is a wonder that no one": Tuthill, "Virginia Dare," 585.

278 "living here quite alone": Nathaniel Hawthorne, *The Works of Nathaniel Hawthorne*, 182.

279 "We have recently seen a photograph": *New-York Tribune*, February 19, 1858.

279 "the National Statue": Louisa Lander, "The National Statue, Virginia Dare," *Dwight's Journal of Music* 25, no. 1 (1865).

279 "essentially and entirely American": Melissa Dabakis, *A Sisterhood of Sculptors: American Artists in Nineteenth-Century Rome* (University Park: Pennsylvania State University Press, 2014), 166.

280 "This design shows": Laura R. Prieto, *At Home in the Studio: The Professionalization of Women Artists in America* (Cambridge, Mass.: Harvard University Press, 2001), 81.

280 "red men of America": Mary Mason, "The White Doe Chase," *Raleigh Register*, April 3, 1861, 2.

281 "the patron saint of manifest destiny": Arner, "Romance of Roanoke," 52.

282 "stirring the ashes of historic memories": *Elizabeth City (N.C.) Weekly Economist*, May 31, 1892.

282 "Bethlehem story": Sallie Southall Cotten, *The White Doe: The Fate of Virginia Dare* (Philadelphia: J. B. Lippincott, 1901), 27

282 "that inevitable John the Baptist": Chandler, *Colonial Virginia*, 13.

282 "the first white child born": Gillespie and McMillen, *North Carolina Women: Their Lives and Times*, 234.

282 "foisted on just about everyone she met": Sally G. McMillen, *North Carolina Women*, 224.

283 "supreme importance in the history": Edward Graham Daves, "Raleigh's 'New Fort in Virginia'—1585," *Magazine of American History with Notes and Queries* 29 (Jan.–June 1893): 459.

283 Manteo White Supremacy Club: Wright and Zoby, *Fire on the Beach*, 254.

283 "with a grand white supremacy rally": "White Supremacy Club Engaged in a Good Work."

283 "at last disenfranchised the Negro": Jonathan Sarris, "Biographical Summary of Sallie Southall Cotten," East Carolina University Student Affairs, 3.

283 "complete supremacy of the white race": "Virginia Makes Every Voter Count," Editorial Board, *The New York Times*, Nov. 17, 2017.

283   "for a man to be both": W. E. B. Du Bois, *The Souls of Black Folk: Essays and Sketches* (Chicago: A.C. McClurg & Company, 1903): 4.

283   "She, the heir of civilization": Cotten, *White Doe.*

284   "that would have done credit": Arner, "Romance of Roanoke," 25.

284   "its people are a hopelessly mixed race": Tara McPherson, *Reconstructing Dixie: Race, Gender, and Nostalgia in the Imagined South* (Durham, N.C.: Duke University Press, 2003), 191.

284   "The ancient Greeks would doubtless": "Virginia Dare Made Symbol of Earliest U.S. Womanhood," Asbury Park Press, August 30, 1926.

285   "infant child of pure": W. Fitzhugh Brundage, *The Southern Past: A Clash of Race and Memory* (Cambridge, Mass.: Belknap Press of Harvard University Press, 2009), 30.

285   "a new and distinct ethnic type": Roosevelt, *Theodore Roosevelt Cyclopedia* (Roosevelt Memorial Association, 1941), 11.

285   "White civilization is triumphant": *Raleigh News and Observer,* Nov. 1, 1908, 7.

285   "not degrade the memory": Mary Hilliard Hinton, *The North Carolina Booklet* (Raleigh: The North Carolina Society Daughters of the Revolution, April 1911), 174.

287   "Virginia Dare will appeal to every": Paul Garrett, *The Art of Serving Wine* (Garrett and Company, 1905), 24.

287   "the menace of the negro woman's vote": Leonard Rogoff, *Gertrude Weil,* 130.

289   "purest Anglo-Saxon blood": "Five Thousand Pay Tribute." *Tampa Bay Times,* Aug. 30, 1926, 4.

289   "most fallacious of all modern": "America Found World Leader," Ibid.

289   Adolf Hitler had just published: Adolf Hitler, *My Struggle* (Madurai, India: LeoPard Books, 2017), 267.

289   "Blackberry cordial, / Virginia Dare wine": Langston Hughes, "Harlem Sweeties," in *The Collected Poems of Langston Hughes* (New York: Vintage, 1995), 245.

290   "a hair's breadth this side": Arner, "Romance of Roanoke," 37.

291   "the heritage, identity, and future": "University of Florida Denies Richard Spencer Event, Citing 'Likelihood of Violence,'" NPR, Aug. 16, 2017, www.npr.org.

291   "America's voice on patriotic": VDARE.com.

291   "leading white nationalists": Congressman Sires's statement on the appointment of Steve Bannon to a top White House post, Nov. 16, 2016, press release, www.sires.house.com.

291   "for the defense of America": Andrew Kaczynski and Chris Massie, "In College, Trump Aide Stephen Miller Led Controversial 'Terrorism Awareness Project' Warning of 'Islamofascism,'" CNN, Feb. 15, 2017, www.cnn.com.

292   "dedicated to preserving": VDARE.com; see also Peter Brimelow, *Alien Nation: Common Sense About America's Immigration Disaster* (New York: Random House, 1995).

292 "You need to have everybody": David Weigel, " 'Racialists' Are Cheered by Trump's Latest Strategy," *Washington Post,* Aug. 20, 2016.

292 "we can't restore our civilization": Philip Bump, "Rep. Steve King Warns That 'Our Civilization' Can't Be Restored with 'Somebody Else's Babies,' " *Washington Post,* March 12, 2017.

292 "to enable us to continue to defend": VDARE.com.

292 "It is in the name of Virginia Dare herself": Ibid.

293 "She is the archetypal mother": Hudson, *Searching for Virginia Dare,* 136.

297 "a Marble Lady": Elizabethan Gardens, "Virginia Dare Statue History." www.elizabethangardens.org.

CHAPTER 13: SWAMP SAINTS AND RENEGADES

302 "a mixed crew, a lawless people": Eric Hannel, *Reinterpreting a Native American Identity: Examining the Lumbee* (Lanham, Md.: Lexington Books, 2015), 82.

302 "a number of free negroes": North Carolina General Assembly, Minutes of the Lower House of the North Carolina General Assembly (December 21, 1773), 768.

303 "In a sense, Henry Berry Lowrie": Guy B. Johnson, "Personality in a White-Indian-Negro Community," *American Sociological Review* 4, no. 4 (1939): 516–23.

303 "we don't kill anybody": Magdol and Wakelyn, *Southern Common People,* 201.

303 "his roving propensities": *New York Herald,* March 8, 1872, 3.

305 "a person of negro descent": North Carolina, *The North Carolina Criminal Code and Digest: A Complete Code* (Edward & Broughton, 1892), 330.

305 "your petitioners are a remnant": U.S. Government Printing Office, *Congressional Edition* (1915), 36.

305 "After the year 1835": McMillan, *Sir Walter Raleigh's Lost Colony,* 17.

305 "We have always been friends": Ibid., 3.

306 dismissed the Lost Colony connection as "baseless": Frederick Webb Hodge, ed., *Handbook of American Indians North of Mexico* (Smithsonian Institution, Bureau of American Ethnology, 1911), 365.

306 "spoke in a high, almost falsetto voice": Alexander Hume Ford, "The Finding of Raleigh's Lost Colony," *Appleton's Magazine,* July 1907, 29.

307 "They pronounced it": Johnson, "Personality in a White-Indian-Negro Community," *American Sociological Review* 4 (August 1939), 520.

307 "the earliest white settlements": U.S. Congressional Serial Set, Serial No. 15016, Senate Reports Nos. 332–55, 84.

307 "the most neglected minority group": Cindy D. Padget, "The Lost Indians of the Lost Colony," *American Indian Law Review* 21, no. 2 (1997), 409.

309 "The survival of colonists' names": Adolph L. Dial and David K. Eliades, *The Only Land I Know: A History of the Lumbee Indians* (Syracuse, N.Y.: Syracuse University Press, 1975), 13.

310   "The whole situation": William Loren Katz, *Black Indians: A Hidden Heritage* (New York: Atheneum, 1986), xii.

315   "It is one thing for Indians": Karen I. Blu, *The Lumbee Problem: The Making of an American Indian People* (Cambridge, U.K.: Cambridge University Press, 1980), 32.

316   "either earlier European contact": Estes, "Where Have All the Indians Gone?"

CHAPTER 14: RETURN TO ROANOKE

321   "It is an odd fact": Raf Sanchez, "Jerusalem Syndrome," *Telegraph*, March 26, 2016, www.telegraph.co.uk.

326   "Although there be deer": John Smith, *Advertisements for the Inexperienced Planters of New-England, or Anywhere; or, The Pathway to Experience to Erect a Plantation* (London: John Haviland, 1631), 11.

326   "all the corn, peas": David B. Quinn, *Roanoke Voyages*, 531.

327   "in reward of his faithful services": Ibid.

327   "The Indians from the back country": James Sprunt, *Chronicles of the Cape Fear River, 1660–1916* (Raleigh, N.C.: Edwards & Broughton, 1916), 14.

329   "It is probable that some of the Roanoke colonists": Kupperman, *Roanoke*, 137.

329   "Ralegh's colonists were lost": Oberg, *Head in Edward Nugent's Hand*, 146.

330   "Intermarriage had been indeed": Beverley, *The History and Present State of Virginia*, 30.

330   "hanged, sunburned, some broken up": Sams, *The Conquest of Virginia*, 154.

330   "find these Indian girls": Lawson, *New Voyage to Carolina*, 194.

331   "And thus we see how apt human nature": Ibid., 66.

331   "no arguments, entreaties, no tears": James M. Volo, *Daily Life on the Old Colonial Frontier*, 244.

331   "no European who has tasted": Colin G. Calloway, *New Worlds for All: Indians, Europeans, and the Remaking of Early America* (Baltimore: Johns Hopkins University Press, 1998), 155.

331   "there is no persuading him": Walter Isaacson, *A Benjamin Franklin Reader*, 157.

331   "We have no examples": James Axtell, *The White Indians*, 57.

332   "Never let anyone persuade you": Hinton, *North Carolina Booklet*, nos. 10, 4, 174.

332   "We are forced to accept": David B. Quinn, *Set Fair for Roanoke*, 342.

332   loophole called the "Pocahontas exception": Rachel F. Moran, *Interracial Intimacy: The Regulation of Race and Romance* (Chicago: University of Chicago Press, 2001), 49.

335   "of such dismal swamps": Oberg, *Head in Edward Nugent's Hand*, 158.

335   "a handful of Indians": Robert J. Cain, ed., *The Church of England in North Carolina: Documents, 1699–1741* (Raleigh: Division of Archives and History, North Carolina Department of Cultural Resources, 1999), 185.

335 "the few remains of the Altamuskeet": *Colonial Records of North Carolina*, 6:563.

335 "Eastern North Carolina Indians learned": David La Vere, *The Tuscarora War*.

336 "enjoyed a social status": Patrick H. Garrow, *The Mattamuskeet Documents: A Study in Social History* (Raleigh, N.C.: Archaeology Section, Division of Archives and History, Department of Cultural Resources, 1975), 34.

336 "are of the Algonquian stock": Frank G. Speck, "Remnants of the Machapunga Indians of North Carolina," *American Anthropologist* 18, no. 2 (1916): 271–76.

336 "In North Carolina there are a number": Frank G. Speck, "The Ethnic Position of the Southeastern Algonkian," *American Anthropologist* 26, no. 2 (1924): 184–200.

337 "a new social order": Patricia Click, *Time Full of Trial*, 83–84.

338 "Today, the ancestry of these people": Gary S. Dunbar, "Hatteras Indians of North Carolina."

CHAPTER 15: AN OLD BUCK CHRISTMAS

348 "brings us face to face": Heinz Dietrich Fischer, *Drama / Comedy Awards, 1917–1996* (Munich: K. G. Saur, 1998), xxvii.

348 "I want to take a representative": John Herbert Roper, *Paul Green: Playwright of the Real South* (Athens: University of Georgia Press, 2003), 185.

348 "all about races mixing": Ibid.

348 "Come to your bed": Green, *Paul Green Reader*, 133.

349 "the integration of all things": Roper, *Paul Green*, xiii.

353 "Agony of rain in first act": Laurence G. Avery, *A Southern Life: Letters of Paul Green, 1916–1981* (Chapel Hill: University of North Carolina Press, 1994), 269n2.

355 "The last yaupon gatherers": Gary S. Dunbar, "Historical Geography of the North Carolina Outer Banks" (PhD diss., Louisiana State University, 1956), 167.

355 "a perennial erosional hotspot": Gibbons, "Morphology, Geologic History, and Dynamics of Wimble Shoals," abstract.

359 "industrious and self-sustaining": David Wright and David Zoby, *Fire on the Beach*, 23.

360 "The horns that grew on his head": G. Newnes, "The Christmas Mummers' Play," *John O'London's Weekly*, Issues 1250–1275 (1945), 145.

CODA: A BRAVE KINGDOM

363 "An armada should be assembled": John Franklin Jameson, *American Historical Review* (American Historical Association, 1895), 450.

363 To keep his cover, Ecija: Fullam, *Lost Colony of Roanoke*, 169.

364 "where the said English were settled": John H. Hann, *Translation of the Ecija Voyages of 1605 and 1609 and the González Derrotero of 1609* (Tallahassee, Fla.: Bureau of Archaeological Research, 1986), 28.

364   "And thus we went sailing": Ibid., 32.

364   "as close to land": Ibid., 33.

364   "And all during this period": Ibid.

365   "And as we came abreast of it": Ibid.

365   "But we were not able to speak to them": Ibid., 34.

365   "And as we were turning away": Ibid.

365   "following us at a full run": Ibid.

365   "made by foreigners": Ibid.

365   "the season is much advanced": Ibid., 39.

366   "was a signal that they had for the ships": Ibid., 34.

367   "Be not afeard, the isle": Shakespeare, *The Tempest*, act 3, scene 2, lines 137–38.

Bibliography

The literature related to the Roanoke voyages is vast and ever expanding; some of the more useful books and articles are listed below. For curious readers, Quinn's two-volume set, *The Roanoke Voyages, 1584–1590*, provides much of the essential source material, while his *Set Fair for Roanoke* offers a readable summation.

Abrahams, Israel. "Joachim Gaunse: A Mining Incident in the Reign of Queen Elizabeth." *Transactions (Jewish Historical Society of England)* 4 (1899): 83–101.

Abrams, Ann Uhry. *The Pilgrims and Pocahontas: Rival Myths of American Origin.* Boulder, Colo.: Westview Press, 1999.

Adams, Stephen. *The Best and Worst Country in the World: Perspectives on the Early Virginia Landscape.* Charlottesville: University Press of Virginia, 2001.

Adamson, J. H., and H. F. Folland. *Sir Walter Ralegh and His Times.* Boston: Gambit, 1969.

Agricola, Georg, Herbert Hoover, Lou Henry Hoover. *De Re Metallica.* Courier Corporation, 1950.

Alexander, John, and James Lazell. *Ribbon of Sand: The Amazing Convergence of the Ocean and the Outer Banks.* Chapel Hill: University of North Carolina Press, 2002.

Almeida, Bruno. "On the Origins of Dee's Mathematical Programme: The John Dee–Pedro Nunes Connection." *Studies in History and Philosophy of Science* 43, no. 3 (2012).

Ambers, Janet, Joanna Russell, David Saunders, and Kim Sloan. "Examination of

Patches on a Map of the East Coast of North America by John White." *British Museum: Technical Research Bulletin* 6 (2012).

Anderson, J. M. *The Honorable Burden of Public Office: English Humanists and Tudor Politics in the Sixteenth Century.* New York: Peter Lang, 2010.

Andrews, Kenneth R. *Trade, Plunder, and Settlement: Maritime Enterprise and the Genesis of the British Empire.* Cambridge, U.K.: Cambridge University Press, 1984.

Annual Report of the American Historical Association. Washington, D.C.: GPO, 1895.

Appleby, John C. *Outlaws in Medieval and Early Modern England: Crime, Government, and Society, c. 1066–c. 1600.* Farnham: Ashgate, 2009.

———. *Under the Bloody Flag: Pirates of the Tudor Age.* Stroud: History Press, 2011.

Armitage, Christopher M., ed. *Literary and Visual Ralegh.* Manchester University Press, 2016.

Armitage, David. *The Ideological Origins of the British Empire.* Cambridge, U.K.: Cambridge University Press, 2000.

Arner, Robert D. *The Lost Colony in Literature.* Raleigh: America's Four Hundredth Anniversary Committee, North Carolina Department of Cultural Resources, 1985.

———. "The Romance of Roanoke: Virginia Dare and the Lost Colony in American Literature." *Southern Literary Journal* 10 (Spring 1978): 5–45.

Ashton, John. *The Adventures and Discourses of Captain John Smith.* London: Cassell, 1883.

Axtell, James. *White Indians of Colonial America.* Ye Galleon Press, 1991.

Bacon, Francis. *The Essays; or, Counsels Civil and Moral of Francis Bacon.* Boston: D. C. Heath, 1908.

Bailyn, Bernard. *The Barbarous Years: The Peopling of British North America: The Conflict of Civilizations, 1600–1975.* New York: Vintage, 2013.

———. *The Peopling of British North America: An Introduction.* New York: Knopf, 1986.

Baine, Rodney M. "Another Lost Colony? Charles de Rochefort's Account of English Refugees and the Apalachites." *Georgia Historical Quarterly* 83, no. 3 (1999): 558–64.

Bancroft, George. *A History of the United States.* Boston: Samuel Dickinson, 1892.

Barbour, Philip L. *The Earliest Reconnaissance of the Chesapeake Bay Area: Captain John Smith's Map and Indian Vocabulary.* Richmond: Virginia Historical Society, 1971.

———, ed. *The Complete Works of Captain John Smith, 1580–1631.* Chapel Hill: University of North Carolina Press, 1986.

———. *The Jamestown Voyages Under the First Charter, 1606–1609.* Vol. 2. London: Hakluyt Society, 2010.

Barcía Carballido y Zúñiga, Andrés González de. *Barcia's Chronological History of the Continent of Florida from the Year 1512, in Which Juan Ponce de Leon Dis-*

covered Florida, Until the Year 1722. Gainesville: University of Florida Press, 1951.

Barlowe, Arthur. *The First Voyage to Roanoke, 1584.* Chapel Hill: Academic Affairs Library, University of North Carolina, 2002.

Beck, Stephen V., and Kenneth F. Kiple, eds. *Biological Consequences of the European Expansion, 1450–1800.* Vol. 26 of *An Expanding World.* London: Routledge, 1997.

Beer, Anna. *My Just Desire: The Life of Bess Ralegh, Wife to Sir Walter.* New York: Ballantine Books, 2003.

Bent, Samuel Arthur. *Short Sayings of Great Men: With Historical and Explanatory Notes.* Boston: J. R. Osgood, 1882.

Bernstein, William J. *A Splendid Exchange: How Trade Shaped the World.* New York: Grove Press, 2009.

Beverley, Robert. *The History and Present State of Virginia.* UNC Press Books, 2014.

Beverley, Robert, and Charles Campbell. *The History of Virginia: In Four Parts.* Richmond: J. W. Randolph, 1855.

Binkley, Cameron, and Steven Davis. *Preserving the Mystery: An Administrative History of Fort Raleigh National Historic Site.* Atlanta: Cultural Resources, Southeast Region, National Park Service, 2003.

Birch, Thomas, and William Oldys. *The Life of Sir Walter Ralegh.* Vol. 1 of *The Works of Sir Walter Ralegh.* Oxford: University Press, 1829.

Birmingham, David. *Trade and Empire in the Atlantic, 1400–1600.* London: Routledge, 2005.

Black, J. B. *The Reign of Elizabeth, 1558–1603.* 2nd ed. Oxford: Clarendon Press, 1959.

Black, Jeannette D., ed. *The Maps.* Vol. 1 of *The Blathwayt Atlas.* Brown University Press, 1970.

Blanton, Dennis B. "Drought as a Factor in the Jamestown Colony, 1607–1612." *Historical Archaeology* 34, no. 4 (2000): 74–81. doi:10.1007/bf03374329.

———. "If It's Not One Thing It's Another: The Added Challenges of Weather and Climate for the Roanoke Colony." In *Searching for the Roanoke Colonies: An Interdisciplinary Collection,* edited by E. Thomson Shields and Charles R. Ewen. Raleigh: North Carolina Department of Cultural Resources, Office of Archives and History, 2003.

Blanton, Dennis B., and Robert A. DeVillar. "Archaeological Encounters with Georgia's Spanish Period, 1526–1700: New Findings and Perspectives." *Journal of Global Initiatives: Policy, Pedagogy, Perspective* 5, no. 1 (2010).

Blanton, Dennis B., and Julia A. King, eds. *Indian and European Contact in Context: The Mid-Atlantic Region.* Gainesville: University Press of Florida, 2005.

Bleichmar, Daniela, Paula De Vos, and Kevin Sheehan, eds. *Science in the Spanish and Portuguese Empires, 1500–1800.* Stanford, Calif.: Stanford University Press, 2009.

Botkin, B. A., ed. *A Treasury of Southern Folklore: Stories, Ballads, Traditions, and Folkways of the People of the South.* New York: Crown, 1949.

Bourne, William. *A Regiment for the Sea, and Other Writings on Navigation*. Edited by E. G. R. Taylor. Cambridge, U.K.: published for the Hakluyt Society at the University Press, 1963.

Brooks, Max. *The Zombie Survival Guide: Complete Protection from the Living Dead*. London: Gerald Duckworth, 2013.

Brotton, Jerry. *The Sultan and the Queen: The Untold Story of Elizabeth and Islam*. Penguin Books, 2016.

Brown, Alexander, ed. *The Genesis of the United States: A Narrative of the Movement in England, 1605–1616, Which Resulted in the Plantation of North America by Englishmen, Disclosing the Contest Between England and Spain for the Possession of the Soil Now Occupied by the United States of America*. 2 vols. Boston: Houghton, Mifflin, 1890.

Burns, Eric. *The Smoke of the Gods: A Social History of Tobacco*. Philadelphia: Temple University Press, 2007.

Burton, Robert. *The Anatomy of Melancholy*. Philadelphia: Moore, 1857.

Bushnell, George Herbert. *Sir Richard Grenville: The Turbulent Life and Career of the Hero of the Little Revenge*. London: G. G. Harrap, 1936.

Cameron, Catherine M. *Captives: How Stolen People Changed the World*. Lincoln: University of Nebraska Press, 2016.

Cañizares-Esguerra, Jorge. *Puritan Conquistadors: Iberianizing the Atlantic, 1550–1700*. Stanford, Calif.: Stanford University Press, 2006.

Cass, Lewis. *A Discourse Pronounced at the Capitol of the United States, in the Hall of Representatives, Before the American Historical Society, January 30, 1836*. Washington, D.C.: P. Thompson, 1836.

———. *Speeches, Etc*. Washington, D.C.: P. Thompson, 1836.

Cave, Alfred A. "Richard Hakluyt's Savages: The Influence of 16th Century Travel Narratives on English Indian Policy in North America." *International Social Science Review* 60, no. 1 (1985): 3–24.

Cell, Gillian T. *English Enterprise in Newfoundland, 1577–1660*. Toronto: University of Toronto Press, 1969.

Chandler, J.A.C. *Colonial Virginia*. Richmond: Times-Dispatch, 1907.

Charles Rivers Editors. *The Lost Colony of Roanoke: History's Greatest Mysteries*. 2015. www.mediabeavers.com.

Chitwood, Oliver Perry. *A History of Colonial America*. New York: Harper, 1961.

Click, Patricia C. *Time Full of Trial: The Roanoke Island Freedmen's Colony, 1862–1867*. Chapel Hill: University of North Carolina Press, 2003.

Clough, Cecil H., and Paul Edward Hedley Hair, eds. *The European Outthrust and Encounter: The First Phase c. 1400–c. 1700: Essays in Tribute to David Beers Quinn on His 85th Birthday*. Liverpool: Liverpool University Press, 1994.

Clucas, Stephen, ed. *John Dee: Interdisciplinary Studies in English Renaissance Thought*. Dordrecht: Springer, 2006.

Congressional Serial Set. Washington, D.C.: U.S. Government Printing Office, 1915.

Cooper, John. *The Queen's Agent: Francis Walsingham at the Court of Elizabeth I*. New York: Pegasus Books, 2013.

Corbett, Julian Stafford. *Papers Relating to the Navy During the Spanish War, 1585–1587*, no. 11 (Navy Records Society, 1898).

Cormack, Lesley B. *Charting an Empire: Geography at the English Universities, 1580–1620*. Chicago: University of Chicago Press, 1997.

Cotten, Sallie Southall. *The White Doe: The Fate of Virginia Dare*. Philadelphia: J. B. Lippincott, 1901.

Covington, James W. "Drake Destroys St. Augustine: 1586." *Florida Historical Quarterly* 44, no. 1/2 (1965): 81–93.

Cressy, David. "Early Modern Space Travel and the English Man in the Moon." *American Historical Review* 111, no. 4 (2006): 961–82.

Crowley, Roger. *Conquerors: How Portugal Forged the First Global Empire*. London: Faber & Faber, 2015.

Cumming, William P. *Mapping the North Carolina Coast: Sixteenth-Century Cartography and the Roanoke Voyages*. North Carolina Office of Archives and History, 1988.

Cushing, Eliza Lanesford. "Virginia Dare; or, The Lost Colony." *Ladies' Companion*, Dec. 1837, 80–92.

"Dare We? New Methods Could Untangle Brenau's Rocks Riddle." *Brenau Window* (Spring 2011): 14–15.

Davies, J. D. *Britannia's Dragon: A Naval History of Wales*. History Press, 2013.

Davis, Richard Beale and J. A. Leo Lemay. *Essays in Early Virginia Literature Honoring Richard Beale Davis*. Stroud, UK: History Press, 2013.

Dawson, Scott. *Croatoan: Birthplace of America*. Infinity, 2009.

DeCosta, B. F. *Ancient Norombega; or, The Voyages of Simon Ferdinando and John Walker to the Penobscot River, 1579–1580*. Albany, N.Y.: Joel Munsell's Sons, 1890.

Dee, John. *The Private Diary of Dr. John Dee and the Catalogue of His Library of Manuscripts*. Edited by J. O. Halliwell-Phillipps. London: Camden Society, 1842.

Delbourgo, James, and Nicholas Dew, eds. *Science and Empire in the Atlantic World*. New York: Routledge, 2008.

Dentamaro, Nick. "History Channel's 'America Unearthed' Segment Features Jim Southerland and Dare Stones." *Brenau Update*, Feb. 1, 2013.

DePratter, Chester B., and Marvin T. Smith. "Sixteenth Century European Trade in the Southeastern United States: Evidence from the Juan Pardo Expeditions (1566–1568)." *Notebook* 19, no. 1–4 (1987): 52–61.

Detweiler, Robert. "Was Richard Hakluyt a Negative Influence in the Colonization of Virginia?" *North Carolina Historical Review* 48, no. 4 (1971): 359–69.

Dolan, Robert, and Kenton Bosserman. "Shoreline Erosion and the Lost Colony." *Annals of the Association of American Geographers* 62, no. 3 (1972): 424–26.

Donegan, Kathleen. *Seasons of Misery: Catastrophe and Colonial Settlement in Early America*. Philadelphia: University of Pennsylvania Press, 2013.

Donno, Elizabeth Story, ed. *An Elizabethan in 1582: The Diary of Richard Madox, Fellow of All Souls*. London: Hakluyt Society, 1976.

Drake, Francis. *Sir Francis Drake's West Indian Voyage, 1585–86.* Edited by Mary Frear Keeler. Farnham: Ashgate, 1981.

Drake, Francisco, and G. Jenner. "A Spanish Account of Drake's Voyages." *English Historical Review* 16, no. 61 (1901): 46–66.

Dunbar, Elizabeth. *Talcott Williams: Gentleman of the Fourth Estate.* R. E. Simpson & Son, 1936.

Dunbar, Gary S. "The Hatteras Indians of North Carolina." *Ethnohistory* 7, no. 4 (1960): 410–18. doi:10.2307/480877.

Duncan, T. Bentley. *Atlantic Islands: Madeira, the Azores, and the Cape Verdes in Seventeenth-Century Commerce and Navigation.* Chicago: University of Chicago Press, 1972.

Elliott, John Huxtable. *Empires of the Atlantic World: Britain and Spain in America, 1492–1830.* New Haven, Conn.: Yale University Press, 2008.

Estes, Roberta. "Where Have All the Indians Gone? Native American Eastern Seaboard Dispersal, Genealogy, and DNA in Relation to Sir Walter Raleigh's Lost Colony." *Journal of Genetic Genealogy* 5, no 2. (2009): 96–130.

Estes, Roberta J., Jack H. Goins, Penny Ferguson, and Janet Lewis Crain. "Melungeons, a Multi-ethnic Population." *Journal of Genetic Genealogy*, April 2012. Accessed May 25, 2012.

Evans, Phil, Eric C. Klingelhofer, and Nicholas M. Luccketti. *An Archaeological Brief for Site X: A Summary of Investigations of Site 31BR246.* Durham, N.C.: First Colony Foundation, 2015.

Evans, Phillip W., Eric C. Klingelhofer, Nicholas M. Luccketti, Beverly A. Straube, and E. Clay Swindell. *2008–2010 Archaeological Excavations at Fort Raleigh National Historic Site: Roanoke Island, North Carolina.* Durham, N.C.: First Colony Foundation, 2016.

Ewen, Cecil L'Estrange. *The Golden Chalice. A Documented Narrative of an Elizabethan Pirate.* Paignton: printed for the author, 1939.

Ewen, Charles R., Thomas R. Whyte, and R. P. Stephen Davis Jr., eds. *The Archaeology of North Carolina: Three Archaeological Symposia.* Carolina Archaeological Council Publication 30, 2011.

Fauvel, John, Raymond Flood, and Robin Wilson, eds. *Oxford Figures: Eight Centuries of the Mathematical Sciences.* Oxford: Oxford University Press, 2013.

Fernández-Armesto, Felipe. *The Americas: A Hemispheric History.* New York: Modern Library, 2005.

"The First Charter of Virginia, April 10, 1606." Avalon Project: Documents in Law, History, and Diplomacy. avalon.law.yale.edu.

Fox, Robert. *Thomas Harriot and His World: Mathematics, Exploration, and Natural Philosophy in Early Modern England.* Farnham: Ashgate, 2012.

Frampton, John. *Ioyfull Nevves out of the Newe Founde Worlde: Wherein Is Declared the Rare and Singular Vertues of Diuerse and Sundrie Hearbes, Trees, Oyles, Plantes, and Stones, with Their Aplications, as well for Phisicke as Chirurgerie . . .* London: In Poules Churche-yarde, by Willyam Norton, 1577.

Franks, Michael. *The Court, the Atlantic, and the City: Sir Walter Ralegh v. William Sanderson.* Mapledurwell: South and West Books, 2009.

Frazier, Charles. *Thirteen Moons.* New York: Random House, 2006.

"Frightening Halloween Festivities on the Outer Banks." blog.kittyhawk.com. Last modified Oct. 6, 2015.

Fuente, Alejandro de la, César García del Pino, and Bernardo Iglesias Delgado. "Havana and the Fleet System: Trade and Growth in the Periphery of the Spanish Empire, 1550–1610." *Colonial Latin American Review* 5, no. 1 (1996): 95–115. doi:10.1080/10609169608569879.

Fullam, Brandon. *The Lost Colony of Roanoke: New Perspectives.* Jefferson, N.C.: McFarland, 2017.

Fuller, Basil, and Ronald Leslie-Melville. *Pirate Harbours and Their Secrets.* London: St. Paul, 1935.

Gabriel-Powell, Andrew. *Richard Grenville and the Lost Colony of Roanoke.* Jefferson, N.C.: McFarland, 2016.

Gaskill, Malcolm. *Between Two Worlds: How the English Became Americans.* New York: Basic Books, 2014.

General Archive of Simancas. *Dept. of State,* no. 2588, fol. 22.

Gibbons, Ryan Michael. "Morphology, Geologic History, and Dynamics of Wimble Shoals, Rodanthe, NC." Master's thesis, East Carolina University, 2017.

Gillespie, Michele and Sally G. McMillen, eds. *North Carolina Women: Their Lives and Times.* University of Georgia Press, 2014.

Gillis, John R. *Islands of the Mind: How the Human Imagination Created the Atlantic World.* New York: Palgrave Macmillan, 2009.

Gitzen, Garry D. *Francis Drake in Nehalem Bay 1579: Setting the Historical Record Straight.* Lulu Press, Inc., 2013.

Glasgow, Tom. "H.M.S. 'TIGER.'" *North Carolina Historical Review* 43, no. 2 (1966): 115–21.

Goetz, Rebecca Anne. *The Baptism of Early Virginia: How Christianity Created Race.* Baltimore: Johns Hopkins University Press, 2012.

Goodman, Ruth. *How to Be a Tudor: A Dawn-to-Dusk Guide to Tudor Life.* New York: Liveright, 2017.

Gorman, M. Adele Francis. "Jean Ribault's Colonies in Florida." *Florida Historical Quarterly* 44, no. 1/2 (1965): 51–66.

Gradie, Charlotte M. "Spanish Jesuits in Virginia: The Mission That Failed." *Virginia Magazine of History and Biography* 96, no. 2 (1988): 131–56.

Granger, J. *A Biographical History of England, from Egbert the Great to the Revolution.* W. Baynes and Son, 1824.

Grassl, Gary C. "Joachim Gans of Prague: The First Jew in English America." *American Jewish History* 86, no. 2 (1998): 195–217. doi:10.1353/ajh.1998.0011.

Gray, Nancy. "Unearthing Clues to Lost Worlds: An Archaeological Dig on the Outer Banks of North Carolina Reveals Evidence of the Croatan Indians and Possible Links to the Lost Colony." *ECU Report* 28 (September 1997): 2.

Great Britain Public Record Office. *Calendar of State Papers: Colonial Series.* London: Longman, Green, Longman, & Roberts, 1893.

———. *Calendar of State Papers: Calendar of State Papers, America and West*

Indies: Volume 12 1685–1688 and Addenda 1653–1687. Edited by J. W. Fortescue. London: Her Majesty's Office, 1899.

Green, Paul. *A Paul Green Reader*. Edited by Laurence G. Avery. Chapel Hill: University of North Carolina Press, 1998.

Grens, Kerry. "Lost Colony DNA: Genotyping Could Answer a Centuries-Old Mystery About a Vanished Group of British Settlers." *Scientist*, Jan. 1, 2012.

Guasco, Michael. *Slaves and Englishmen: Human Bondage in the Early Modern Atlantic World*. Philadelphia: University of Pennsylvania Press, 2014.

Gullberg, Jan. *Mathematics: From the Birth of Numbers*. New York: W. W. Norton, 1997.

Haag, William G. *The Archeology of Coastal North Carolina*. Edited by James P. Morgan and Richard J. Russel. Baton Rouge: Louisiana State University Press, 1958.

Hackler, M.B. and Ari J. Adipurwawidjana, eds. *On and Off the Page: Mapping Place in Text and Culture*. Cambridge Scholars Publishing, 2009.

Hakluyt, Richard. *A Discourse Concerning Western Planting*. Cambridge, Mass.: Press of J. Wilson, 1877.

———. *Divers Voyages Touching the Discovery of America and the Islands Adjacent*. Edited by John Winter Jones. London: Hakluyt Society, 1850.

———. *The Principal Navigations, Voyages, Traffiques, and Discoveries of the English Nation*. Glasgow: J. MacLehose and Sons, 1903–5.

Hall, Joseph. "Glimpses of Roanoke, Visions of New Mexico, and Dreams of Empire in the Mixed-Up Memories of Gerónimo de la Cruz." *William and Mary Quarterly* 72, no. 2 (2015): 323–50. doi:10.5309/willmaryquar.72.2.0323.

Hally, David J., and Marvin T. Smith. "Sixteenth-Century Mechanisms of Exchange." *Journal of Global Initiatives: Policy, Pedagogy, Perspective* 5, no. 1 (2010).

Harkness, Deborah E. *The Jewel House: Elizabethan London and the Scientific Revolution*. New Haven, Conn.: Yale University Press, 2007.

Harrington, J. C. "Archeological Explorations at Fort Raleigh National Historic Site." *North Carolina Historical Review* 26, no. 2 (1949): 127–49.

———. *Search for the Cittie of Ralegh: Archeological Excavations at Fort Raleigh National Historic Site, North Carolina*. Washington, D.C.: National Park Service, U.S. Department of the Interior, 1962.

Harriot, Thomas. *A Briefe and True Report of the New Found Land of Virginia*. New York: Dover, 1972.

Hawks, Francis Lister. *History of North Carolina*. Fayetteville, N.C.: E. J. Hale, 1857.

Hawthorne, Julian. *Nathaniel Hawthorne and His Wife*. Houghton Mifflin, 2016.

Hawthorne, Nathaniel. *The Words of Nathaniel Hawthorne* 15. Houghton Mifflin, 1884.

Hedrick, P. W. "Hopi Indians, 'Cultural' Selection, and Albinism." *American Journal of Physical Anthropology* 121, no. 2 (2003): 151–56.

Henneton, Lauric, and L. H. Roper Brill, eds. *Fear and the Shaping of Early American Societies*. Leiden: Brill, 2016.

Hill, Richard. "The Maritime Connection." In *History of the Middle Temple*, edited by Richard Havery. Portland, Ore.: Hart, 2011.

Hinton, John Howard. *The History and Topography of the United States*. London: R. Fenner, Sears, 1830–32.

Hitler, Adolf. *My Struggle*. Madurai, India: LeoPard Books, 2017.

Hodge, Frederick Webb, ed. *Hand Book of American Indians North of Mexico*. Washington, D.C.: Government Printing Office, 1907.

Hoffman, Paul E. *Florida's Frontiers*. Bloomington: Indiana University Press, 2002.

————. *A New Andalucia and a Way to the Orient: The American Southeast During the Sixteenth Century*. Baton Rouge: Louisiana State University Press, 2004.

————. "New Light on Vicente Gonzalez's 1588 Voyage in Search of Raleigh's English Colonies." *North Carolina Historical Review* 63, no. 2 (1986): 199–223.

————. *Spain and the Roanoke Voyages*. Raleigh: America's Four Hundredth Anniversary Committee, North Carolina Department of Cultural Resources, 1987.

Hoffman, Ronald, Mechal Sobel, and Fredrika J. Teute, eds. *Through a Glass Darkly: Reflections on Personal Identity in Early America*. Chapel Hill: University of North Carolina Press, 1997.

Honour, Hugh. *The European Vision of America: A Special Exhibition to Honor the Bicentennial of the United States Organized by the Cleveland Museum of Art with the Collaboration of the National Gallery of Art, Washington, and the Réunion des Musées Nationaux, Paris*. Cleveland: Cleveland Museum of Art, 1975.

Horn, James. *Kingdom Strange: The Brief and Tragic History of the Lost Colony of Roanoke*. New York: Basic Books, 2011.

————. "Roanoke's Lost Colony Found? New Ideas—and Archaeological Evidence—May Provide Answers to Colonial North America's Longest-Running Mystery." *American Heritage* 60, no. 1 (2010).

Horning, Audrey J. *Ireland in the Virginian Sea: Colonialism in the British Atlantic*. Chapel Hill: University of North Carolina Press, 2013.

Houston, Lebame, and Barbara Hird, eds. *Roanoke Revisited: The Story of the First English Settlements in the New World and the Fabled Lost Colony of Roanoke Island*. Manteo, N.C.: Penny Books, 1997.

Hudson, Marjorie. *Searching for Virginia Dare: On the Trail of the Lost Colony of Roanoke Island*. 2nd ed. Winston-Salem, N.C.: Press 53, 2013.

Humber, John L. *Backgrounds and Preparations for the Roanoke Voyages, 1584–1590*. Raleigh: North Carolina Office of Archives and History, 1986.

"Instructions for the Virginia Colony, 1606." *American History: From Revolution to Reconstruction and Beyond*. www.let.rug.nl.

Irwin, Margaret. *That Great Lucifer: A Portrait of Sir Walter Ralegh*. London: Chatto & Windus, 1960.

Isil, Olivia A. *When a Loose Cannon Flogs a Dead Horse There's the Devil to Pay: Seafaring Words in Everyday Speech*. Camden, Maine: International Marine, 1996.

Isaacson, Walter. *A Benjamin Franklin Reader*. Simon and Schuster, 2005.

James, Erin. "The Lost Colony May Now Be Found." *Virginian-Pilot*, Nov. 1, 2010.

Jenkins, Philip. *A History of the United States*. London: Macmillan, 1997.

Jewett, Clayton E., and John O. Allen. *Slavery in the South: A State-by-State History*. Westport, Conn.: Greenwood Press, 2004.

Johnson, Charles. *The Long Roll*. Wentworth Press, 2016.

Johnson, F. Roy, and Thomas C. Parramore. *The Lost Colony in Fact and Legend*. Murfreesboro, N.C.: Johnson, 1983.

Jones, Evan. *Inside the Illicit Economy: Reconstructing the Smugglers' Trade of Sixteenth Century Bristol*. Farnham: Ashgate, 2012.

Jones, H. G. *Raleigh and Quinn: The Explorer and His Boswell*. Chapel Hill: North Caroliniana Society and the North Carolina Collection, 1987.

Jones, Phil. *Ralegh's Pirate Colony in America: The Last Settlement of Roanoke, 1584–1590*. Charleston, S.C.: Tempus, 2001.

Jowitt, Claire. *Pirates? The Politics of Plunder, 1550–1650*. Springer, 2006.

Kelso, William M. *Jamestown: The Buried Truth*. Charlottesville: University of Virginia Press, 2008.

Kelso, William M., and Beverly Straube. *Jamestown Rediscovery, 1994–2004*. Richmond: Association for the Preservation of Virginia Antiquities, 2004.

Klingelhofer, Eric C. "Progress Report on 2012–13 Multidisciplinary Research at Salmon Creek, Bertie County, North Carolina." First Colony Foundation, 2013.

———, ed. *First Forts: Essays on the Archaeology of Proto-colonial Fortifications*. Boston: Brill, 2010.

Klooster, Wim, and Alfred Padula. *The Atlantic World: Essays on Slavery, Migration, and Imagination*. Upper Saddle River, N.J.: Pearson, 2005.

Knapp, Jeffrey. "Elizabethan Tobacco." *Representations*, no. 21 (Winter 1988): 26–66. doi:10.2307/2928376.

Knight, Charles. *London 1-2*. London: Charles Knight and Co., 1841.

———. *An Empire Nowhere: England, America, and Literature from "Utopia" to "The Tempest."* Berkeley: University of California Press, 1994.

Konstam, Angus. *The Great Expedition: Sir Francis Drake on the Spanish Main, 1585–86*. Oxford: Osprey, 2011.

Kupperman, Karen Ordahl. *America in European Consciousness, 1493–1750*. Chapel Hill: University of North Carolina Press, 1995.

———. "Apathy and Death in Early Jamestown." *Journal of American History* 66, no. 1 (1979): 24–40.

———. *Indians and English: Facing Off in Early America*. Ithaca, N.Y.: Cornell University Press, 2000.

———. *Roanoke: The Abandoned Colony*. 2nd ed. Lanham, Md.: Rowman & Littlefield, 2007.

Lacey, Robert. *Sir Walter Raleigh*. London: Phoenix Press, 2000.

Lane, Kris. *Pillaging the Empire: Piracy in the Americas, 1500–1750*. Armonk, N.Y.: M. E. Sharpe, 1998.

Lane, Ralph. *Raleigh's First Roanoke Colony: An Account by Ralph Lane.* Chapel Hill: Academic Affairs Library, University of North Carolina, 2002.

Larson, Lewis H. *Aboriginal Subsistence Technology on the Southeastern Coastal Plain During the Late Prehistoric Period.* Gainesville: University Presses of Florida, 1980.

Laughton, John Knox. *The Defeat of the Spanish Armada.* New York: Burt Franklin, 1894.

La Vere, David. *The Lost Rocks: The Dare Stones and the Unsolved Mystery of Sir Walter Raleigh's Lost Colony.* Wilmington, N.C.: Dram Tree Books, 2010.

————. *The Tuscarora War: Indians, Settlers, and the Fight for the Carolina Colonies.* Chapel Hill: University of North Carolina Press, 2013.

Lawrence, D. H. *Studies in Classic American Literature.* New Delhi: Atlantic, 1995.

Lawson, John. *A New Voyage to Carolina.* Whitefish, Mont.: Kessinger, 2004.

Lawson, Sarah, and W. John Faupel. *A Foothold in Florida: The Eye-Witness Account of Four Voyages Made by the French to That Region and Their Attempt at Colonisation, 1562–1568.* West Sussex: Antique Atlas Publications, 1992.

Lenman, Bruce. *England's Colonial Wars, 1550–1688: Conflicts, Empire, and National Identity.* Routledge, 2014.

Lester, Toby. *The Fourth Part of the World: The Race to the Ends of the Earth, and the Epic Story of the Map That Gave America Its Name.* New York: Free Press, 2009.

Lewis, Clifford M., and Albert J. Loomie. *The Spanish Jesuit Mission in Virginia.* Chapel Hill: University of North Carolina Press, 1953.

Lipson, Ephraim. *The Economic History of England.* Vol. 1. London: A. and C. Black, 1959.

Locklear, Erica Abrams. "'What Are You?': Exploring Racial Categorization in Nowhere Else on Earth." *Southern Literary Journal* 39, no. 1 (2006): 33–53. doi:10.1353/slj.2007.0009.

Loker, Aleck. *Thomas Harriot: Mathematician, Scientist, Explorer of Virginia.* Williamsburg, Va.: Solitude Press, 2007.

Lorimer, Joyce, ed. *Settlement Patterns in Early Modern Colonization, 16th–18th Centuries.* Brookfield, Vt.: Ashgate, 1998.

Luccketti, Nicholas M. *Fort Raleigh Archaeological Project: 1994/1995 Survey Report.* Virginia Company Foundation, 1996.

Lyon, Eugene. *The Enterprise of Florida: Pedro Menéndez de Avilés and the Spanish Conquest of 1565–1568.* Gainesville: University Press of Florida, 1999.

MacMillan, Ken, and Jennifer Abeles, eds. *John Dee: The Limits of the British Empire.* Westport, Conn.: Praeger, 2004.

Macrakis, Kristie. *Prisoners, Lovers, and Spies: The Story of Invisible Ink from Herodotus to Al-Qaeda.* Yale University Press, 2014.

Magdol, Edward, and Jon L. Wakelyn. *The Southern Common People: Studies in Nineteenth-Century Social History.* Westport, Conn.: Greenwood Press, 1980.

Magnaghi, Russell M. "Sassafras and Its Role in Early America, 1562–1662." *Terrae Incognitae* 29, no. 1 (1997): 10–21.

Maine Historical Society. *History of the State of Maine* 2. Portland, Maine: Lefavor-Tower, 1877.

Malcolmson, Cristina. *Renaissance Poetry*. Routledge, 2016.

Mallinson, David J. *Past, Present, and Future Inlets of the Outer Banks Barrier Islands, North Carolina: A White Paper*. Greenville, N.C.: East Carolina University, 2008.

Mallios, Seth. *The Deadly Politics of Giving: Exchange and Violence at Ajacan, Roanoke, and Jamestown*. Tuscaloosa: University of Alabama Press, 2006.

Mancall, Peter C. *Hakluyt's Promise: An Elizabethan's Obsession for an English America*. New Haven, Conn.: Yale University Press, 2007.

———, ed. *The Atlantic World and Virginia, 1550–1624*. Chapel Hill: University of North Carolina Press, 2007.

Mann, Rob. *Smoking and Culture: The Archaeology of Tobacco Pipes in Eastern North America*. Knoxville: University of Tennessee Press, 2004.

Manning, Charles, and Merrill Moore. "Sassafras and Syphilis." *New England Quarterly* 9, no. 3 (1936): 473–75.

Marchand, Philip. *Ghost Empire: How the French Almost Conquered North America*. Toronto: McClelland & Stewart, 2005.

Martin, François-Xavier. *The History of North Carolina, from the Earliest Period*. New Orleans: A. T. Penniman, 1829.

Mathis, Mark A., and Jeffrey J. Crow. *The Prehistory of North Carolina: An Archaeological Symposium*. Raleigh: North Carolina Division of Archives and History, Department of Cultural Resources, 1983.

Maudlin, Daniel, and Bernard L. Herman, eds. *Building the British Atlantic World: Spaces, Places, and Material Culture, 1600–1850*. Chapel Hill: University of North Carolina Press, 2016.

McGrath, John T. *The French in Early Florida: In the Eye of the Hurricane*. Gainesville: University Press of Florida, 2000.

McIlvenna, Noeleen. *A Very Mutinous People: The Struggle for North Carolina, 1660–1713*. University of North Carolina Press, 2009.

McIntyre, Ruth A. "William Sanderson: Elizabethan Financier of Discovery." *William and Mary Quarterly* 13, no. 2 (1956): 184–201. doi:10.2307/1920532.

McMillan, Hamilton. *Sir Walter Raleigh's Lost Colony: An Historical Sketch of the Attempts of Sir Walter Raleigh to Establish a Colony in Virginia, with the Traditions of an Indian Tribe in North Carolina. Indicating the Fate of the Colony of Englishmen Left on Roanoke Island in 1587*. Wilson, N.C.: Advance Presses, 1888.

McMullan, Philip Sidney, Jr., and Frederick Lawson Willard. *Hidden Maps, Hidden City: A Search for the Lost Colony*. Edited by Kathryn Louise Sugg. Williamston, N.C.: Lost Colony Center for Science & Research, 2016.

McMullen, George. *One White Crow*. Norfolk, Va.: Hampton Roads, 1994.

Middleton, Arthur Pierce. *Tobacco Coast: A Maritime History of Chesapeake Bay in the Colonial Era*. Newport News, Va.: Mariners' Museum, 1953.

Miller, Lee. *Roanoke: Solving the Mystery of the Lost Colony*. New York: Penguin Books, 2002.

Milton, Giles. *Big Chief Elizabeth: The Adventures and Fate of the First English Colonists in America*. New York: Farrar, Straus and Giroux, 2000.

Mira, Manuel. *The Portuguese Making of America: Melungeons and Early Settlers of America*. Franklin, N.C.: PAHR Foundation, 2001.

Mires, Peter B. "Contact and Contagion: The Roanoke Colony and Influenza." *Historical Archaeology* 28, no. 3 (1994): 30–38.

Moran, Michael G. *Inventing Virginia: Sir Walter Raleigh and the Rhetoric of Colonization, 1584–1590*. New York: Peter Lang, 2007.

———. "Ralph Lane's 1586 Discourse on the First Colony: The Renaissance Commercial Report as Apologia." *Technical Communication Quarterly* 12, no. 2 (2003): 125–54. doi:10.1207/s15427625tcq1202_1.

More, Thomas, Francis Bacon, and Henry Neville. *Three Early Modern Utopias*. Oxford: Oxford University Press, 1999.

Morgan, Edmund S. *American Slavery, American Freedom: The Ordeal of Colonial Virginia*. New York: W. W. Norton, 1975.

———. "John White and the Sarsaparilla." *William and Mary Quarterly* 14, no. 3 (1957): 414–17.

Morison, Samuel Eliot. *The European Discovery of America: The Northern Voyages, A.D. 500–1600*. New York: Oxford University Press, 1971.

Morrison, David. " 'Dare Stones' Authenticity Theories Rock On," *Brenau Update* (blog), Feb. 6, 2013.

Morrison, Jim. "In Search of the Lost Colony." *American Archaeology*, Winter 2006–7.

Mortimer, Ian. *The Time Traveler's Guide to Elizabethan England*. New York: Penguin Books, 2014.

Mundy, Barbara E. *The Mapping of New Spain: Indigenous Cartography and the Maps of the Relaciones Geográficas*. Chicago: University of Chicago Press, 1996.

Nicholls, Mark. "George Percy (1580–1632 or 1633)." *Encyclopedia Virginia*. Virginia Foundation for the Humanities, 28 Dec. 2016. Web.

Nicholls, Mark, and Penry Williams. *Sir Walter Raleigh: In Life and Legend*. London: Bloomsbury Continuum, 2011.

Nichols, A. Bryant, Jr. *Captain Christopher Newport: Admiral of Virginia*. Newport News, Va.: Sea Venture, 2007.

Noël Hume, Ivor. *The Virginia Adventure, Roanoke to James Towne: An Archeological and Historical Odyssey*. Charlottesville: University Press of Virginia, 1997.

Oberg, Michael Leroy. "Between 'Savage Man' and 'Most Faithful Englishman': Manteo and the Early Anglo-Indian Exchange, 1584–1590." *Itinerario* 24, no. 2 (2000): 146–69.

———. *Dominion and Civility: English Imperialism and Native America, 1585–1685*. Ithaca, N.Y.: Cornell University Press, 2003.

———. "Gods and Men: The Meeting of Indian and White Worlds on the Carolina Outer Banks, 1584–1586." *North Carolina Historical Review* 76, no. 4 (1999): 367–90.

———. *The Head in Edward Nugent's Hand: Roanoke's Forgotten Indians*. Philadelphia: University of Pennsylvania Press, 2008.

Ostovich, Helen, Mary V. Silcox, and Graham Roebuck, eds. *The Mysterious and the Foreign in Early Modern England*. Newark: University of Delaware Press, 2008.

Padfield, Peter. *Maritime Supremacy and the Opening of the Western Mind*. Woodstock, N.Y.: Overlook Press, 2000.

Padget, Cindy D. "The Lost Indians of the Lost Colony: A Critical Legal Study of the Lumbee Indians of North Carolina." *American Indian Law Review* 21, no. 2 (1997): 391–424.

Pagden, Anthony. *Lords of All the World: Ideologies of Empire in Spain, Britain, and France, c. 1500–c. 1800*. New Haven, Conn.: Yale University Press, 1998.

Park, George Brunner. *Richard Hakluyt and the English Voyages*. New York: American Geographical Society, 1928.

Parramore, Thomas C. "The 'Lost Colony' Found: A Documentary Perspective." *North Carolina Historical Review* 78, no. 1 (2001): 67–83.

Parramore, Thomas C., and Barbara M. Parramore. *Looking for the "Lost Colony."* Raleigh, N.C.: Tanglewood Press, 1984.

Parry, Glynn. *The Arch Conjuror of England: John Dee*. New Haven, Conn.: Yale University Press, 2013.

Pearce, Haywood J. "New Light on the Roanoke Colony: A Preliminary Examination of a Stone Found in Chowan County, North Carolina." *Journal of Southern History* 4, no. 2 (1938): 148–63. doi:10.2307/2192000.

Pearson, Fred Lamar. "Early Anglo-Spanish Rivalry in Southeastern North America." *Georgia Historical Quarterly* 58 (1974): 157–71.

Peck, Douglas T. "Lucas Vásquez de Ayllón's Doomed Colony of San Miguel de Gualdape." *Georgia Historical Quarterly* 85, no. 2 (2001): 183–98.

Percy, George. "Jamestown: 1607, the First Months." In *Discourse of the Plantation of the Southern Colony in Virginia by the English, 1606*. London, 1608.

Perdue, Theda, and Christopher Arris Oakley. *Native Carolinians: The Indians of North Carolina*. Raleigh: North Carolina Department of Cultural Resources, Office of Archives and History, 2010.

Peterson, Larry Len. *American Trinity: Jefferson, Custer, and the Spirit of the West*. Helena, Mont.: Sweetgrass Books, 2017.

Picard, Liza. *Elizabeth's London: Everyday Life in Elizabethan London*. New York: St. Martin's Press, 2014.

Pickett, Margaret F., and Dwayne W. Pickett. *The European Struggle to Settle North America: Colonizing Attempts by England, France, and Spain, 1521–1608*. Jefferson, N.C.: McFarland, 2011.

Pittman, Louisa. "The Myth in the Memory: Towards a New Archaeology of Hatteras Island." PhD diss., University of Bristol, 2014.

Pluymers, Keith. "Taming the Wilderness in Sixteenth- and Seventeenth-Century Ireland and Virginia." *Environmental History* 16, no. 4 (2011): 610–32.

Porter, Charles W. "Fort Raleigh National Historic Site, North Carolina: Part of the Settlement Sites of Sir Walter Raleigh's Colonies of 1585–1586 and 1587." *North Carolina Historical Review* 20, no. 1 (1943): 22–42.

Porter, H. C. *The Inconstant Savage: England and the North American Indian, 1500–1660*. London: Gerald Duckworth, 1979.

Powell, Andrew Thomas. *Grenville and the Lost Colony of Roanoke: The First English Colony of America*. Leicester, U.K.: Matador, 2011.

Powell, William S. *North Carolina Through Four Centuries*. Chapel Hill: University of North Carolina Press, 1990.

———. *Paradise Preserved: A History of the Roanoke Island Historical Association*. Chapel Hill: University of North Carolina Press, 1965.

———. "Who Were the Roanoke Colonists?" In *Raleigh and Quinn: The Explorer and His Boswell*, edited by H. G. Jones, ed. Chapel Hill: North Caroliniana Society and the North Carolina Collection, 1987.

Prentice, Guy, Lou Groh, and John Walker. *Tallahassee, Fort Raleigh National Historic Site Archaeological Overview and Assessment*. Tallahassee, Fla.: Southeast Archaeological Center, National Park Service, 2010.

Purchas, Samuel. *Hakluytus Posthumus; or, Purchas His Pilgrimes*. Cambridge, U.K.: Cambridge University Press, 2014.

Quattlebaum, Paul. *The Land Called Chicora: The Carolinas Under Spanish Rule, with French Intrusions, 1520–1670*. Gainesville: University of Florida Press, 1956.

Quinn, Arthur. *A New World*. New York: Berkley, 1995.

Quinn, David B. *The Elizabethans and the Irish*. Ithaca, N.Y.: Cornell University Press, 1966.

———. *England and the Discovery of America, 1481–1620*. New York: Alfred A. Knopf, 1974.

———. "James I and the Beginnings of Empire in America." *Journal of Imperial and Commonwealth History* 2, no. 2 (1974): 135–52. doi:10.1080/03086537408582402.

———. *North America from Earliest Discovery to First Settlements: The Norse Voyages to 1612*. New York: Harper & Row, 1977.

———. "Preparations for the 1585 Virginia Voyage." *William and Mary Quarterly* 6, no. 2 (1949): 208–36. doi:10.2307/1919870.

———. *The Roanoke Voyages, 1584–1590*. London: Hakluyt Society, 1955.

———. *Set Fair for Roanoke: Voyages and Colonies, 1584–1606*. Chapel Hill: University of North Carolina Press, 1985.

———. "Some Spanish Reactions to Elizabethan Colonial Enterprises." *Transactions of the Royal Historical Society* 1 (1951): 1–23. doi:10.2307/3678560.

———. "Thomas Harriot and the Virginia Voyages of 1602." *William and Mary Quarterly* 27, no. 2 (1970): 268–81. doi:10.2307/1918653.

———. *Thomas Harriot and the Problem of America*. Oxford: Oriel College, 1992.

———. "Turks, Moors, Blacks, and Others in Drake's West Indian Voyage." *Terrae Incognitae* 14, no. 1 (1982): 97–104.

Quinn, David B., ed. *Early Maryland in a Wider World*. Detroit: Wayne State University Press, 1982.

———. *The Hakluyt Handbook*. 2 vols. London: Hakluyt Society, 1974.

————. *North American Discovery Circa 1000–1612*. Columbia: University of South Carolina Press, 1971.

————. *Raleigh and the British Empire*. London: English Universities Press, 1962.

————. *The Roanoke Voyages, 1584–1590*. 2 vols. London: Hakluyt Society, 1955.

————. *Voyages and Colonization Enterprises of Humphrey Gilbert*. London: Hakluyt Society, 1940.

Quinn, David B., Kenneth R. Andrews, Nicholas P. Canny, and P. E. H. Hair, eds. *The Westward Enterprise: English Activities in Ireland, the Atlantic, and America, 1480–1650*. Liverpool: Liverpool University Press, 1978.

Quinn, David B., and Alison M. Quinn, eds. *The English New England Voyages, 1602–1608*. New York: Routledge, 2011.

————. *The First Colonists: Documents on the Planting of the First English Settlements in North America, 1584–1590*. North Carolina Department of Cultural Resources, Division of Archives and History, 1982.

Quinn, David B., Alison M. Quinn, Susan Miller, eds. *New American World: A Documentary History of North America to 1612*. Vols. 1–3. New York: Arno Press, 1979.

Rabb, Theodore K. "Investment in English Overseas Enterprise, 1575–1630." *Economic History Review*, n.s., 19, no. 1 (1966): 70–81. doi:10.2307/2592793.

Raleigh, Walter. *The Works of Sir Walter Raleigh*. Vol. 2. London: Dodsley, 1751.

————. "A Discourse of the Invention of Ships, Anchors, Compass, &c." *The Works of Sir Walter Raleigh*, 8. The University Press, 1829.

"Raleigh's Lost Colony." *Raleigh (N.C.) Morning Post*, March 4, 1990.

Randolph, Edmund. *History of Virginia*. Charlottesville: University Press of Virginia, 1970.

Riggs, Stanley R., et al. *The Battle for North Carolina's Coast: Evolutionary History, Present Crisis, and Vision for the Future*. Chapel Hill: University of North Carolina Press, 2011.

Roanoke Colony Memorial Association. *Virginia Dare Day: Annual Celebration by the Roanoke Colony Memorial Association, Old Fort Raleigh, Roanoke Island, North Carolina, August 18, 1926*. Raleigh, N.C.: Edwards & Broughton, 1926.

Robertson, William. *The History of America: Books IX and X*, no. 59. Philadelphia: James Humphreys, 1799.

Rodger, N. A. M. "Atlantic Seafaring." *Oxford Handbooks Online*, 2011. doi:10.1093/oxfordhb/9780199210879.013.0005.

Rogoff, Leonard. *Gertrude Weil: Jewish Progressive in the New South*. Chapel Hill: University of North Carolina Press, 2017.

Roper, L. H. "Fear and Genesis of the English Empire in America." In *Fear and the Shaping of Early American Societies*, edited by Lauric Henneton and L. H. Roper. Leiden: Brill, 2016.

Rowse, A. L. *The Elizabethans and America: The Trevelyan Lectures at Cambridge 1958*. Westport, Conn.: Greenwood Press, 1959.

————. *Sir Richard Grenville of the* Revenge. Boston: Houghton Mifflin, 1937.

Ruby, Robert. *Unknown Shore: The Lost History of England's Arctic Colony*. New York: Henry Holt, 2001.

Salley, Alexander Samuel, ed. *Narratives of Early Carolina, 1650–1708*. New York: C. Scribner's Sons, 1911.

Sams, Conway Whittle. *The Conquest of Virginia; the Third Attempt 1610–1624*. Reprint Company, 1973.

Sauer, Carl Ortwin. *Sixteenth Century North America*. Berkeley: University of California Press, 1971.

Scammel, G. V. "The English in the Atlantic Islands, c. 1450–1650." *Mariner's Mirror* 72, no. 3 (Aug. 1986).

Schmidt, Ethan A. *The Well-Ordered Commonwealth: Humanism, Utopian Perfectionism, and the English Colonization of the Americas*, 2010. www.tandfonline .com.

Schrift, Melissa. *Becoming Melungeon: Making an Ethnic Identity in the Appalachian South*. Lincoln: University of Nebraska Press, 2013.

Schwartz, Seymour I. *The Mismapping of America*. Rochester, N.Y.: University of Rochester Press, 2008.

Schwartz, Seymour I., and Ralph E. Ehrenberg. *The Mapping of America*. Edison, N.J.: Wellfleet Press, 1980.

Seaworthy, Gregory. *Nag's Head; or, Two Months Among "the Bankers": A Story of Sea-Shore Life and Manners*. Chapel Hill: Academic Affairs Library, University of North Carolina, 2001.

Secrets in the Sand: Archeology at Fort Raleigh, 1990–2010: Archeological Resource Study. Manteo, N.C.: National Park Service, 2011.

Seed, Patricia. *American Pentimento: The Invention of Indians and the Pursuit of Riches*. Minneapolis: University of Minnesota Press, 2001.

———. *Ceremonies of Possession in Europe's Conquest of the New World, 1492–1640*. Cambridge, U.K.: Cambridge University Press, 1995.

Semans, Sandy. "Ft. Raleigh? New Find on Roanoke Island Creates Stir." *Outer Banks Sentinel*, Feb. 17, 2007.

Sharpe, Jim. *Witchcraft in Early Modern England*. New York: Routledge, 2014.

Sheehan, Bernard. *Savagism and Civility: Indians and Englishmen in Colonial Virginia*. Cambridge, U.K.: Cambridge University Press, 1980.

Shields, David S. "The Atlantic World, the Senses, and the Arts." *Oxford Handbooks Online*, 2011. doi:10.1093/oxfordhb/9780199210879.013.0008.

Shields, E. Thomson, and Charles Robin Ewen, eds. *Searching for the Roanoke Colonies: An Interdisciplinary Collection*. Raleigh: North Carolina Office of Archives and History, 2003.

Shirley, John W. *Sir Walter Ralegh and the New World*. Raleigh: North Carolina Division of Archives and History, 1985.

———. *Thomas Harriot: A Biography*. Oxford: Clarendon Press, 1983.

———, ed. *Thomas Harriot: Renaissance Scientist*. Oxford: Clarendon Press, 1974.

Skowronek, Russell K., and John W. Walker. "European Ceramics and the Elusive 'Cittie of Raleigh.'" *Historical Archaeology* 27, no. 1 (1993): 58–69.

Sloan, Kim. *European Visions: American Voices*. London: British Museum, 2009.

Sloan, Kim, and Joyce E. Chaplin. *A New World: England's First View of America*. London: British Museum, 2007.

Smith, John. *The Journals of Captain John Smith: A Jamestown Biography*. Washington, D.C.: National Geographic Society, 2007.

————. *Travels and Works of Captain John Smith, Part 1*. New York: B. Franklin, 1910.

————. "A True Relation of Such Occurrences and Accidents of Note as Hath Happened in Virginia, etc." In *The Transplanting of Culture, 1607–1650*. Vol. 1 of *Colonial Prose and Poetry*, edited by William P. Trent and B. W. Wells. New York: T. Y. Crowell, 1901. www.bartleby.com.

Smith, John. *The General Historie of Virginia, New England & The Summer Isles* 1. Glasgow, Scotland: James MacLehose and Sons, 1907.

Smith, John. *Works, 1608–1631*. Birmingham: Unwin bros., 1884.

Sparkes, Boyden. "Writ on Rocke: Has America's First Murder Mystery Been Solved?" *Saturday Evening Post*, April 26, 1941.

Stahle, Daniel K., Dorian J. Burnette, and David W. Stahle. "A Moisture Balance Reconstruction for the Drainage Basin of Albemarle Sound, North Carolina." *Estuaries and Coasts* 36, no. 6 (2013): 1340–53. doi:10.1007/s12237-013-9643-y.

Stahle, David W., Dorian J. Burnette, Jose Villanueva, Julian Cerano, Falko K. Fye, R. Daniel Griffin, Malcolm K. Cleaveland, Daniel K. Stahle, Jesse R. Edmondson, and Kathryn P. Wolff. "Tree-Ring Analysis of Ancient Baldcypress Trees and Subfossil Wood." *Quaternary Science Reviews* 34 (2012): 1–15. doi:10.1016/j.quascirev.2011.11.005.

Stahle, David, Malcolm K. Cleaveland, Dennis B. Blanton, Matthew D. Therrell, and David A. Gay. "The Lost Colony and Jamestown Droughts." *Science Magazine*, April 24, 1998.

Stephenson, Robert L. "Report of Observations Regarding 'the Dare Stones.'" Institute of Archaeology and Anthropology, University of South Carolina, April 15, 1983.

Stern, Philip J. "British Asia and British Atlantic: Comparisons and Connections." *William and Mary Quarterly*, 3rd ser., 63, no. 4 (2006): 693–712.

Stick, David. *Roanoke Island: The Beginning of English America*. Chapel Hill: University of North Carolina Press, 1983.

————, ed. *An Outer Banks Reader*. Chapel Hill: University of North Carolina Press, 1998.

Strachey, William. *The Historie of Travaile into Virginia Britannia Expressing the Cosmographie and Comodities of the Country, Together with the Manners and Customes of the People, Gathered and Observed As Well by Those Who Went First Thither*. Edited by Richard Henry Major. Farnham: Ashgate, 2010.

Strickland, Agnes. *Letters of Mary, Queen of Scots: Now First Published from the Originals, Collected from Various Sources, Private as well as Public, with an Historical Introduction and Notes*. Vol. 2. London: H. Colburn, 1845.

Sumner, Samuel. "The Remote Sensing of the McMullen Site." *Expedition* 6 (1998), 20.

Taylor, Alan. *American Colonies: The Settling of North America*. Edited by Eric Foner. New York: Penguin Books, 2002.

Taylor, Charles S./UPI. "Dare Stones: Hoax or Clue to Lost Colony?" *Ludington Daily News,* April 11, 1977.

Taylor, E. G. R. "Richard Hakluyt." *Geographical Journal* 109, no. 4/6 (1947): 165–71.

———. "Roger Barlow: A New Chapter in Early Tudor Geography." *Geographical Journal* 74, no. 2 (1929): 157–66. doi:10.2307/1785313.

———, ed. *The Troublesome Voyage of Captain Edward Fenton, 1582–83.* Cambridge, U.K.: Hakluyt Society, 1959.

Tepaske, John, ed. *Three American Empires.* New York: Harper & Row, 1967.

"Town's Shock as Residents from Mystery US 'Twin' Turn Up Bearing Gifts." *Daily Mail Online,* Oct. 20, 2006.

Tracy, Don. *Roanoke Renegade.* New York: The Dial Press, 1954.

Trebellas, Christine, and William Chapman. *Fort Raleigh National Historic Site: Historic Resource Study.* Southeast Regional Office, National Park Service, U.S. Department of the Interior, 1999.

Trevelyan, Raleigh. *Sir Walter Raleigh: Being a True and Vivid Account of the Life and Times of the Explorer, Soldier, Scholar, Poet, and Courtier—the Controversial Hero of the Elizabethan Age.* New York: Henry Holt, 2014.

Trichopoulou, A. "Low-Carbohydrate–High-Protein Diet and Long-Term Survival in a General Population Cohort." *European Journal of Clinical Nutrition* 61 (2006). doi:oi:10.1038/sj.ejcn.1602557.

Tuthill, Cornelia L. "Virginia Dare; or, The Colony of Roanoke." *Southern Literary Messenger* 5 (1840).

U.S. Library of Congress. *Records of the Virginia Company of London.* Washington, D.C.: GPO, 1933.

VanDerBeets, Richard, ed. *Held Captive by Indians: Selected Narratives, 1642–1836.* Knoxville: University of Tennessee Press, 1973.

Vaughan, Alden T. *American Genesis: Captain John Smith and the Founding of Virginia.* Edited by Oscar Handlin. Boston: Little, Brown, 1975.

———. "Sir Walter Ralegh's Indian Interpreters, 1584–1618." *William and Mary Quarterly* 59, no. 2 (2002): 341–76. doi:10.2307/3491741.

Vigneras, L. A. "A Spanish Discovery of North Carolina in 1566." *North Carolina Historical Review* 46, no. 4 (1969).

Volo, James M. and Deneen Volo. *Daily Life on the Old Colonial Frontier.* Greenwood Publishing Group, 2002.

Wallace, Willard Mosher. *Sir Walter Raleigh.* Princeton, N.J.: Princeton University Press, 2015.

Wallis, Patrick. "Exotic Drugs and English Medicine: England's Drug Trade, c. 1550–c. 1800." *Social History of Medicine* 25, no. 1 (2011): 20–46. doi:10.1093/shm/hkr055.

Ward, H. Trawick, and R. P. Stephen Davis. *Time Before History: The Archaeology of North Carolina.* Chapel Hill: University of North Carolina Press, 1999.

Warner, Thomas E. "European Musical Activities in North America Before 1620." *Musical Quarterly* 70, no. 1 (1984): 77–95.

"Warren on Amendment." *Raleigh (N.C.) Morning Post,* March 4, 1990.

Weaver, Jace. *The Red Atlantic: American Indigenes and the Making of the Modern World, 1000–1927*. Chapel Hill: University of North Carolina Press, 2014.

Weber, David J. *The Spanish Frontier in North America*. New Haven, Conn.: Yale University Press, 1992.

Wellard, James. *The Search for Lost Cities*. London: Constable, 1980.

West, W. Richard. *The Changing Presentation of the American Indian: Museums and Native Cultures*. Seattle: University of Washington Press, 2015.

Wheat, David. *Atlantic Africa and the Spanish Caribbean, 1570–1640*. Chapel Hill: University of North Carolina Press, 2016.

White, John. "A Wife of an Indian 'Werowance' or Chief of Pomeiooc" (1585–93). This and all other cited White drawings held by the British Museum. www.britishmuseum.org.

"White Supremacy Club Engaged in a Good Work." *Raleigh (N.C.) Morning Post*, June 3, 1990.

Williams, Allan, and Monica Lucinda Fonseca. "The Azores: Between Europe and North America." In *Small Worlds, Global Lives*, edited by Russell King and John Connell. London: Pinter, 1999.

Williams, Talcott. "The Surroundings and Site of Raleigh's Colony." *Annual Report of the American Historical Association for 1895*, 47–61.

Williamson, Hugh. *The History of North Carolina*. Vol. 1. Philadelphia: Thomas Dobson, 1812.

Wright, David, and David Zoby. *Fire on the Beach: Recovering the Lost Story of Richard Etheridge and the Pea Island Lifesavers*. New York: Oxford University Press, 2002.

Wright, Irene A. "Spanish Policy Toward Virginia, 1606–1612: Jamestown, Ecija, and John Clark of the Mayflower." *American Historical Review* 25, no. 3 (1920): 448–79. doi:10.2307/1836882.

———, ed. *Further English Voyages to Spanish America, 1583–1594: Documents from the Archives of the Indies at Seville Illustrating English Voyages to the Caribbean, the Spanish Main, Florida, and Virginia*. London: Hakluyt Society, 1951.

Wright, Louis B. "Elizabethan Politics and Colonial Enterprise." *North Carolina Historical Review* 32, no. 2 (1955): 254–69.

Wroth, Lawrence. *The Voyages of Giovanni da Verrazzano, 1524–1528*. New Haven, Conn.: Yale University Press, 1970.

York, Robert, and John Brooke-Little. *The Grant of Arms to the City of Raleigh 1586*. Manteo, N.C.: Elizabethan Rendezvous Productions, 1984.

Youings, Joyce. *Ralegh's Country: The South West of England in the Reign of Queen Elizabeth I*. Raleigh: America's Four Hundredth Anniversary Committee, North Carolina Department of Cultural Resources, 1986.

Zerubavel, Eviatar. *Terra Cognita: The Mental Discovery of America*. New Brunswick, N.J.: Rutgers University Press, 1992.

"Zombie Colony of Roanoke." Zombie Research Society. Last modified Oct. 22, 2009. zombieresearchsociety.com.

Index

Page numbers in *italics* refer to illustrations and maps.